Contents

British Fascist Antisemitism and Jewish Responses, 1932–40

Praise for *British Fascist Antisemitism and Jewish Responses, 1932–40*

'Just when we thought that there could really be little more to say on the subject of British fascism and the Anglo-Jewish response to it in the 1930s, Dr Tilles has taken our breath away with a thoroughly researched investigation that challenges much received wisdom concerning this most sensitive subject. Using new material as well as reinterpreting well-thumbed existing accounts, he offers us a provocative but at the same time compelling re-telling of the narrative, focussing especially on the deep divisions that characterised Anglo-Jewry's confrontation with domestic fascism in the early 1930s, and the efforts made to bind these wounds after 1936.'

Geoffrey Alderman, Michael Gross Professor of Politics & Contemporary History, University of Buckingham, UK

'Daniel Tilles has produced the most detailed and nuanced account of the British Union of Fascists' antisemitism and Jewish responses to it. Utilising new sources and re-assessing old ones, he provides a thought-provoking analysis of the nature of BUF antisemitism, including that of its leader, Oswald Mosley. Tilles also shows the complex and, he argues, successful Jewish actions against the vile attacks of Britain's largest fascist movement during the 1930s.'

Tony Kushner, Director of the Parkes Institute, University of Southampton, UK

'This book brings a breath of fresh air to the study of the British Union of Fascists and of Jewish responses to the threat it posed. In clear, forceful prose, Daniel Tilles demolishes two long-standing interpretations: that the BUF embraced antisemitism belatedly and only after Jews disrupted their meetings, and that the response of the Jewish communal elite was timid by comparison with the militant response of Jewish workers and Communists. His argument, which draws in large part on hitherto unavailable archival materials, is compelling and has far reaching implications.'

Todd Endelman, Professor Emeritus of History and Judaic Studies, University of Michigan, USA

A Modern History of Politics and Violence

Series Editor: Paul Jackson

A Modern History of Politics and Violence is a new book series that scrutinizes the diverse history of political violence in the modern world.

It includes original studies, edited collections and reference works that explore the cultural settings and key actors that have allowed violent solutions to become seen as desirable somehow at certain points in history.

Published:
A British Fascist in the Second World War, Claudia Baldoli
and Brendan Fleming (2014)
British Fascist Antisemitism and Jewish Responses, 1932–40, Daniel Tilles (2015)

Forthcoming:
The Comparative History of Fascism in Eastern Europe, Constantin Iordachi (2015)
A Comparative History of Persecution and Victim Experience, Kitty Millet (2015)
Colin Jordan and Britain's Neo-Nazi Social Movement, Paul Jackson (2015)
Transnational Fascism in the Twentieth Century, Matteo Albanese
and Pablo del Hierro (2015)
Civil Uprisings in Modern Sudan, W. J. Berridge (2015)

British Fascist Antisemitism and Jewish Responses, 1932–40

Daniel Tilles

Bloomsbury Academic
An imprint of Bloomsbury Publishing Plc

BLOOMSBURY

LONDON • OXFORD • NEW YORK • NEW DELHI • SYDNEY

Bloomsbury Academic

An imprint of Bloomsbury Publishing Plc

50 Bedford Square	1385 Broadway
London	New York
WC1B 3DP	NY 10018
UK	USA

www.bloomsbury.com

BLOOMSBURY and the Diana logo are trademarks of Bloomsbury Publishing Plc

First published 2015
Paperback edition first published 2016

© Daniel Tilles, 2015

Daniel Tilles has asserted his right under the Copyright, Designs and
Patents Act, 1988, to be identifi ed as Author of this work.

British Library Cataloguing-in-Publication Data
A catalogue record for this book is available from the British Library.

ISBN: HB: 978-1-4725-1057-0
PB: 978-1-4742-8642-8
ePDF: 978-1-4725-0725-9
ePub: 978-1-4725-0568-2

Library of Congress Cataloguing-in-Publication Data
Tilles, Daniel, author.
British Fascist antisemitism and Jewish responses, 1932-40 / Daniel Tilles.
pages cm – (A modern history of politics and violence)
Revised version of the author's thesis (doctoral)–University of London, 2011.
Includes bibliographical references and index.
ISBN 978-1-4725-1057-0 (hardback) – ISBN 978-1-4725-0725-9 (epdf) –
ISBN 978-1-4725-0568-2 (epub) 1. Fascism–Great Britain–History–20th century. 2. British
Union of Fascists. 3. Antisemitism–Great Britain–History–20th century. 4. Jews–Great
Britain–History–20th century. 5. Great Britain–Ethnic relations. I. Title.
DA578.T55 2014
305.892′404109043 – dc23
2014020197

Series: A Modern History of Politics and Violence

Typeset by Integra Software Services Pvt. Ltd
Printed and bound in Great Britain

In memory of Professor David Cesarani, my former doctoral supervisor, without whose patience, generosity and guidance this book would never have been completed, and to whom I owe the greatest of debts, professionally and personally.

Acknowledgements

I acknowledge my gratitude, above all, to the supervisor of the doctoral research on which this book is based, David Cesarani, for his guidance, advice and constructive criticism. I also appreciate greatly the insights offered by the many who have given their thoughts on my work, particularly David Feldman and Thomas Linehan, my examiners; Dan Stone and Helen Graham, who conducted my PhD upgrade examination; Salvatore Garau, for his invaluable comments throughout; and to Nigel Copsey, Matthew Feldman (not least for sparking my initial interest in British fascism and supervising my early research as an undergraduate), Aristotle Kallis, Graham Macklin, Edward Marshall, Stanley Bill, Matthew Barnes, Margaret Webb, Boris Veselinovich, Elaine Baker and Amy Lo.

My research would have been far more difficult to undertake without the financial assistance provided by Royal Holloway, in the form of a research scholarship, as well as two contributions – a doctoral grant and financial support to convert my doctoral thesis into a book – from a funding body that, as a general policy, asks for its name not to be publicized. Similarly, I am also grateful for the assistance of numerous archivists and librarians at the institutions, listed in the bibliography, where I have conducted my research. They have often gone well out of their way to answer my inquiries. In particular, I appreciate the help of the staff at the CST and of Sandra Clarke at the Board of Deputies in allowing me regular and privileged access to material in the Board's defence archives. I am grateful to the University of Southampton Library for granting me permission to reproduce material from their Anglo-Jewish archives. And last, but certainly not least, my heartfelt thanks must also go to my family for their patience, assistance and understanding throughout the whole process.

List of Abbreviations

AJEX	Jewish Ex-Servicemen's Legion (from 1939, Association of Jewish Ex-Servicemen)
AJY	Association of Jewish Youth
AJFS	Association of Jewish Friendly Societies
BF	British Fascisti/Fascists
BUD	British Union of Democrats
BUF	British Union of Fascists
CoC	Co-ordinating Committee (from 1938, Jewish Defence Committee)
CMSJ	Council of Manchester and Salford Jews
CPGB	Communist Party of Great Britain
EMAF	Ex-Servicemen's Movement Against Fascism
FQ	*Fascist Quarterly*
FW	*Fascist Week*
IFL	Imperial Fascist League
JC	*Jewish Chronicle*
JLC	Jewish Labour Council
JPC	Jewish People's Council Against Fascism and Anti-Semitism
JUDA	Jewish United Defence Association
LAC	London Area Council
LBWS	Legion of Blue and White Shirts
LCC	London County Council
LJY	League of Jewish Youth
MCP	Militant Christian Patriots
NCCL	National Council for Civil Liberties
NSDAP	*Nationalsozialistische Deutsche Arbeiterpartei* (National Socialist German Workers' Party)
NL	Nordic League
NSL	National Socialist League
NWF	New World Fellowship
POA	Public Order Act
TAC	Trades Advisory Council
YCL	Young Communist League

General Introduction

Fascism and antisemitism are not subjects that have been neglected by scholars. Neither, despite a relative lack of severity by comparison to their European counterparts, have British manifestations of these two phenomena struggled for academic attention. Indeed, British fascism's explicit hostility towards Jews – unprecedented in the country's political life – is the aspect of its history that has left the strongest imprint on collective memory. Similarly, the targets of this campaigning, Britain's Jews, have not, especially given their small number, been wanting for research. In particular, their experiences of and responses to domestic fascism in the 1930s have come to be regarded as a central feature of modern Anglo-Jewish history.

Nevertheless, there remain significant gaps within, as well as between, these fields. The burgeoning discipline of fascist studies, for example, has had relatively little to say on antisemitism's position within fascist ideology,[1] while it has also devoted scant attention to fascism's British variant. Work dedicated to British fascism has, equally, tended to make minimal reference to developments in the wider field of fascist studies, or to locate its subject within this context.[2] Moreover, while the importance of antisemitism to British fascist history is recognized, the forms that it took and the ways in which it was presented, as well as its relationship to fascist ideology and to native patterns of anti-Jewish thought, have been explored only fragmentarily.[3] Similarly, scholars of British antisemitism have at times been guilty of disregarding domestic fascism, partly as a result of its relative obscurity but also, perhaps, because of a desire to move away from the study of 'Continental' types of extreme and politicized antisemitism and towards the divination of more indigenous forms of prejudice.[4]

Work on British fascism and anti-fascism, meanwhile, has tended to touch only incidentally upon Jewish forms of opposition. Where they have been explored in their own right, accounts tend to be rather static and simplistic, concentrating almost exclusively on just one brief period and sketching a dichotomy between two, allegedly opposing forms of reaction. Moreover, researchers of all stripes have focused primarily upon the activity favoured by just one section of Anglo-Jewry – young, working-class Jews of recent immigrant extraction, who pursued an active, confrontational approach to fascism – to the exclusion of other groups.[5] Above all, despite the histories of interwar British fascism and Anglo-Jewry being so closely intertwined, the two have been examined largely in isolation, with studies tending to approach their relationship exclusively from the perspective of one side or the other. Scholars of British fascism rely little on Anglo-Jewish sources and vice versa, resulting in accounts that fail to offer comprehensive and balanced coverage. Indeed, the present work is the first to bring the two together, helping shed new light on both.

The first part of this study will focus on British fascist antisemitism, taking as its main subject Oswald Mosley's British Union of Fascists (BUF), by some distance the country's most prominent and sophisticated interwar fascist organization.[6] It will examine how and when antisemitism was incorporated into the party's ideology and programme; the ways in which anti-Jewish sentiment was expressed in its discourse over time; and what beliefs and motivations underlay these developments.[7] These insights will then be used to reflect on broader issues.

These include, first of all, the question of whether antisemitism, which was initially absent from the party's official programme, should be regarded an authentic element of its ideology, or if, instead, it was an artificial addition to it, forced upon the BUF's leadership by external or internal forces, or exploited by them for cynical political gain. The role of Mosley, the movement's dominant figure, in this process will also be considered. Second, the study will assess the degree to which the fascists' antisemitism stemmed from indigenous attitudes towards Jews, or, by contrast, how far it was inspired by foreign influences. Additionally, the ways in which the BUF's anti-Jewish position related to – and affected relations with – other groups on the British and European radical right will be touched upon. Finally, the above will provide the basis for discussion of the wider relationship between antisemitism and fascism as a generic phenomenon, and in particular the extent to which the former – or any other form of exclusionary prejudice – is inherent to the latter, and why.

Subsequently, attention will turn to the ways in which Britain's Jews reacted to the emergence, for the first time in British history, of an explicitly antisemitic political party with a substantial base of support. By surveying a far broader range of Jewish responses to domestic fascism over the period 1932–40 than previous accounts – and by revealing how they evolved, overlapped and interacted with one another – a more comprehensive and representative picture will emerge. This, in turn, will provide a framework within which to examine a number of other themes.

First, the question of why Jewish approaches to fascism evolved over time will be discussed: the extent to which this was, on the one hand, a response to external circumstances – such as the changing nature of the fascist threat – or whether, on the other, it was driven internally, by discussion among Jews themselves. The effect that this 'defence debate' had on relations between various sections of Britain's Jewish community will also be explored in depth, and related to wider shifts in the balance of communal power during this period. We will also observe the role that Jews played in Britain's anti-fascist movement, and how they interacted with the various other groups, institutions and individuals who were opposed to fascism. Finally, the issue of identity will be considered: the ways in which responses to fascism were influenced by – and how, in turn, they influenced – Jews' sense of their Britishness and Jewishness, and the balance between them.

By scrutinizing British fascist antisemitism and Jewish responses side by side in this way, this study will also be able to assess the impact that the two had on one another. This, first of all, will comprise an assessment of the concept of 'interactionism'. This is an idea that, while not always given this specific label, has become firmly established in the historiography of British fascism, referring to an alleged vicious circle that developed over the 1930s: early Jewish hostility towards the fascists encouraged the latter to adopt antisemitism as official policy, which in turn exacerbated Jewish antagonism, thereby further hardening the fascists' stance. This premise will be re-examined, with the relationship between the two sides, and their influence (or lack of influence) on one another, explored in detail. Second – and related to this – the effectiveness of Jewish efforts to restrict the fascists' activity, thwart their political ambitions and counteract their antisemitic propaganda will be analysed.

While this book will, then, both cover new ground and reconsider certain established views, it also faces the question of significance: why is its subject matter important? This is an issue that has perennially confronted historians of British fascism and Anglo-Jewry, both of which can appear to be of limited historical relevance and interest, not only on an international scale, but even in the British context.

In his seminal *History of Fascism*, for instance, Stanley Payne devotes just a page and a half of text to what he describes as the 'political oxymoron' of British fascism, remarking that the voluminous historiography devoted to the subject can appear 'inversely proportionate' to its actual significance.[8] More bluntly, Anthony Julius, in his study of English antisemitism, argues that the country's fascists

> contributed nothing to the understanding of their times; they included no thinkers or strategists of distinction or even mediocrity; there was nothing original or even engaging in their programmes; they produced nothing of political or cultural value; their newsletters and pamphlets were dreary, somewhat hysterical and most of all just *wrong* about the events they reported.[9]

In a similar vein, David Vital's *The Jews in Europe* describes the experience of Britain's Jews as something of an 'oddity' when compared to that of their co-religionists elsewhere on the continent. The British historian David Cannadine is even more forthright, arguing that, due to Anglo-Jewry's small size, high level of assimilation, and the relative lack of prejudice and hostility it faced, its history is 'little more than a bland and lukewarm chronicle', one that 'in the context of international history … is neither very interesting, nor very exciting … [and] in the context of British history … just not that important'.[10]

Yet, while Britain's fascists and Jews may superficially appear peripheral, there are important reasons for their histories – and the intersections between them – to be acknowledged, understood and incorporated into the wider scholarship. Far from being outliers, both individually provide instructive and representative examples of broader developments, and taken together contribute to an understanding of the relationship between Jews and fascists across interwar Europe.

Payne's jibe towards British fascism notwithstanding, the trend in fascist studies over recent decades has been to take more seriously the study of smaller, less successful fascist movements, and to use them to refine our understanding of fascism as a generic phenomenon. As Roger Griffin argues, Italian Fascism and German Nazism, despite dominating the scholarship, should actually be regarded as 'freak examples' of fascism. They were the only two interwar fascist parties that were able to form regimes, making them exceptions to the general rule of fascist failure across the rest of interwar Europe. Instead, he believes, it was the much wider range of small, 'abortive' movements that better characterized the way in which fascism developed.[11] Taking the case even further, Zeev Sternhell claims that the inevitable compromises forced upon any political movement once it reaches power mean that it is only smaller opposition groups that offer a 'pure ... unmuddied' version of fascism.[12] In this light, the BUF – a small party, but with a clearly defined, consistent and undoubtedly 'fascist' ideology – provides a case study on the use of antisemitism by fascist parties that is both valuable in its own right and, as we shall see, sheds light on broader trends that have received relatively little academic attention.

Additionally, as both Griffin and Robert Paxton contend, the fortunes of individual fascist parties were dictated as much by environmental factors as by their inherent qualities.[13] This, first of all, reinforces the notion that a lack of political success should not in itself diminish the importance of studying a particular strain of fascism. But it also emphasizes the importance of both understanding those external conditions that caused fascism to fail and discerning any common factors that made this failure so pervasive across interwar Europe.

In Britain the countervailing forces against fascism were manifold. Most obviously, its development was hindered by the country's inhospitable political culture, with its tradition of stability and gradual change, an electoral system that inhibits the progress of small parties, and widespread acceptance of liberal democracy. (Griffin warns, however, against the 'Whiggish belief' that Britain's political culture was somehow uniquely resistant to extremism. Fascism was, he notes, stymied by 'structural feature[s] of all but the most defective liberal democracies anywhere in the world'.)[14] In addition to such intrinsic impediments, fascism was also constrained by the broad opposition it aroused in Britain. Indeed, these two sets of inhibitory factors were closely related to one another, with Nigel Copsey arguing that the study of anti-fascism 'tell[s] us much about the popular resilience or otherwise of "democratic" values in the inter-war period'.[15] Jews, as we shall see, played an integral role across Britain's spectrum of anti-fascist forces, one that has not been fully acknowledged as an explanatory factor in the suppression and marginalization of British fascism.

The story of this highly effective resistance to fascism in Britain also has wider relevance for European Jewish history, as an alternative narrative of the relationship between Jews and fascists during the interwar period and Second World War. Attention in this regard has, understandably, focused on Nazi Germany and the territories that fell under its sphere of influence, resulting in a prevalent perception of Jews as victims of, refugees from or heroic but ultimately doomed rebels against fascism. Jürgen Matthäus and Mark Roseman caution in the introduction to their volume on Jewish responses to Nazi persecution in Germany that, as much as they hope to present Jews 'as actors, not simply as passive witnesses', the 'massive imbalance in the power relationship' between Jews and their fascist oppressors means that 'the potential for Jewish agency was restricted from the start and increasingly diminished over time'.[16] Yet in Britain, where this balance of power was to some extent inverted, we find that Jews had a far wider and more palatable range of options open to them, which they pursued to great effect, playing an active role in shaping fascism's path of development.

This may, on the one hand, reinforce the idea that Anglo-Jewry is an 'oddity', set apart from the experiences of its continental peers. Yet, rather than detract from the importance of its history, this is surely a powerful argument in its favour. If the experiences of British Jews do not fit comfortably into wider paradigms, then it is important to understand what it is that made Britain, and its Jews, different. Alternatively, it may be the case that, as with the general study of fascism, the attention paid to Nazi Germany has obscured alternative Jewish interactions with fascism elsewhere, with Britain fitting into a broader story of Jewish resistance to the European radical right, particularly before 1939.

Finally, an understanding of Jewish interactions with interwar fascism can, it is hoped, contribute to the wider question of how minorities respond to organized political prejudice directed against them. This is an issue not only of historical interest but also, given the continued existence – and recent renewed prominence – of the ultranationalist, xenophobic radical right, one with contemporary resonance. The circumstances of interwar Britain's Jews – a small community, widely perceived as alien to and even incompatible with the native culture, facing relatively pervasive suspicion and hostility – are characteristic of many minority groups across different time periods and national contexts. The emergence of a political movement that harnessed such prejudices and advocated placing restrictions upon, or even completely removing, certain minorities is also an experience far from unique to Jews. And here Britain provides a more widely applicable historical model than, say, Nazi Germany or Fascist Italy, given that the modern radical right is, in virtually all European countries, still a small, fringe force, whose impact is felt more through stirring public disorder and ethnic tensions than in terms of any formal political power.

Yet, while it is hoped that the present work can in some way contribute to this range of fields – and reference will be made throughout to the relevant literature – the study itself will focus relatively narrowly on the use of antisemitism by Britain's interwar fascists – in particular the BUF – and on the ways in which the country's Jews responded. As such, it is worth, to provide some context for what is come, offering a brief overview of the history of Britain's fascists and their opponents during the relevant period, how this history has been interpreted by scholars, and in what ways this study will augment and challenge the existing scholarship.

The outlines below are divided into two parts – on fascist antisemitism and Jewish responses – that replicate the division made in the rest of the book. This structure has been chosen, in part, for reasons of clarity, as well as because of the different methodological approaches taken for each of the two subjects under consideration. But it also reflects a central aspect of this study's findings, which is to reject the widely held idea that Jewish actions were responsible for the fascists' adoption of antisemitism. Instead, it will be demonstrated that the latter developed independently of the former, and as such merits consideration in its own right. That is not to say, however, that the two sides were completely disconnected. There were a number of ways in which they intersected with one another, and these points of contact will be made clear throughout.

The BUF and antisemitism

As suggested above, assessments of the impact made by the BUF on British society usually place it somewhere between an irrelevance and an inconvenience. With relatively low membership for most of its existence, defeat in the few elections it contested and an extremely limited contribution to mainstream political and intellectual discourse, the party's presence was felt chiefly through the public-order problems it provoked. Richard Thurlow, a leading historian of British fascism, accepts that the BUF was of 'only marginal significance to British politics', a 'nuisance' at worst.[17] Yet this has not prevented a profusion of work appearing since serious academic research into British fascism began in the 1960s, with the field now encompassing comprehensive surveys (from Colin Cross' early work, *The Fascists in Britain*, through to more recent efforts, such as Thurlow's *Fascism in Britain* and Thomas Linehan's *British Fascism*),[18] portraits of individuals' figures (most notably Robert Skidelsky's biography of Mosley)[19] and studies of local Blackshirt activity.[20]

A particularly interesting avenue of inquiry has been the party's ideology. Mosley, an accomplished thinker and previously a rising star in both the Conservative and Labour Parties, produced a programme that, Thurlow argues, was 'intellectually the most coherent and rational of all the fascist parties in Europe', representing a sophisticated synthesis of 'English radical economics, fascist politics and German idealist philosophy'.[21] Scholars of fascism concur, with Paxton observing that 'Mosley probably had the greatest intellectual gifts ... of all the fascist chiefs', making his party 'one of the most interesting [fascist] failures' of the interwar period. Even Payne admits that the BUF possessed an 'elaborate', 'decidedly modernist' programme, combining complex economic theory and concepts of 'scientific production' with vitalist and Shavian philosophical influences.[22]

Fascism has also been used as a prism through which to view other aspects of British politics and society. Martin Pugh and Richard Griffiths, for example, have explored the sympathy felt towards fascism by some on the conventional political right, describing the 'flourishing traffic in ideas and personnel' between the two sides. This, Pugh argues, dispels the 'comforting and widely held view' that British fascism was destined to fail, and instead reveals the influence it had on interwar politics.[23] As his words suggest, others – Mike Cronin being one example – have used British fascism's failings to argue for a resistance to extremism allegedly inherent to Britain's political character.[24] Meanwhile Griffin, as we have seen, employs the British case as an illustration of the difficulties fascism faces in achieving power without a specific set of favourable circumstances.[25]

Although scholars differ on many of the details, there is broad agreement on the general path of the BUF's history.[26] Founded in late 1932, following the collapse of Mosley's proto-fascist New Party,[27] it initially took Italian Fascism as its chief inspiration (and received discreet funding from Benito Mussolini). The party adopted many of the typical trappings of fascism: uniforms, processions, a quasi-military structure and ethos, an emphasis on physical training and youth, and absolute dedication to the cause and to 'the Leader', as Mosley styled himself.

Additionally, as intimated above, its ideology was quintessentially fascist, predicated on a gloomy diagnosis of the economic, social, cultural and political decay supposedly afflicting Britain, and proposing a revolutionary remedy to purge the influences seen to be responsible for this state of affairs, thereby inaugurating a reborn and revitalized nation populated by a 'new fascist man'. In terms of the party's programme, this was manifested in a balance between negative aspects – opposition to communism, international finance, the 'Old Gang' of political parties and various other forces allegedly detrimental to national wellbeing – and a more positive image of the Britain Mosley promised to (re)create. Seeking to place itself above the traditional division between political right and left, the BUF from the start laid out a detailed picture of the corporatist political and economic system it proposed to establish and the ways in which this would transform the British economy through modern, scientific methods; ameliorate industrial relations by balancing the interests of employers, employees and consumers; and improve the lot of domestic businesses and workers by insulating the British market from deleterious international influences.[28]

While asserting that his followers would be prepared to meet with force any revolutionary threat from the far left, Mosley always expressed his preference for a lawful, electoral path to power. This necessitated the cultivation of a respectable image, meaning that the more disreputable aspects of Italian and German fascism – particularly violence and antisemitism – were initially suppressed. Violence, where it did take place, was usually 'defensive' in nature (though carried out with relish by many Blackshirts, particularly members of the specially trained 'defence force').[29] And while many within the party harboured, and often openly articulated, negative sentiment towards Jews, antisemitism was consistently repudiated in official pronouncements during the party's early days.

These aspirations to enter the political mainstream were boosted in early 1934, when the press magnate Lord Rothermere – proprietor of, among other titles, the *Daily Mail*, one of Britain's most widely circulated newspapers – threw his support behind the BUF. Already attracting considerable interest, the party now grew even more rapidly. It reached a peak membership of around 50,000 in 1934, with support drawn largely from the working class and unemployed, veterans of the Great War and middle-class youths.[30] (As a frame of reference, the British Fascists (BF), the most prominent fascist organization of the 1920s, briefly had perhaps a few thousand members at their peak, while during the 1930s membership of the Communist Party ranged between 2,500 and 18,000.)[31] The Blackshirts also had notable success in attracting female members, who made up an estimated 25 per cent of support.[32]

Over the summer and autumn of 1934, however, the BUF suffered a dramatic reversal of fortunes. A wave of organized anti-fascist disruption at its events was met with a violent response from Mosley's stewards, most conspicuously at the Olympia Hall meeting of June 1934. This, along with a concurrent escalation of Nazi brutality in Germany, irrevocably tarnished fascism's image in Britain, driving away the majority of the BUF's more respectable supporters, including Rothermere. Meanwhile, with Britain's economy beginning to recover from the Great Depression,[33] Mosley's economic policies, the centrepiece of his programme, held progressively less relevance and appeal. As a result, his party entered a period of instability and decline, with membership falling as low as 5,000 in 1935.[34]

A further cause of the BUF's growing disrepute was its increasingly explicit hostility towards Jews. This culminated in the formal 'adoption' of antisemitism in autumn 1934, justified by Mosley on the grounds that Jews had been guilty of attacking his party. It quickly became apparent that this feature of propaganda was proving popular in areas with traditions of tension between Jewish immigrants and other communities. This was particularly the case in London's East End, an economically deprived area that housed the country's largest concentration of Jews. From late 1935, the BUF began to focus its efforts there, mounting an intensive campaign of street-corner meetings, marches and propaganda drives, its activity dominated by a coarse and vicious antisemitism.[35] This inspired a hostile response from anti-fascists, whose ranks were swelled by large numbers of Jews, leading to a worsening cycle of violence between the Blackshirts and their opponents. Matters came to a head at the famous 'Battle of Cable Street' in October 1936, where a crowd of 100,000 or more demonstrators forcibly prevented a column of Blackshirts headed by Mosley from marching through the streets of east London.

Although successful in attracting support in a narrow range of localities, the BUF largely collapsed as a national force during this period. As a consequence, it also struggled financially, a problem that was exacerbated by Mussolini's decision to cut back his subsidies as Mosley drifted closer to the Nazis.[36] This lack of funds, as well as the party's failure to win a single seat at local elections in 1937, forced Mosley to implement drastic cutbacks in personnel and administrative costs, leading to the departure of many leading members.

Subsequently, the BUF re-orientated away from the East End and attempted to return to the national stage. In particular it aimed to exploit public concern over events in Europe, with Mosley launching a passionate crusade to avert the impending war with Germany and to prevent the arrival of (mostly Jewish) refugees from central Europe.[37] This helped spark a revival of interest in his party, with membership estimated to have grown to perhaps 20,000 in 1939.[38] After the outbreak of war, suspicions over where the allegiance of British fascists lay led, in 1940, to the forcible dissolution of the BUF by the government and the internment of many of its members, including Mosley.

No scholar disputes that antisemitism played a significant role in the above developments. Yet, as we will see in the following chapter, it has in many regards been relegated to a secondary position within the historiography, treated as an artificial appendage to the BUF's programme, rather than an organic element of it. Consequently, while various facets of the party's history – its ideology, membership, structure, activity, the opposition it aroused and so on – have been examined in their own right, antisemitism tends to be discussed almost entirely in terms of its relationship to these issues.

The only monograph devoted specifically to this subject – W.F. Mandle's *Anti-Semitism and the British Union of Fascists* – was written four decades ago.[39] Given the wealth of primary material and secondary research that has since emerged, his analysis shows its age. More recent accounts tend to spend little time examining the antisemitism itself: the ways in which it was expressed, the beliefs that underlay it and its relationship to the BUF's wider programme. Instead, they focus on the reasons for and consequences of its use – certainly important issues, but indicative of the idea that antisemitism is simply a prism through which to examine other aspects of BUF history. Tellingly, equal or greater attention is often paid to the anti-Jewish output of other organizations on interwar Britain's radical-right fringe, despite their minuscule size and complete lack of impact, even in comparison to the BUF. This, it seems, is because antisemitism is regarded as being a more authentic component of their ideology than it was of the BUF's.[40]

Part One of this study aims to contest such a notion and to advance this aspect of the scholarship on British fascism. First, through a combination of a quantitative survey of anti-Jewish rhetoric in the BUF press and more traditional analysis of primary sources, a comprehensive picture of the evolving use of antisemitism over the party's entire existence will be drawn. This will challenge the standard narrative in a number of ways, demonstrating, above all, that the BUF's anti-Jewish outlook was absolutely evident throughout its history, including the periods before its formal 'adoption' in autumn 1934 and after the turn away from the East End in 1937. Indeed, it will be shown that the crude antisemitism of the East End campaign in 1936–7 – which has attracted the most historical attention – was very much an interruption to the longer-term development of a distinctive, consistent and sophisticated anti-Jewish position, one that was closely integrated across the party's wider programme.

This understanding will then be used to explore the relationship between the BUF's antisemitism and its ideology, revealing that the former was always an authentic and fundamental aspect of the latter, thereby refuting any suggestion that outside influences, such as Jewish anti-fascism, played a part in compelling the party to oppose Jews. This will be shown to be symptomatic of fascism's necessary rejection of out-groups deemed incompatible with its idealized vision of a pure nation; but, equally, we will also see that the BUF's antisemitism was not at all imitative of other fascist movements, instead representing a synthesis – and, it will be argued, a 'fascistization' – of various native traditions of anti-Jewish thought. Throughout the foregoing, the conspicuous presence of Mosley will be observed, and in Chapter 4 his dominant role in the formulation and presentation of the BUF's anti-Jewish position will be explored, challenging the perception of him as a reluctant antisemite.

While these findings rest upon extensive primary research, it should be noted that – in contrast to the second part of the book, which will take advantage of much underused or completely new material – archival holdings pertaining to British fascism are well explored and, other than the occasional release of files by the National Archives, rarely produce completely novel sources. However, given the sheer volume of material available, examining certain parts of it more thoroughly than others have been able, approaching them from a different perspective or applying novel forms of analysis allows new understandings to emerge. Even three decades ago Colin Holmes admitted that his work on BUF antisemitism was not 'breaking into uncharted territory', but emphasized the continued value of 'rigorous and probing analysis of the evidence'. Fifteen years and a further deluge of research later, Kenneth Lunn warned that 'the notion that we no longer have anything to say about any particular aspect of

British fascism's history' simply because the available sources have been exhausted is a 'methodology long since discredited'.[41]

The National Archives remain the richest resource. The contents of its files relating to the BUF do, it should be noted, have a strong bias towards the issues that most interested the authorities – particularly public order and national security – and towards events in London. But this is, in fact, rather helpful for the present study. The police, Home Office and government regarded antisemitism as a key factor in fascist-related disorder and were concerned about links between British fascists and their German counterparts, with mutual opposition to Jews a cornerstone of this relationship. Moreover, a disproportionate amount of BUF activity, and particularly its anti-Jewish campaigning, took place in London.

The BUF itself left behind a wealth of published material, now available at a variety of archives and libraries: books, pamphlets and leaflets; an academic-style journal, *Fascist Quarterly* (*FQ*); and three national newspapers, *Blackshirt*, *Action* and *Fascist Week* (*FW*). It is these that will form the basis of the analysis of the party's anti-Jewish discourse, with the quantitative study of its newspapers, contained in Chapter 2, offering a good example of how applying fresh methodological approaches to well-used sources can tease out new insights. Relatively little, however, remains in terms of the BUF's internal records (or at least little that is available to scholars), but much of what does is held at the Universities of Birmingham and Sheffield. In particular, Mosley's papers, housed at Birmingham, demonstrate the efficacy of thoroughly reviewing previously examined sources. They provide, in the form of handwritten notes ignored by earlier researchers, unique evidence of Mosley's personal thoughts on the use of antisemitism, which will be used to support a fresh understanding of his involvement in this aspect of policy.

Anti-fascism and Anglo-Jewry

Despite far outnumbering their opponents, and proving extremely successful in subduing them, Britain's anti-fascists have received significantly less historical attention. In part, this reflects the fact that they were not a single, cohesive force, but rather a variegated and evolving collection of groups and individuals who opposed fascism for varying reasons and in different ways, often completely uncoordinated – and at times even in conflict – with one another. Even defining whom to place within this category has proved divisive. Many choose to focus primarily on those who confronted the fascists directly, an approach that has characterized various local histories, which detail efforts to physically oppose the Blackshirts in places as diverse as Oxford, Aberdeen and the Medway Towns of Kent.[42] These forms of activity often had a strongly political, and in particular left-wing, flavour.

Copsey, who has produced the most authoritative and rigorous work on the subject, criticizes accounts that deal only with this type of 'hostile activism'. Instead, he proposes a more 'pluralistic' approach, one that also incorporates 'liberal' (i.e. non-confrontational) and even 'passive' (i.e. non-active) anti-fascism. This allows for a far broader and more textured picture of the forces that were arrayed against British fascism. His most recent volume, *Varieties of Anti-Fascism*, co-edited with Andrzej Olechnowicz, includes contributions on the Labour, Conservative and Communist Parties, the press, émigré intellectuals, women, Christians and the British state.[43]

Copsey acknowledges, however, that holes remain in the research, and that 'much more needs to be said about the historic and contemporary complexities of anti-fascism'.[44] One group that has, in particular, been neglected in his work are Britain's Jews. In *Varieties of Anti-Fascism*, Jewish individuals appear from time to time, but only briefly, and as Conservative MPs, Labour councillors, intellectuals and so on, rather than as Jews.[45] Copsey's earlier survey, *Anti-Fascism in Britain*, provides greater coverage of Jewish involvement; yet, despite his calls for a wider definition of anti-fascism, he is himself guilty of focusing almost exclusively on left-wing, activist forms of Jewish opposition to the BUF.[46]

This has been the case elsewhere, too. Research on the BUF has, understandably, concentrated on the types of Jewish activity that most directly impinged on the party, which tends to mean disruptive and confrontational anti-fascism. More surprisingly, Anglo-Jewish historians have also presented a rather one-sided account. Their primary interest has been the vigorous and assertive response to fascism among some Jews – often young, working class and of recent immigrant stock – in the East End and Manchester. These individuals were active and influential participants in a coalition of groups, centred around the Communist Party of Great Britain (CPGB), that was responsible for the most visible opposition to the BUF. Their story is an important one, yet its domination of the historical narrative has come at the expense of other forms of Jewish activity. Where these are acknowledged, it is usually in the form of criticism of the Anglo-Jewish communal leadership for allegedly failing to take seriously the fascist threat and, consequently, pursuing only a half-hearted and ineffective defence policy. Additionally, accounts tend to focus on the periods when disruptive anti-fascism was at its most intense, 1934 and 1936–7, to the neglect of important developments before, after and between (a similar, and related, temporal bias has also characterized the study of BUF antisemitism).[47]

Part Two of this book attempts to address some of these deficiencies, and to expand and enhance our understanding of Jewish anti-fascism, by looking beyond the most visible and direct forms of activity. Adopting a more traditional, linear structure than the first half of the study, it will comprise a broadly chronological account – divided into three periods, each representing a separate stage of development – of the ways in which different elements of the Jewish community perceived and reacted to the emergence of the BUF and other groups on the domestic radical right, and tracing the ways these responses evolved over time and interacted with one another, as well as with non-Jewish forms of opposition. By encompassing a much wider range of responses than previous studies, and over a longer period of time, a far more textured picture of Jewish anti-fascism will emerge than the standard portrayals of an antithetical division between working-class activists and passive elites. In particular, perceptions of the attitude and actions of the latter group will be revised, revealing far greater urgency and activity from the Jewish leadership than the prevalent narrative allows. Throughout, the prominent and decisive role Jews played at all levels of Britain's highly successful anti-fascist movement will be revealed.

These findings will be used to reflect more widely upon issues of communal dynamics and identity. The 1930s were a time of enormous upheaval for Anglo-Jewry, as growing tension over the balance of power within a community whose complexion had changed rapidly over preceding decades came to a head. The threat of fascism – both at home and abroad – and the heated debate it provoked among Jews over how best to respond are traditionally portrayed as fitting neatly into this wider process of communal reform, with an increasingly assertive immigrant community forcefully challenging the authority of the traditional anglicized elites, who were failing to properly represent the interests of Anglo-Jewry in its entirety. Yet, while it is true that the emergence of the BUF exposed pre-existing divisions within Anglo-Jewry, it will be shown that, over time, there developed a cohesive Jewish response, with broad agreement on the forms that communal defence should take and the fact that it should be coordinated by the Board of Deputies of British Jews, the community's official representative body. This, in turn, played a part in smoothing an evolution – rather than radical transformation – towards a leadership that better embodied the community it served.

We will also see how these developments encouraged reflection by Jews on their position within British society. The BUF's antisemitism acted as a powerful reminder that Jews continued to be regarded as alien by a substantial section of the British population, while the worsening fate of Jews at the hands of fascists elsewhere in Europe put into perspective some of the disputes that had previously divided Anglo-Jewry's disparate elements, and emphasized the common interests that they shared. Equally, however, Jews were by and large well integrated into their surrounding society, and we find that their approaches to fascism were strongly informed by a sense of attachment to Britain. How Jews negotiated the balance between their various identities, and the reciprocal relationship between this process and Jewish defence activity, will be explored.

The account presented in Part Two relies in large part on the exploitation of sources previously unavailable to or neglected by scholars, and therefore will contain a great deal of material that has never before appeared in print. In particular, the defence archive of the Board of Deputies, housed separately from its main collections, contains a wealth of material that, perhaps as a result of its relative inaccessibility,[48] has barely been touched. As well as offering an invaluable insight into the attitude and actions of the Jewish communal leadership – much of which was unpublicized at the time and has remained hidden since – it also covers a broad range of other Jewish groups and individuals with whom the Board, as Anglo-Jewry's representative body, was in contact or whose activity it closely monitored. Additionally, the Board's defence committee collected more comprehensive intelligence on British fascism than any institution other than the British state itself (indeed, the authorities themselves often sought information from the Board). Its archives, therefore, provide extensive details of fascist activity, including unique glances into the internal workings of various radical-right organizations from the Board's network of informants.

Two further sources that have received relatively little attention are the large (but uncatalogued) collection of material on the British radical right gathered by the Institute of Jewish Affairs, housed at University College London, and the Anglo-Jewish archives held by the Parkes Institute at Southampton University. From the latter, this study has made particular use of the private papers of Neville Laski, the president of the Board for most of the 1930s; his successor, Selig Brodetsky; Robert Waley Cohen, a communal luminary whose collection is a recent addition to the Institute's holdings; and the eponymous James Parkes himself, a clergyman and scholar who maintained close contact with various Jewish groups interested in combating fascism and antisemitism. Together, these provide further details of the discussions that took place between a variety of actors, both inside and outside the Jewish community, and the activity that consequently arose.

On the anti-fascist activity of working-class and left-leaning Jews, the People's History Museum and Working Class Movement Library, both in Manchester, are of particular value, while the same city's Jewish Museum possesses a comprehensive collection of written and oral-history material. Hull University Library also holds useful sources in this regard, particularly the archives of the National Council of Civil Liberties (known today as the pressure group Liberty). Two contemporary personal collections – those of Lazar Zaidman, a prominent figure in the CPGB and the Workers' Circle friendly society, and David Spector, a leading member of the Association of Jewish Ex-Servicemen, housed at Sheffield University and the Wiener Library, respectively – provide further repositories of information. Finally, although far from being underused, the back catalogue of the *Jewish Chronicle* (*JC*), Anglo-Jewry's main newspaper, is an indispensible source on activity and opinion across the entire spectrum of Anglo-Jewry, as well as on the development of domestic fascism, which the *JC* closely monitored.

Part One

British Fascist Antisemitism

1

Introduction

British antisemitism

Modern British forms of antisemitism have long been deemed relatively trivial by comparison to their counterparts in many parts of Continental Europe, seen to lack the latter's severity, variety and pervasiveness. The historical stereotype is of modern Britain as a tolerant society, perhaps harbouring a degree of social prejudice and economic jealousy towards its Jewish minority, but free of the extreme and politicized antipathy found elsewhere. Indeed, scholars have even highlighted the popular enmity felt in Britain towards more explicit forms of antisemitism, with this sometimes cited as a factor in the BUF's decline in support from 1934.[1]

Early scholarship on Anglo-Jewish history generally ignored the issue of gentile antagonism altogether. This reflected a desire, in the post-emancipation period, to avoid being seen as ungratefully denigrating British hospitality, to discourage perceptions of Jewish solidarity and to avoid the risk of reviving historical complaints against the community by drawing attention to them. As David Cesarani notes, in its omission of this topic the early historiography was itself 'shaped by antisemitism'.[2] After the Second World War, the study of antisemitism was, for obvious reasons, dominated by its more radical and violent manifestations; in particular, attempts were made to explain what, psychologically, could make individuals susceptible to hatred of Jews. Such work focused predominantly on continental Europe, where these forms of prejudice had recently had such a horrific impact. When scholars did turn their attention to Britain, they tended to replicate this preoccupation, taking British fascism, and its extreme brand of antisemitism, as their subject.[3]

In the 1970s, efforts to examine British antisemitism in its own right began to emerge. The first, Gisela Lebzelter's 1978 *Political Anti-Semitism in England*, still struggled, however, to emerge from the shadow of Nazism, taking as its yardstick 'total' antisemitism with the final aim of the eradication of Jewry. By these standards, Lebzelter finds a complete 'absence of a historical tradition of anti-semitism in Britain'.[4] By contrast, Colin Holmes, in his seminal study, *Anti-Semitism in British Society*, published a year later, describes a visible and at times influential tradition of antisemitism specific to Britain, though he sees this as reflective of a general hostility towards immigrants, rather than Jews exclusively. Of particular pertinence to the present study, he offers a partially 'interactionist' analysis, arguing that antisemitism came about not simply from some inherent and irrational antipathy towards Jews, but also as a result of 'an identifiable core of grievances' stemming from Jewish behaviour.[5]

Holmes' work, as well as that of Geoffrey Field soon after, did much to begin to reveal the vibrancy and diversity of the various strands of anti-Jewish thought native to Britain. These ranged from anti-alienism – motivated by economic competition and cultural tension with Jewish immigrants – through the wariness many socialists felt towards the Jews' role as financiers, industrialists and employers, to the work of writers such as Leo Maxse, Hilaire Belloc and the Chesterton brothers, Cecil and G.K. The latter figures articulated many of the fears regarding national decline, corruption and decadence that inspired fascists of later years, and central to their attacks, and to those of less prominent but more ardently antisemitic polemicists such as Arnold White, Nesta Webster and Joseph Bannister, was the supposedly pernicious influences of Jews, who were alleged to be responsible for many of the ills afflicting British society.[6]

Yet such hostility, Holmes admits, was 'of a less severe and intense kind than that which manifested itself in certain other countries'. It took, Field adds, 'vaguer', 'less political' and 'quieter forms'. The latter author offers a number of explanations for this: a relative lack of opposition to Jewish emancipation, a tradition of religious tolerance and admitting refugees, a reluctance to openly express prejudice, and a widespread acceptance of the economic liberalism that elsewhere was negatively associated with Jews. Presaging future developments in the field, he concludes that Britain experienced its own 'particular form of anti-Semitism'.[7]

This final comment hints at the main criticism that has been levelled at early attempts to understand British attitudes towards Jews: that they employ foreign models of antisemitism as a benchmark. By searching for the types of anti-Jewish prejudice found in other parts of Europe – which were indeed relatively weak in Britain – they neglected other, more peculiarly British forms of intolerance. But growing attention to the study of immigration – both gentile perceptions of it and the experiences of migrants themselves – began to reveal further layers of popular resentment towards Jews, who reached Britain (mostly from eastern Europe) in large numbers over the six decades preceding the Second World War. Such negative sentiment – which permeated political discourse and public attitudes, and found legislative expression in the Aliens Act of 1905 and further legal restrictions at the beginning and end of the First World War – represented, Cesarani contends, 'a specific, indigenous form of xenophobia', one which helps demonstrate that 'Continental-style racism was not the most appropriate yardstick to use when judging the presence or absence of antisemitism in Britain'.[8]

As a new school of thought on British antisemitism emerged, two further established beliefs came in for challenge: the idea of interactionism; and the notion that liberalism and antisemitism are somehow inversely correlated, with the strength of the former in Britain impairing the development of the latter. Bryan Cheyette, in particular, has vigorously attacked interactionist theories, warning that by choosing to treat anti-Jewish beliefs as rational and rooting them in concrete economic and social realities, they 'confuse the contextualisation of anti-Semitism with a coercively assimilationist construction of racism that argues that ethnic minorities should adopt the dominant culture to avoid race-hatred'. Anti-Jewish attitudes grew, in fact, from established representations of the Jew that existed not just in the minds of extremists, but more widely throughout society, he contends.[9]

Many of these representations, as Cheyette, Frank Felsenstein and Anthony Julius have demonstrated, arose from anti-Jewish tropes in popular culture: from the recurring figure of the 'Wandering Jew', through Shakespeare's Shylock, to the work of T.S. Eliot. These helped establish and perpetuate negative cultural stereotypes of 'the Jew', in particular his supposedly sinister, avaricious and predatory nature, as well as his inveterate foreignness. The persistence of such characterizations challenges the complacent perception of British tolerance, revealing 'the extensive undergrowth of anti-Semitic allusion' that has long existed in the depths of public discourse and reminding us that the coming of modern, liberal Britain 'did not eradicate but merely altered the nature of anti-Semitism'. Moreover, such stereotypes provided rich source material for political antisemites to draw upon. Given that they had established a popular image of the Jew as 'threaten[ing] to overturn and confound the fabric of the social order' and as 'the perpetual outsider whose unsettling presence serves to define the bounds that separate the native Englishman from the alien Other', it is not hard to envisage their utility for British fascists.[10]

Cheyette's reference above to 'coercive' pressures alludes to another native strand of thought regarding Jews, explored by Holmes and later described by Bill Williams as the 'anti-Semitism of toleration'. This refers to the demand made of Jews to fulfil their side of the 'emancipation bargain': that in return for being granted equality and acceptance, they were expected to prove their loyalty and worth to the nation, and to abandon any elements of their Jewish identity regarded as incompatible with their embracement of Englishness. 'The expectation', Holmes suggests, was 'that Jews would cease to be Jewish.' Moreover, if antisemitism subsequently persisted, this was the Jews' own fault, for not making sufficient effort to integrate.[11] The prevalence of such attitudes, and the burden they placed on the Jewish community, undermines the axiomatic belief that British liberalism regarded Jews benevolently, and instead reveals some of the manifold pressures that created, in Cesarani's words, the 'more highly textured picture of prejudice, discrimination and stereotyping that persisted without difficulty within a liberal society that officially rejected racism'.[12]

Building on such work, Tony Kushner has delineated two principle forms of prejudice towards Jews in modern Britain. To the 'anti-semitism of liberalism', which mirrors Williams' conception, he adds the 'anti-semitism of exclusion': a widespread sentiment, prevalent among conservatives, that many Jews were incorrigibly alien. This, therefore, left Britain's Jews on the one hand accused of not trying hard enough to assimilate, while on the other being told they were not able to do so. Anglo-Jewry was, Kushner concludes, 'caught in a vice' between these two conflicting gentile perceptions, causing severe 'neuroses' and inhibiting the formation of a positive identity. Moreover, because such thinking pervaded the political mainstream, it also had concrete effects, influencing anti-alien legislation in the early twentieth century and the treatment of Jewish refugees from Nazism in the 1930s and 1940s.[13]

The most recent – and, in terms of scope, ambitious – thesis has been put forward by Julius, who traces four distinct traditions of English antisemitism: the 'radical prejudice of defamation, expropriation, and murder' that prevailed during medieval times, culminating in the Jews' expulsion from England in 1290; the literary antisemitism that emerged during the subsequent absence of Jews and continues to 'flourish' to this

day; the 'modern anti-semitism of insult and partial exclusion' that developed after the
Jews' readmission, becoming 'pervasive but contained', never preventing emancipation
or economic advancement; and, finally, contemporary anti-Zionism, which 'now
constitutes the greatest threat'.

Most pertinent to this study is the third category. Yet its breadth (ranging from
'everyday' popular prejudice to conspiracy theories of Jewish power) and its omissions
(many anti-alien agitators and exclusionary nationalists of the first half of the twentieth
century advocated far more than 'insult and partial exclusion') make it rather a blunt
tool of analysis. Presumably aware of such deficiencies, Julius admits that this type
of antisemitism absorbed aspects of its more extreme medieval predecessor and also
'coexisted for some time with the immense ideological anti-semitisms of the European
Continent, in part replicating them (but in diminished form)'.[14] Yet such a position
neglects the contemporary, native patterns of thought from which even the more
radical varieties of modern British antisemitism grew, as well as the variegated forms
that they took.

It should be acknowledged that the 'British school' of thought represented by the
likes of Cesarani, Kushner and Cheyette is not universally accepted.[15] David Feldman,
for example, acknowledges that English antisemitism was 'home-produced', and that
there remained, even after emancipation, a 'difficult relationship between Jews and
the state ... and the nation', with many wondering 'whether Jews could be patriots'. But
he also believes that work has focused too narrowly on Jewish experiences and on
traditions of liberal thought, rather than understanding the varying and evolving ideas
of 'Englishness' among different sections of British society and the broader context
within which the Jewish question was placed. Yes, Jews were expected to acculturate;
but 'acculturat[e] to what?', he asks.[16]

Todd Endelman was initially a more outspoken critic, disputing the existence of
these alleged pressures on Anglo-Jewry (especially the idea of 'liberal' antisemitism)
and reiterating that, in comparison to many other places, Britain's Jews experienced
an extremely tolerant environment, one conducive to their rapid economic and social
advancement.[17] In more recent work, however, Endelman has modified his view. He
continues to maintain that, from the eighteenth to twentieth century, 'it was easier
to be a Jew in Britain than anywhere else in Europe', but also admits that 'this is not
the whole story': as part of the 'price to be paid for inclusion and acceptance', Jews
experienced 'subtle and diffuse' pressure to 'suppress, tone down, or reconfigure their
Jewishness', which had a powerful 'disintegrative effect on the maintenance of Jewish
identity'.[18]

This appears a fair assessment. One can understand modern British anti-Jewish
attitudes as distinct, prevalent and insidious while also accepting that they resulted in far
less of a threat to Jews' physical wellbeing, social acceptance and personal advancement
than in many other parts of the world. Moreover, it is undeniable that more radical and
explicit forms of antisemitism struggled to gain any traction, whether through some
inherent British immunity to them or simply because the right circumstances for their
activation were never present. Additionally, much of the popular prejudice that Jews
did face has proved not to be particular to them, having also been experienced by other
minority groups at various stages.[19]

But, for the purposes of this study, the strength and pervasiveness of British antisemitism is of less concern than the forms that it took, and the patterns of thought upon which fascists could build. In this regard, Kushner's division between exclusionary and liberal prejudices, complemented by the work of Holmes, Field and others on the various forms of antisemitism that emerged in early-twentieth-century Britain, serves as a useful framework, to which we will later return.

Fascism and antisemitism

The association between fascism and Jews understandably brings to mind an extreme and overriding political antisemitism, grounded in pseudo-scientific theory, along with organized persecution leading, potentially, to mass murder. Such a perception has, of course, been shaped by the fanatical and destructive antisemitism of the Nazis and their collaborators, and by the fact that by the outbreak of war most fascist movements had come to adopt an anti-Jewish position, often seemingly as a result of Nazi influence. Yet it is important to remember that a relationship between fascism and antisemitism is not inevitable, and in fact has been far from ubiquitous historically. Indeed, fascism's inaugural Italian manifestation – the dominant paradigm before Hitler's rise to power – officially eschewed antisemitism for the first nineteen of its twenty-six years of existence, while up to the early 1930s a significant portion of Europe's fascist organizations expressed little interest in the Jewish question.

Given popular misconceptions, it is somewhat surprising that the wealth of historical and theoretical work on fascism in recent decades has devoted scant attention to this issue. While there has been great debate over whether fascism was revolutionary or reactionary, modernizing or conservative, located on the left or the right of the political spectrum (or outside of it altogether), whether it should be defined by its ideology or practice, how wide or narrow any such definition should be and what components should comprise it, the position of antisemitism and racism within fascist thought has been little discussed.[20]

This perhaps results from a degree of accord on the issue. Griffin and Payne broadly concur that fascism's inherent ultranationalism and ethnicism predispose it to a belief in racial superiority, although not necessary to Nazi-style biological, 'Nordic' or Social Darwinian racism, nor to antisemitism per se.[21] Paxton, similarly, regards racism as a by-product of fascists' need to 'diabolise some enemy' and purge the nation of alien or impure elements. He also stresses that Jews need not be the target of this drive.[22] In a similar vein, Aristotle Kallis sets out how two objectives that were at the heart of the fascist project, cleansing and rebirth, were intimately connected to one another, with the former being 'both the precondition and the consequence' of the latter. By 'purging the national community from allegedly threatening and/or harmful "others"' – often, but not always, Jews – fascists would inaugurate their 'desired utopian state of wholeness and purity'.[23] Mark Neocleous, who sees fascist ultranationalism as 'necessarily xenophobic … and thus always … an invitation to antisemitism and racism', can also be placed within this camp.[24]

What follows from this interpretation is that the adoption and development of antisemitism is more a product of the context within which a given movement develops – with interwar Europe providing a rich tradition of antipathy towards Jews for fascists to absorb and build upon and a near-ubiquitous Jewish minority to oppose – than it is of fascism itself, whose latent exclusionary nationalism can take a variety of forms. Moreover, even for the most extreme racial fascists, racism represents a *means* of achieving their ultimate goal – national purification and rebirth – rather than an end in itself.

Others, admittedly, might choose to place themselves outside this consensus. Kevin Passmore, on the one hand, claims that 'fascism is unabashedly racist' and that 'racism pervade[s] all aspects of fascist practice'.[25] At the other extreme, A. James Gregor claims that 'racism is not even necessary to "fascism" as a concept'.[26] While superficially contradictory, both these views can in fact be reconciled within the above position: racism did indeed come to dominate the activity of most interwar fascist groups, but often as a consequence of the prevailing conditions within which they operated, which activated their inherent predisposition to xenophobic prejudice, rather than being an essential and inevitable aspect of fascist development.

Where there has been significant disagreement is over the extent to which National Socialism, along with its powerful and idiosyncratic brand of antisemitism, should influence our perception of fascism: whether it, alongside Italian Fascism, should be regarded as fascism's most fully formed and characteristic 'prototypes';[27] or if, instead, it was just one manifestation among many, politically more successful but ideologically no more representative than any other.[28] Some, indeed, suggest excluding Nazism from our conception of fascism altogether.[29] A further complication, however, is that to whatever degree one accepts Nazism as representative of fascism, it is indisputable that Hitler's creed had a strong influence on the development of contemporaneous fascist movements, particularly in regard to their racial thought. But, again, little effort has been made to trace the evolution of and relationship between various incarnations of fascist antisemitism.

The first real attempt to explore these issues in detail – to ascertain antisemitism's position within 'generic' fascist ideology, to trace the development of its specific manifestations during the interwar period and to evaluate the influence of National Socialism on this process – has recently been undertaken by Kallis. He accepts that European interwar fascist groups adopted 'highly diversified attitudes' towards Jews, each reflecting 'country-specific strategies for the defence and strengthening of the national community' that 'fus[ed] … generic fascist values with indigenous anti-Jewish currents and trends'. But, he asks, if this was the case then why did fascist antisemitism, which had been 'conspicuous by its absence' in the 1920s, suddenly proliferate and radicalize across the continent during the mid-to-late 1930s, apparently under the influence of German National Socialism?

Kallis' answer is that fascist movements were keen to replicate the success that antisemitism had apparently yielded for the Nazis, but without necessarily mimicking its specific form. Furthermore, as the 1930s progressed, fascists felt an increasing sense of unitary purpose, of participation in a final confrontation between themselves and the international forces of Bolshevism, liberal democracy and capitalism. Jews had of course long been popularly associated with these 'enemies', and antisemitism, in its various guises, now became the common cause that rallied these movements behind the Nazi 'spearhead' in this crusade of liberation, cleansing and rebirth.[30]

The BUF provides a fitting example of the radicalization and unification process Kallis describes. While the party initially adopted an outwardly non-committal position on the Jewish question, antisemitism became an increasingly evident feature of its activity, programme and ideology. This was, moreover, a process that coincided with a growing sense of pan-European fascist alignment – and in particular a drift towards the Nazis' sphere of influence – yet, equally, one that produced an antisemitism that was far from imitative, instead being rooted in native patterns of anti-Jewish thought.

BUF antisemitism

All work on the BUF has broached the issue of antisemitism, which by the mid-1930s had become a central plank of Blackshirt campaigning. As mentioned above, it is this facet of the party's brief existence that is perhaps most strongly associated with the movement in the public mind, given the rarity of such explicit prejudice in British political history, the violence and disorder it provoked and its perceived association with the concurrent racial policies of the German Nazis. As a result, more popular accounts of British fascism often resort to unhelpful generalizations. Stephen Dorril's recent biography of Mosley, for example, posits that 'anti-Semitism united all sections of the BUF in their hatred of Jews'.[31]

By contrast, academic research has tended to treat the BUF's antisemitism as a secondary issue, often using it as a lens through which to examine other aspects of the party's history. Thus, Pugh's *Hurrah for the Blackshirts!* includes a chapter on 'Anti-Semitism and the Reorganisation of Fascism 1936–8', relating the development of this aspect of policy to internal factional disputes within the BUF over a limited period.[32] Others have analysed antisemitism in the context of the conflict that emerged between the Blackshirts and their opponents, particularly in mid-1934 and during the peak of East End activity in 1936–7.[33] In this regard, much attention has been paid to the violence provoked by the BUF's antisemitism. This is not surprising, given the visibility and unprecedented nature of such activity, but it often distracts from the content and expression of the party's anti-Jewish position. (It is, moreover, symptomatic the way in which fascism, unlike most other political movements, is perceived primarily in terms of its activity rather than its ideas.[34])

As the above suggests, scholars have principally been interested in the causes and effects of BUF antisemitism, rather than the antisemitism itself. In particular, they attempt to explain the motivation behind its adoption and development as official policy from late 1934, and the extent to which this decision stemmed from, and subsequently influenced, the party's political fortunes. Most researchers advocate some combination of six explanations for the BUF's move towards explicit antisemitism: the hostility it faced from Jewish anti-fascists; the party's marginalization from mainstream politics and declining support; Britain's improving economy, which made Mosley's original programme far less appealing; the influence of antisemitic members within the BUF on Mosley; the growing prominence and success of the Nazi model of fascism; and the popularity of anti-Jewish propaganda in east London. What these theories have in common, of course, is their implication that antisemitism was not initially intended to form part of the BUF's programme, and that Mosley was compelled by these various factors to incorporate it.

Colin Cross claims that by 1934 there was 'pressure... at every level in the BUF' for Mosley to adopt antisemitism, which he 'found... difficult to resist'. Both Cross and another early scholar of British fascism, Robert Benewick, believe that Jews served as a useful and tangible target for BUF campaigning once it had begun to falter in 1934.[35] They do accept, as does Mandle, that there were visible 'undercurrents' of antisemitic sentiment in the BUF from its earliest days; but it was only in October 1934, during an infamous address at the Albert Hall, that Mosley 'signalled the real beginning of the BUF's campaign against the Jews'.

Mandle does, however, betray some confusion over why this step was taken. First he contends that the 'decision... was made with an eye, naturally, to political advantage': the BUF's declining membership and tarnished reputation, alongside Britain's economic recovery, meant that Mosley 'needed an issue' to reinvigorate his party. Having observed Hitler's successes in Germany, he turned to antisemitism. But in the very same section of the book, Mandle contradictorily warns that it is 'erroneous' to talk of any conscious decision: the BUF had, in fact, 'been compelled to become anti-Semitic'. This compulsion was provided in part by Jews themselves, due to their involvement in anti-fascist disruption and physical confrontation.[36]

The latter is a theme that was taken up by Robert Skidelsky, whose 1975 biography of Mosley placed much of the blame for the BUF's adoption of antisemitism on Jewish anti-fascists. He did subsequently qualify his account somewhat, admitting that it had 'not sufficiently explain[ed] the surplus [fascist] hostility to which opposition by Jews gave rise', nor the pre-existing antisemitic stereotypes that their actions 'activated' in Mosley and others. But he continues to maintain that the BUF was not inherently antisemitic or violent, but had 'been pushed in these ways by the opposition it aroused'.[37] This position is supported to some extent by Holmes, who cites Jewish actions as one of a range of factors that contributed to the BUF's antisemitism. But, like Skidelsky, he admits that the forms that antisemitism took far transcended the set of 'identifiable issues' that underlay them.[38]

Scholars of Anglo-Jewish history and British antisemitism have, by contrast, tended to reject any suggestion that interaction with Jews pushed the BUF towards antisemitism. Lebzelter, for example, points instead to the influence of antisemitic party members and a shift in emphasis from domestic to foreign policy as the key factors behind the growing opposition to Jews.[39] Cheyette, too, has extended his broader criticism of interactionism to take account of the BUF. The suggestion that Jews themselves were in some way responsible for antipathy towards them comes worryingly close to Mosley's own defence that he attacked Jews for 'clearly discernible reasons', Cheyette cautions, and risks exculpating the BUF and its leader of blame for the adoption of antisemitism.

Interestingly, from the perspective of the present study, Cheyette advocates a 'discourse' approach, which sees antisemitism as a series of representations, rather than authentic depictions, of Jews. Such anti-Jewish narratives were already well established in Britain and could readily be drawn upon.[40] In summarizing the views of Cheyette and others in the 'British school', Kushner and Lunn note that 'in terms of British racism, "the problem exists not at the level of specific instances of conflict … but in the realms of ideology" '.[41] This will be shown in the present work to be an important consideration with regard to the BUF.

While acknowledging such concerns, work on British fascism continues to suggest that Jews themselves were to some extent responsible for the BUF's turn to antisemitism, be it by their economic activity, their ethnic visibility or, most often, their involvement in anti-fascism. D.S. Lewis, for example, maintains that in many ways the separation between interactionism and scapegoat theories is 'artificial'. While BUF antisemitism grew in part from within the movement – due to the influence of antisemites around Mosley and the need for 'an alien but flexible enemy' – it also inevitably elicited a response from the Jewish community, leading to 'a degree of interaction'.[42]

Thurlow, despite admitting that antipathy towards Jews had been 'incipient' in the BUF from the outset, believes that its incorporation into official policy was the 'result of the interaction of bitterly opposed fascist and anti-fascist elements'. This was not entirely the Jews' fault, however, as the Blackshirts, deprived of press coverage, sought out confrontation as the best means to obtain publicity. Later, when the BUF had 'all but collapsed as a national force' and with its central ideology holding little appeal, antisemitism was developed as a 'virulent political weapon' in certain localities, most notably the East End, as part of a wider 'strategy … to foment local and regional grievances in populist campaigns'.[43]

The most recent academic studies of British fascism have suggested a familiar set of factors that pushed the BUF towards antisemitism. Pugh cites the party's declining popularity, anti-fascist hostility and the fact that it had already become associated with Nazism in public perception. He also underscores the influence of internal party dynamics, with a struggle between various factions over 1934–7 playing an important role in the shifting use of antisemitism.[44] Linehan's 'multi-causal analysis' of the BUF's antisemitism incorporates 'the interaction context' and socio-economic factors, Mosley's opportunism in exploiting these, and the role of 'xenophobic racist anti-semites within the decision-making hierarchy' who were 'pushing for a more aggressive anti-Jewish policy'. As part of this mix, however, Linehan also acknowledges the influence of the party's ideology and of established British representations of Jews – crucial observations, to which we will shortly return.[45]

With regard to antisemitism's impact upon the BUF's political fortunes, almost all scholars agree that it played a negative role,[46] although their interpretations as to why this was the case differ. Some, such as Thurlow, believe that it helped push the BUF 'beyond the pale' of respectable opinion and into the 'political sub-culture' of east London, guaranteeing its continued marginalization from the mainstream.[47] But others, notably Lebzelter and Mandle, argue that, in fact, the BUF suffered from not being antisemitic enough: its anti-Jewish rhetoric was 'half-hearted', 'clumsily handled' and was never formed into a convincing and comprehensive case against the Jews.[48] It will be argued in this study that, in actual fact, Mosley constructed a relatively sophisticated anti-Jewish position, one that was built upon native patterns of thought and carefully integrated into his programme.

Similarly, Pugh believes that, at a time when public opinion on Nazi Germany was divided, and the question of Jewish refugees was high on the agenda, the BUF allowed itself to be 'outflanked' on Jewish issues by other, even more extreme groups.[49] His claims appear, however, to be an exaggeration. Of the other organizations he cites, the Imperial Fascist League (IFL) and National Socialist League (NSL) had minute memberships and made barely a mark on public consciousness; the Nordic League (NL) was a secretive underground body that held small private meetings for obsessive antisemites; and the BF had ceased to exist altogether in 1935. None was able to harness popular anti-Jewish sentiment to build a base of popular support – not even to the limited extent that the BUF managed. His evidence of the 'success' of another group, The Link, is that its membership rose to 4,300 by June 1939. Yet he takes this figure from its own journal – hardly an impartial source, especially given the propensity of those on Britain's radical right to greatly exaggerate their popularity. In any case, even if one were to accept its veracity, the number is only around a fifth of estimated BUF membership at this time, making it hard to believe that The Link was more effective in exploiting anti-war and anti-refugee sentiment.

While much of historiographical discussion of the BUF's antisemitism has been devoted to the question of why the party chose to incorporate this aspect of policy, far less attention has been paid to exactly when and how this happened, and the subsequent process of development. This reflects the fact that there is a broad consensus over the path of this progression: initially, abuse of Jews occurred infrequently and without official endorsement; then, following a summer of anti-fascist disruption and declining popularity, the BUF 'adopted' antisemitism as policy in the autumn 1934; its use rapidly accelerated following the onset of the East End campaign in late 1935; finally, the migration away from the East End after 1937 saw a diminishment in anti-Jewish rhetoric, with a brief spike in 1939 as a corollary of Mosley's 'Peace Campaign'.[50]

Although some scholars may deviate slightly in places, this general outline has become almost axiomatic. This appears, however, to have in part arisen from a readiness to skim over important aspects of BUF history. In particular, the period after 1937's London County Council (LCC) elections has often been perceived simply as the anticlimactic aftermath of the East End campaign, leading some, such as Alan Sykes in his brief summary of BUF antisemitism, to ignore it entirely and others, like Mandle in his far more comprehensive survey, to claim that 'anti-Semitism was virtually dropped as a major issue from 1938 onwards'.[51]

The first year and a half of the movement's history has been similarly neglected. Skidelsky, for example, claims that that official attitudes towards Jews remained unchanged for the first two years of the party's existence – a claim that is contradicted by even his own evidence of a hardening line over late 1933 and 1934. Even when such indications of an incipient antisemitism are acknowledged, they are usually accompanied by little analysis, with accounts tending to begin in proper with Mosley's 'conversion' to antisemitism over the summer and autumn of 1934.[52] The chapter of Linehan's *British Fascism* on the BUF mentions nothing of its activity before mid-1934, while the years 1938–9 are summarized extremely concisely, thus reducing three and a half years – 50 per cent of the BUF's peacetime existence – to a single page of thirty devoted to the history of the movement.[53]

One partial exception has been Lewis, who acknowledges that 'the consistent elements of anti-Semitism were all there' by the end of 1933, 'suggest[ing] that an as yet undecided variety of anti-Semitism had become official BUF policy'. Mosley's subsequent speeches the next autumn were therefore 'not an aberration but rather a further stage in the development of an anti-Semitic process which had begun considerably earlier'. This is a particularly important point, and will be expounded in far greater detail throughout the present study. Lewis' account is less helpful in tracing subsequent developments, however. He tersely dismisses the 1937–8 period as one of rapidly declining antisemitism (which, as we shall see, it was not), ignores 1939 altogether and otherwise focuses entirely on the East End campaign.[54]

The abovementioned deficiencies are significant, because a firm understanding of *when* and *how* the BUF's antisemitism evolved is first necessary before one can reliably suggest *why* it did. For example, if it can be shown that the BUF had openly set itself against Anglo-Jewry by the end of 1933, or that the rise in anti-Jewish rhetoric over the summer of 1934 commenced before Olympia – both of which will be demonstrated below – then this raises serious questions over the validity of interactionist theories. More generally, by shifting attention away from the East End campaign and treating the periods 1932–5 and 1938–9 in their own right, rather than as a 'before and after', a more representative picture emerges.

A second, related problem is that the attention paid to the causes and consequences of the BUF's antisemitism has come at the expense of substantial analysis of the antisemitism itself. The one real exception is Mandle's account; yet, published forty-five years ago, at a time when sources relating to the BUF were scarce and memories of the war still fresh, its findings do not stand up to close scrutiny today. Taking Nazism as his gauge, Mandle concludes that the BUF had 'most of the characteristics of anti-Semitic movements of modern times[.] ... Its motivation and activities paralleled, in microcosm, larger and more successful contemporary ones'. His justification for this claim, though, presents various inconsistencies. Having declared that the BUF fits a five-point model of Nazi antisemitism conceived by Leon Poliakov, he is forced to admit that there are some doubts over two of those categories: the fourth, anti-Jewish propaganda appealing to sexual passions, which Mandle notes was little used by the BUF; and the fifth, the use of violence, which in the BUF's case was 'mild' and pursued in a 'curiously defeatist' way. In addition to these anomalies, the present study also takes some issue with his classification of the BUF within categories one (portraying Jews as an indistinguishable whole) and three (deeming Jews an inferior race).[55]

The main reason why so little has been done to explore anti-Jewish discourse in the wealth of research on the BUF conducted in the decades since Mandle's study appears to be that, as we have seen, antisemitism is regarded as an artificial and belated addition to the BUF's programme, either forced upon Mosley by Jewish attacks or exploited opportunistically to boost his party's fortunes. As such, it has tended not to be seen as an authentic – or at the least not a central – element of the party's ideology.

Holmes, for example, has produced a chapter dedicated to the BUF's antisemitism. Yet after only minimal discussion of its content and typology, he quickly moves on to what, strangely, he believes are the issues that have been neglected by scholars: 'the causes of the BUF's anti-semitism and its subsequent containment in the inter-war years' (at the time of publication, these were precisely the issues that had already interested Skidelsky, Benewick and others). In particular, he devotes attention to the receptiveness of the British public to the party's anti-Jewish line, which, though interesting, is a separate issue from the antisemitism itself. His brief analysis of the form of Blackshirt antisemitism does, however, offer the seeds of a promising approach, noting that Jewish policy was 'linked and related to the general ideology of the movement'; that 'anti-semitism was present in the BUF from the beginning', simply becoming 'a more significant element of ideology' after 1934; and that the East End campaign, and its attendant antisemitism, developed separately from the party's central ideology.[56]

In a chapter comparing the BUF's antisemitism to that of other British fascist organizations, Thurlow distinguishes two separate strands of anti-Jewish thought. The 'Mosley tradition' approached the question of race in neo-Lamarckian, vitalist terms, differentiating between 'good' and 'bad' Jews. By contrast, the materialist, determinist approach taken by racial nationalists elsewhere on the radical-right fringe dictated that Jews be regarded as an indistinguishable, incorrigible and intolerable whole. While this is an accurate and valuable observation, such a distinction – premised chiefly on differences over whether race should be defined culturally or biologically – is rather reductionist, taking account of only one (admittedly important) factor. Each party's anti-Jewish position comprised numerous facets, and they usually had more in common than set them apart. Given Britain's diversity of fascist organizations, a series of overlapping circles seems a more appropriate model to map their views than does the neat, single-issue dichotomy suggested by Thurlow.

Thurlow also argues that, for the BUF, antisemitism 'never became a total ideological explanation of all the imagined ills of British society' in the way that it did for many other domestic fascist groups, such as the IFL. It always remained 'something entirely different' from 'the real inner core' of ideology, which was focused on the creation of 'the new fascist man', who would 'transform himself and his society to create a new stage in the evolutionary development of mankind'. Antisemitism, by contrast, was largely a means by which to attract followers in certain areas, who were then indoctrinated with the true 'beliefs of inner fascism'. This is why, Thurlow claims, Mosley's central programme often bore little relation to the populist rhetoric found in BUF publications.[57] In actual fact, as we shall see, the line delivered through the party's propaganda organs – including their anti-Jewish rhetoric – corresponded extremely closely to Mosley's own pronouncements. The Leader's words were prominently reported in his newspapers and he himself periodically contributed articles. It will be demonstrated that this was indicative of the fact that antisemitism formed an integral part of his, and thereby the BUF's, core ideology.

This is something that others have begun to acknowledge. Stephen Cullen, though maintaining that the BUF's initial attitude towards Jews was 'ambivalent', does believe that some of its 'original basic beliefs' – ultranationalism, an autarchic economic philosophy, the desire for peace, and anti-communism – 'facilitated, though did not compel, any [sic] movement towards anti-semitism'.[58] His discussion of the issue, however, does not go much further. David Baker – although his work focuses more narrowly, on just one of the BUF's leading figures, A.K. Chesterton – emphasizes that his subject's antisemitism was 'an integral part of a wider set of cultural and economic attitudes and beliefs' and must be understood 'within the framework of his fascist ideology', pointing in particular to the fusion of 'Spenglerian historicism, cultural anti-Semitism and utopianism' that lay at its heart.[59]

Linehan's more recent analysis, while comprising largely a standard discussion of the motivation behind the use of antisemitism, rather than its form, takes a significant further step. Like Thurlow, he notes that the BUF had little time for the biological theories espoused by some other British fascists; the justification for its antisemitism was primarily cultural. But where he differs from Thurlow is in regarding this as having a 'genuinely held … ideological underpinning'. In particular, he believes that the 'mythic palingenetic ultra-nationalist core at the heart of BUF ideology' and a 'gloomy preoccupation with decadence … decay and decline … underlay much of Mosley's ethnocentric anti-semitism'. Jews were made to represent 'a welter of apparently "decadent" modern culture forms and developments', with their removal seen as a prerequisite to 'bring[ing] about a glorious national rebirth'.[60]

This nascent acknowledgement of the relationship between the BUF's ideology and its antisemitism is something upon which this study will build. Moreover, it will argue that the party's fascist beliefs were not merely compatible with, or even simply conducive to, the development of an anti-Jewish position, but were the very driving force behind it. Consequently, the influence of Mosley, who took a dominant role in the formulation and propagation of the party's doctrine, must also be reconsidered.

2

The Evolution of Anti-Jewish Discourse

The use of quantitative analysis

Most historical scholarship rests upon a foundation of qualitative findings, with individual contentions supported by reference to a handful of sources, leaving the reader to trust that this offers a fair representation of the available material. Such an approach is, of course, usually perfectly valid; but equally, it is not difficult to use a small and unrepresentative set of examples to support a certain interpretation – deliberately or through unconscious confirmation bias – or to examine only a limited range of sources and reach a misleading conclusion.[1]

In certain cases, the likelihood of any such distortion can be reduced by the collection and analysis of a large and representative sample of data. While such a methodology is most obviously applicable to areas where numerical data are readily accessible, it can be used more creatively in other cases, particularly given the growing availability of primary material in digital form and the development of computerized data-collection and -analysis tools. Political scientists, for example, have used these tools to assess the ideological content of party manifestos, newspapers and judicial opinions.[2] Historians, of course, often do not have sufficient sources available to carry out such forms of analysis; yet in many cases it is possible either to piece together enough evidence to reach qualified conclusions – as some historians have done with regard to the BUF's membership (see below) – or to draw wider inferences from a rich and representative sample of data, as this study will do.

There will be understandable scepticism towards any suggestion of numerically quantifying something as subjective and complex as antisemitism. However, it should be noted that this aspect of the study is confined to tracing the prevalence of anti-Jewish rhetoric in the discourse of a single organization over time. It is accepted that this type of methodology alone can offer only limited insights, providing just a broad outline of trends and themes. These findings will then be supplemented by a more traditional qualitative assessment of the substance, tone and context of propaganda. It is only through a combination of these two types of analysis that any conclusions will be drawn. Indeed, when employed together, these complementary approaches produce a far more comprehensive picture of the development of BUF antisemitism than either alone, and will help challenge and refine aspects of the standard historical narrative.

The acceptance of such an undertaking will also be made more difficult by the most prominent previous effort to quantitatively gauge antisemitism, William Brustein's study of anti-Jewish activity and attitudes in five European states. In addition to the inherent difficulties of making direct comparisons across such different national contexts, his methodology and interpretation of results are also deeply flawed. Chief among these faults, and most relevant as far as this study is concerned, is Brustein's attempt to ascertain public attitudes towards Jews by way of newspaper analysis. In addition to the questionable premise that newspapers are an accurate measure of public opinion, his method of sampling – examining only one newspaper in each country – leaves much to be desired. The danger of this approach is aptly demonstrated by his choice of newspaper in Britain, the *Daily Mail*, whose political position (extending to supporting British fascism for a time) strongly influenced its content. This problem is, in fact, confirmed by Brustein himself, who takes a smaller test sample from another newspaper, the left-leaning *Daily Herald*, for comparison, and finds its attitude towards Jews to be appreciably different from the *Mail's*.[3] However, while this and numerous other issues make Brustein's work a warning of the dangers of a poorly executed quantitative analysis, it should not preclude future, better designed and implemented, studies, and highlights some important pitfalls to be avoided. With regard to the current study, it should be noted that as it uses the BUF's own publications to gauge the attitude of that party's leadership towards Jews, it completely avoids the particular methodological problem in Brustein's work outlined above.

Various forms of data collection and statistical analysis have already been productively applied to the study of the BUF, in particular in assessing the composition and level of the party's support. John Brewer, for example, in his study of West Midlands fascism, breaks down figures on local membership into various categories, though he readily admits that his sample of fifteen former members is far too small to offer any conclusive findings. On a larger scale, Linehan has gathered data on local membership in east London and south-west Essex to reveal patterns in social and professional distribution. Various efforts have also been made to use the fragmentary available evidence to estimate national membership figures, with G.C. Webber offering the most comprehensive methodology and detailed findings. Finally, Cullen has mined police records for figures on fascist-related disorder, in an attempt to produce a more comprehensive and impartial picture.[4]

This chapter will survey the expression of anti-Jewish sentiment within BUF discourse through quantitative analysis of the party's three national newspapers, almost full sets of which survive and are available in scanned, digitized form. Although *Blackshirt* represented the chief ideological outlet for much of the 1930s, and will be used for the majority of this analysis, there were two periods (January to May 1934 and March 1938 onwards) when it became the party's internal bulletin, reporting on local branch activity, organizational matters and other practical concerns. For these periods, *FW* and *Action*, respectively, will be used, as both took over propaganda duties from *Blackshirt*.[5]

The party, of course, had other means of ideological propagation, but various limitations render them less representative of the BUF's discourse as a whole than its newspapers. Numerous books and pamphlets were produced, but often focused on specific aspects of the party's programme, were usually written by a single author, and are difficult to assess in a systematic way over time. The *FQ* journal hosted some of the movement's more thoughtful minds, but was only launched in 1935 and catered to a limited readership. And the fascist message was broadcast through speeches at thousands of public meetings, but these were often tailored to local concerns, occurred unevenly (both temporally and geographically), and were not always under the control of the central leadership. By contrast, the party's newspapers, which were published weekly and hosted a variety of authors writing on all aspects of policy and activity, served as the BUF's main forum for expounding its doctrine on a national scale to both members and non-members,[6] and therefore provide a consistent and representative gauge of its discourse.[7]

For the analysis, a systematic, representative and extremely large sample of articles was created, constituting 21 per cent of all content in the BUF's main weekly newspaper from March 1933 (the first month in which more than one issue was published) to August 1939 (the last month before wartime censorship restricted the ability of the BUF to express itself freely). Each article within this sample that mentions Jews was recorded, and then categorized in various ways: most importantly, whether or not negative sentiment towards Jews was expressed within it; second, if Jews or Jewish issues were the primary focus of the article; finally, whether there were present certain established 'types' of antisemitism and certain common themes within BUF discourse. (For a fuller explanation of this methodology, see Appendix One.)

It is acknowledged that the decisions made on these various classifications are to some extent subjective, dependent upon the author's judgement. But equally, analysis of primary sources in any area of historical research relies on individual interpretation, and this methodology at least offers a more comprehensive, consistent and transparent means of doing so (and one that is supported by extensive qualitative analysis of the same material, including numerous excerpts from it).

The five phases of anti-Jewish discourse

To trace the prevalence over time of anti-Jewish rhetoric within BUF discourse, the continuous (upper) line in Figure 2.1 offers a graphical representation of the most important dataset collected: the monthly proportion of sampled articles in the BUF press that expressed negative sentiment towards Jews. In addition, a basic gauge of the intensity of anti-Jewish rhetoric is offered by the dashed (lower) line, which depicts the percentage of sampled articles that are 'negative' *and* focus primarily on Jewish issues.

These data can be further broken down into five distinct (though overlapping) phases (see Figure 2.2), which will be discussed individually over the course of this chapter, with quantitative findings providing the foundation for more detailed discussion of the content of discourse and policy within each. It should be borne in mind throughout, however, that these periods are defined in large part on the basis of the prevalence of anti-Jewish rhetoric within each. With regard to its content, it will

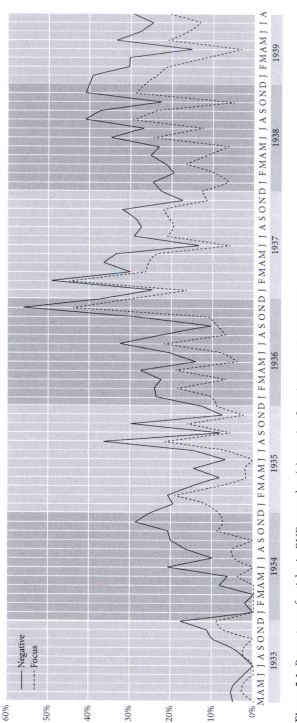

Figure 2.1 Percentage of articles in BUF press that (a) mention Jews in a negative context (continuous line) and (b) are 'negative' and focus on Jews (dashed line)

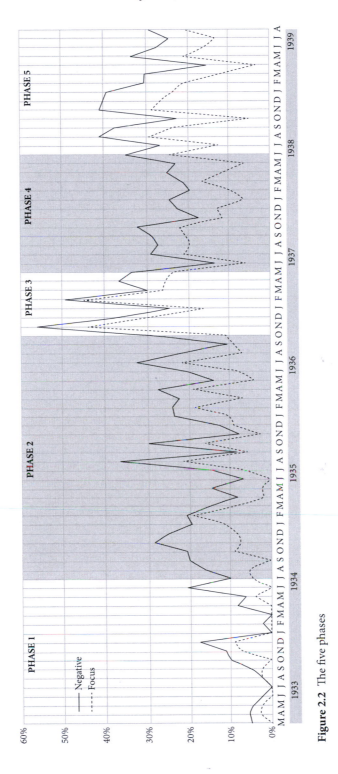

Figure 2.2 The five phases

be argued below and in the following chapters that a number of consistent themes characterized the first, second, fourth and fifth phases. By contrast, the third, which ran from late 1936 to early 1937 (coinciding with the peak of the East End campaign), represented a brief departure from earlier and later developments.

Phase one: Suppression and emergence (October 1932–Summer 1934)

The findings from the initial period of the BUF's existence present the strongest challenge to the established picture of its use of antisemitism. Although scholars have recognized that occasional attacks on Jews crept into BUF rhetoric at this time, and that the party harboured influential antisemitic members, the consensus is that it was not until after the dramatic events of mid-1934 that its leadership committed the party to an antisemitic course. This perception, moreover, is used to support the prevailing belief that Jews themselves, who were involved in attacks on the BUF, particularly over the summer of 1934, helped push the party – and convert Mosley – to an antisemitic position, which was announced in the autumn.

Closer study of the BUF press, alongside other contemporary sources, suggests a different pattern of events, with anti-Jewish rhetoric, in fact, becoming a feature of discourse before the end of 1933 (see Figure 2.2). Indeed, at the BUF's very first major public event, at London's Memorial Hall in October 1932, Mosley's address contained the two key components of the BUF's nascent antisemitism. First, he labelled members of the noisy anti-fascist contingent in the audience 'class warriors from Jerusalem' – a comment which, as was no doubt intended and in a pattern that would be repeated regularly over the following eight years, triggered disorder in the crowd. Second, as a correspondent for the *Times* noted, during the speech 'hostility to Jews was directed against those who financed Communists or were pursuing anti-British policy'.[8]

These statements were not anomalous, or simply provoked by Jewish anti-fascists in the crowd. Prior to the meeting, Mosley had issued a statement clarifying his new party's attitude towards Jews. While it would 'never attack Jews because they are Jews', and guaranteed that those who were 'loyal citizens of Britain and who serve this country rather than its enemies will always have a square deal from us', it would have no compunction in 'attack[ing] Jews if they are engaged in subversive activities such as the direction of the Communist Party or ... international financial transactions'.[9]

Thus, at its very formation, the BUF had chosen to single out Jewish involvement in 'subversive activity', and had demonstrated a proclivity for conspiracy theories that tied together 'Jewish' finance and communism. Furthermore, it had already laid down the primary foundation upon which its antisemitism would be built: that Jews themselves – by opposing the BUF and involving themselves in the types of 'anti-national' activity that fascism opposed – were to blame for the movement's growing antagonism towards them.

However, as is clear from the data, Jewish issues did not feature prominently in the party's public agenda over the nine months or so after October 1932. This, of course, coincided with Hitler's rise to power in Germany, and may therefore have been the consequence of a desire to disassociate the BUF from the Nazis' antisemitism. A front-page *Blackshirt* article, entitled 'Fascism and the Jews', assured that the 'Jewish question is no issue of Fascism' and therefore 'Jew-baiting in every shape and form [is] forbidden' within the party. Nevertheless, in the very same article it is not difficult to detect signs of the BUF's true feelings. In attempting to justify Nazi policies, the writer distinguished between 'loyal' German Jews, who had nothing to fear, and those who were involved in subversive activity, remarking that one 'cannot blame the Nazi movement for the ruthless severity with which it has removed its enemies'.[10]

Insinuations of Jewish involvement in anti-fascism began to appear more and more frequently, usually accompanied by a reminder of the BUF's official rejection of antisemitism – further 'evidence' that it was Jews themselves who were forcing the party to gradually abandon this position (see Figure 2.3). As will be detailed in Chapter 6, spring 1933 saw a series of clashes between Jews and Blackshirts in the West End of London, and many of the earliest negative allusions to Jews were associated with these and similar events: opponents were described as 'alien hooligans' or 'ghetto mobs', who slunk 'back to Whitechapel' (an East End district with a large Jewish population) after attacking the fascists.[11]

There were also increasing indications of a more insidious underlying attitude that belied the official renunciations of antisemitism. This was exemplified in May, when an editorial denial of antisemitism in *Blackshirt* appeared incongruously alongside an article attacking Jewish political influence that offered the most explicit expression thus far of the BUF's conspiratorial antisemitism. The regular columnist 'Lucifer' (probably the pen-name of William Joyce, Mosley's most notoriously antisemitic lieutenant) described Jews as 'among the biggest purchasers of Honours in England', with politicians their 'servants'. This power, the writer alleged, was being used to press the British government into condemning Nazi treatment of Germany's Jews.[12]

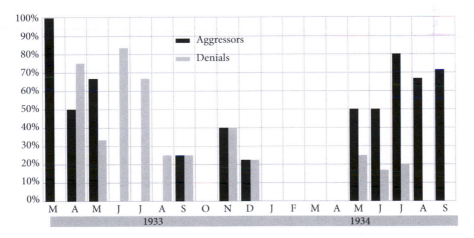

Figure 2.3 Percentage of articles mentioning Jews (a) that portray them as aggressors towards fascism (black bars) and (b) that deny antisemitism (grey bars)

Three months later, the same author went further, penning a diatribe against the 'alien drug-traffickers and white-slavers, who flourish like fat slugs on the decayed body of "bourgeois" society' and the 'financial criminals who have battened...on the economic miseries of the country'. Although not explicitly identifying such miscreants as Jews, he left the reader in little doubt as to their identity by referring to the persecution of Jews in Germany, before promising that the guilty in Britain would also be 'brought to book'. Concluding with the darkest of humour, he suggested that these 'money-lords' could be 'certified dead', putting an end to their legal existence, with 'Golders Green Crematorium...allocated to them as a Country Club' (Golders Green being another area known for its large Jewish population).[13]

The latter article inaugurated a change in approach over the second half of 1933, with a rise in anti-Jewish attacks and concomitant decline in denials of antisemitism. In September, the persecution of Jews in Germany was again linked with the need for Britain to purge 'the unscrupulous monopoly-holder, the gambler against British interests, the white-slave trafficker, and the wage-slave trafficker'. Reporting that a Jew had been found guilty of assaulting a fascist in the West End, *Blackshirt* warned that 'when Fascism comes to power in this country, and deals faithfully and justly with such vermin, we shall be accused of atrocities'.[14]

Further invective appeared at the end of the month, with an article on 'The Alien Menace' demonstrating how feeble had become the facade erected to disguise an increasingly unambiguous anti-Jewish position. While masquerading as a protest against the threat posed to British workers by immigrants who accepted lower wages, the piece quickly descended into condemnation of those Jews who were 'pillar[s] of international finance' and members of communist 'razor gangs', before finishing with a discussion of BUF race policy. These aliens, it was claimed, were 'debasing the life of this nation'; they were 'a cancer in the body politic which require[s] a surgical operation'. Such concerns far transcended the employment issues supposedly in question, and revealed much about the anonymous author's true motives.[15]

Thinly veiled attacks on 'aliens' continued, before November saw another escalation – and a watershed in the BUF's commitment to antisemitism – when Mosley penned an unsigned piece entitled 'Shall Jews Drag Britain to War?' It is important to place the article in context: a mainstream newspaper, the *Daily Express,* had earlier in the year headlined 'Judea Declares War on Germany' in response to a widely supported Jewish boycott of German goods, while the Board of Deputies had publicly condemned unilateral Jewish action aimed at Nazi Germany.[16] But the BUF's analysis took the case much further. It unequivocally accused Jews of deliberately agitating for war, and supported this charge with various 'revelations' regarding the 'Jewish money power' that allegedly controlled politics and the press.

The article also announced a shift in policy. Mosley now revealed that, although his movement had thus far eschewed antisemitism, this stance had always been open to adjustment should it become apparent that 'Jews as an organised body within the State were pursuing an anti-British policy'. This boundary had now been breached, with clear evidence that 'Jews are striving to involve Britain in a war'. The BUF therefore openly declared its new stance towards Britain's Jews: 'We oppose them'. This point was reinforced by a subtle but significant change in tone: whereas up to this point 'good', patriotic Jews had been acknowledged (and even commended), Mosley now demanded that '*if* there are Jews in Britain who ... set the interests of Britain before racial passion, let them come forward'. The existence of such Jews was no longer taken for granted; it was their duty to prove themselves. This was, of course, a disingenuous challenge, one couched in terms that the BUF knew would be impossible for Jews to meet, thereby providing further justification for the policy of antisemitism it was now – and, as we shall see, had always been – committed to.[17]

Two weeks later, the party's position was clarified further. After issuing the standard preface to antisemitic pronouncements – that the BUF stood for 'religious tolerance' and was 'against no Jew because he is a Jew' – *Blackshirt* warned that it would not tolerate harmful financial activity, agitation for war, 'hordes of aliens ... swamp[ing] the labour market' and criminal behaviour. These, it was asserted, were reasonable policies; it was not the party's fault if, having criticized someone for their involvement in such activity, 'we find out that individual is of the Hebraic faith'. Again, the emphasis was placed on British Jews to come forward and declare where their allegiances lay, and the article concluded with a crude doggerel distinguishing between the Jewish 'upright citizen' who is fascism's 'brother', and the 'oily, material, swaggering ... pot-bellied, sneering, money-mad Jew'.[18]

This early escalation of antisemitism was, however, quickly suppressed, with Jewish issues disappearing almost completely from BUF discourse in the opening months of 1934 (see Figure 2.1). Opposition was now directed against 'international' rather than 'alien' finance, while references to communism and anti-fascism rarely alluded to Jewish involvement in either.[19] This dramatic change in direction coincided with the formalization of the party's relationship with Lord Rothermere.

Rothermere had long taken a positive interest in fascism, hailing its 'many advantages' in 1930 and, from at least December 1931, encouraging Mosley to position himself as a British Mussolini or Hitler, promising the support of his press empire if he did so. The following year, after the failure of the New Party venture, the press magnate again urged Mosley to continue his journey towards fascism.[20] Nevertheless, after the BUF's formation the two men remained wary of one another. Not until January 1934 was Rothermere prepared to announce publicly his support for the party – infamously declaring, in a *Daily Mail* headline, 'Hurrah for the Blackshirts!' – and over the following months he did much to advertise Mosley's movement.[21] That the incipient emergence of antisemitism in the party's publications ceased at precisely the time a formal alliance with Rothermere was announced suggests that the two developments were related.[22]

Yet the link may not be quite so clear cut. During his previous expressions of sympathy towards German fascism, Rothermere had been prepared to accept – and even defend – its associated antisemitism. In 1930, he celebrated the NSDAP's strong performance in Reichstag elections as heralding a 'new era' for Germany. He did, at the same time, criticize the Nazis' 'Jew-baiting' as a 'stupid survival of medieval prejudice'; yet he blamed such sentiment on Jews themselves. They had 'brought great unpopularity upon their community' by their 'political unwisdom' in pushing for a Jewish homeland in Palestine, by their attempts 'by every means – financial, social, political and personal – to influence' government policy, and by their 'leadership of the Bolshevist campaign against civilisation and religion'. These 'defects of the children of Israel' were, he alleged, apparent among Britain's Jews as well as their counterparts in Germany.[23]

Three years later, with the Nazis now in power, Rothermere penned a glowing tribute in his *Daily Mail* to the 'swift and momentous' changes taking place in Germany. Previously, the country had been 'rapidly falling under the control of its alien elements', with 'Israelites of international attachments ... insinuating themselves into key positions in the German administrative machine'. Fortunately, a leader had now been found 'who can combine for the public good all the most vigorous elements in the country'.[24]

There is no evidence of any direct input by Rothermere with regard to the BUF's antisemitism. Certainly, he attempted to push the party in a less radical, more conservative direction. Such efforts may have included the suppression of antisemitism, which – in explicit form at least – was not traditionally a prominent feature of Britain's political environment and, with regard to fascism, was associated in the public mind with German Nazism. Only as he abandoned the BUF in July 1934 did Rothermere – in a letter to Mosley informing him of this decision – state publicly that he had 'made it quite clear in my conversations with you that I could never support any movement with an anti-semitic bias'.[25]

Again, however, there are reasons to treat Rothermere's words sceptically. In the same letter, he also claimed that he could not be associated with a movement that had dictatorship and the creation of a corporate state as stated aims. Both had, of course, always been explicit and central parts of the BUF's programme. They do not, therefore, appear to have been genuine concerns for Rothermere – and in this light there is no reason to believe that antisemitism, which had also been evident in BUF discourse since before Rothermere's formal support, was either.[26] Moreover, he continued to praise, both publicly and privately, the far more radically antisemitic Nazis and their dictatorial leader until 1939.[27]

A more plausible explanation for the split from Mosley – as well as for the 'sudden irrelevant burst of applause for the Jews' that the *Times* observed in Rothermere's newspapers at the same time[28] – was that Jewish companies, angered by his support for the BUF, had threatened to withdraw advertising money. Mosley himself claimed that this was the real reason behind Rothermere's decision, although his account should, as always, be treated with scepticism. This is particularly the case in this instance, given that the idea of powerful Jewish businessmen attacking fascist supporters fits perfectly into Mosley's wider narrative employed to justify his 'adoption' of antisemitism in late 1934.[29] Nevertheless, Skidelsky and Pugh do place some credence in Mosley's claims, though both also point to 'fundamental differences of policy' between he and Rothermere, with Pugh arguing that the latter's support cooled as he began to realize that Mosley was not as pliable as he had hoped.[30] A final possibility is that public revulsion at two incidents in June – the BUF's violent Olympia meeting and the 'Night of the Long Knives' in Germany – led Rothermere to deem any association with fascism too damaging.[31]

Whatever the reason for the sudden disappearance of anti-Jewish rhetoric from the BUF's press in January 1934, as Rothermere's letter to Mosley in July suggests, by the summer it had begun to re-emerge. In April, John Beckett, a former Labour MP who had joined the BUF earlier in the year, authored a front-page article in *FW* condemning Conservatism as 'the catspaw of the banker and cosmopolitan financier' and observing that 'Tory backers are as varied a crowd of names as any that could be found on a Committee of the Third International'. Two pages later, Robert Gordon-Canning, another prominent figure, to whom we shall later return, attacked the 'alien' corruption of British cinema, singling out the Jewish director Alexander Korda for particular disdain.[32]

While such allusions retained a degree of ambiguity, an editorial the next month left little doubt that the movement was picking up where it had left off in December. It was announced that Jews were now barred from BUF membership, on the grounds that 'the great majority ... have placed the interests of their own race before the interests of the country in which they reside'.[33] The extent to which antisemitism had now become internalized was revealed later in May. In jest, a letter allegedly from a Bernard Cohen offering to supply the BUF with black raincoats was published under the headline 'Business Is Business'. The premise underlying the joke – that no Jew should possibly want to do business with the fascists – revealed much about the movement's self-perception at this stage, and laid bare the insincerity of its declared belief in 'good' Jews.[34]

The above has significant implications for the widely accepted interactionist explanation of the BUF's antisemitism. We can see that the outline of anti-Jewish policy was in place at the party's formation; a year later, its leader openly declared his opposition to the Jewish community – the majority of whom were cast as incorrigible, undesirable aliens – while putting the onus on any 'good' Jews, should they exist, to prove their loyalty. Jews were alleged to exercise a powerful influence over politics, the press, international finance and communism, and to participate in criminal activity, while their physical features and personal habits were disparaged. That such sentiment existed – and had been openly expressed – at a stage when, as we shall see in Chapter 6, relatively few Jews were involved in domestic anti-fascist activity demonstrates the extent to which antisemitism was an innate aspect of the BUF's programme, rather than a policy forced upon the party by Jewish attacks or declining membership, both of which begun in earnest months later (and were to a large degree induced by the BUF's hostility towards Jews, rather than vice versa).

Certainly, anti-Jewish rhetoric was at times suppressed, but this coincided with external events that necessitated a degree of tactical restraint: the Nazis' seizure of power in Germany and the alliance with Rothermere. There is no reason to believe that, had the latter not occurred, the rise in antisemitism witnessed over the second half of 1933 would not have continued. Yet even so, it was in the spring that the familiar pattern re-emerged – *before* the wave of organized anti-fascist disruption that took place at Olympia and elsewhere in June. Jewish involvement in such activity was subsequently exploited (and exaggerated) by the fascists to justify their increasingly radical position, but it was clearly not the genuine motivation behind this process, which had begun much earlier.

Phase two: Indecision and oscillation (Summer 1934–September 1936)

Although from the summer of 1934 onwards antisemitism always remained a regular feature of BUF discourse, the following two years saw great fluctuation in its expression. Overall, a slight upward trend can be discerned from the data for this period, but in a highly inconsistent pattern, rarely rising or falling for any two consecutive months nor maintaining a steady level (see Figure 2.2).

While this new phase would be officially inaugurated at three large set-piece events addressed by Mosley in autumn 1934, the BUF press sharpened its tone slightly earlier. In August, *Blackshirt* provided readers with a 'topical quotation' from Hitler's *Mein Kampf* that described how 'the international world-Jew is slowly, but surely strangling us'.[35] Later that month, Alexander Raven Thomson – after Mosley, the party's leading ideologist and a figure whose influence on the direction of its antisemitism has been somewhat overshadowed by the more extreme and vociferous contributions of other leading members – authored a detailed critique of the Jews' economic power (to which we will later return).[36] And regular charges were made that the present wave of anti-fascist disruption was dominated by Jews: opposition at a rally in Hyde Park in September 'positively reeked of aliens'.[37]

But it was Mosley himself who was chiefly responsible for the intensification of rhetoric. At Hyde Park, his oration was marked by a 'furious anti-Semitic outburst' aimed at 'Jewish financiers' and 'the Jewish-Socialist mob'.[38] A few weeks later, at Belle Vue in Manchester, he further condemned 'Yiddish finance', accusing it of 'undermining the prosperity of Britain' by investing abroad and flooding domestic markets with cheap foreign goods. He quickly passed from these perverse, but at least superficially rational claims into the realm of conspiracy, repeating the accusations made a year earlier that the media and parliament were 'ruled by Jewish finance', which was pushing Britain towards war with Germany.[39]

The next month, at London's Albert Hall, the Leader reiterated and amplified his attack, promising to 'deal with organised Jewry in this country'. His new position, however, was portrayed not as a choice, but as a necessity forced upon him. Jews had shown themselves to be a dangerous minority, 'which owes allegiance not to Britain, but to another race in foreign countries'. Despite the Blackshirts' regular renunciations of antisemitism, Jews had 'mobilised against Fascism' – through organized Jewish mobs hired by wealthy Jews to attack BUF events, and by financially blackmailing fascist supporters – in order to defend their 'system of international usury' and 'racial interests' against the 'national revival' fascism had set in motion. The BUF, therefore, had choice but to 'take up th[eir] challenge'.[40]

Despite such categorical language, repeated by Mosley at another speech in Manchester later the same month and reinforced by the likes of Joyce, Beckett and Chesterton (cousin of the aforementioned Chesterton brothers and another of Mosley's trusted advisors and propagandists) in print,[41] 1935 saw confusion over how, and indeed whether, to tackle this 'challenge'. This reflected factional struggles within the party over its future direction, which will be discussed in greater detail in Chapter 4. The first half of the year witnessed a marked reduction in the quantity and severity of anti-Jewish rhetoric in the party's press, with even the more radical figures noticeably toning down their language. Where Jews were mentioned, it was often in passing, rarely as the focus of propaganda.

Nevertheless, a constant undercurrent of anti-Jewish sentiment remained, particularly after the introduction in February of a regular feature entitled 'The Jews Again', compiled by Joyce's protégée Angus MacNab. This long-running column (later renamed 'Jolly Judah') reported in a derisive but light-hearted manner on 'Jewish' affairs, selecting items from the press (often from Jewish publications) that allegedly exposed Jews' criminal, avaricious and alien nature, and ridiculing their physical characteristics. Over the following years it became a key component in the propagation of antisemitism, extending it beyond the realm of serious policy and into the sphere of 'entertainment', all the while helping perpetuate and internalize a distorted and pernicious caricature of Jews.[42]

From the end of the summer, anti-Jewish attacks resumed as a regular feature of discourse. Reports of activity in east London also began to appear, describing the 'vigorous' struggle against 'Jewish influence' in the area.[43] However, contrary to the impression given in many historical accounts, the commencement of the East End campaign in late 1935 did not lead to a dramatic rise in antisemitism at the national level. In fact, fluctuation continued, without any great overall increase over the first three-quarters of 1936. This emphasizes two important points. First, that growing activity in east London did not immediately, or even quickly, transform the BUF into an obsessively antisemitic, single-issue party. It was only from October 1936, a year or so after the East End campaign had begun in earnest, that the BUF could be described in these terms, and even then only ephemerally, as we shall see.

Second, although the movement always tailored its message to suit different audiences, there was at this point a particular divergence between local campaigning in east London and the central programme. With Mosley granting the likes of Joyce, Raven Thomson and local activists 'Mick' Clarke and 'Bill' Bailey free rein to run the East End campaign, antisemitism quickly became, as the *JC* recorded, an 'all-embracing' focal point of propaganda in the area, promulgated through street-corner meetings and locally distributed publications, and accompanied by physical and verbal 'Jew-baiting'.[44] But in mid-1936 antisemitism in the national BUF press, in quantitative terms at least, differed little from the autumn of 1935 or even late 1934, reflecting the enduring hope of building a broad, national base of support (in November 1936 the party announced its aim to stand 100 candidates at the next general elections, and reiterated its pursuit of a 'constitutional path to power').[45]

That is not to say, however, that national propaganda remained completely insulated from the party's drift towards more extreme forms of antisemitism in east London. Despite little growth in the frequency of anti-Jewish attacks, there was a perceptible hardening of tone. From July 1935 the BUF's central code – the 'Ten Points of Fascism' – replaced opposition to 'Aliens and International Finance' (which had been introduced in early 1934) with the more specific 'Jewish finance' and 'Jewish usury'.[46] The same month, *Blackshirt*, reporting on Mosley's first major address in east London, quoted the Leader giving what appears to be his earliest public commitment on how he proposed to resolve the Jewish problem: by deporting those Jews that failed to put the national interest first. 'Judged by that test,' he joked, 'boats going out would be very full.'[47] Increasingly positive reports on Germany – including endorsements of the Nazis' anti-Jewish measures – also featured in the Blackshirt press.[48] Mosley openly compared his own 'forced' conversion to antisemitism to the *Führer's*, proclaiming that 'even Hitler was not anti-Semitic before he saw a Jew'.[49]

The increasing pursuit of working- and lower-middle-class support – in east London particularly, but also in parts of Manchester and Leeds, two cities with large Jewish populations – also had an impact on the tenor of the national BUF press. The BUF had long differentiated between 'big' and 'little' Jews, and propaganda now increasingly focused on the latter, who was 'driving Gentiles out of business' using 'every kind of filthy chicanery', 'exploiting British workers' and comported himself in an ostentatious, offensive and, above all, alien manner.[50]

In particular, *Blackshirt* – rebranded as 'The Patriotic Worker's Paper' – espoused a progressively cruder form of antisemitism. This was especially manifest in the newspaper's political cartoons, which had long offered a means of conveying the anti-Jewish message.[51] Any pretence of subtlety in these drawings now disappeared, supplanted by vulgar and unsophisticated imagery, reminiscent of that employed by the Nazis' *Der Stürmer* newspaper. A typical instance in May 1936 saw a bloated, grotesque 'Briddish' Jew sitting atop his tailoring business, a money-bag (representing 'financial strangulation') alongside him and a 'sweated girl labour[er]' dangling from his hand. Beneath him, British workers and small traders protested to 'keep Britain clean'. Below the image, Alex Bowie, the BUF's regular cartoonist, who often supplemented his sketches with short texts, warned that 'these people who were our guests would be our masters[.] ... The soul of Britain ... shall arise and purge this menace from our land'.[52]

Phase three: The East End phase (October 1936–Spring 1937)

Though there had thus far remained some distinction between national and East End campaigning, events in east London now saw the two align, as the BUF moved into the next, and most extreme, stage of its antisemitism. In particular, the Battle of Cable Street, in October 1936, had a dramatic effect on the quantity and severity of anti-Jewish rhetoric (see Figure 2.2). The events of the day itself, and their consequences, will be examined in Chapter 7, but, from the BUF's perspective, they provided a further opportunity to draw attention to Jewish involvement in (or, as it claimed, domination of) the anti-fascist movement.

The demonstration was immediately labelled 'Jewry's Biggest Blunder', and the police, who had ordered Mosley to call off his march, were accused of 'surrender[ing] to alien mobs'.[53] The event did indeed mark the culmination of months of progressively more belligerent anti-fascist activity on the part of the Jewish community (although this had itself developed largely in response to the BUF's own 'Jew-baiting' in the East End). However, just as alleged Jewish actions had been used in 1934 as a convenient pretext for an escalation of antisemitism that was already underway, so they were again exploited to justify a further hardening of policy that had been set in motion earlier.

In July 1936 the BUF had announced it would be putting forward six candidates for East End seats at the following March's London Country Council elections. From the outset these had been advertised as a choice 'between us and the Parties of Jewry', a clear indication that the movement's first ever election campaign would be fought on a primarily antisemitic platform.[54] The party's campaign leaflet was predictably monothematic, mentioning Jews or aliens twenty-two times in just two pages of text.[55] 'No one knows better than the people of East London the stranglehold that Jewry has on our land,' ran the appeal, the 'Jewish domination which keeps them in subjugation and housed in slums.'[56]

Over the late summer, the party's ideological heavyweights used *Blackshirt*, edited since June by Beckett,[57] to lay the foundations for an escalation of Jewish policy. Raven Thomson was again to the fore, penning a front-page piece on 'The Jews and Fascism', while Chesterton followed with two further articles. Both writers appealed directly to East End residents to lead the way in this struggle.[58] Behind the scenes, Joyce and others were agitating for a radicalization of the party's anti-Jewish position, as we will see in Chapter 4.

Although, then, there were portents of an imminent shift in position, it was only after Cable Street that this change became fully manifest. To illustrate this in quantitative terms, in the six months before October around 21 per cent of articles sampled from *Blackshirt* expressed some form of negative sentiment towards Jews (without any strong upward trend); in the equivalent period subsequently, this figure almost doubled, to 39 per cent. The content of propaganda, too, indicated that a new phase was in evidence, and the data collected on the types of antisemitism used during each of the five periods reveal some striking insights.

Economically grounded criticism of Jews declined to its lowest rate for the movement's entire existence (though still remained a significant feature of propaganda), challenging the assumption that the East End campaign relied especially on aggravating economic tension between Jews and gentiles (see Figure 1, in Appendix Two). The same trend is apparent in the use of conspiratorial allegations of Jewish power (Figure 2, Appendix Two), which fell even more dramatically. Instead, three others lines of attack were increasingly pursued: accusations of Jewish criminality (Figure 3, Appendix Two), the portrayal of Jews as culturally alien (Figure 4, Appendix Two) and negative caricaturing of Jewish features and traits.[59] These changes suggest that antisemitism was being 'dumbed down' for an East End audience: the more complex aspects of the BUF's economic arguments and conspiracy theories were discarded (although their more populist elements remained) in favour of crude attacks on Jews' alleged physical and cultural distinctiveness and undesirability.

A barrage of articles now reported on alleged cases of Jewish impropriety, often in a sensationalist, emotive manner. Jews were accused of siphoning off charitable donations for their personal gain; of making fraudulent insurance and bankruptcy claims; of stealing, breaking trading laws and selling counterfeit goods.[60] Insinuations of sexual deviancy were also made: Jews lived off the 'immoral earnings' of women, and were importing American-style 'strip tease dances' to Britain. A published letter from one supporter even provided biblical references to 'prove' that Jews had immemorially profited from prostitution, engaged in incestuous relationships and abided only by their own laws rather than those of the host society.[61]

As well as a continuation of their offensive depiction in Bowie's illustrations,[62] Jews were described in increasingly derogatory terms ('slimy', 'oily' 'parasites' with 'hooked noses'), their accents were mocked (they were 'voikers', or engaged in 'bithnes') and their levels of hygiene were disparaged.[63] Taken individually, such instances were often relatively trivial; but together they represented a sustained effort in this period to create a repulsive, dehumanized representation of Jews, and to protest that Britain, and in particular the East End, had become a 'refuse heap' for this 'discarded muck'.[64]

Another addition to the BUF's antisemitic armoury during this period, albeit one that was used only sporadically, was religiously associated attacks on Jews, aimed primarily at east London's Catholic population. In the most direct appeal, entitled 'Can Catholics Support Fascism?', the values of these two 'faiths' were conflated, with the persecution of Jews justified as merely an extension of opposition to fascism's enemies, international financiers and communist revolutionaries, both groups that all good Catholics should also find objectionable.[65] Reports of atrocities in the Spanish Civil War were also readily exploited: while news of the bombing of Guernica was queried as a possible 'red ruse for sympathy', stories of Republicans murdering nuns and burning down churches were credulously recounted. Moreover, they were tied into the fascists' wider analysis of the conflict, which from the start had associated the Republican side with 'the predatory activities of the Jew'. How, it was asked, could the world so vociferously condemn the Nazis' persecution of a religious group, yet stand idly by while 'the Church of Christ may be crucified afresh in Russia and Spain by ... [the] leaders of Jewry'? Bowie, as ever, was keen to reinforce such imagery, depicting the conflict in Spain as a stereotypically 'Jewish'-looking figure holding a bloodied young woman up against a cross with a knife to her throat.[66]

While these few months marked by far the most intensive stage of BUF antisemitism, quantity came at the cost of quality. There was little to match the clearly articulated, coherent and consistent anti-Jewish narrative that characterized much of the rest of the party's existence. Instead, crude and populist xenophobia aiming to exploit anti-alien traditions in the East End, but with little appeal elsewhere, saturated propaganda.[67] It is therefore somewhat misleading – although not surprising, given the highly visible, provocative and violent nature of East End campaigning – that this brief period is the one for which the BUF is best remembered, and where so much historical attention has focused.

Phase four: The Chesterton period (Spring 1937–Summer 1938)

Although the BUF polled relatively well at the LCC elections in the East End constituencies it contested,[68] it failed to win a single seat. In addition to this embarrassing setback, the party was now beset by financial difficulties. Its growing disrepute had deterred many wealthy sponsors and reduced proceeds from membership and newspaper sales, while the move closer to the Nazis had led Mussolini to reduce his subsidies, which ended altogether in 1937.[69] This forced significant cutbacks, with expenditure reduced by 70 per cent and over half of personnel at headquarters leaving, including many figures who had played a prominent part in East End campaigning.[70] Moreover, it encouraged another change in strategy, with national campaigning once again decoupled from activity in the East End.

The clearest indication of this was an abrupt drop in the level and ferocity of antisemitism in national propaganda. This has been well documented in the historiography, but surveying the party's newspapers reveals two important details that have been overlooked: that the subsequent period saw neither a trough in the movement's use of anti-Jewish rhetoric, nor any downward trend. Negative sentiment towards Jews was actually expressed with greater frequency than it had been before Cable Street, and now became a more consistent, stable element of discourse, and one that steadily grew in prevalence over the final years of the decade. In fact, if one looks at the level of negative coverage of Jews in the BUF press over the entire 1933–9 timeframe with the brief East End phase excluded, a continual upward incline can be observed (see Figure 2.4), again indicating that the intense but evanescent stage of East End antisemitism was something of an anomaly that interrupted longer-term developments.

The defining feature of propaganda during this period was its dominance by one individual, Chesterton, who edited *Blackshirt* from August to December 1937 (before it was refashioned as an internal newsletter) and *Action* in February–March 1938 (before his own departure from the BUF). He also authored significant individual publications, most notably an antisemitic treatise, 'The Apotheosis of the Jew', and a hagiography of Mosley, *Portrait of a Leader*.[71] Given that Beckett, Joyce and MacNab had been among those forced out of the party in March, the stage was set for Chesterton – supported by Raven Thomson and the increasingly prominent Gordon-Canning – to shape policy and propaganda, which was now permeated by his idiosyncratic brand of cultural-conspiratorial antisemitism, reinforced by a devout belief in the spiritual, regenerative mission of fascism. An early editorial in *Blackshirt* set the tone, promising that the BUF would 'stand alone' in the struggle against 'the sinister and disruptive powers ... [of] the corrupt Judaic Internationale' that threatened 'the survival of our race'.[72]

While the East End phase had seen a focus on the 'small' Jew, attention now returned to his 'big' counterpart. In what masqueraded as a serious journalistic exposé, Chesterton revealed the ways in which Jews maintained and exploited Britain's 'financial democracy' (a favourite catchphrase during this period) to keep the country 'under the heel'. 'Whenever Jewish financial interests are involved,' he explained, 'the Government ... succumbs to them[.] ... They dominate Britain's affairs; their money-power is law.'[73] Raven Thomson, in his 1937 pamphlet 'Our Financial Masters', went into intricate detail on how Jewish financiers allegedly controlled the world financial system, using this 'money power [to] strangle the world' and destroy British trade and industry.[74] As ever, the party was also keen to demonstrate that these powerful forces

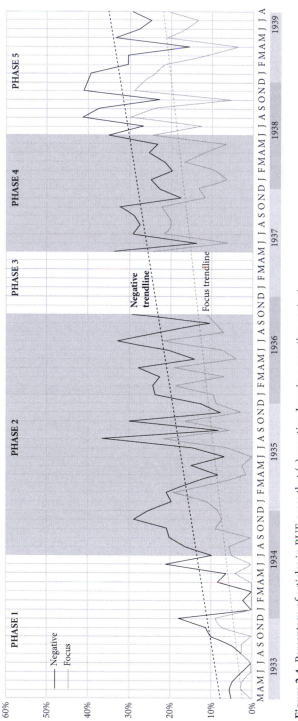

Figure 2.4 Percentage of articles in BUF press that (a) mention Jews in a negative context (black line) and (b) are 'negative' and focus on Jews (grey line) (phase 3 removed; showing trend line for each set of values)

were arrayed against British fascism, with Mosley's speech on the anniversary of the BUF's formation describing 'five years of rough marching and hard fighting ... in [the] face of Money power, Press power and Jewish power'.[75]

During this period, the BUF's anti-Jewish position also appeared to be converging with that of others on the domestic radical right. In December, an advert appeared in *Blackshirt* for the *Protocols of the Elders of Zion*, the infamous text that purportedly revealed plans for Jewish world control but had been debunked as a forgery as far back as 1921. Previously, the BUF, unlike many other antisemitic organizations, had distanced itself from this discredited document; now, it was recommended as 'the most astounding book ever published', one that 'every Fascist should read'.[76] Potential solutions to the Jewish problem – which others on the British radical right had long pondered but on which the BUF had been reluctant to publicly commit itself – were more regularly discussed. Raven Thomson suggested, as an answer to dangerous and intractable 'Jewish racialism', segregation along the lines of that forced upon Blacks in the American South.[77] Writing in *Blackshirt*, Joseph Bannister, the infamous British antisemite, proposed that 'no jewish [sic] or coloured doctors' be allowed 'anything to do with English or other white women patients'. *Action* added that 'Jews, under no circumstances, should be allowed to employ white women'.[78] Meanwhile, growing identification with 'national socialism' in general, and with its German manifestation in particular, continued apace. Following a sojourn in Germany, Chesterton indulged himself with an eleven-part series of panegyrical studies on 'Aspects of the German Revolution'. Such explicit sympathy towards Nazi Germany brought the BUF closer in line with the likes of the IFL, the Militant Christian Patriots (MCP), the NL and The Link, a development that will be discussed in the following chapter.[79]

Increased coverage of Germany reflected a wider emphasis on foreign affairs, another noticeable change from the more parochial character of the East End period. Antisemitism was internationalized too, with the BUF increasingly regarding itself as part of a European struggle against the Jews. Central to this process was Gordon-Canning, a regular contributor to both *Blackshirt* and *Action* who from January 1938 became editor of the latter's foreign-affairs page.[80] In addition to regular articles on Europe's Jewish problem, Gordon-Canning, an Arabist and avowed anti-Zionist, devoted particular attention to Palestine, which was under British mandate. Jews were blamed for the mounting violence in the territory, thereby putting British lives at risk in peacekeeping efforts; Zionists were accused of threatening to use 'the filthy power of their gold' to bring down the British Empire should their demands not be met. Above all, the fascists expressed empathy with Palestinian Arabs, another native population facing the Jewish 'alien who comes to their land and does not become one of them ... [but] tries to foist on the nation his own base customs ... [and] to enslave [them] with his chains'.[81] A cartoon illustrated the ways in which Jews were 'bringing culture' to Palestine, portraying an incredulous Arab surveying a selection of Jewish stereotypes: the communist agitator, the racketeer, the jazz musician, the cut-price merchant and purveyors of 'feelthy [sic] postcards', 'leg shows' and other immoral temptations.[82]

As such imagery suggests, attempts to convey the Jews' undesirability often focused on their alleged debasement of the arts and culture. This was not a new preoccupation:

as mentioned earlier, in April 1934 Gordon-Canning had complained of alien filmmakers producing 'sentimental trash, sexual aphrodisiacs and criminal heroics'. Over the following three years further attacks were made in the BUF press on the 'blight of the Jew' in the theatre, cinema, music, literature and art. The 'allurements and relaxations of Negroid-Jewish culture' were presented as the very antithesis of the homogenous, disciplined, traditionalist fascist ideal.[83]

Now, under the direction of Chesterton, himself a member of a famous literary family and formerly a theatre critic, such concerns were given greater prominence. The British film industry was being corrupted by Jews, such as Isidore Ostrer and the Korda brothers, who had no understanding of British cultural mores;[84] boxing, once a noble pursuit, had been commercialized and degraded by Jewish 'crookery'.[85] There was even a lament for the traditional British holiday resorts of the south coast, which were now overrun with Jews, both as businessmen – running shops selling 'cheap foreign goods' and overseeing a proliferation of 'Kosher Hotels with Jewish symbols brazenly displayed' – and as tourists, 'wallowing like porpoises' in all the best spots on the beach.[86]

The latter description indicates one vestige of the East End campaign that did remain, and indeed proliferated. Negative characterizations of Jews' physical and dispositional traits peaked during this period. This was exemplified by regular extracts from the 'Diary of Klemens Brunovitch', a fictitious account of the life of an East End Jew and his collection of greedy, swindling and comically foreign companions, fulfilling many of the functions of the defunct 'Jolly Judah' column, which had petered out after MacNab's departure.[87] Chesterton described Britain's alleged rulers as 'a gang of greasy gesticulating Jews'; his predecessor as editor, Geoffrey Dorman, remarked that Jews were identifiable by their 'unmistakable facial uniform'.[88] In a further sign of the ridicule and contempt with which Jews were to be treated, an editorial decision was made in September 1937 to de-capitalize the first letter of the word 'Jew' and its derivatives each time they were used – a fixation that extended even to headlines completely in capitals, which now referred to 'jEWS'.[89]

Above all, this period saw greater consistency in the BUF's antisemitism, as its main strands – fear of the Jews' political power, economic influence and cultural corrosion, along with a sense of fascist victimhood at their hands – became increasingly intertwined and mutually reinforcing, forming a more cohesive narrative and more stable aspect of discourse. This was reflected in two publications, which for the first time presented the party's Jewish policy as a comprehensive and integrated whole.

The first, 'The British Union and the Jews', written by 'Mick' Clarke, one of the party's most effective antisemitic orators, began by outlining the ways in which 'the Jew has brought upon himself the wrath of many Englishmen': his immoral and avaricious attitude in business dealings; his clannish, alien character; 'his creeping influence … in business, politics, sport, cinema and industry'; and his attempts 'to drag [Britain] into a war'. Fascism had challenged the Jews' interests, causing them to 'set all the forces of finance controlled democratic machinery to work' against the BUF. This was why, in response, the party had been forced to adopt an anti-Jewish position. Should the Blackshirts come to power, those Jews who had transgressed in any way would be firmly encouraged to leave the country, while the remainder could stay, but 'as an alien people' denied the rights of British subjects.[90]

The second, a pamphlet entitled 'Britain and Jewry', provided an identical list of concerns in various subtitled sections – 'Jewish Finance', 'Jewish Racialism', 'Jewish Crime', 'Communism is Jewish' – which were summarized thus:

> the presence of an alien racial minority in the midst of the British People is intolerable, when that minority exercises great financial power, is active in seditious activities, directs publicity through its monopoly control over advertising, and uses these influences to advance its international racial interests throughout the world.

As a solution, it suggested (as did Clarke) finding a suitable homeland to which Jews could emigrate, 'where their racialism can take a healthy patriotic instead of an unhealthy parasitic form'.[91]

Phase five: The internationalization of the Jewish problem (Summer 1938 onwards)

With the movement's anti-Jewish narrative now reaching a more settled form, but still failing to act as a significant recruiting spur outside east London, it was international developments – ironically, the consequences of Nazi aggression – that provided the context for its appeal to widen. First, mounting tension in Europe and the growing likelihood of war allowed Mosley to advertise more prominently, and to a more receptive audience, a central plank of his case against the Jews: that they were pushing the country towards a dangerous and unnecessary international conflict, which would further their own interests but damage Britain's. Second, with tens of thousands of Jewish escapees from Central Europe reaching Britain, the escalating refugee crisis made the BUF's anti-alienism far more germane outside the confines of the East End.

Turning first to the data, this final period saw a continuation of the previous upward trend in the quantity of anti-Jewish rhetoric, a rise that was significant but gradual and relatively consistent, in contrast to the sudden injection of antisemitism that marked the start of the East End period or the oscillation of the first two phases (see Figure 2.2). Conspiratorial and economic themes continued to take a central place, while the departure of Chesterton from the movement coincided with a diminution in efforts to maliciously caricature Jewish traits and in cultural attacks, though the latter remained a substantial element of propaganda (see Figures 1–4, Appendix Two).

The issue that came to dominate the agenda above all was the 'Peace Campaign', into which the various threads of antisemitism developed over earlier years were woven. This was not a novel element of policy: Mosley's founding treatise, *Greater Britain*, had endorsed universal disarmament, described aggressive imperialism as 'folly' and expressed the BUF's desire to 'help in the organisation of world peace'.[92] Nor was its association with Jews anything new: by November 1933, the Leader had openly accused them of attempting to drive Britain into conflict with Germany, and this always remained central to his justification for antisemitism.[93] And the focus had never been solely on Germany: in 1935, Mosley had declared that over the Abyssinian Crisis rose 'the stink of the Jews', who allegedly controlled the Bank of Ethiopia; later, they were alleged to be stirring up conflict in Spain for their own economic gain.[94] But it was developments over 1938–9, as war with Germany became ever more likely, that gave greater resonance to such calls, finally providing the BUF's programme with a focal point that tied antisemitism to a mainstream concern (see Figure 2.5).

The fascists propounded their pacifist position from two main angles: attempting to excuse German aggression and repudiate criticism of the country; and accusing those pressing for war of pernicious ulterior motives, while offering the counter-argument that any conflict was contrary to Britain's interests. The former tactic at times subtly employed antisemitism. For example, the German annexation of the Sudetenland was defended using a corruption of a case regularly made against Germany with regard to its treatment of Jews: the German minority in Czechoslovakia, Mosley maintained, were victims of 'racial oppression'; if the Western Powers truly believed in protecting minorities, Sudeten Germans should be allowed to willingly reunite with their brethren.[95]

But it was the second approach that more readily incorporated attacks on Jews, who, it was claimed, were desperate to engineer the downfall of the Nazi regime, not simply because of their co-religionists' persecution at its hands (reports of which had in any case been exaggerated, the Blackshirts maintained), but also 'because Germany has struck a blow at the world domination of Jewish usury' at home, and was now threatening to do so outside its borders. Czechoslovakia, for example, was an 'outpost of Jewish Communism and Jewish finance', *Action* declared; hence the campaign to prevent it from falling into fascist hands.[96]

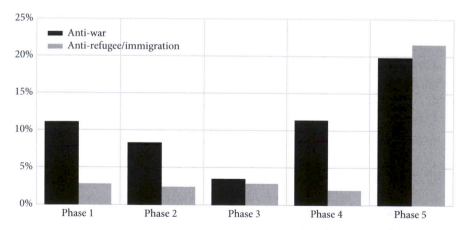

Figure 2.5 Percentage of articles expressing negative sentiment towards Jews that (a) associate Jews with agitation for war (black bars) and (b) express anti-refugee/immigration sentiment (grey bars)

The BUF, of course, aimed to replicate the Nazis' achievements in Britain, and this, the movement had long claimed, was the reason it faced such ardent opposition from Anglo-Jewry. The anti-Jewish aspects of the Peace Campaign were, then, simply an extension of longstanding patterns of thought further into the realm of foreign policy, with the BUF increasingly identifying its own struggle in Britain with a wider conflict between fascism and Jews at the international level. This belief was reinforced when Italy joined the fray, adopting anti-Jewish racial laws in summer 1938.[97]

The BUF argued that Britain was on the wrong side of Europe's emerging cleavage, aligned with the 'decadent, democratic' countries rather than the 'vigorous, resurgent' authoritarian states. This, of course, was the result of Jewish manipulation:

> Germany is not stronger than Britain today so much because she has got something we have not … [but] because she has freed herself of the parasitic cancerous growth of International Jewish Finance, which still exploits and strangles the British people … [who must] at last rise in their wrath, and demand a foreign policy based not upon foreign entanglements but upon British interests.[98]

This case was buttressed with 'evidence' of Jewish financial and political power. In August 1938, a purportedly investigative piece in *Action* gave 'exclusive disclosures' of how 'Jewish money-lords' were engineering the replacement of Prime Minister Neville Chamberlain, who was pursuing a policy of appeasement towards Germany, with the war-mongering Anthony Eden.[99] Supposed corroboration of the BUF's position from neutral sources was regularly invoked. Another *Action* article, which was also distributed in leaflet form, drew attention to recent claims in a Jewish journal, the *American Hebrew*, that Jews held prominent political positions in Britain, France and Russia, and would use their power to 'send [Hitler] to hell'.[100] An extract from the *Daily Telegraph* illustrating Jewish financial interests in eastern Europe was cited, along with quotes from a speech by the historian and prospective Labour parliamentary candidate Hugh Ross Williamson, in which he echoed precisely the BUF's position: that German aggression threatened the 'great profiteers who rule England'; that the media was controlled by the likes of Julius Elias and Victor Gollancz (both Jews); and that war would only be in the interests of 'the great Capitalists, the Jews and the Communists'.[101]

Concurrent with the anti-war campaign emerged strident opposition to the reception of refugees (see Figure 2.5). Previously, the BUF's anti-immigrant rhetoric had been directed against relatively poor arrivals from eastern Europe and their descendants, focusing primarily on their cultural distinctiveness. But now, with comparatively affluent and less visibly 'alien' central-European Jews arriving, cultural attacks declined and economic arguments were adjusted (although much of the language of earlier years remained: Britain was still a 'dumping ground' that was being 'systematically invaded' by 'refujews').[102]

Following claims that refugees were helping develop Lancastrian industry and create local jobs, *Action* countered that they were in fact no different to other Jewish employers, who sweated British workers or moved production overseas. Elsewhere, under the headline 'Refugees to have *your* boys' jobs', it was claimed that Jewish financiers were assisting their incoming co-religionists in finding employment at the expense of the British unemployed.[103] The alleged wealth of the newcomers was highlighted and caricatured, with the newspaper dispatching a photographer to Liverpool Street Station to document the arrival of these 'fat, swarthy ... fur-coated' individuals, 'reek[ing] of affluence'. In a microcosm of what it perceived to be the wider relationship between gentiles and Jews, *Action* detailed the indignity of English porters 'learning how to work for the refugees[,] ... struggling under piles of luggage'.[104] Most galling of all, these undeserving exiles were the recipients of enormous charitable generosity, and here, as with the anti-war campaign, the BUF presented itself as the only guardian of true British interests. It complained that while over a million pounds had been raised from the public to assist Jewish refugees, British citizens continued to 'endure existences of almost intolerable misery'. 'Who is being persecuted?' *Action* asked, before accusing those who gave to refugee charities of high treason.[105]

There was, however, occasionally a hint of pragmatic sympathy with those forced out of continental Europe. Although it was felt that the Jews' were themselves to blame for their persecution, and that it was certainly not Britain's place to harbour them, a sensible solution had to be found.[106] *Action* welcomed reported German attempts to come to some kind of financial arrangement with its departing Jews, and suggested setting aside an 'undeveloped colonial area' (British Guiana was mooted) as a national home for the Jews. There, freed from being a 'parasitic minority', they could develop their culture in a healthy and productive direction. The aim, of course, would be for Britain at some stage to send its own Jewish 'irritant' to this territory.[107]

The consideration of such practicalities was emblematic of the more serious and less polemical approach to the Jewish question that had been taken since the end of the East End phase. Individual publications now presented antisemitic charges behind a veneer of scholarly rigour. Gordon-Canning's booklet *The Holy Land: Arab or Jew?*, for example, offered an academically presented and coherently argued thesis, supported by footnotes and numerical data. Its intention was to expose 'the great influence of Jewry, British and International, on British Governments', which was being used to further Jewish aims in Palestine, to the detriment of the native Arab population.[108] In similar, 'factual' style, Raven Thomson used the pamphlet 'Our Financial Masters' to analyse in detail the means by which Jews supposedly manipulated markets and 'strangle[d] the world'.[109]

Indeed Raven Thomson, the movement's political director, along with Dorman, editor of *Blackshirt* and *Action* for most of the period from April 1937 to April 1939, appear to have been integral to shaping the anti-Jewish message. Under their guidance, antisemitism no longer acted as the dominant, obsessive, but unstructured focus of propaganda that it had been during the East End campaign. Instead, it became a more considered and integrated component of policy, interwoven through other aspects of the party's programme and expressed in such a way as to broaden its appeal among those who, while they may have had little sympathy for Jews, would have been repelled by the crude antisemitic rhetoric employed over 1936–7.

This was evident in the two major campaigns outlined above, where the main facets of policy – opposition to foreign military engagements and to immigration – existed and were expressed in their own right,[110] but were regularly supplemented by antisemitism, which was couched in terms less vicious than before. A more prosaic, but equally instructive, example was *Action's* regular 'British Countryside' column, aimed at the movement's rural supporters – not a group that traditionally paid great attention to the Jewish question. Its compiler, Jorian Jenks, interspersed his articles with antisemitism, but did so in a way designed to appeal to his particular audience. Anthropomorphic analogies were employed to explain the issue: Jews were like rooks, flocking onto newly sown fields to gorge on farmers' oats; or they were an infestation of rabbits, ostensibly 'poor defenceless creatures' but who 'ultimately take possession' of the land and consume its bounty, necessitating their 'abolition' by 'systematic ... modern methods'.[111] More explicitly, Jenks argued that it was natural for farmers to dislike Jews, given the role they played in exploiting agriculture as international financiers and commercial middlemen. Finally, as war approached, he lamented that the 'alien hands' of Jewish refugees were being used to work British soil – this, in his fascist eyes, was the 'final degradation'.[112] Such references were sporadic, and rarely took a prominent place in the column, but demonstrated the insidious integration of antisemitism across the BUF's programme.[113]

Finally, in attempting to build a more rational and palatable case against Jews, the Blackshirts also made efforts to contextualize their antisemitism. Jews, *Action* noted, had throughout history faced oppression in a variety of different host societies, from ancient Egypt and Rome, through to Tsarist Russia and now much of modern-day Europe. Clearly they must have 'done something to merit it'; there is no 'effect without a cause'. Moreover, while the persecution of non-Jewish minorities around the world was allowed to go unchallenged, Germany was roundly condemned for its actions. Why did the world remain silent over America's treatment of its black citizens (or 'Roosevelt's Mad Racialism', as *Action* described it)? Did not the Jews themselves persecute Arabs in Palestine? Jewish influence over governments and the media, it appeared, had made them a 'privileged race', granted special protection and held to different standards than others; any discussion of their faults was stifled and those raising such questions were demonized. Yet the BUF, against whom the Jews' immense power was now levelled, was fully alive to the danger they posed to British and European interests. With the Jewish threat becoming more palpable as war approached and the refugee crisis mounted, the Blackshirts encouraged the British people to experience the same epiphany.[114]

3

Cleansing the Nation: Antisemitism and Ideology

While, then, one can discern distinct stages of development in the BUF's anti-Jewish rhetoric, these correspond largely to changes in its presentation – its quantity, tone and emphasis. In terms of content, certain consistent themes permeated the party's discourse over its entire existence (with the exception of the East End phase, when local campaigning in that particular area briefly dominated the party's activity). These were laid down in the earliest days, and over time were shaped into a singular, comprehensive and consistent narrative, intimately integrated with the BUF's wider ideology.

Above all, the rationale that underpinned antisemitism remained constant. The BUF regularly made clear that it did 'not attack Jews on racial or religious grounds' – and its discourse did indeed contain almost nothing by way of biologically or religiously justified criticism of Jews.[1] In other words, blanket prejudice predicated on some deficiency inherent to Jews or their religion was (officially, at least) rejected, deemed 'not only unfair, but … undiscriminating and ineffective', as even Joyce (in his guise as Lucifer), one of the party's most ardent antisemites, put it.[2] Instead, and in keeping with the cerebral brand of fascism Mosley aimed to present, antisemitism was portrayed as a rational position. Jews were blamed for the specific and identifiable behaviour that many of them allegedly chose to undertake, rather than for some innate and unalterable defect. As Joyce, again, explained, the BUF 'does not attack Jews by reason of what they *are*, it resists them by reason of what they *do*'.[3]

Such a position, of course, had a logical flipside: if any Jew did 'put Britain first', then prejudice against him need not exist. As we have seen, in the party's early days it was keen to emphasize that 'good' Jews had 'nothing to fear from Fascism', which only opposed 'the low type' of Jew.[4] Though anti-Jewish rhetoric hardened significantly over subsequent years, and explicit acknowledgement of 'good' Jews largely disappeared, their theoretical existence remained essential in the justification for antisemitism. In 1938, Mosley still continued to distinguish between 'Jews who have placed the interests of Jewry before those of Britain', and would therefore be deported, and 'those against whom no such charge rests [, who] will not be persecuted'.[5] One should, of course, question the sincerity of such words. It is unlikely they would have been translated into practice under a BUF government given that, as we shall see, the presence of distinctive out-groups was incompatible with the fascist vision of Britain. But nevertheless, this remained the logical cornerstone that buttressed the party's case against the Jews.

With antisemitism thus framed, the BUF was obliged to construct a case that demonstrated these alleged Jewish offences. This centred on three central premises, distinct, but overlapping and mutually reinforcing: that Jews maintained an alien and dangerous culture and identity; that they held great power and wealth, which was employed for nefarious purposes; and that their presence damaged the economic interests of the British people.[6] While a sense of each of these themes has already emerged, it is worth examining each – as well as the relationship between them and with the party's fascist ideology – in closer detail.

Central to the BUF's mission was a renewal of national culture, whose perceived erosion and corruption at the hands of various international forces was regarded as symptomatic of Britain's wider decline. This revival was to play an integral role in precipitating the national rebirth envisioned by the fascists.[7] Thus Francis McEvoy, writing in *Action*, decried the 'soulless' modern state, which granted naturalized aliens equality with those 'whose collective ancestors have lived and died in Britain'. This was bringing about the 'death' of true national culture, whose resuscitation represented the 'primary motive-power of the great movements of regeneration which are conquering Europe today', such as the BUF.[8] Expressing these fears in more populist form, Mosley lamented the disappearance of 'the Britain we knew and loved', warning that the 'entry of alien standards and alien life ... is going to change the whole character of English life and English people[,] ... destroy[ing] the things that were noble and the things that were beautiful'.[9]

The Jews' character was regarded as ostentatious, loud, effete, clannish and immoral – the very antithesis of noble British qualities. Because of the growing Jewish presence, Britain's identity and heritage were under threat at all levels, from the trivial – Epping Forest becoming littered with matzo boxes – to the more serious – the East End turning into an 'international settlement'.[10] As we have already seen, Jews were accused of debasing the arts, popular culture and sport. *Blackshirt* bemoaned the effect that Jewish jazz music was having on Britain's 'afflicted modern youth[,] ... produc[ing] a general neurasthenia in which Hebrew influence may ascend'. The newspaper cast an admiring glance towards Nazi Germany, where music had been restored as a 'social service[,] ... uniting [people] in team spirit, team action, unified impulse'. Chesterton promised that 'one of the first duties of Fascism will be to recapture the British cinema for the British nation', purging it of 'bastardised Judaic-American pseudo-culture'.[11]

To raise these concerns, it was emphasized, was not to denigrate Jews, simply to stress their incompatibility. The fascists believed that nations could thrive only as self-contained, homogenous entities, and that cultural miscegenation was harmful to all concerned. Describing his 'spiritual' conception of nationhood, McEvoy argued that, by 'the fusion of its diverse racial elements throughout the centuries', Britain had developed 'a basic homogeneity of culture, language and tradition'.[12] As such, the assimilation of outsiders risked corrupting this distinct and carefully nurtured identity: the BUF would not welcome '400,000 Frenchmen or other foreigners' either, Mosley declared. These ideas pervaded right down the movement, with even Bailey, responsible for some of the party's worst racial invective, claiming that that he had 'nothing against the individual Jew'; rather, he was 'anti-Semitic only as a nationalist[,] ... because there is no room in one nation for another'.[13]

Maintaining ethnic exclusivity was also, Mosley argued, in the Jews' own interests, given that they 'ha[ve] always maintained that they were a separate nationality'.[14] 'When [a Jew] pretends to be an Englishman,' claimed Beckett, 'he merely makes himself both a bad Englishman and a bad Jew'.[15] To support this contention, the movement regularly invoked (highly selective) quotes from Jewish figures. The words of Gerald Soman, chairman of an obscure group called the World Jewry Fellowship, regularly appeared at the head of the 'Jolly Judah' column: 'You cannot be English Jews[.] ... Our mentality is of a Hebraic character, and differs from that of an Englishman'.[16]

The primacy of this alleged alien identity not only rendered Jews culturally incompatible; it had another, equally troubling corollary: that they held stronger allegiance to their international co-religionists than to their host societies. Fascism, above all else, demanded devotion to and service of the nation. Mosley had made clear from the founding of the BUF that he required all personal and sectional interests to be 'subordinated to the welfare of the community as a whole'; he could not tolerate any 'state within a state'. On this basis, he had used his very first speech as leader of the BUF to single out Jews for criticism, charging them with pursuing activities that were contrary to the national interest.[17] Within eighteen months, he claimed to have found that 'oriental patriots ... [are] organise[d] against the State', advising them 'to choose between Britain and Jewry'.[18] Over the following years Jews were repeatedly accused of 'anti-British conduct' and 'spiritual allegiance ... to co-racialists' abroad.[19] Even the types of crime that Jews were allegedly prone to – fraudulent bankruptcy, drug smuggling, the white-slave trade – were regarded by the BUF as 'crimes against society rather than crimes against the person', carried about by 'people who feel no sort of responsibility for the welfare of the nation as a whole, but only towards their own minority race'.[20]

While the presence of a disloyal group was undesirable enough, the situation was made especially troubling given the immense power and wealth this particular group was purportedly able to employ in pursuit of its interests. Though Skidelsky claims that only in late 1934 did the BUF's anti-Jewish rhetoric begin to take a conspiratorial tone,[21] we have seen that in a statement on the party's founding Mosley was already alluding to Jewish involvement in the 'subversive activities' of communism and high finance, staples of all good anti-Jewish conspiracy theorists. The following spring and autumn, these charges were reinforced with even less ambiguous attacks on alleged Jewish power and the harmful ends to which it was employed.

This crude outline was subsequently painted into a complex picture of the 'Jewish aim at world domination'. 'Jewish finance' was 'the nameless, homeless and all-powerful force which stretches its greedy fingers from the shelter of England to throttle the trade and menace the peace of the world'; it controlled both 'decadent democratic capitalism' and 'hideous fratricidal Communism', using them as tools to bring about the 'enslavement ... of entire nations'. It dominated the United States, Soviet Union and much of Europe, and sought to engineer war against the one nation, Germany, that had fully escaped its grip and threatened to dismantle its 'international network of intrigue'.

Britain was simply another of its puppets, with the 'dark face' of the Jew 'glower[ing] savagely behind our decadent Government and Press, relentlessly, pitilessly, urging the country to pursue a course that will end in barbarism and tragedy'.[22]

The final of the three central charges levelled against Jews was that their presence was economically harmful to gentiles. Here the BUF distinguished, as we have seen, between 'big' and 'small' Jews – though both were dangerous in their own right. The former, international financiers, invested capital abroad, facilitated the expansion of large conglomerates at home and manipulated the price of gold, all of which put Britons out of work, undercut traditional producers and traders, and weakened the domestic economy.[23] The latter, working- and middle-class Jews, were the target of many of the typical allegations directed towards immigrant groups: that they stole jobs, housing and other resources from their British counterparts; drove native competitors out of business; and exploited gentile employees and tenants.[24]

It was this aspect of anti-Jewish campaigning that was most tailored to local audiences. In Lancashire, Jews were accused of financing the Indian cotton industry, thus devastating British production. Herbert Samuel, a leading Jewish Liberal and staunch opponent of trade tariffs, and the Sassoon merchant family were singled out for blame.[25] In Yorkshire, home to the Jewish-owned Burton chain of clothes shops, the BUF condemned 'the Jews' grip of the clothing trade' and promised to 'defend the interests of the small manufacturer and native Yorkshireman against … growing Jewish influence'.[26] Elsewhere, miners were told that Jewish investment in foreign oil production had decimated the coal industry;[27] small businessmen, a particular target in the late 1930s, heard that Israel Sieff, vice chairman of Marks & Spencer, 'has declared that 500,000 small traders must be destroyed'.[28]

Areas containing large and visible Jewish populations saw a focus on 'small' Jews. Such attacks played upon the negative cultural stereotypes outlined above; Jews were not portrayed simply as economic competitors, but as playing by different rules altogether. Their supposedly low ethical standards meant they were prepared to sweat, swindle and subvert gentile employees, customers and competitors; their clannishness led them to favour fellow Jews over natives in business dealings; their religion allowed them to flout the Sunday-trading laws that others were required to abide.[29] Indeed, it was argued that the capitalist system itself was ideally suited to the Jews' character. In 1934, Raven Thomson, setting out fascism's vision for 'economic justice' between employers, workers and consumers, criticized prevailing 'bourgeois' capitalism, which, he claimed, rewarded 'cupidity and self-seeking' and punished 'nobility and generosity'. In this light, 'the predominance of Jews in our present state of decadence is not surprising … [as] they possess the very attributes suitable to survive under these conditions'. Meanwhile, the obsession with the material over the spiritual encouraged by Jews served only to further 'degenerate the [British] race'.[30]

As these latter examples indicate, the three central strands of antisemitism cultivated by the BUF were readily interwoven, spun into a narrative portraying Jews as a powerful and subversive alien minority responsible for impoverishing and enslaving Britain and its people, corroding national culture and enmeshing the country in their international web. Chesterton, after Mosley perhaps the chief exponent of this vision, described in typically histrionic fashion the 'spirit[ual] cancer' and 'national neurosis' afflicting British society, into which 'came forth the Jew openly to claim his financial masterdom'. Not content simply as 'parasitical overlords', exploiting Britain's empire and leaving its citizens poor and hungry, these 'Lords of Decadence ... break down what remains of a healthy, virile nationalism that alone could check and defeat the international rampage of usury and the international crowning of decay'.[31]

An illustrative example of this vision being translated into a practical area of policy came in the preoccupation with Jews' dominance of the means of cultural production. This allowed them to not only enrich themselves and put Britons out of work, but to promulgate a distorted and dangerous version of British culture that, by morally corrupting (and even physically degenerating) the British people, strengthened the Jewish grip over the country.[32] This narrative extended right down to the lowest levels: the 'alien' Jews of east London, for example, were accused of controlling local councils and using their power to favour their co-religionists in the distribution of housing and trading licences, to the economic detriment of the gentile population.[33]

Additionally, modern economic developments – particularly the globalization of trade and capital and the rationalization of industries, both encouraged by the allegedly Jew-controlled liberal, free-market system – were claimed to have had the greatest negative impact on professions that were regarded as the lifeblood of the nation, such as small traders, farmers, miners and textile producers. Their demise was not only economically damaging to those involved, it also ripped the heart out of whole communities: mining villages and factory towns stripped of their existential purpose; local shops selling British goods replaced by soulless Jewish chain stores peddling mass-produced, low-quality imported products; the traditional rural way of life disappearing. Jenks lamented that not only had agriculture 'been sacrificed ... because its activities interfere with the flow of tribute to Mammon' under Britain's 'plutocratic dictatorship', but its disappearance was also accelerating Britain's 'degenerat[ion]' slowly into a community of town-bred, undernourished weaklings, a parasite nation dependent for its very existence upon the charity of international financiers'. 'The Britain of Elizabeth and Victoria, of Drake and Nelson' had lost its 'true nationhood', becoming 'the slave of usury'.[34]

In response, the BUF presented itself as the embodiment of Britain's suffering at the hands of Jewry's creeping encroachment, and fascism as the only means by which to reverse this process.[35] After the government's prohibition of political processions in the East End, *Blackshirt* claimed that 'financial democracy' and 'Soviet-subsidised Communist[s]' had colluded to inhibit lawful fascist activity in the interests of a 'small alien population'. In effect, the authorities had 'hand[ed] over this quarter of London to Jewry, as the Jews' own territory', something that gentile residents, thousands of them BUF supporters, would not take lightly.[36] Likening their struggle to that of the American revolutionaries, who had similarly rebelled against 'financial tyranny', the newspaper declared 4 July 'British Independence Day', calling on people to throw off 'the alien yoke of Jewish International Finance' that threatened 'to make Britain a subservient state'.[37] The BUF placed itself at the vanguard of this bitter struggle, which pitted 'the jewish [sic] Union of Decay against the British Union of people's revolution'.[38]

As should now have become clear, antisemitism was not just a prominent feature of the party's ideology, it was integral to it. For the BUF, fascism was a political, economic and cultural project, with the goal of purging, purifying and revitalizing these three spheres of British life, each of which had succumbed to decay and degeneration at the hands of various modern, 'international' forces. Jews, the most conspicuous 'foreign' presence in Britain, were already popularly (though that is not to say fairly) associated with many of these forces: socialism and communism; liberal democracy; immigration and ethnic mixing; the internationalization of trade, production and finance; modern art, music and other novel forms of culture; 'unproductive' middleman professions; agitation for, and profiteering from, war. Moreover, for a movement that held the ambition of creating a pure, homogenous society, the presence of a relatively large and distinctive out-group was inevitably problematic.

In this context, Jews provided a tangible embodiment of the alien influences that fascism so vehemently opposed, and which could otherwise appear somewhat disparate and nebulous. Hostility towards them was justified on the basis of precisely the political, economic and cultural concerns that were at the heart of fascist ideology. That is not to say, however, that they were simply a convenient scapegoat, or that antisemitism was an opportunistic addition to the fascist programme. Rather, the two complemented and reinforced one another. There was significant overlap between the preoccupations and outlook of fascists and many antisemites, both of whom were often those who had lost out in, or simply felt disconnected from, the modern world. By contrast, Jews were seen to have been a chief beneficiary of developments over the last century, winning full citizenship rights and becoming a visible and successful section of society. To some, it appeared that these achievements had come at the expense of the native population, and that the interests of the two groups were mutually incompatible.

The fascists simply took such sentiment to its extreme conclusion, making the removal of Jewish influence from all aspects of life a fundamental prerequisite for Britain's rebirth. When it came to the conflict between 'British rights and Jewish interests', the BUF declared, 'we must govern our own country'; if not, 'then the nation is committing suicide'.[39] As early as October 1933, a *Blackshirt* cartoon depicted the broom of fascism literally sweeping away Britain's 'undesirable aliens', aptly symbolizing this purgatory aim.[40] Within a few years, it could be expressed more explicitly:

> The power of Jewry ... dominates our press, our politics, our cinemas, our finance, our economy; it is anti-British; it is anti-national; it is decadent; it must be controlled, and, if necessary, expurgated[.] ... The rising storm [of fascism] will herald the dawn of Britain's rebirth, when she will be cleansed at last from these evil, alien influences, and those noble words 'Britain' and 'British' shall once more have restored to them their full and finest meaning.[41]

Most telling were the words of Mosley himself, who in late 1934 outlined his conception of a synthesis between fascism's mission and the struggle against the Jews. First, in late September, he argued that Jews, 'more than any other single factor', were 'undermining the prosperity of Britain today', and that he could 'not tolerate those who sabotage the nation'. Tying the fate of Britain's Jews explicitly to his envisioned national rebirth, Mosley declared that he aimed to inspire 'a new spiritual revival of British manhood against [these] aliens'; by 'put[ting] them down ... we shall put the nation up'.[42] A month later, in a speech trumpeted as 'the most decisive in the history of British Fascism', this vision was further expounded. Mosley accused Jews of 'ow[ing] allegiance not to Britain but to another race in foreign countries', and of using their great power to 'destroy the foundations of our national life' and 'rob us of our heritage'. In another typically fascist rallying call, he appealed to Britain's 'epic generation' to rally to his 'movement of national revival', to overturn the 'decadent, rotting, reeking' system of 'corruption and decay', 'to sweep away, to destroy, and then to build again'. Reporting on the meeting, *Blackshirt* made clear the centrality of antisemitism to the Leader's message: two 'forces are arrayed – on the one hand the great cleansing spirit of Fascism, and on the other, organised Jewry, representing unclean, alien influence on our national and imperial life'.[43]

That Mosley delivered these words in autumn 1934, at events which announced the formalization of antisemitism as official policy, demonstrates that, while the severity, prominence and pervasiveness of anti-Jewish rhetoric may have subsequently increased, its underlying rationale, its central themes and its symbiotic relationship with fascist ideology were in place from the outset. Indeed, as we have seen, this position had been adumbrated at the party's formation – when Mosley publicly singled out Jews as opponents of fascism and accused them of involvement in the types of international, anti-British activity his movement could not tolerate – and was further revealed over 1933, when Jews were charged with war agitation, involvement in a variety of 'social crimes' and of foreign allegiance. That it took another year for the full picture to be revealed was the result of deliberate, tactical concealment, rather than because antisemitism was not yet part of the fascists' mindset. In the next chapter, we will return to look more closely at the relationship between Mosley's antisemitism and his fascist beliefs, and the reasons why he revealed this only in stages over 1932–4.

Fascist antisemitism or 'fascistized' antisemitism: The genealogy of the BUF's anti-Jewish thought

If, then, antisemitism is to be regarded as a fundamental aspect of the BUF's ideology, this raises two further sets of questions relating to fascism as a wider, generic phenomenon. First, is antisemitism inherent to fascism itself, and if so, why? Second, is there a single type of fascist antisemitism, and is it used in the same way and for the same reasons by different groups and individuals?

On the first of these issues, as outlined earlier, fascism innately rejects the presence of out-groups incompatible with its vision of a homogenous society, and sets itself against various perceived 'anti-national' influences. In interwar Europe, Jews represented an almost ubiquitous 'alien' minority and were popularly associated with a wide range of activities that fascism opposed, making them a natural target. In other contexts, however, Jews need not play this role. In Italy, a country with a tiny and relatively acculturated Jewish population, Mussolini's National Fascist Party paid comparatively little heed to the Jewish question prior to 1938; indeed, it counted a number of Jews among its members, including some leading figures. Instead, far greater attention was devoted to the prevention of miscegenation in Italy's

African territories, and to concerns about Slavs, Pentecostals and homosexuals, all of whom were regarded as threats to the Italian 'race' (which tended to be defined culturally, rather than biologically, despite the pseudo-scientific language of 1938's racial laws).[44]

Similarly, many on today's extreme right (though one can, of course, debate the extent to which they should be deemed 'fascist') aim their hostility towards minority groups more germane to the context in which they operate: Romani, Muslims, homosexuals, blacks and so on. Jews, admittedly, remain a target for some, reflecting in part the powerful vestigial influence of interwar fascism (and particularly Nazism), as well as the enduring myth of Jews as a powerful and malevolent international force. Nevertheless, while intolerance of certain minorities is essential to fascism's functioning, this need not be manifested as prejudice towards Jews.

On the question of a common fascist form of antisemitism, there has long been an impression that it was the Nazi model of racial thought that most inspired other interwar fascists. Mussolini's adoption of anti-Jewish laws in 1938, for example, was traditionally regarded as a product of his improving relationship with Hitler, a view that is only now being challenged, as scholars draw attention to the native roots and long-term development of Italian Fascist antisemitism.[45] The BUF has tended to suffer a similar perception. Many contemporaries saw the party's use of antisemitism as a result of direct or indirect German influence, claiming it was an imported, rather than home-grown, problem. As we have seen, historians, in explaining the development of the BUF's antisemitism, also stress the importance of its drift towards Hitler's sphere of influence, and their analyses of Mosley's anti-Jewish position are often comparative.

Holmes is one who does acknowledge the 'need to take account of an existing tradition of anti-semitism in Britain' when studying the BUF, noting that certain 'features of BUF policy…predisposed it towards a concentration upon Jews'. His list of these features, however, extends only to 'Britain for the British' populism and opposition to finance capital. As we have seen, many other aspects of the movement's programme inclined it towards antisemitism.[46]

Writing soon after Holmes, Lunn tackled the issue more substantively, in what remains the most comprehensive effort to understand British fascism's native roots. He attempts to 'shift the emphasis away from British anti-semitism as "a pale Continental importation" and concentrate on its roots in the native cultural experience', tracing 'important linkages between…the pre-1914 period and the activity of the inter-war years', which suggest 'a continuity of thought indicative of a tradition of British anti-semitism'.[47] His findings chimed with the changes underway in the wider study of British antisemitism, where a new generation of historians similarly condemned the 'preoccupation with the Nazi model', warning that searching for 'continental'-type antisemites in Britain is a largely futile endeavour.[48]

One such scholar, Kushner, turning his attention fleetingly to the BUF, finds that, while many of the more extreme aspects of its antisemitism never caught the public imagination, in as far as it helped reinforce and exacerbate negative stereotypes of Jews – in particular, that they were alien – its rhetoric can be situated within the 'anti-semitism of exclusion' that was widespread on the political right. In this regard, 'fascist ideology was not fundamentally different from popular discourse on Anglo-Jewry, in that Jews were commonly seen as un-British'; fascism only 'differed ... [in] demand[ing] a political programme in which antisemitism would be prominent'. Moreover, the only 'major difference between fascist demands and state policy on the Jews was that the former did not differentiate among Jews': fascists wanted to remove them all, whereas the state accepted 'Englishmen of the Hebrew faith' but rejected aliens. Kushner's claims in some ways go too far: as we have seen, Mosley and his party always continued to distinguish (theoretically at least) between Jews that 'must leave' Britain and those that would be allowed to stay. But in others, not far enough: the BUF, as will be shown below, drew on a far wider range of influences in formulating its anti-Jewish position than just conservative exclusionary traditions.[49]

Yet despite advances over the 1980s and 1990s in the understanding of native forms of antisemitism, little equivalent progress was made in the field of British fascist studies, prompting Lunn to repeat his criticism of the tendency to relate the development of British fascism to its more prominent continental counterparts.[50] More recently, however, work has begun to place greater emphasis on the intellectual and ideological antecedents of the British radical right, though the focus has tended to be on individuals and minor organizations, rather than the BUF.

Dan Stone, for example, outlines the 'indigenous ways of thinking ... [and] longstanding concerns' that produced home-grown forms of fascism, such as that offered by the English Mistery (a completely marginal group, even by British fascism's standards). Yet, by contrast, he dismisses the BUF as an 'obvious imitator' of foreign fascisms.[51] Griffiths, too, begins by describing traditional British attitudes towards Jews as 'the bed-rock on which more extreme anti-Semitism could flourish', but goes on to relate this chiefly to the 'lunatic fringe' that gathered around Archibald Ramsay in the late 1930s.[52]

Others have sought a compromise between native and European influences. Claudia Baldoli contends that 'the BUF always offered an anglicised version of European fascism', though her argument includes the dubious claim that in 1939 the party accepted German biological racism. She, like others, relates the development of anti-Jewish ideology to a 'shift from a Roman to a Teutonic model of fascism'.[53] Thurlow, in his delineation of two trends in British fascist racial thought, also cannot resist international comparisons, claiming that the 'Mosley tradition' 'was closer to the Italian idealist fascist view of race', while the 'racial nationalism' of the IFL and the Britons 'bore more similarities to Nazism'.[54] Meanwhile, Gary Love argues that, although Mosley developed a distinctive, British form of fascism, it was overshadowed by, and therefore influenced by and to some degree imitative of, the Italian and German models: it was 'a cocktail of native and derivative influences, but ... also part of a wider European fascist view'. Such an observation is difficult to dispute, but is so sweeping as to offer little valuable insight. On antisemitism specifically, despite dismissing the idea that its adoption was part of an effort to ape the Nazis, and despite his stated objective to take BUF ideology seriously, Love still regards it as partly an opportunistic appendage to the party's programme (the Jews were a useful 'soft target') and partly a response to Jewish anti-fascism. Antisemitism is thus denied an authentic place in the movement's doctrine.[55]

In the latest research on the BUF, a more promising approach has begun to emerge. Thurlow acknowledges that Mosley's antisemitism had 'deep roots in late Victorian and Edwardian politics', particularly in its anti-alienism and conspiratorial accusations against Jews.[56] Pugh, meanwhile, has charted the intersection between the BUF and the mainstream political right, finding that fascist antisemitism was 'obviously compatible with orthodox Conservatism'. But, as with Kushner's similar approach, Pugh's focus leads him to neglect the extent to which fascism drew inspiration from, and aimed to appeal, across the political spectrum, not just the right.[57] This is a point highlighted by Linehan, whose study of east London fascism reveals how the BUF was able to play upon longstanding associations of Jews with harmful financial and business activity in a way that appealed to those with leftist leanings.[58] In his most recent work, Linehan emphasizes that 'the domestic context is crucial to an understanding of [fascism's] intellectual lineage'. Britain, he points out, possessed a 'potent and highly articulate' tradition of antisemitism upon which fascists could draw, and the BUF was able to successfully 'manipulat[e] ... these cultural and historical anti-Jewish prejudices'.[59]

With regard to any lingering charges of imitation, the first point to make is that the framework for the BUF's antisemitism had already been set in place over 1932–3, at a time when the Nazis were only just coming to power and when Italian Fascism was still years away from official endorsement of antisemitism. Given that Mosley's anti-Jewish message subsequently remained fairly consistent, this suggests that factors other than mimicry of foreign models were at play in its formulation. (Improving ties with the Nazis from 1934 and the introduction of the Italian racial laws in 1938 did appear to have an effect on the quantity and tone of the BUF's antisemitic rhetoric, but not on its substance, other than an increasing sense of fascist unity in the struggle against the Jews.)

For its part, the BUF always made clear that it took a different approach to the Jewish question from its German and Italian counterparts. Some may ascribe this to a desire to distance itself from the Nazis, whose anti-Jewish measures were unpopular in Britain – and this no doubt played some role.[60] Yet the BUF had no compunction in excusing Hitler's 'relatively mild persecution of a few thousand Jews', while at the same time promising that such actions would 'not be repeated in Fascist Britain'.[61] The reason, it was explained, was that every country faced a unique Jewish problem: Italy, with few Jews, had little reason to tackle the issue; Germany, with many more, was forced to take a hard line; Britain rested somewhere between the two. 'By reason of the differences of the problem,' Mosley explained in 1934,

> as well as the difference – vast difference – in our national character, our attitude towards [Jews] must be different from the Italian or the German, just as in every part of our policy our attitude is peculiarly British and is not foreign.

Indiscriminate persecution along racial or religious lines, while perhaps appropriate in Germany, was 'altogether foreign to the English mind', not to mention incompatible with Britain's multiracial, multifaith empire.[62]

This reasoning remained constant over the years. In 1936, Mosley likened his struggle against the Jews to Hitler's, but promised that he would employ only 'good British methods' to achieve his goals.[63] Two years later, E.D.F. Hart, an *Action* columnist, disputed claims that Italy's new racial legislation was a result of German pressure. Antisemitism had been forced upon Mussolini, as it had upon Mosley, by domestic circumstances: the expansion of the Italian empire, the arrival of central-European refugees and Jewish involvement in domestic anti-fascism. 'That it would please Germany was an agreeable, but subordinate consideration'. Despite the BUF's undisguised admiration for the Nazis, Hart regarded their antisemitism as 'too bitter' to provide a useful solution to the Jewish problem outside Germany.[64] Even Joyce, later a wartime propagandist for Hitler, claimed in 1937, on establishing his post-BUF party, the NSL, that it would reject the trappings of foreign fascism, which 'repel the great majority of Englishmen'; there would be no swastikas, no military-style organization and no dictator.[65]

In the rare glimpses of private policy discussions that are available, we see such sentiment being expressed behind the scenes, too. Writing to Mosley in early 1936, J.F.C. Fuller, chairman of the movement's publications arm, advised that neither the Italian nor the German model of fascism was suited to the British environment.[66] Even the BUF's addition of 'National Socialists' to its official title in 1936 was not the straightforward indicator of German emulation it may seem (as is suggested by the apparent contradiction above between Joyce's rejection of fundamental aspects of Nazism and his new party's name). The BUF, seeking support in working-class areas, genuinely wished to present itself as a progressive but patriotic force, in contrast to the international outlook of many on the traditional left; the term 'national socialism' expressed this position perfectly. Additionally, the phrase was deemed to hold less of a foreign connotation than the word 'fascism', hence its use among patriotic, working-class audiences to stress the BUF's native credentials. A set of instructions on campaigning for the 1937 LCC elections gave guidance on the subject of 'National Socialist Revolution', directing speakers to appeal to left-leaning audiences by stressing that the BUF would succeed where Labour had failed in the workers' struggle against international finance.[67]

Yet the clearest indication of the movement's independent approach to the Jewish question comes from simply examining its discourse. As we have seen, criticism of Jews that invoked religion or biology – the staple of many foreign antisemitic political movements – was extremely rare.[68] No scientific racial theory was ever advanced by any senior figure in the party, and religiously justified attacks played little role other than in occasional appeals to targeted groups. Instead, as we have seen above, an approach was favoured that focused not on inherent deficiencies in the Jews or their religion, but on the harmful activity they chose to undertake. This position, and the ways in it was expressed, conformed closely to native traditions of anti-Jewish thought.

Indeed, the very fact that the BUF worked so hard to justify its opposition to Jews on the basis of their alleged misconduct in itself indicated the strength in Britain of the 'antisemitism of tolerance' described by Williams and others: the notion that Britain was prepared to accept Jews on the condition they contributed positively to society;

but that if they did not, ill-feeling towards them was deserved. Thus Herbert Morrison, a leading figure in the Labour Party and active opponent of fascism, argued in 1936 that it was in part Jews themselves who 'creat[ed] anti-alien feeling', recommending that they should strive to be 'super-correct in their ... conduct'.[69] Hilaire Belloc, a popular writer and sometime Liberal MP, like the BUF repudiated 'abhorrence of Jewishness *per se*', Cheyette notes, instead basing his 'rational' case against the Jews on certain 'facts'. 'No-one can say with truth that I have ever objected to the practice of Judaism,' Belloc wrote, 'but I do object most strongly to Jewish cosmopolitan financial influence'.[70] The explicit distinction that Mosley made between 'good' and 'bad' Jews was another firmly established aspect of British discourse. In the wake of the First World War, Jews deemed to fall into the latter category had been deported by the British authorities, a solution the BUF also suggested, though on a far larger scale.[71]

The ways in which the BUF attacked the Jews' allegedly deleterious cultural influence and foreign allegiance bore the hallmarks of the second prevalent pattern of thought described earlier: the perception, particularly among conservatives, that Jews were incorrigibly alien in culture and identity, and that their presence and participation in society should therefore be restricted. William Joynson-Hicks, Britain's Tory home secretary from 1924 to 1929, publicly deprecated 'those who put their Jewish ... before their English nationality'. He feared an 'England flooded with the whole of the alien refuse from every country in the world'.[72] The *Times*, meanwhile, described immigrant Jews as 'stand[ing] aloof – not without a touch of oriental arrogance – from their fellow citizens. They look upon us with suspicion and a certain contempt[.] ... These people remain an alien element in our land'.[73]

Such sentiment was readily expressed in literary circles, too. T.S. Eliot, in a statement that mirrored almost precisely the BUF's warnings regarding cultural miscegenation, maintained that 'the population should be homogenous; where two or more cultures exist in the same place they are likely either to be fiercely self-conscious or both become adulterated'. This made 'any large number of free-thinking Jews undesirable'. As Cesarani observes, Jewish characters in Eliot's works often represented the 'deracination, corruption, decay and degeneracy' he associated with modernity – themes that suffused fascist thought.[74]

The fascists, of course, took the case a step further, not only questioning the Jews' loyalty and compatibility, but accusing them of deliberately pursing their interests to the detriment of the host society. Such claims were, again, already well established in British political discourse. It had long been felt in certain quarters that Jewish concerns conflicted with British ones; and it was often insinuated that Jews exploited the great power and wealth they supposedly possessed to advance their own cause. In the 1870s, at the time of the Eastern Crisis in the Balkans, Britain's ethnically Jewish Conservative prime minister, Benjamin Disraeli, was accused by opponents of attempting to push the country into a 'Jewish war, waged with British blood to uphold the objects of Jewish sympathy'.[75] This idea went on to gain great traction, particularly on the political left. The Anglo-Boer conflict in southern Africa at the turn of the century, for example, was widely alleged to have been instigated by Jewish financiers who held interests in the region. John Burns, a Labour MP, accused 'the financial Jew [of] operating, directing, [and] inspiring the agencies that have led to this war'; *Reynold's*, a respectable newspaper with a wide circulation, argued that 'at the bottom of the war … [is] the sinister figure of the financial Jew who is gradually enmeshing the world in the toils of the money-web'.[76]

The most comprehensive critique was provided by the anti-imperialist economist J.A. Hobson, an influential voice on the left. His *War in South Africa* contained a checklist of concerns that could have been transcribed into a BUF pamphlet. Until he had arrived in the country, he 'had no conception of [the Jews'] number or their power'; Johannesburg had become 'essentially a Jewish town … [where] greed, gambling, and every form of depravity' abounded. While these Jews professed to be British, they were in fact aliens, and could be divided between the 'highly intelligent, showy, prosperous … upper crust' and 'rude and ignorant' small traders. The former, a 'little ring of international financiers[,] already control the most valuable resources', including the stock exchange, mines, the alcohol and gambling trades, money-lending syndicates and, worst of all, the press (in Britain, as well as South Africa), which they employed as an instrument of 'agitation'. To maintain these vast interests they had first established 'control [of] politics and legislation by bribery and other persuasive arts', and more recently had used this influence to drag Britain into conflict with the Boers. This 'disastrous war', Hobson argued, was merely an attempt 'to place a small international oligarchy of … financial Jews … in power'.[77] Through the claims of Hobson and others, the BUF was provided with a ready-made template of conspiratorial, anti-capitalist antisemitism. It is no coincidence that Mosley's most frequent single charge against the Jews was that they were agitating for a war to protect their financial and political interests.

The mainstream political right had not been averse to conspiracy theory either. A prominent conservative weekly, the *National Review*, in 1905 referred to 'a committee of Jews … [who] determine international policy'.[78] Its editor, Leo Maxse, worried that Jews were attempting to 'intrigue against British interests and to work for our … enemies'.[79] After the First World War, further concerns were evoked by the Bolshevik Revolution, the growing prominence of Jews in the British Communist Party and the publication of the *Protocols of the Elders of Zion* in English. In 1920, the *Morning Post* ran a series of articles based on the *Protocols*, which the newspaper's editor regarded as 'a most masterly exposition' that revealed 'the aim of the political Jews, which is the domination of the world'. Even in parliament, Cesarani notes, many on the 'Die Hard' wing of the Conservative Party 'believed fervently in the existence of a world Jewish conspiracy that was subverting the British Empire at home and abroad'.[80] Such concerns were readily exploited by the BUF to bolster another of its core aims: the defence of society against various 'subversive' movements, particularly those associated with the far left.

Finally, in its economic attacks, the BUF could rely on established depictions of both 'small' and 'big' Jews. Forty years earlier, various anti-alien groups, most prominently the British Brothers League, had campaigned in the same deprived areas as the BUF, likewise promising to protect British workers from the large-scale immigration of poor, east-European Jews. They received support from elements in the Conservative Party, such as Stepney's MP, William Evans-Gordon. His 1903 book, *The Alien Immigrant*, argued not only that mass Jewish entry was causing socio-economic problems as a result of increased competition and overcrowding, but suggested, as the BUF later would, that the Jews' very disposition was to blame: 'wheresoever the Jews are congregated in numbers two types make their appearance and become prominent – the parasitical and the predatory'. As a solution, Evans-Gordon proposed creating a homeland for Jews, a place where they could feel pride in their own nation, rather than 'exploiting the *Goim*', towards whom they felt no responsibility.[81] The BUF later endorsed precisely the same policy, with identical justification.

The success of the anti-alien agitators in building a wide base of support demonstrates, David Feldman believes, how this cause 'was able to mobilise a coalition of diverse interests into a significant political movement ... [with] values and practices crossing class boundaries'. Moreover, he sees their efforts as an 'attempt to construct a national community ... influenced by the growing threat to Britain's imperial predominance ... [and] inevitably based upon a series of inclusions and exclusions'.[82] The precedent this set for fascism – which sought cross-class appeal on a platform of exclusionary nationalism and warnings of national decline – is clear, and was not lost on the BUF, which instructed its speakers to invoke the spirit and success of the British Brothers League when addressing East End audiences.[83]

The 1905 Aliens Act notwithstanding, the Tories continued to exploit this issue. Their leader, Stanley Baldwin, promised during his successful 1924 general election campaign that 'no alien should be substituted for one of our own people'; his appointee as home secretary, Joynson-Hicks, enthusiastically enforced anti-alien legislation.[84] Again, such sentiment was not limited to just one region of the political landscape: Linehan demonstrates how negative perceptions of Jews as middlemen and exploiters of the working classes became firmly embedded among trade unionists and socialists. 'It was through this medium of traditional left-wing ambivalence towards Jewish economic and business behaviour,' he observes, 'that the BUF made a direct appeal to Gentile labour.'[85]

A negative association between Jews and high finance was also well grounded in political discourse on both left and right – and dated far back in literary tradition, too, to Shakespeare's Shylock and beyond.[86] In 1901, an east London newspaper warned that 'with the sceptre of finance the Jew ... [is] forging the chains with which he is preparing to load those miserable Gentiles'; another contemporary worried that 'the appalling ascendency ... of this gifted Asiatic tribe' makes 'the struggle for life proportionately harder for the inferiorly equipped Englishman'.[87] Two financial scandals in the 1910s – the Indian Silver affair and the Marconi scandal – prompted concerns about Jewish influence at the highest levels of finance and politics, articulated most forcefully by the Chesterton brothers and Belloc, who warned of the 'Anglo-Judaic plutocracy' that dominated national affairs.[88]

Such attitudes were, of course, not unique to Britain; nor were Jews the exclusive target. Conspiracy theories, cultural chauvinism and animosity towards immigrants and minority middlemen have been common throughout the world and across time. Yet, as historians have convincingly demonstrated, one can divine peculiarly British (or English, in some cases) themes, motives and modes of expression regarding Jews, and these pervaded the BUF's rhetoric, often down to the level of specific words and phrases. With such a rich heritage to drawn upon, the party had little need to look abroad for inspiration.

The movement did, though, differ in two important ways from those who had come before it. First, it fused these diverse traditions of antisemitism into a singular narrative that was more comprehensive and coherent than anything produced by earlier groups, doing so in much the same way that fascism as a broader ideology synthesized a variety of disparate political and intellectual influences.[89] Second, it integrated this narrative into nearly all aspects of a sophisticated political programme, making the removal of Jewish influence an essential component of its revolutionary project. In other words, it 'fascistized' existing antisemitism, harnessing and developing native patterns of thought and employing them in pursuit of its purgatory and palingenetic goals.

This all, of course, repudiates any suggestion of a single 'type' of fascist antisemitism. As discussed above, fascists were predisposed to oppose out-groups, and in interwar Europe Jews represented the most obvious target. But, as befitted an ultranationalist creed, the forms that fascist antisemitism took were dictated to a large degree by indigenous attitudes towards Jews. The resultant variety of positions on the Jewish question was demonstrated at the 1934 'World Congress' of fascists in Montreaux, where antisemitism became the most divisive issue among the delegates, who were representing fascist movements from a dozen European countries. Eventually, it was agreed that 'each Fascist organisation has the right of autonomy in dealing with its [Jewish] affairs according to local circumstances'.[90]

The obvious caveat to this picture of heterogeneity, though, and one highlighted by Kallis, is that there was a palpable radicalization of antisemitism among fascist movements over the 1930s that appeared to take place as a consequence of growing Nazi influence. The BUF certainly fitted this pattern, with its anti-Jewish rhetoric becoming more prominent as the decade progressed. This process, Kallis suggests, resulted from a growing sense of unity among Europe's fascist movements, as they sensed that a final confrontation with the democratic states and the Soviet Union was edging closer. Given that Nazi Germany was the de facto figurehead of the fascist camp, and that antisemitism represented one of the few ideological features that most fascist parties had in common and that could readily be internationalized, the struggle against the Jews offered a cause around which they could rally.[91] Again, we find evidence of this process in BUF discourse.

From its earliest days the party had been keen to cultivate international ties, and not only with its initial sponsor and archetype in Italy. In 1933 Mosley – in whose study hung a portrait of Hitler alongside one of Mussolini – sent a BUF delegation to the Nuremberg rally.[92] Senior party figures maintained regular contact with their Nazi counterparts over 1934, and supplied them with material for antisemitic propaganda relating to Britain.[93] This reflected the fact that leading Blackshirts already saw fascism as a universal European creed. Mosley explained that the various national manifestations of fascism were all part of 'the same Movement, finding different expressions in different countries in accord with different national and racial characteristics'.[94] W.E.D. Allen, a trusted confidant of Mosley who been with him since his New Party days, argued that 'Fascism – National Socialism – whatever we like to call it, is essentially a European movement – a political and spiritual transformation, having its roots and taking its expression from the oldest seats of European culture'. Like Mosley, he claimed that, while fascism took on distinct forms suited to various national contexts, these were 'complementary rather than disruptive', together making 'diverse contributions to ... World Fascism'.[95]

Once antisemitism became a central part of BUF policy, it was integrated into this vision of a universal fascist struggle. In 1935, during a friendly exchange of telegrams with Julius Streicher, the infamous Nazi propagandist, Mosley expressed solidarity with his counterpart, declaring that 'the forces of Jewish corruption must be conquered in all great countries before the future of Europe can be made secure in justice and peace'. He believed that Jews were engaged in an 'anti-Fascist crusade ... [against] the West', requiring a unified response.[96] Taking up the same theme, Joyce distinguished between Westerners, who had much in common with one another, and 'Oriental' Jews, 'who have no sense of obligation to the West and no sense of kinship with Western peoples'. In Europe, he warned, 'no National movement can tolerate [the] menace' of a Jewish presence; 'organised Jewry, on the other hand, is bound to fight any National movement'.[97] The BUF's pamphlet on Jewish policy, mentioned above, advised that the only way to 'break Jewish power ... [is] to dissolve the International System which gives such advantages to a dispersed race'; in order to do so, each nation needed to 'put its own house in order'.[98]

By the end of the decade, this imagined pan-continental insurrection had taken firmer shape, with the BUF identifying itself as one of the 'great movements of regeneration ... conquering Europe'.[99] It was presumably not by chance that the rise in anti-Jewish rhetoric that marked the beginning of the final (and most 'international') phase of BUF antisemitism coincided with Mussolini's introduction of anti-Jewish racial laws, suggesting a renewed feeling of confidence now that the second great fascist power had joined the crusade against the Jews. The BUF envisioned the 'great Nordic nations' leading 'a united Europe in the struggle for Western Civilisation ... [against] International Jewish Finance'.[100] 'Gentiles in every land', it was predicted, will 'rise up in protest against [the Jews'] international network of intrigue',[101] helping bring about the final goal of 'ultimate European purification',[102] with 'each nation ... a spirit reborn'.[103] Previously, the BUF had been rather negative and defensive in its antisemitic imagery, portraying itself, like the British people, as a victim of the Jews. But now, standing alongside its powerful allies, the party called upon 'the Jewish Jackal ... who has skulked too long at the [British] Lion's heels to feast on his kills, [to] try conclusions with the German Eagle, if he dares'.[104]

This process of convergence was mirrored in the domestic sphere too, where Britain's various radical-right groups grew progressively closer to one another, with a shared antisemitism again the primary driving force. In the BUF's early days, there had been much tension with other fascist organizations. In fact, some of its most violent early confrontations had come not with anti-fascists, but with rivals such as the IFL and the BF.[105] In particular, the BUF's initial ambiguity on the Jewish question had aroused suspicion among these other groups. The IFL labelled the Blackshirts 'Kosher Fascists' and their party the 'British Jewnion'; in 1933, it published a leaflet reassuring the public that, despite their similar black uniforms, the League had nothing to do with the 'Judaic Fascism' of the newly formed BUF. The BF's publications also made sure readers were aware they had 'no connection with Mosley or Moses'.[106]

But subsequently, once the BUF had made its anti-Jewish stance explicit, had been completely marginalized from mainstream politics and had aligned itself more closely with the Nazis, collaboration with others on the British radical right became far more feasible. In March 1937, the BUF put out feelers to the IFL to form a united fascist front, a move that appears to have been received positively, with Special Branch noting a warming of attitudes towards the BUF from IFL speakers.[107] But it was developments over 1938–9 that did most to transform relations. Just as the growing threat of war helped to rally fascists internationally, so too it brought them together at home, where preventing a 'Jewish war' with Germany became a shared obsession for various pro-Nazi groups.

In particular, the NL, an underground society headed by Archibald Ramsay, a Conservative MP and ardent Nazi sympathizer, acted as a forum for extreme antisemites to gather in the late 1930s. Indeed, it had been created precisely to perform such 'co-ordinating efforts', its founder noted. Figures such as Robert Blakeney (associated variously with the BF and IFL), Fuller (BUF), Henry Beamish (the Britons), Houston (BUF, Nationalist Association), Serrocold Skeels (United British Party, IFL), Joyce (BUF, NSL), Arnold Leese (IFL) and Chesterton (BUF, British People's Party) spoke at its meetings, invariably railing against the Jewish menace. Its secretive, ticketed gatherings were advertised through the BUF, IFL, NSL, MCP, the Britons, the Liberty Restoration League and the United Ratepayers Advisory Association.[108] At a meeting in the summer of 1939 organized by the MCP, Ramsay and Chesterton spoke. During his address, the latter appealed for Britain's anti-Jewish forces to unite behind a single leader, a call the audience responded to with loud chants of 'Mosley!'[109]

The *New Pioneer*, published by Viscount Lymington, a leading figure in the English Mistery, acted as an equivalent to the NL in print. Founded in December 1938, its pages hosted various figures from across the radical right.[110] Meanwhile, behind the scenes, senior figures in the BUF discussed common aspects of policy and potential collaboration with their counterparts in the Mistery, and hosted a dinner for leading members of The Link, a pro-German, antisemitic organization.[111]

In addition to their mutual admiration of Hitler, what bound these organizations and individuals together was agreement that at the heart of the multitude of social, economic and political problems they diagnosed in British society lay the Jews, whose urgent removal was required. This shared ambition sprung, above all, from a common desire for a pure Britain, purged of injurious alien influences.[112] While it is true that the BUF's position was not founded upon the type of the pseudo-scientific racial theories advanced by the IFL and others, too much emphasis is often placed on this distinction. In practical terms, it mattered little whether a fascist's desired racial purity was defined biologically or culturally; in either case the Jews' incompatibility was regarded to be inherent and immutable and, consequently, the solution to this 'problem' – their removal – was the same. The IFL's proposal that Jews be forcibly resettled in Madagascar and, before they left, made to repay 'what they have robbed from the English people' was completely compatible with official BUF policy to find a separate homeland for Britain's Jews.[113]

The BUF did, admittedly, maintain its theoretical notion of 'good' Jews, who would supposedly be treated less harshly (though they were rarely mentioned by Blackshirt speakers and writers by the late 1930s). But this should, as mentioned above, be regarded as an attempt to justify its position and conform to native patterns of thought, rather than a genuine belief. Indeed, as we shall see in the following chapter, this area represented the one real tension between Mosley's idealized fascist vision, which required the entire removal of incompatible out-groups, and his efforts to portray his antisemitism as rational.

Mosley, Fascism and Antisemitism

If, as has been demonstrated so far, the foundations for the BUF's antisemitism were in place from the outset, its form remained relatively consistent over the following years, and it was an authentic, integrated and central aspect of the party's programme and ideology, this points to a further conclusion: that antisemitism had always been intended to play a role in BUF policy. This, in turn, raises questions as to exactly when, how and why Mosley – the architect and arbiter of that programme and ideology, but who had shown no inclination towards political antisemitism in his pre-fascist career – decided that opposition to Jews should form part of his doctrine.

In the Leader's own version of events, presented in his autobiography, he claimed that, while he may have had 'a quarrel... with certain Jews', this was 'for political reasons' and 'had nothing to do with anti-semitism'. He 'never attacked the Jews as a people', merely opposed those who threatened British interests. Moreover, he had 'not the slightest doubt' that Jews themselves were responsible for initiating this conflict. But, magnanimously, he forgave them: given concurrent events in Germany, 'it is comprehensible that they were in a state of considerable alarm and liable to jump to unjustified conclusions'; indeed, had he been a Jew, he 'might possibly have felt and acted as they did'. He was prepared to admit that some 'hard-boiled anti-semites' had been drawn to the BUF, and that occasionally 'foolish, abusive and violent things were said and written' by them. But, while such individuals were often a 'nuisance', Mosley made 'no apology for having accepted the[ir] support', given that the Jews had picked this fight.[1]

However implausible much of Mosley's account is, a prevailing sense remains in the historiography that antisemitism was an area of policy that was largely out of his control, run by more radical elements around him or forced upon him by Jewish aggression. At the very worst, he was a cynical opportunist, harnessing anti-Jewish sentiment to boost his failing movement. Thurlow believes that Mosley was 'not an ideological anti-semite'; instead, his hostility towards Jews stemmed from his 'concept of personal honour and his rational analysis of the activities of some Jews against the BUF, and their role in British society, [which] convinced him that assaults by enemies on the movement should be resisted by defensive force'.[2] Pugh, too, thinks that there is 'some validity in Mosley's claim ... [that] he had not envisioned anti-Semitism as a central element of his movement', and considers his early attacks on communists and international financiers to have been 'only incidentally critical of Jews'. On Mosley's later 'mistake' of adopting antisemitism, Pugh argues that he was 'buffeted by forces beyond his control', namely the influence of the Nazis and of prominent antisemites in the BUF. Lewis, similarly, claims that Mosley was 'the victim of influential hard-line anti-Semites within the party', that he exploited antisemitism 'in pursuit of political gain' and that interaction with Jewish opponents played a part.[3] As we saw in Chapter 1, the likes of Cross, Holmes and Lebzelter have also all argued for some combination of external and internal compulsion on Mosley.

Skidelsky mounts the staunchest defence. He believes that Mosley always saw 'the Jewish issue as more of a liability than an asset, a diversion from his main task', and cites various mitigating circumstances to explain Mosley's 'evil' side: 'a process of interaction' with Jews, who 'act[ed] in specific ways, under specific conditions', causing a 'genuine' problem that required a 'solution'; the extremists around Mosley, whose antisemitism 'rub[bed] off' on him; a 'demand' in east London 'for a political campaign along ethnic lines to redress the local balance of power'; the 'unreflective cultural anti-semitism which Mosley shared with even enlightened members of his class'; and the 'breakdown in moral standards' during the interwar period. Even when Skidelsky admits that Mosley 'erected an anti-semitic superstructure' that included specious claims of Jewish power, he contends that this was a consequence of 'intellectual and moral carelessness', rather than any design.[4]

Recently, Linehan has rightly criticized other scholars for 'fail[ing] to recognise that [Mosley's] anti-Jewish rhetoric had its basis in anti-semitic beliefs that were genuinely held ... [and] cannot be viewed in isolation from the remainder of ... [his] fascist ideology'. His own account, however, does not go quite far enough. Mosley's anti-Jewish views were more than just 'conspiratorial and ethnocentric', as Linehan claims, and it is inaccurate to say that 'little attempt was made at the level of official party ideology to develop a systematic anti-semitic theory'.[5] As we have already seen, a wide-ranging framework of antisemitism was developed and integrated into nearly all aspects of BUF policy. As will be argued below, this process was initiated and overseen by Mosley himself.

Mandle, too, refuses to believe that Jewish policy was dictated by those around the Leader, insisting that 'the particular nature of the anti-Semitism used, its emphasis and its direction was clearly Mosley's decision'. Yet he also argues – wrongly, as we shall see – that Mosley publicly distanced himself from its propagation and was never fully committed to it as a policy, perhaps because he was not himself 'totally' antisemitic. Mandle offers three possible explanations for the descent of this gifted thinker – who had previously shown 'no signs of the irrational eccentricity' characteristic of dedicated antisemites – to gutter racial politics. First are the two standard hypotheses that he was responding to Jewish anti-fascism or that he exploited antisemitism for political profit.

More interestingly, Mandle's final, and favoured, theory is that Mosley always 'needed a powerful force to challenge, a mighty opponent to defeat, and the more generalised and amorphous it was, the better it served his purpose'. This had been expressed first through his opposition to the traditional political system and the 'old Gang' that populated it, before expanding to include 'international finance', and finally the Jews. Additionally, Mosley's reluctance to admit his own failings meant that he tended to ascribe them to outside forces. In late 1934, realizing that his party was in decline, that he had failed to control the violent elements within it and that he had not managed to forge ties with the political establishment, he 'inflated a minor opponent into a major cause of failure'. Thus his opposition to Jews was 'both sincere and self-deluding'.[6]

Another to argue that Mosley was in control of the BUF's antisemitism is Dorril, who criticizes 'the theory of the reluctant Mosley' as unduly 'absolv[ing] him from his responsibility' for an anti-Jewish policy that 'he fully endorsed'. Yet Dorril himself fails to offer a convincing and consistent alternative narrative explaining Mosley's approach to this issue. Initially he argues – as the present chapter also will – that Mosley's antisemitism was part of a 'pre-planned … campaign' that 'worked to a timetable'. This feature of policy was only to be unveiled when the BUF was 'strong enough to confront the inevitable backlash' from Britain's powerful Jews. Yet if that was the case, it appears odd that, as we have seen, antisemitism was employed in sustained bursts during the party's early existence, not least by Mosley himself. Then, subsequently, with the BUF at the peak of its powers during the alliance with Rothermere, anti-Jewish language was suppressed. When antisemitism was finally adopted as official policy in late 1934, this came not at a time of strength, but when the party was in rapid decline after the disastrous events of the preceding months.

Subsequently, Dorril himself somewhat contradicts the idea of a fixed 'timetable', suggesting that Mosley was flexible on this issue, prepared to 'bend' anti-Jewish policy depending on the circumstances. When attempting to win favour with Mussolini, antisemitism was downplayed; its subsequent escalation from 1934 was designed to win support from Hitler. Complicating matters further, elsewhere the author seems to imply that there was no genuine intention of pursing an anti-Jewish policy at all. He claims that 'Mosley's attitude towards Jews was outlined in [W.E.D.] Allen's book', an officially sanctioned study of the BUF published in 1934 (when Mosley was supposedly attempting to impress the Nazis), which stated that 'the English race … [is] strong enough to ignore – and to absorb – the Jews'.[7]

Through this chapter it will be argued that not only was Mosley's direct influence evident, both publicly and behind the scenes, at every major juncture in the development of the BUF's anti-Jewish policy, but that antisemitism had been an integral element of his thought from the very start. Indeed, Mosley's attraction to Jewish conspiracy theories actually appears to have begun even before he founded his fascist party. In April 1932, he had invited two of Britain's most notorious antisemites, Arnold Leese, leader of the IFL, and Henry Beamish, founder of the Britons, to address the New Party's youth wing (which later formed the core of the early BUF) on the subject of 'The Blindness of British Politics under the Jew [sic] Money-Power'. The diary of Harold Nicolson, a former parliamentary candidate for the New Party, reveals that Mosley's original draft of *The Greater Britain* had contained criticism of Jews. The exact nature of these attacks is unknown ('Jewish banking houses' are the only of Mosley's targets mentioned in the diary), but they were vehement enough for Nicolson, whom Mosley had asked for advice on his text, to warn that their 'Nazi note' would alienate British audiences.[8]

Mosley heeded his friend's counsel, removing any direct references to Jews from the final version of the book. He did, however, in a section on the financial industry, decry the 'alien elements, which arrogate ... power above the State, and ha[ve] used that influence to drive flaccid governments of all political parties along the high road to national disaster'.[9] Moreover, as we have seen, in an official statement on the party's formation, and again at its first public meeting, the Leader raised concern over Jews' supposed involvement in 'subversive activity' and suggested that they held anti-British aims, setting out the precise pattern his party's antisemitism would subsequently follow.[10]

The escalation of anti-Jewish rhetoric in late 1933 once again saw Mosley to the fore. It was he who penned November's infamous 'Shall Jews Drag Britain to War?' article, which announced his party's open opposition to Anglo-Jewry. As well as allegations of war-mongering, it contained wide-ranging attacks on the 'Jewish money power' that controlled the Conservative Party and the 'Jewish intellectuals' who dominated socialism, leading both the Tories and Labour to 'dance to the Jewish tune' (Leese and Beamish's lecture had clearly made an impression). Jews also held a 'corrupt monopoly' over the press, cinema 'and other organs for the creation of public opinion'; they were 'an alien and anti-national minority organising within the state', using their power 'not for the benefit of Britain, but for their own race'. In fact, Mosley already saw this as an international conspiracy: 'all over the world, they [the Jews] organise against the Fascist revolution'. At a public meeting later that month, he again railed against 'Jewish interests and organisations ... urging England to march against Germany'.[11]

Subsequently, although explicit expressions of antisemitism were discouraged during the early stages of the Rothermere alliance, Mosley was unable to resist continuing his earlier line of attack, using veiled but transparent language. In January 1934 he warned that his fascists would 'attack the alien forces in the City of London[,] ... crack the whip over their heads, and drive'; later the same month he promised to 'deal faithfully with the alien interests of high finance who use the money power of Britain to serve her enemies'.[12]

Moreover, disclosures provided by three disgruntled senior figures in the party suggest that any official suppression of anti-Jewish rhetoric at this time was merely a tactical decision on Mosley's part. One, speaking anonymously to the *News Chronicle* in February 1934, claimed that antisemitism was endemic in the BUF, but that members were forced to officially deny it.[13] By July, in an outburst that had clearly been brewing for some time, Robert Forgan, the party's second-in-command, privately declared that it had become 'impossible to work with' Mosley due to 'his anti-Semitic utterances and the anti-Semitic trend of the Fascist movement' under his leadership.[14] Later in the year, Charles Dolan, a former national propagandist who had now abandoned the BUF, claimed that Mosley's denials of antisemitism had always been 'for political reasons only'.[15]

The growing unease of the party's more moderate figures was contrasted by the rapid ascent through the ranks of those who became the chief exponents of anti-Jewish policy. It cannot have been without Mosley's blessing that, well before the summer of 1934, the BUF's propaganda wing had come to be dominated by the likes of Joyce, Beckett, Chesterton and Raven Thomson. By the end of 1933, for example, Joyce had risen to become the party's director of research. He already regularly 'deputised for the

Leader' at public meetings, *FW* noted, 'assisting in the promulgation of Fascist policy'. At one such event, in January 1934, Joyce had condemned 'Jewish renegades', declaring that 'the flower of Israel shall never grow in ground fertilised by British blood'. When contacted by the *JC*, Raven Thomson, the BUF's director of policy, refused to distance the party from Joyce's words; in fact, he endorsed them, declaring that if Jews 'place the interests of th[eir] race before the interests of this country', it was only 'natural that there should be a difference of opinion between ourselves and the[m]'.[16]

During the public re-emergence of antisemitism in the spring and early summer, Mosley again led from the front. In March 1934, at a speech in Bristol, he confirmed that Jews were prohibited from joining his party on the basis that he could not 'invite an enemy to come into my camp'. The same month, he disparagingly referred to 'those so-called Englishmen with foreign names, who are enemies of Britain and the British people'. By April, the message was less ambiguous: 'Oriental patriots who exploit the people for their own greed' were advised 'to choose between Britain and Jewry' and 'not to organise as they are doing to-day'. Should they fail to heed these warnings, then, under a fascist government, 'the right[s] of the minority [would] be sacrificed' for the good of the majority.[17] In May, Mosley accused the Tories of worshipping 'at the shrine of an Italian Jew', Benjamin Disraeli, 'danc[ing] like portly dervishes before the altar of their Eastern Divinity'. A few days before Olympia, he again claimed that the Conservative Party and the City of London were dominated by 'alien hands'; at the meeting itself, he attacked the three mainstream political parties for following an 'Italian Jew', a 'German Jew' (Karl Marx) and 'that typical John Bull, Sir Herbert Samuel' (the Jewish leader of the Liberals). His own creed, by contrast, represented the only truly British option.[18]

It was then Mosley's addresses at Hyde Park, Belle Vue and Albert Hall in the autumn – each presenting a progressively more explicit, comprehensive and vituperative anti-Jewish message – that, as we saw in the previous chapter, confirmed and elucidated the relationship between his party's antisemitism and its fascist ideology. Publicly, of course, he portrayed this as a recent (and reluctantly taken) decision, forced upon him by Jewish involvement in the wave of anti-fascism that had struck his party over the summer. Decades later Mosley still maintained that it was only during this period, having learnt the extent of the Jews' opposition to his movement, that he decided to change tack. It was in October 1934 that he had criticized Jews 'for the first time', having 'rarely...even mentioned' them previously.[19] Few examples better attest to the dishonesty of his account.

Chesterton, similarly, recalled how, so 'puzzled' had Mosley been by the outpouring of Jewish opposition in 1934, that he 'ordered a thorough research' into the matter. This was carried out by Chesterton himself, who 'discovered' that Jews held great sway over international finance, the retail trade, the cinema and theatre, the press and all political parties, exploiting this power 'to the detriment of Britain'. Mosley realized he had 'stumbled upon the secret of Jewry's bitter attack on his movement': they were involved in all the types of harmful activity that fascism promised to bring to an end. Chesterton lamented the sad irony that fascism, which simply wished 'to preach a straightforward doctrine of patriotism and economic reform', had 'been driven into a racial policy by the very people who had most to lose from the implementing of that policy'.[20]

Scepticism at such claims should stem, first, from the fact that Chesterton's 'findings' were nonsense: Jews possessed nothing like the power, wealth or influence he alleged, while charges of early Jewish involvement in anti-fascism were greatly exaggerated. (As we will see in Chapter 6, by this stage only a tiny proportion of the Jewish community had been involved in active opposition to the BUF; the majority were wary of, but not yet actively hostile to, Mosley, while a handful even took a positive interest in his movement). But, even if we were to take Chesterton's report seriously, the idea that he and Mosley experienced a sudden epiphany in mid-1934 is ludicrous. In 1932 Mosley was already making insinuations of Jewish involvement in these types of 'anti-British' activity, and by late 1933 these had turned into explicit attacks. A year after the official adoption of antisemitism, Mosley publicly contradicted his previous claims of naivety, admitting that when his movement was founded, he already 'knew something of the force which would be rallied against us[,] ... this one small alien clique ... us[ing] its power against the nation'.[21]

As the latter quote suggests, it is also difficult to believe that in mid-1934 Mosley was 'puzzled' by alleged Jewish opposition to his party, or by the reasons for it. Indeed, he had made reference to this issue well before then, declaring in November 1933, for example, that Jews 'fear and hate us because we ... challenge their corrupt power'; it was 'the[y], not we, who have forced the struggle'. Two weeks later, *Blackshirt* claimed that there had been 'a declaration of war by Jewry against us ... long before [now]'.[22] Perhaps most tellingly, in April 1934, during a major address at the Albert Hall, Mosley announced: 'When [Jews] talk of declaring war on Fascism, my answer is "Get on with it!" '[23]

In this light, a far more plausible explanation presents itself, one that will be further developed over the course of this chapter: that the Blackshirts' early anti-Jewish outbursts were intended to goad Jews into attacking them, with the aim of only fully revealing their antisemitism when it could be presented as a response to Jewish aggression. The concerted anti-fascist disruption of BUF events in the summer of 1934 – in which Jews had played a role, although not to the extent the fascists claimed – finally provided Mosley with his pretext.

Yet these clear grounds for scepticism have not stopped scholars taking the fascists' version of events at face value. Thurlow, in a credulous affirmation of Chesterton's account, argues that in the summer of 1934 Mosley was 'genuinely puzzled by growing Jewish hostility to the BUF', and believes that Chesterton's report 'convinced Mosley of Jewish dominance in British society'. It was then Mosley's Albert Hall speech in October that 'signalled ... [the] turn to anti-semitism'.[24] Skidelsky, too, suggests that 'Jews were responsible for the ... escalation' of hostility in the summer of 1934. This was largely due to their participation in the disruption of fascist meetings, but also, as mentioned in Chapter 2, because it 'may have been true' that, as Mosley claimed, Jewish advertisers pressured Rothermere to abandon the BUF and wealthy Jews financed the anti-fascist movement. Neither Skidelsky nor Mosley offer any sources to substantiate these claims.[25]

Additionally, many believe that, once adopted, this aspect of policy was shaped in large part by factional dynamics within the party. There is no consensus on the precise composition of these groups, but it is unanimously agreed that on one side was a coterie of doctrinal fascists that favoured an emphasis on propaganda and ideology, comprising the likes of Raven Thomson, Chesterton, Beckett and Joyce, the latter having been appointed director of propaganda in 1934. Another bloc – led by Fuller, a renowned military strategist, and F.M. Box, a former Tory electoral agent – aimed to take the BUF in the direction of a more conventional political party, building up its electoral machinery and toning down the more radical aspects of its programme and activity. Antisemitism lay at the heart of their differences: the former faction supported its use; the latter was more circumspect (Box strongly opposed it; Fuller, who was a dedicated antisemite, argued that it should be employed with great care). The party's changing approach to Jewish issues, it is argued, depended in large part on which group held Mosley's ear at various times.[26]

An internal party report, written at some point between August and December 1934, appears, superficially at least, to support such a notion. Authored by G.S. Gueroult, a member of the more moderate faction and previously the BUF's director of propaganda, the document discusses the crisis then facing the movement. Among other concerns, Gueroult warns that the growing use of anti-Jewish rhetoric by platform speakers and in *Blackshirt* had 'produced very grave repercussions' in terms of a loss of both public sympathy and many 'sound, level-headed' members. There was a feeling within the party that Mosley was being 'jockeyed' by Joyce 'in directions known to suit the personal predilections of this Officer'. Gueroult requested that the Leader take greater control of propaganda himself.

However, handwritten annotations added to the text suggest that Gueroult's account should not be taken at face value. In particular, the latter two of his comments outlined above – those that referred to Mosley directly – clearly irked the reader of the report: unlike the rest of the document, they are marked with numerous exclamation and question marks. Given that the copy in question resides in Mosley's personal collection of papers, it is likely that it was he who made these notes, suggesting he disagreed with accusations that the party was being taken in an antisemitic direction at Joyce's bidding and without his knowledge or consent.[27] Indeed, given that Mosley himself was responsible for the worst of the platform rhetoric Gueroult complained about, was a contributor to *Blackshirt* on the Jewish question and would have sanctioned the promotion of Raven Thomson and Joyce ahead of Gueroult in the party's policy and propaganda apparatus, it is improbable that he was a passive bystander to Joyce's machinations.

Nevertheless, that is not to doubt that such machinations were taking place. At around the time of Gueroult's report, police sources documented the 'internal decay' afflicting the BUF, brought about by a combination of financial difficulties, personal rivalries and 'inept' organization. The loss of respectable support after Olympia, in particular, had exacerbated these problems, while the poor fascist turnout at September's Hyde Park rally had 'made Mosley look ridiculous'. Various individuals around the Leader were now vying for influence over the movement's future direction, fostering an 'atmosphere of distrust' between them. Joyce, in particular, had become a 'storm centre' for these disputes, which revolved around differences over the use of violence and antisemitism. Such was the degree of internal antagonism that two members of headquarters staff were put before a 'court martial' to face charges of conspiring with five others to divide the party. Other members – including prominent moderates Forgan and Rex Tremlett, the former editor of *Blackshirt* – simply decided to abandon Mosley altogether.[28]

Another subplot in these intrigues, and one that touches upon the party's growing use of antisemitism, concerns the figure of George Pfister, the head of the BUF's Foreign Relations and Overseas Department. As his title suggests, Pfister's work encompassed establishing relations with overseas fascist organizations. Drawing on German archival sources, Dorril claims that Pfister's communications with senior Nazis demonstrate the extent to which Mosley had by 1934 committed to a policy of antisemitism, as part of his efforts to win support from Berlin. In April, for example, Pfister informed the Germans that Mosley was now 'completely unambiguous' in his opposition to Jews; in June, he quoted Mosley's words, allegedly verbatim, from a private meeting, at which the Leader had promised to 'take the most drastic measures as soon as we are in power' against 'our opponents of non-Aryan race'.[29]

These findings do, to some extent, endorse the version of events presented in this chapter. Yet there are reasons to be cautious in placing too much weight on these sources. It appears that most, if not all, of the words and sentiments attributed to Mosley in the reports concerning Pfister's activity are recounted only second or third hand, through Pfister himself or the Germans with whom he met. This is particularly troublesome in the context of the circumstances around Pfister at this time – barely acknowledged by Dorril – that raise doubts as to how faithfully he was representing his leader.

Pfister's efforts to cultivate links with the Nazis on Mosley's behalf appear not to have been entirely successful, with the highest-ranking figures, including Hitler himself, remaining unconvinced of Mosley's value.[30] In the circumstances, it would not have been surprising if Pfister had taken it upon himself to exaggerate, or at least distort, the nature of Mosley's views, especially regarding Jews, in order to win over the Nazis, who had made clear that they hoped for the BUF to adopt a more explicitly antisemitic stance.[31]

That this may have been the case is indicated by Pfister's dramatic fall from grace in the autumn, when Mosley closed down his entire department and forbade further communication with Germany. According to the police's information, Pfister had been punished for 'intrigue with Austrian Nazis', suggesting he was seen to have overstepped the mark in his dealings with foreign fascists.[32] In August, Forgan had warned Mosley that Pfister was showing 'excessive zeal' in his work, and that other senior figures 'resent [his] intrusion' into areas of policy. Joyce was particularly hostile, and appears to have played a key role in engineering Pfister's downfall.[33] The following year, Pfister was suspended from the party without pay after it was discovered he had continued to correspond with Berlin against Mosley's explicit orders – reinforcing the notion that in dealings with the Nazis he was prepared to act independently, even in direct contravention of his leader's wishes.[34]

Dorril's own evidence indicates that, after Pfister's departure, relations improved between the BUF and the German Nazis, with Mosley invited to meet Hitler in April 1935. It was recorded that 'the word Jew was never mentioned' during their hour-long conversation, while Dorril also suggests that Hitler warmed towards

Mosley once he realized that he was not simply a 'copyist' who imitated Nazi ideas.[35] This raises further doubt as to the extent to which Pfister's focus on antisemitism when communicating with the Nazis was his own initiative, rather than at Mosley's behest. A final question mark over Pfister's role is MI5's claim that he had been working as a Nazi agent within the BUF. After leaving Mosley, he resettled in Germany and joined the Nazi Party.[36]

Whatever the precise composition, role and interests of the various groups and individuals active within the BUF at this time, it seems clear that the failure of any faction to completely win Mosley over – certainly for any significant period of time – had a tangible impact on the party's presentation of policy, in particular with regard to antisemitism. The oscillation in anti-Jewish rhetoric over 1934–6 described in Chapter 2 mirrored closely events behind the scenes. First, from mid-1934, the ideologists were in the ascendancy, reflected in the growing use of antisemitism. By early 1935, the Box–Fuller faction held greater sway, with attacks on Jews consequently diminishing. Yet their resumption soon after demonstrated Box's failure to assert his will on the party, leading to his resignation later in the year. The radicals did not subsequently have everything their way, however. They now vied for power with a further group, centred around Neil Francis Hawkins, who was made director-general of the BUF in early 1936, which favoured an emphasis on the aesthetic, 'emotional' and militaristic aspects of activity (uniforms, marches, music and the like), rather than ideological propagation. This appears to explain the continued inconsistency in the use of antisemitism over the first three-quarters of 1936, and the fact that it did not yet become a dominant aspect of discourse.[37]

Yet as we have seen, one should not confuse these tactically motivated shifts in the prominence of antisemitism with changes to its form, which remained within the framework laid down by Mosley over 1932–4. Nor should one doubt the Leader's continued commitment to this aspect of policy. In March 1935, at a time when his press was downplaying the Jewish question, Mosley, again speaking at the Albert Hall, launched what was described as 'one of the bitterest anti-Jewish tirades of his career'.[38] Two months later, reports emerged of his telegram to Streicher calling for the elimination of 'the forces of Jewish corruption … in all great countries'. When contacted by the Jewish Telegraphic Agency to ascertain whether the quotes were genuine, the BUF confirmed that they were completely consistent with Mosley's position.[39]

Mosley's personal papers also offer a unique, if fleeting, indication of his mindset. In the margin of one document, scribbled in Mosley's distinctive script, is the only extant example of his unguarded personal thoughts on Jewish policy. The text in question is another report on the state of the movement, compiled by Fuller, probably in mid-to-late 1934. Like Gueroult, he warned that the majority of British people were wary of both radical politics and the erosion of personal liberty. This dictated that the BUF should be more 'pro' than 'anti' in its programme. In particular, if fascism was to be portrayed as a 'binding and not a separating philosophy' then it should be implied that there was 'a place for all British subjects'; consequently, 'British Jews cannot be excluded' entirely, 'however undesirable the bulk of them may be'. Indeed, indiscriminate antisemitism was exactly what the 'big Jews yearn for', as it would 'lead to a popular outcry in their favour', allowing them to 'exploit the situation' to 'destroy

Fascism'. At all costs, therefore, the BUF should not 'condemn [Jews] as a race' or make physical attacks upon them. Instead, it should denounce 'only such sections as are connected with illegal and criminal undertakings', on the basis of the same rules that 'apply to all people'. It should be shown that fascism, 'like the human body', 'assimilate[s] what is beneficial to it and evacuate what is useless and injurious to its health'.

This, of course, fitted perfectly with the impression Mosley had always sought to convey: that opposition was directed only against those Jews who involved themselves with the types of harmful behaviour incompatible with fascist values. His complete agreement with Fuller is confirmed by the approving comment added alongside this specific section of text (with many words, unfortunately, entirely or partially illegible): 'This is a [...ull] arg[ume]nt in favour of the strategy of [...ing] the onus of aggression onto the Jews. It may be shown from now [in?] [illegible] that the Jew is the aggressor and the [...ter] [...ession] may be launched [with?] a good [illegible] of [further?] [support?]'.[40]

Skidelsky, writing in 1980, claimed that a lack of evidence pertaining to private discussions within the BUF over June–October 1934 made it impossible to know how the decision to adopt antisemitism was reached. Above all, it is 'impossible to be certain' whether it 'was [Mosley's] initiative, or represented his concession to his militants'.[41] Mosley's reaction to Fuller's advice, along with the other evidence presented above and the clear and continuous correlation between party policy and Mosley's own rhetoric, firmly point to the former conclusion. The BUF's leader, while happy to listen to those around him, was fully in control.

Moreover, this particular glimpse behind the scenes suggests two further conclusions. First, that, by mid-1934, internal discussion had moved well beyond the question whether or not Jews were harmful to British and fascist interests. Fuller was not trying to persuade Mosley that the 'the bulk of them' were 'undesirable'; this was taken for granted and was not his main concern. The issue under discussion at this stage was how opposition to Jews should most effectively be pursued – in Mosley's own words, it was a question of 'strategy'. Second, in terms of the motivation behind Mosley's attitude towards Jews, his comments show not a man being impelled to adopt antisemitism by Jewish attacks (or even baffled or angered by them, as he publicly claimed to be). Rather, he appears to see in them an opportunity to publicly justify a pre-existing antisemitic position. Both of these conclusions, of course, contradict Mosley's own version of events, and those of many subsequent scholars.

There is, though, evidence to suggest that subsequently, as the East End campaign began to dominate BUF activity, Mosley's supremacy over this aspect of policy was challenged. The police observed over August and September 1936 that the BUF leadership was urging speakers to tone down the cruder forms of 'Jew-baiting' in order to avoid legal action (again, evidence that variations in the external presentation of antisemitism were purely tactical). This had not pleased 'an influential section of the headquarters', which 'strongly deprecates any suggestion that the party should modify its policy in regard to the Jewish question'. This group had, without the involvement of Mosley, discussed a plan to deliberately court prosecution through anti-Jewish speeches. On 15 September, Joyce gathered the party's main speakers to advise them that they 'should be prepared to face imprisonment rather than comply with the dictum of the authorities that they were not to attack Jewry'. The same month, Raven Thomson was arrested for using insulting words towards Jews from the platform.[42]

On the eve of the 4 October 'Cable Street' march – at which, the police had learned, Joyce was planning for a leading speaker to make a particularly inflammatory antisemitic speech – Mosley took the unusual and highly significant step of penning a front-page article for *Blackshirt* advising his followers on 'the right way and the wrong way' to combat the Jews. The piece appears to have been a direct riposte to those agitating for more extreme forms of anti-Jewish rhetoric and activity. Moreover, it reveals the extent to which Mosley aimed to disguise the real reason for his opposition to Jews – a desire for Britain to be 'racially' pure – behind more rational public presentation of this aspect of policy.

He began by observing that, while there had been numerous antisemitic organizations in Britain, all had failed after being outsmarted by the 'big Jews'. The BUF, therefore, had to follow a 'cleverer' approach. Making 'violent or foolish' accusations merely allowed Jews to portray themselves as victims and the fascists as 'liars and lunatics', thereby 'alienating public sympathy' for the BUF. Mosley confirmed that he was 'fully aware of the racial differences between Jews and ourselves', and promised to 'take any measures necessary for the preservation of the British race'. But, he warned, this could not be the basis for policy; Jews should only be condemned for specific, demonstrable anti-British or anti-fascist behaviour. Finally, he reiterated his belief that the party should seek to gain an electoral mandate to tackle the Jewish problem and always remain 'entirely within the law'. 'Violence is illegal and injures our cause. Mere abuse [of Jews] is bad propaganda.'[43]

Despite these exhortations, the period after Cable Street, as we have seen, saw a dramatic change in the BUF's anti-Jewish rhetoric, deviating both quantitatively and qualitatively from the pattern that characterized the periods before and after. Yet this is very much the exception that proves the rule. At this time, with attention focused on campaigning in the East End for the LCC elections, it seems that Mosley saw his control over the party's message temporarily diluted, with local firebrands such as Clarke and Bailey, as well as the likes of Joyce and Raven Thomson, who were both standing as candidates, taking a more prominent role.[44] We see, therefore, that at the time when Mosley had his weakest grip on the content and dissemination of propaganda, there was a marked change in its form; throughout the rest of the BUF's existence, when policymaking was centralized around the Leader, a consistent anti-Jewish narrative can be traced.

Indeed, Mosley's dissatisfaction with the state of affairs during the 'East End phase' was demonstrated in spring 1937, when he brutally reasserted his authority by forcing the more radical elements out of the party. Cover for this operation was provided by the BUF's financial difficulties, which necessitated a dramatic cull of paid staff. The previous December, Joyce complained to Mosley and Raven Thomson that his salary had been reduced to an unacceptable level; in March, it was cut altogether, along with that of Beckett and many others in the propaganda department, which was hit disproportionately by Mosley's belt-tightening. Many of these individuals now left the party altogether. That differences over policy and strategy, rather than budgetary requirements, had been behind the primary factor this decision was later confirmed by both Joyce and Beckett. The latter claimed he and Joyce had been 'expelled ... without any consultation', the reason being that 'we told [Mosley] the truth' whereas he preferred to be 'surrounded by flatterers'. Joyce complained of the difficulties caused by Mosley's 'insistence on personal autocracy'. The memoirs of another Blackshirt, Jeffrey Hamm, state that disagreements over antisemitism had been the chief cause of this split. Tellingly, the new party established by the outcasts, the NSL, declared that it would have no 'figurehead' dictating policy.[45]

Following this purge, the pre-Cable Street pattern of antisemitism immediately re-established itself, supplanting the crude, vicious rhetoric favoured in the East End. This did not make Mosley popular. In June, Fuller privately condemned his 'absurd' decision to refocus on national campaigning rather than concentrating on the 'gutter-electorate' of east London, where Fuller now believed the greatest opportunities lay. In November, claiming he had 'lost faith with ... Sir Oswald', Bailey resigned from the party after being instructed by headquarters to 'tone down the violent anti-Jewish tenor' of his speeches. Charles Wegg-Prosser, who had also stood for the BUF at the LCC elections, departed the party in 1938, denouncing Mosley's 'increasingly dictatorial' methods.[46] Such discontent, coming particularly from those who had been involved in East End campaigning, suggests that Mosley was firmly back in control of Jewish policy.

Yet while this aspect of discourse was now expressed in a more measured fashion than it had been during the East End phase, one should not confuse this with any diminishment in its centrality to BUF ideology. Thurlow observes that in Mosley's 1938 outline of policy, *Tomorrow We Live*, only four pages of seventy-two were devoted to antisemitism. This, he believes, offers further evidence of the disparity between official ideology, which was little concerned with the Jewish question, and the anti-Jewish rhetoric more common in the party's newspapers and speeches. Yet closer examination reveals some important details that are overlooked by Thurlow.

First, parts of the book not dealing specifically with Jewish policy also contain coded but, by this stage, completely clear references to Jews: for example, at least six disparaging attacks on 'alien finance', including a promise to deport those involved with it. More significantly, 'The Jewish Question' is granted a chapter entirely of its own, placing it on a par with the other core elements of the BUF programme. As Mosley stated in the very first sentence of this section, he believed that 'the Jewish question should receive proper space in relation to national affairs in any book which deals with the modern problem'. Admittedly, the chapter appears towards the end of the book. But this fitted precisely Mosley's preferred presentation of antisemitism: first, he set out his analysis of Britain's political, social and economic decay, before then explaining how he had come to realize, after Jews begun so vehemently to oppose his attempts to tackle these problems, that they were responsible for a large proportion of them.

It is true that, as Thurlow notes, the relevant chapter is rather short. But this is explained, first, by the fact that the types of problems allegedly caused by Jews had already been outlined in preceding chapters: political corruption, monopolization of the press, poverty, the erosion of Britain's economic supremacy and so on. Mosley simply now had to name the perpetrators. But also, relatively little space was needed because Mosley's 'final solution' to the Jewish 'problem' was, unlike many of his other policies, extremely straightforward: Jews guilty of involvement in undesirable activity would be deported; those who were not could remain (though as foreigners, not British citizens). With regard to the former category, he wanted Britain to lead the way in international efforts to locate a suitable territory for their settlement. It should be somewhere unoccupied by any other group (ruling out Palestine, which belonged to the Arabs) but fertile, where the Jews could 'escape the curse of no nationality and may again acquire the status and opportunity of nationhood'. Given that Jews were unwelcome in their various host societies, had themselves chosen to maintain a distinct identity and desired the recreation of a Jewish homeland, such a policy was not persecution, but 'justice' for all concerned.[47]

Subsequently, during 1938–9 Mosley was the chief architect and exponent of the BUF's two major campaigns: opposition to war and the reception of refugees. As we have seen, these drew together and synthesized all the themes of earlier years, creating a coherent and comprehensive anti-Jewish message, and one with potential appeal to a much wider audience.[48] It is instructive to note that this was achieved once Joyce, Beckett and Chesterton had left the movement, and others, such as Gordon-Canning and Fuller, were known to be disillusioned with Mosley.[49] It seems that, without the distraction of factional infighting and the attendant discord over Jewish policy, Mosley was finally able to perfect his anti-Jewish message.

Certainly, other figures had contributed to the precise formulation of the party's antisemitism at various stages – Chesterton, for example, with regard to Jews' alleged cultural influence; Gordon-Canning on the international aspect of the Jewish question; Raven Thomson in the economic sphere. But it is implausible to suggest that Mosley – the undisputed leader of a party that preached autocratic rule, its leading ideologist and one of the primary contributors to its funds[50] – was not, for the vast majority of the time, in control of policy, let alone that he was 'buffeted' or 'compelled' into making decisions he was not comfortable with.

Moreover, Mosley's own anti-Jewish position (like all the central components of his fascist doctrine) remained absolutely consistent over the years. Whether in 1933 or 1939, he accused Jews of pursuing their interests to the detriment of Britain's; of exploiting their great wealth and power to do so; of retaining a separate, incompatible and dangerous culture and identity; and of opposing fascism. Always wishing to present himself as a rational thinker, he maintained that this position was not founded on some inherent, ubiquitous deficiency in the Jews – be it racial or religious – but on the specific activity they chose to undertake. Thus the idea of the 'good' Jew always remained.[51]

These were, as we saw throughout the previous two chapters, precisely the premises upon which the BUF's antisemitism was always based, and the contributions of other leading propagandists nearly always remained within the parameters laid down by Mosley. Of course, at various stages certain themes were emphasized or downplayed in response to external circumstances or as a result of internal party dynamics. And it is not difficult to find individual members, particularly at the local level, occasionally straying from the party line. But, other than for a brief period over late 1936 to early 1937, one always finds Mosley's imprint on the content of official BUF discourse.

Coming, finally, to the question of whether Mosley was an 'ideological antisemite'. This depends, to some degree, on what one means by the term. Certainly, prior to his founding of the BUF, there is nothing to indicate any hostility towards Jews. In fact, quite the opposite: in 1931 he had suggested to Nicolson that Ted 'Kid' Lewis, the famous Jewish boxer and a New Party candidate in the general election of that year, could be made 'the symbol of our Youth Movement'.[52] Yet it is clear that, by late 1932, antisemitism had become an integral part of his political outlook. Even Skidelsky admits that during the intervening period it seems Mosley began an 'education in the "realities" as opposed to the "surface appearances"' of the Jewish question.[53]

But in many ways Mosley's personal feelings are immaterial. More important is the relationship between his fascism and his antisemitism: the further his devotion to the former grew, the closer he was drawn to the latter. The problems his fascist mind now diagnosed in British society – the pernicious effects of various international forces, particularly communism and high finance; exploitative middle-man professions; cultural and moral corruption; Britain's economic decline – led him each time to the Jews – or, more accurately, to a set of existing stereotypes of the Jews.

Whether Mosley was aware of the spuriousness of his claims, and simply saw the imagined Jewish enemy as necessary to bind together his ideology, or whether he felt that he had made a genuine 'discovery' is impossible to say with certainty, though there is some evidence pointing to the former conclusion. In his autobiography, Israel Sieff alleged that Mosley had announced at a dinner party in early 1932 that his new party needed to find something to hate, and he had settled upon the Jews.[54] Mosley, for his part, vehemently denied that the incident took place and there is no corroboration elsewhere.[55] His opposition in the post-war period to black immigrants, Britain's new 'other', does, however, suggest that his exclusionary nationalism was simply aimed at the most relevant target.[56]

Perhaps the strongest indication that Mosley did not hold a genuine grudge against Jews can be inferred from the logical inconsistency that lay at the heart of his case against them. As we have seen, he declared that, under a fascist government, even 'good' Jews – those who had served Britain and avoided any undesirable activity – would be denied full citizenship and forced to live as foreigners, on the nonsensical basis that they should be 'treated as the majority of their people have elected to be treated'.[57]

For the proudly rational Mosley, such a contortion of logic – to constantly claim that he opposed Jews purely for the activity they chose to undertake, but then to punish those who were innocent of wrongdoing for the sins of others – points to a fundamental discrepancy between his own beliefs and the fascist credo. As his earlier attitude towards Lewis (an East End Jew, born Gershon Mendeloff) revealed, Mosley had always been happy to accept Jews as British. Yet the homogeneous conception of nationhood dictated by fascism compelled him to forsake this view, and classify even the most patriotic and honourable of Jews 'as a foreigner', 'physically, mentally and spiritually…alien to us'. In offering some justification, he added that any other large mass of foreigners – be they French, German, Italian or Russian – would be treated similarly if they, too, chose to 'maintain themselves as a community in our midst, owning [sic] spiritual allegiance to their original nation'. But, again, he contradicts himself, immediately admitting that Jews represented a special case because unlike Europeans, who were culturally Western, they were 'Oriental', and therefore particularly incompatible.[58]

Mosley himself appears, certainly in later years, to have been somewhat uncomfortable about this clear discrepancy in his position. After Skidelsky had argued in his biography that this 'complete *non sequitur*' in Mosley's otherwise 'genuine political argument' with Jews 'constitutes the greatest blemish on his whole career', Mosley responded personally to the author. He conceded that he had 'made mistakes' in his dealings with Jews, and 'use[d] methods … which may even be repugnant'. On his specific 1930s policy to strip even faultless Jews of their British citizenship, Mosley attempted to backtrack, claiming that 'in practice it is inconceivable' that it would have been applied to the 'thousands of Jews who had been for generations in this country', as well as any others who conducted themselves 'in a entirely British fashion'. He cited Herbert Samuel and Alfred Mond as two anglicized Jews who would have avoided such measures.[59]

As with so much of his subsequent revisionism, Mosley's claims are not consistent with the facts. His statements as leader of the BUF had been clear: all Jews, including the 'good' ones, would suffer in some way. Indeed, even the two supposedly honourable Jews cited by Mosley in the 1970s had once been targets of the BUF's scorn. Mosley himself, during his Olympia speech, had labelled Samuel as typical of the un-British Jews who dominated national politics and whom fascism aimed to usurp. Alfred Mond had passed away before the BUF was formed, but his son, Henry, was attacked in official Blackshirt literature as precisely the type of Jewish monopolist who would have to be dealt with under a fascist government.[60]

Whatever his personal feelings on the issue really were, the clear contrast between Mosley's publicly stated attitude towards Jews during, on the one hand, the periods before and after his active fascist career and, on the other, as leader of the BUF serves merely to reinforce how intimately connected were his fascism and his antisemitism. He absorbed from his political creed its desire for purity and its attendant need to oppose certain alien enemies, the elimination of whom would help bring about national rebirth. In seeking (consciously or not) such enemies, Mosley understood, as he himself put it, that antisemitism was 'an old English growth';[61] this, along with the Jews' status as the most prominent 'alien' minority in 1930s Britain, made them the almost-inevitable target for his exclusionary ultranationalism.

Mosley was not, therefore, an ideological antisemite in the sense that hatred of Jews motivated his political thought and action. Rather, it was the other way round: his ideology, fascism, compelled him to oppose Jews. Unlike many of his peers, whose visceral antisemitism had driven them towards fascism as a vehicle through which to act out their hatred, Mosley travelled in the opposite direction.[62]

Part Two

Jewish Responses to British Fascism

Introduction

British fascism is rightly seen to have had only a limited impact on interwar British society. Yet for the country's Jews it presented a disproportionate threat – the greatest, indeed, since their readmission to England in the seventeenth century. For the first time in modern British history, a political movement with substantial support had made the removal of the majority of Anglo-Jewry a central aspect of its programme, and was responsible for a systematic campaign of physical and verbal intimidation against the community. Moreover, while domestic fascism may have been weak in isolation, concurrent events in Germany and, from 1938, Italy offered a chilling vision of the potential dangers it posed to Jews.[1]

Equally, however, Anglo-Jewry was well placed to defend itself, certainly in comparison to the victims of political antisemitism in many other parts of Europe. The community, around 350,000 strong, greatly outnumbered the poorly supported fascists. A number of Jews held influential positions in politics, industry and elsewhere.[2] They could also count on the support of a large section of society – within which opposition to fascism was strong – and the state itself, which endeavoured to restrict extremist political activity, particularly the Jew-baiting that did so much to provoke disorder.[3] The Jewish community was, therefore, able to offer an effective response – or rather a variegated set of responses – both independently and in tandem with Britain's other anti-fascist forces, contributing significantly to British fascism's marginalization and failure.

Yet despite this, Sharon Gewirtz notes, 'attempts to write a history of specifically Jewish opposition to fascism are thin on the ground[.] ... When Jews are mentioned, it is usually as nameless inhabitants of the East End, faceless victims of fascism and antisemitism, or as institutions'. Her complaint was made in 1990, but still largely holds true. Ten years later, Kushner and Nadia Valman again called for 'more detailed and precise work' to be carried out, adding that the focus on Jewish activism in east London has led to the neglect of other elements of the community. Geoffrey Alderman, similarly, stresses that 'the importance of the East End to the Anglo-Jewish experience in the 1930s ... should not be over-emphasised'.[4] At a more general level, Stuart Cohen has pointed to the 'curious bibliographical gap' regarding any comprehensive attempt to examine Anglo-Jewish responses to antisemitism.[5]

Where histories of Anglo-Jewry have devoted attention to responses to fascism, they have tended to draw a rather reductionist picture of two broad types, which are seen to have been in bitter opposition to one another: confrontational anti-fascism, centred in the East End and often with a left-wing and working-class character; and the more passive, low-profile approach favoured by the communal elites, particularly the Board of Deputies. This dichotomy was first set out by Gizela Lebzelter in 1978, with subsequent scholars deviating little from her account.

She describes how the Board cautioned against direct engagement, preferring instead to focus on factually refuting antisemitic charges while otherwise trusting in the authorities to deal with the fascist threat. Although it eventually relented somewhat, establishing in mid-1936 a body to direct defence policy, Lebzelter feels that this was done purely to alleviate intra-communal pressure and prevent the appropriation of defence work by independent Jewish groups. The Board's own analysis of the situation had not changed, and its activity remained low key and of limited efficacy.[6] Much of this pressure had emanated from east London, where Jews, who experienced Blackshirt provocation first hand, found the Board's conservative line inadequate. Instead, they favoured the energetic approach offered by local defence bodies and various workers' organizations, which endeavoured to tackle fascism itself, rather than just the antisemitism it propagated.[7]

This image of fascism's divisive effect on Anglo-Jewry has since become ingrained in the historical narrative. Cesarani, for example, notes how the emergence of British fascism 'triggered a debate that split Anglo-Jewry', with the growth of independent Jewish defence bodies 'deepen[ing] the fractures'. These disputes are placed within the framework of wider developments during the interwar period, in particular as part of the growing rift between 'old' and 'new' sections of the community, with the pre-eminence of the traditional elites challenged by increasingly assertive Zionist and working-class elements, often of recent immigrant stock, who demanded, and gradually attained, greater representation within the communal power structure. Endelman, for example, claims that, in its response to domestic fascism, the Jewish leadership's 'arrogance, alienation from the fears and concerns of second-generation Jews, and failure to act boldly' had grave long-term consequences for its standing within the community.[8] This version of events will be challenged in the present study, and instead it will be shown how, after 1936, there was growing collaboration across the community on defence work, under the leadership of the Board.

The conflicting approaches to defence have also been used by scholars to reflect on issues of identity within Britain's heterogeneous Jewish community. The anglicized elites, whose forebears had negotiated the long path to emancipation and accepted its implicit assimilatory obligations, felt that Jews remained 'a tolerated, rather than accepted, section of the population'. Though they had attained a relatively secure and prosperous existence, this position remained precarious, they believed, its continuance contingent upon the maintenance of a certain standard of behaviour. As such, they were desperate to avoid the 'public display of Jewishness' that opposition to fascism would entail (in particular, the impression that Jews were acting as a single political interest group), preferring instead to trust that British traditions of tolerance and fair play would prevail. The best way for Jews themselves to ameliorate the situation was to ensure that their own economic and social practices were beyond reproach, thereby removing any possible justification for antisemitism. The general historical consensus is that such demands were at best 'offensive and pointless', as W.D. Rubinstein puts it, and at worst, as Alderman argues, akin to asking the community to accept second-class status by demanding a standard of behaviour exceeding that expected of gentiles.[9]

By contrast, many second-generation immigrants, with shallower roots and less emancipatory baggage, felt less obliged to conform to any prescribed pattern of behaviour, and less willing to trust solely in gentile good nature to counteract fascism. That is not to say that they did not feel British; simply that they interpreted their Britishness differently: as something to employ robustly in their defence, rather than to apologetically protect. As a contemporary later reflected:

> We were the first generation [of recent immigrant Jews] brought up in a free society, instilled with the English traditions and spirit which formed our character[,] ... taught to stand up and fight for ourselves[.] ... We resolved that under no circumstances would we allow Fascists and their propaganda, together with their insults and attacks, to come along to our community where our people were living and working in peace.[10]

The struggle against antisemitism, therefore, had a powerful effect on the character of Anglo-Jewry. 'As the Fascists "turned up the heat,"' Cesarani notes, 'old identities dissolved and new ones formed[,] ... no less infused with Jewish tradition and ... actually more assertive'. Through their participation in anti-fascist events, Kushner and Valman add, Jews 'were asserting both their integration within the local community ... and their demand for respect as Jews'.[11]

Discussing Anglo-Jewish attitudes towards antisemitism more widely, Cohen highlights the importance of Jewish identity in informing responses. He describes an axis, at one end of which stood those for whom 'Jewishness was central to their existence and aspirations' (Zionists, for example), and, at the other, those 'who felt their Jewishness to be peripheral' (such as assimilationists among the Jewish elite, and many Jewish socialists, anarchists and communists). The majority of the community stood somewhere between these extremes, with 'a foot firmly placed in each of the two worlds'. By being 'neither completely integrated nor totally segregated', such Jews felt an uncomfortable 'sense of marginality' and this, Cohen believes, resulted in incoherent and variegated responses to antisemitism.[12]

Another who touches upon this issue is Elisa Lawson, in an article on the racial thought of Anglo-Jewish historian Cecil Roth. Drawing upon the work of John Efron, Lawson describes interwar Anglo-Jewry as facing a 'post-emancipatory crisis of Jewish identity', with (in Efron's words) an 'ethnic pride that had been battered by the winds of assimilation'. These feelings were rendered more acute by the external pressure of antisemitism, fostering among Jewish intellectuals, Efron claims, 'a unique ... venture in Jewish self-definition and self-assertion'. Roth's efforts to conceptualize an 'Anglo-Jewish race[,] ... imbued with an almost volkish connection to the [English] land', which came in response to the worsening antisemitism of the period, were one manifestation of those attempts to 'fill th[e] vacuum' of Jewish identity, Lawson contends.[13]

As we will see over the following chapters, this question of identity was central to the development of Anglo-Jewish defence over the 1930s. The complexities of identity Cohen describes, and the differing paths of assimilation pursued by various sections of the community, helped induce an initially diverse and uncoordinated set of responses to the BUF. Yet as the decade progressed, the growing threat of fascist antisemitism drew together disparate elements of the community in their defence, with anti-fascist activity founded upon an increasingly cohesive sense of Anglo-Jewish identity.

While research into Jewish responses to British fascism has tended to focus on events in London, a handful of local studies have shed light on developments elsewhere. Though they, too, often make the familiar distinction between 'elite' and 'working-class' activity, they at least hint at the ways in which the boundary between the two was at times blurred.

Gerwirtz and Neil Barrett, for example, have provided complementary studies of Manchester's Jewish community, the largest in Britain outside London. Barrett concentrates on the Jewish leadership, challenging those who dismiss its actions 'as timid and half-hearted, without much discussion as to the nature of this response and the logic which underpinned it'. Opinion within the communal leadership, he reminds us, at both the national and local level, was far from homogenous, encompassing a diversity of views. Yet his subsequent account does little to challenge existing perceptions, drawing a picture of a paternalistic elite favouring a low-key approach, set against an immigrant community that pursued activist, and at times violent, anti-fascism, often in association with left-wing political groups.[14]

Gewirtz focuses more closely on working-class elements of Manchester Jewry, tracing the way that strong traditions of political radicalism brought over from eastern Europe were transmitted to subsequent generations. These manifested themselves in a struggle for a Britain in which Jews would be accepted as equals, leading to a firm reaction against fascist campaigning. Gewirtz, like others, believes that the communal elites were slow to react and that, once they did, they favoured apologetic forms of activity. Yet she does demonstrate that the picture was not always quite so clear cut, citing rumours that some within the communal leadership worked alongside Jewish Communists in the struggle against fascism.[15]

Amanda Bergen paints a similar picture in Leeds, whose Jewish community of 30,000, though slightly smaller than Manchester's, was proportionally the largest of any British city.[16] Here, in a familiar pattern, 'there was little consensus as to what constituted an appropriate response'. Many, especially young working-class men with communist sympathies, favoured an aggressive approach. But the communal leadership deplored such activity, preferring instead to work with the local authorities to counter fascist propaganda, and to trust in the 'extraordinary tolerance and decency' of the British people. Interestingly, however, Bergen notes that, over time, 'the external forces which were attempting to destroy the Jews became the means of uniting them', with Leeds Jewry drawing closer together as the 1930s progress.[17] This theme of eventual communal convergence is one that will be further developed in Chapter 8.

Accounts of British fascism and anti-fascism offer little to supplement the above. The former tend to touch upon Jewish activity only where it most obviously coincides with their subject matter, resulting in further emphasis on disruptive and violent forms of anti-fascism. These, as was outlined in Chapter 1, tend to be invoked by scholars as one factor behind the BUF's adoption and radicalization of antisemitism. Skidelsky, in particular, has focused on this issue, placing much blame at the door of Jewish anti-fascists, and in particular Jewish communists, who he suggests were deliberately employed as 'front-line troops in order to expose fascism's anti-semitic potential[,] … show[ing] particular relish for this work'. His claims are, however, founded largely on a credulous acceptance of fascist sources – which, unsurprisingly, blamed communist Jews for the escalating conflict – and on questionable interpretation of police reports.[18]

Recent research on the BUF has offered a more nuanced picture, yet, as we have seen, nevertheless continues to cite confrontational Jewish anti-fascism as a primary contributor to the BUF's hardening stance on the Jewish question.[19] The activity of Jews outside the East End and communist milieus is rarely acknowledged, though Linehan does touch in passing on the Board's detailed monitoring of the BUF and its efforts at burnishing the community's image.[20]

In this light, the work of Copsey has been of particular value, as it broadens the scope of the study of British anti-fascism away from just the more visible and direct forms of action. In particular, he chides scholars who focus primarily on conspicuous events such as Cable Street and the 'popular' anti-fascism they represented. Such an approach 'fails to draw out different anti-fascist analyses and strategic positions', he warns. Instead, he urges an appreciation of the 'full spectrum of different understandings and approaches'.

Yet, when it comes to specifically Jewish responses to fascism, Copsey rather ignores his own advice, concentrating primarily on the disruption of BUF events in 1933–4 and the 'Jewish-Communist alliance' of anti-fascists that emerged over 1935–7. He, like others, draws a distinction between the activism of left-wing Jews and the work of the Board, the latter characterized as indirect and somewhat apologetic. Moreover, as discussed earlier, Copsey's more recent, co-edited volume deals with Jews only incidentally and cursorily, despite them being, as we shall see, a driving force within British anti-fascism. The present study aims to add some texture to the picture of Jewish anti-fascism, which in many ways mirrored the variegated development of wider British anti-fascism that Copsey otherwise so effectively traces.

Another aspect of Copsey's work particularly pertinent to the present study is his proposal of an 'anti-fascism minimum': whether Communist or Conservative, Copsey argues, all opponents of fascism in Britain had 'as their common denominator the democratic ideal "of rule by the people"' and a fundamental commitment to the Enlightenment values of humanism, rationalism, progressivism and universalism. Fascism, by contrast, represented the antithesis of these principles, pursuing an anti-democratic 'counter-Enlightenment'.[21] This, as we shall see, very much applies to the various responses to the BUF offered by the Anglo-Jewish community, all of which were rooted in a deep attachment to democracy and liberal values, albeit interpreted in varying ways by different individuals and groups.

Copsey's framework also allows us to understand the British state as an anti-fascist force. Indeed, its actions – ranging from intelligence-gathering to legal measures restricting political extremism and finally, during the war, internment of leading fascists – were among the most effective in thwarting the ambitions of the BUF and limiting its scope of activity. Thurlow, in particular, has demonstrated the extent to which the police and Home Office were hostile towards British fascism, and the measures they took to constrain it.[22] We will see how the Jewish leadership, recognizing this, lobbied and worked alongside the authorities to combat the domestic radical right.

There are two features characteristic of the above historiography that require particular attention. The first is that the events of 1936 have drawn disproportionate attention. This is not completely unwarranted: the year witnessed some of the BUF's most intensive anti-Jewish campaigning; heated debate within the Jewish community over how best to respond to this (with criticism of the Board at its strongest); the formation of numerous Jewish defence bodies; and, of course, the Battle of Cable Street. Yet acknowledgement of the importance of this period should not come at the expense of tracing longer-term trends, including both early attitudes to the growth of the BUF in 1932–5 and the significant developments that took place over 1937–40.

Second, research has concentrated almost exclusively on the two types of response described above: working-class activism and the work of the communal leadership. This is not necessarily a problem in itself, as these two broad groups did dominate the response to fascism, and indeed will be a primary focus of the present study (though effort will be made to widen the scope of investigation). Where difficulties arise is the portrayal of the two as relatively static, homogenous and in direct opposition to one another. In actual fact, within each camp a diversity of views were held and expressed, and developed over time, resulting in a variegated and constantly evolving approach to defence. Moreover, there were significant areas of overlap between the two 'sides' – who, it must be remembered, were fighting the same cause – and these became increasingly apparent as the decade progressed, contradicting the prevailing perception that the defence debate exacerbated cleavages in the community.

On a more general note, one should also be aware of the methodological approach that has characterized much existing research and the way it has shaped the resultant historical narrative. Scholars give disproportionate weight to the version of events offered by those involved in activist anti-fascism, who, for obvious reasons, tend to present such activity in a positive, uncritical light, and are often disparaging towards the communal leadership.[23] That is not to say that such sources are not of value, simply that the reliance on them has resulted in a rather one-sided perspective. Similarly, many of the best-known accounts of the period have been provided by political figures – such as Phil Piratin and Joe Jacobs, two prominent Jewish Communists – who had their own agendas.[24] Indeed, the very fact the Jewish-Communist version of events takes such a prominent place in itself has a distortionary effect, given that just a small fraction of Anglo-Jewry was affiliated to the CPGB in the 1930s, as will be shown presently.

Furthermore, recollections of such a momentous period, one subsequently written into Jewish and anti-fascist lore, are not always reliable – an effect exacerbated by the fact that many of the oral-history interviews and memoirs which historians have drawn upon were produced long (often decades) after the events had taken place. The occasionally problematic nature of such accounts, and the ways in which personal experience can blend into mythologized history, will be observed in particular with regard to the Battle of Cable Street, the consequences of which – as recorded in contemporary sources – were very different to those subsequently claimed by participants. Far from being a great defeat for the BUF, the event boosted the fascist cause and made life far more unpleasant for Jewish residents of the East End.

By contrast, sources relating to the communal leadership have been largely neglected by researchers. David Rosenberg, whose research focuses on the East End, and Barrett both discuss 'elite' approaches to defence; yet neither makes reference to the Board's own extensive records.[25] Meanwhile, Lebzelter's claim that parts of the Board's work are 'difficult to assess since they were never described in great detail' is no longer valid given the release of much archival material in the three decades since her research was conducted.[26] Those who have consulted these sources refer to them sparingly and selectively. This omission is of particular significance because the Board's most substantial defence work was carried out, by necessity, privately; in public, only its anti-defamation and communal-'improvement' efforts were fully apparent. This encouraged contemporary charges of inactivity and callousness, which, without the injection of new archival research into the historiography, have been transmitted through scholarly accounts with little challenge.

This self-perpetuating narrative is illustrated in Cesarani's claim that Laski's (allegedly complacent) attitude towards fascism is 'well known'. Yet to support this contention he is able only to cite Lebzelter, who admits she had little insight into the Board's internal activity; Alderman's *The Jewish Community in British Politics*, published at a time (1983) when access to the relevant material was still limited; and Laski's own book, *Jewish Rights and Jewish Wrongs*, which reveals only his public position and not the approach he took behind closed doors.[27] Subsequent improvements in access to the Board's own files – as well as to the papers of some of its leading figures, which have received even less attention – reveal a very different picture, providing invaluable testament to the diverse attitudes, motivations and analyses that lay behind not only its own response to the growth of political antisemitism, but also those of the other Jewish groups and individuals with which it had extensive contact as the community's representative body.[28]

Thus, by examining the entire period 1932–40 through as wide a range of sources as possible, Part Two of this volume aims to present a more comprehensive, nuanced and representative account than is provided elsewhere. It will comprise a broadly chronological overview of Anglo-Jewry's attitudes towards and responses to the growth of fascism and political antisemitism over the 1930s, the ways in which they related to and interacted with one another, and how they developed over time. There will be a particular emphasis on those parts of this story that have been neglected by other accounts. Throughout, reflection will be offered on wider questions of Jewish identity and intra-communal dynamics.

Early Responses to the BUF, 1932–5

First reactions

Despite the absence of antisemitism from the BUF's founding programme, the Jewish community expressed an immediate wariness towards the organization. Its concern was elicited by the anti-Jewish character of Britain's other fascist bodies, rumours that antisemitism had been rife within Mosley's New Party and the looming spectre of Nazism in Germany.[1] But above all, it was fuelled by the Blackshirts' own words, which, as we saw in Part One, from the outset belied their regular disavowals of antisemitism.

In particular, Anglo-Jewry's unofficial mouthpiece, the *JC* – which in August 1932 had called attention to the 'sundry premonitory indications' that the New Party was 'a hot-bed of anti-Semitic propaganda'[2] – viewed Mosley's new fascist venture with suspicion. Following his attacks, soon after the BUF's formation, on the 'subversive activities' of Jews, the *JC* declared it 'perplexing' that Mosley could make such charges while simultaneously denying that his party was anti-Jewish. The newspaper warned him that he had 'no right to single out for reprobation the Jewishness... of his adversaries', and feared it could already detect the 'cloven hoof of anti-Semitism peeping out of his statement[s]'. The newspaper did, though, welcome news that Mosley had subsequently promised Lord Melchett, a Jewish industrialist, that antisemitism would form no part of the BUF's programme, hoping that he would now 'find new light' and end this 'idiotic drivel'.[3] Behind the scenes, the Board of Deputies also expressed concern, requesting clarification from Mosley on his position, to which he responded with the standard renunciation of antisemitism.[4]

Over the following months, as we have seen, anti-Jewish rhetoric did indeed largely disappear from BUF discourse, with the movement keen to distance itself from the Nazis following Hitler's ascent to the German chancellorship. The latter issue of course dominated Anglo-Jewish attention, too, and concerns over domestic fascism took a back seat. The two were not, however, unconnected in many eyes, with fears expressed over the relationship between British and German fascism. These manifested themselves explosively in the spring of 1933, in a series of violent clashes in London's West End, a focal point of early BUF activity.

The police noted that Blackshirt campaigners in the area had been attracting 'unfriendly interest' from Jews, who often congregated around Coventry Street on Sundays. Anxious about the increasing persecution of their co-religionists in Germany, they feared that the BUF was using its publications to disseminate Nazi propaganda in Britain. This simmering tension boiled over in April and May, when conflict broke out between the two sides. On 30 April, a crowd of Jews, allegedly 1,000 strong, chanting 'Down with the Nazis; down with the Hitlerites', chased and surrounded a group of fascists, seven of whom were arrested by the police for refusing to leave the area. The skirmishes continued, however, and six Jews were later detained for various offences, including two who had 'seriously pummelled' a Blackshirt. The following week, further trouble arose in the same spot. Again, a large crowd of Jews pursued a small number of fascists, attacking them once they caught up. Five Jews, four of them young men from the East End, were arrested for their involvement. Nearby, two more Blackshirts had become embroiled in a fracas with another group of Jews, and were eventually taken into custody 'for their own safety'.[5]

In Manchester, too, the first serious violence associated with the BUF arose from concern over its attitude towards Jews. In March 1933, Mosley made his first address in the city as a fascist, to an audience of around 4,000 at the Free Trade Hall. The speech itself passed without incident, but afterwards, while written questions were being taken, protestors began to interrupt, demanding details of the party's Jewish policy. In a pattern that would later become familiar, overzealous Blackshirt stewards attempted to silence the hecklers, leading to a violent brawl and police intervention.[6] In contrast to events in the West End, here it was the fascists who appeared to be largely responsible for the clashes. As well as their aggressive stewarding, reports emerged of an attack on three Jews by a group of Blackshirts outside the meeting. Describing the episode, a local newspaper noted that ' "Jew-baiting" has been part of the policy of Manchester Fascists for weeks past. Prominent Jews have been shadowed and subject to all sorts of insults'.[7]

Jewish involvement in such incidents deeply troubled traditional communal institutions, though they were not without a degree of sympathy. In response to the first of the West End disturbances, the *JC*, which had close ties to the Jewish leadership, not least through its editor, Jack Rich, a former secretary of the Board, urged Jews not 'to lose their self-control and respect for law'. But it also wondered if it was wise for the authorities to allow uniformed Blackshirts to campaign 'in an area where many have good reason not to love Fascism'.[8] Following the second incident, the newspaper adopted a firmer line, condemning the 'stupid and disgraceful behaviour' of the Jews involved, who by 'copying the Nazi violence which we loath and detest' were 'betraying' the Jewish cause. Hoping to allay concerns, it arranged an interview with Mosley, in which he claimed that charges of antisemitism were a lie designed to discredit his party. The newspaper accepted the sincerity of his reassurances, but pointedly expressed hope that his followers would heed their leader's words.[9]

Attempts to restrain both sides continued over the rest of the year. Noting a spate of anti-Jewish attacks in London and Manchester in the summer, the *JC* urged proper punishment for the 'miscreants' responsible, so as to discourage further episodes. Any Jews who experienced such provocation were urged to report it to the police, rather than take matters into their own hands.[10] Soon after, Jewish participants in an anti-Nazi march were praised for their 'dignity and orderliness', while those 'few feather-brained individuals' involved in violence were warned that they were doing a 'rank disservice to the Jewish cause'. The newspaper confessed that these words were aimed as much at Mosley as at Jews, in the hope he would accept once and for all that the vast majority of Anglo-Jewry was not involved in attacks on his movement. Both sides were reminded that Mussolini was demonstrating how 'Fascism does not necessarily imply anti-Semitism'; it was only 'the Hitlerites' besotted mentality [that] has confused the two'. Should British fascism adopt the Italian approach, there need be no acrimony with the Jewish community.[11]

Various communal luminaries also called for calm. Leonard Montefiore, president of the Anglo-Jewish Association, and Neville Laski, the recently appointed president of the Board, made a joint public appeal for Jews to avoid violent activity, which, they warned, 'can only be harmful to the general cause which we all have at heart'.[12] This message was reiterated at a meeting with club managers of the Association of Jewish Youth (AJY), who were urged to ensure that their members 'maintain a pacific attitude and keep out of clashing with Fascists'. Displaying the type of insecurity and condescension that characterized the early approach of the Jewish elites, Montefiore warned that Jews remained 'before a jury' and should endeavour to win gentile sympathy, while Laski argued that appearing 'impeccable and blameless to the outside world ... was the best answer [we] could give to Fascism'.[13] The next year, the chief rabbi, Joseph Hertz, who had also put his name to Laski and Montefiore's abovementioned statement, condemned those Jews involved in anti-fascist disturbances as 'irresponsible young men ... [who] bring discredit on their Faith and undermine the position of the Jew in this country'. He, too, cautioned that Jews' wellbeing 'largely depended on the ... morality' of their behaviour.[14]

Despite these public calls aimed at improving Jewish behaviour, behind the scenes the Board was employing its resources and influence in more direct efforts to mitigate the growth of domestic antisemitism. Following an anti-Jewish outburst by a prospective Labour candidate, Laski contacted two leading figures in the party to complain that 'the situation is unpleasant enough without this addition to the creation of anti-Semitism in this country'.[15] In 1934, a request was made to the Home Office that a prosecution be brought against the IFL's Arnold Leese for his antisemitic pronouncements.[16]

Structural changes were also implemented to meet the growing threat. The Board's Press Committee, which had been established in 1919 to respond to a surge of antisemitism in the aftermath of the war, merged in 1933 with the Joint Foreign Affairs Committee. As this suggests, political antisemitism was regarded largely as a foreign import, a belief expressed explicitly in the new body's first annual report, which warned of the growing problem of 'anti-Semitic activities in Great Britain conducted by agents working under instructions from abroad'. The committee immediately began to intensify its intelligence-gathering and anti-defamation efforts, closely monitoring fascist activity, regularly contacting newspapers to correct false information pertaining to Jews, and producing and distributing publications.[17]

Yet these endeavours were deemed insufficient by many, even within the Board itself. At a heated meeting in late November 1933, numerous deputies raised concern at Mosley's mounting anti-Jewish campaign. M. Gordon Liverman, who seven years later would assume the chairmanship of the Board's defence committee, warned that the 'ordinary peace-time methods' currently employed 'were not adequate' anymore. Alexander Easterman, a deputy from the East End, journalist and later political secretary to the British section of the World Jewish Congress, suggested the formation of a special committee of the Board dedicated solely to combating antisemitism.[18] The extent to which such concerns had permeated to the heights of the community was demonstrated the following May, when Nathan Laski, father of Neville and unofficial figurehead of the Jewish community in Manchester, warned an audience that 'in this country the virus of anti-Semitism, disguised as "Fascism", was growing; and Jewish youth had a duty to perform to itself and to the old by unifying itself and using every legitimate means to prevent a ... tragedy happening here.'[19]

By late 1933, the *JC*, too, had finally run out of patience with the BUF's increasingly implausible denials of antisemitism, which, as we saw in Part One, stood in flagrant contradiction to the anti-Jewish rhetoric they accompanied. In November, following *Blackshirt*'s 'Shall Jews Drag Britain to War?' article, the *JC* came to the inescapable conclusion: in an editorial entitled 'Sir Oswald Mosley, Anti-Semite', it accused the BUF of 'an undisguised call to war on the Jewish people', justified by 'a tissue of nonsense and falsehood ... taken from the rag-bags of the peddlers of Continental anti-Semitism'. Following a reply in *Blackshirt*, which declared once more the fascists' belief in 'religious toleration', the *JC* rejected such talk as 'the idlest nonsense', and reaffirmed its belief that Mosley had decisively committed himself to Hitlerite fascism.[20]

With even elements of the communal establishment now making such unequivocal pronouncements, it is not surprising to find that lower down the social rungs of Anglo-Jewry, particularly among its younger elements, calls for a more vigorous response were becoming louder. A lively discussion began to emerge in the pages of the *JC*, which, Cesarani notes, 'remained the only communal forum open to all portions of Anglo-Jewry[,] ... reflect[ing] virtually the entire spectrum of opinion'.[21] Presaging in microcosm the debate that would fixate the community over the following three years, students in Oxford argued the question of defence. John Brown, of Ruskin College, drew attention to fascist provocation of Jews in the city and urged a strong response. In Germany, he warned, 'lethargy and self-deception' had allowed Hitler to rise to power, yet the Anglo-Jewish leadership continued to 'bury their heads in the sands of complacent apathy'. The situation required physical action, not resolutions and speeches: 'fists can be put to better service than propelling pens'.

In response, Abe Harman, president of the Oxford University Jewish Society and a leading young Zionist, criticized Brown's 'highly exaggerated' account, suggesting that it was communists, not Jews specifically, who were on the receiving end of fascist aggression. Yet equally, he acknowledged the inevitability of BUF antisemitism, advising that 'there will be plenty of time for an alliance [against fascism] when Mosley comes forward as a proclaimed anti-Semite'. But for the time being, Jewish involvement in anti-fascism simply brought the 'Jewish question ... [into] the arena of political strife' and made violence more likely. Another student, A. Duschinsky, also saw signs of trouble ahead. Though the BUF denied antisemitism publicly, he observed, it had also attempted to excuse Nazi persecution of Jews, had sent a delegation to the

Nuremberg Rally and spoke disparagingly of 'Ghetto scum' and 'Whitechapel rabbis' – all indicators of a more insidious underlying attitude.[22]

Organizations now began to emerge that catered to such concerns. The first of these,[23] the League of Jewish Youth (LJY – not to be confused with the AJY), was formed in the second half of 1933, seeking to unite young Jews in 'combating the dangers of the anti-Semitic feeling which Fascists were spreading in this country'. Yet its agenda was wider, tinged with a Zionist character: among its other listed goals were the propagation of Jewish national ideals, the study of Jewish tradition and the reestablishment of a homeland in Palestine. By mid-1934, the group had formed branches in north, east and west London and claimed to have almost 1,000 members. Its honorary secretary, D. Polztschik, hoped that by providing Anglo-Jewish youth a single, powerful voice, the LJY would compel the Board to listen to their concerns and to rethink its defence policies. The first of her wishes was indeed granted, with Laski addressing an LJY meeting at Woburn House, the home of the Board, in November 1934. But his speech, which urged Jews to improve their own behaviour and to leave the 'alien' BUF to die out of its own accord, would no doubt have disappointed.[24]

Another body, the Jewish United Defence Association (JUDA), chaired by J.L. Blonstein, a young doctor and talented amateur boxer, was the first to dedicate itself purely to defence. Like the LJY, it attracted predominantly young members. Many were no doubt drawn to the activist approach suggested by its adoption of a uniform, leading the *JC* to fulminate against the thought of Jewish 'youth strutting around in blue shirts and imitating the prevalent tomfoolery'. Members also heard lectures on the situation in Germany and the growth of antisemitism in Britain, and were encouraged to support the boycott of German goods. Within months of its establishment, JUDA boasted at least five branches spread across south, east and west London, and had established affiliations with other Jewish organizations. However, by the summer of 1934 the association appears, for unknown reasons, to have ceased activity.[25]

JUDA's chairman was, though, partly responsible for a fascinating subplot in the story of communal defence, one that offers an indication of the intersections that already existed between the approaches of supposedly divergent elements of Anglo-Jewry. For, despite the Board's disapproval of the type of activity encouraged by JUDA, Blonstein himself was a deputy. In March, he had entered correspondence with the BUF's second-in-command, Robert Forgan, on the subject of the party's antisemitism, and subsequently the two men, both physicians by training, arranged to meet. This appears to have then paved the way for Mosley's lieutenant to hold further meetings with, first, Lionel Cohen, vice-president of the Board and chairman of its Law and Parliamentary Committee, and subsequently Laski himself.

There has been speculation – based largely, it seems, on an unreferenced claim by Colin Cross – that over the first half of 1934 Forgan acted as an intermediary between Mosley and the Jewish community, and even tried to forge a 'Jewish-Fascist agreement'.[26] Certainly the former MP represented the respectable face of the BUF, and was instrumental in establishing its January Club, which aimed to popularize fascism among the political and social establishment (and even managed to attract a number of Jewish members).[27] At one of its meetings, Forgan had reassured Jews that they had nothing to fear from fascism; Harry Nathan, a Jewish MP, was invited to speak, though he used the occasion, to the disappointment of his hosts, to claim that 'racial animosity' was the 'driving force' of fascism.[28] In this light, it is not unthinkable that Mosley might have used Forgan as part of a cynical attempt to appease leading Jews and further obfuscate his antisemitism during the brief 'Rothermere' period – though this would almost certainly not have resulted from any authentic desire to 'improve relations', as Skidelsky argues.[29]

Yet whatever his original remit, by the time Forgan met Laski in late July, it was clear that he no longer retained any ambition of fulfilling it. Instead, he announced that he was abandoning the BUF, finding its 'anti-Semitic trend' intolerable. This, Laski remarked, was no surprise: 'In spite of certain observations by Sir Oswald[,] I for one had no doubt as to the ultimately anti-Semitic character of the Fascist movement in this country. We had sufficient material before us to justify that assertion'. Discussing the BUF's strength, Forgan revealed that the Olympia shambles and Rothermere's desertion had initially increased membership and invigorated the party. Subsequently, however, it had begun to 'disintegrat[e]'. This suggested that the BUF's fortunes rose and fell in direct correlation with the intensity of disruptive anti-fascism (which had peaked in June and diminished over July), reinforcing Laski's belief that direct and visible defence work was counterproductive, whereas starving the BUF of publicity hindered its progress.[30]

Disruptive anti-fascism

Yet Laski's approach remained unacceptable to certain sections of the community, who felt compelled to actively oppose fascism. But the extent of their participation in the more confrontational forms of anti-fascism should not be exaggerated. After the ephemeral and spontaneous violence in Manchester and London's West End in spring 1933, there is little evidence of Jewish involvement in such activity over the following year or so.[31] The wave of organized disruption that struck BUF events around the country in June 1934 and again in the autumn did, however, involve a number of Jews. A neutral observer at Olympia claimed to have seen 'bands of young men, mostly Jews, on their way to the meeting … clearly in a fighting mood'.[32] At Manchester's Belle Vue in October, the police recorded that the anti-fascist contingent of around 350 'consist[ed] mostly of Jews'.[33]

Yet equally, Mosley's claim – invoked to justify his turn to antisemitism – that 50 per cent of the sixty-four people convicted for attacking his party between June and November were Jewish appears a vast exaggeration (not to mention, of course, that even if thirty-two Jews had been guilty of attacking fascists, this would be questionable grounds for opposition to the entire Jewish community). During the period in question, the BUF faced violent disruption in Edinburgh, Gateshead, Leicester and numerous other places where Jews made up a negligible portion of the population. After a single incident in Bristol, nine communists (who alone would have comprised 14 per cent of Mosley's figure of sixty-four) were convicted of public-order offences; none, it appears, was Jewish.[34]

At most, a proportion of 50 per cent may hold true for arrests in London, where Jewish involvement in anti-fascism was more substantial – though even this seems unlikely. Of twelve anti-fascists reported in *Blackshirt* to be facing charges in the aftermath of Olympia, just one can definitively be identified as Jewish, Marks Barnett Becow (who holds the distinction of being imprisoned for violent conduct at both Olympia and the Battle of Cable Street two years later). Of the remaining ten, one more, a woman whose charge of using insulting words was dismissed by the magistrate, had a possibly Jewish-sounding name. Stephen Cullen, who has analysed police records in detail, finds that of those arrested at a sample of 142 BUF meetings (the vast majority in London) over 1934–5, only ten were classified by the police as Jews, representing under 17 per cent of all non-fascist arrests.[35]

The unreliability of Mosley's numbers is also suggested by their constant diminution: the 50-per-cent figure he cited in late 1934 represented a drop from the 80 per cent alleged a couple of months earlier; by 1936, it was claimed that only 20 per cent of those convicted for violence against fascists in 1934 and 1935 were Jewish (despite the fact that growing BUF activity in the East End over 1935 encouraged more, not fewer, Jews to become involved in oppositional activity).[36] There is no doubt that the BUF's increasing use of antisemitism over 1934 encouraged a reaction from Jews, but the numbers involved in disruptive activity at this stage represented a small proportion of both the Jewish community and of Britain's activist anti-fascists.

Jews and political organizations

What is also clear – though the fascists would not have cared to make this distinction – is that many of the Jews who participated most eagerly in early agitation against the BUF did so in part or in whole because of pre-existing political affiliation, rather than as Jews. The interwar period saw, for example, a number of Jews attracted to the CPGB – indeed, they 'constituted an ethnic majority' among East End members, records Henry Srebrnik.[37] Often, however, their reasons for joining had little to do with ethnicity.

Many Jewish youths in urban, working-class areas found communist ideology and activity appealing for precisely the same reasons as their non-Jewish peers. Indeed, those drawn to the CPGB were often somewhat detached from the Jewish community, identifying themselves more as part of the British working class. The Jewish journalist and socialist William Zukerman argued that 'the East End Jew is in reality no Jewish type at all … but the general East End London Labour type', and that support for left-wing movements was an indication of assimilation, not of some lingering, alien political perspective.[38] Many Jewish CPGB members confessed to signing up for social reasons: the Young Communist League (YCL), which organized debates, dances and other events, provided a rare forum in which one could mix with other youths, especially of the opposite sex.[39]

But there were also more specifically 'Jewish' reasons for joining. As Smith notes, the 1930s represented 'a unique decade … in the sense that there was no obvious conflict between Jewish interests and communist interests'. Furthermore, Alderman adds, the 'communists were seen as people who evinced a genuine concern for Jewish needs, and who matched words with deeds'.[40] For one, communism promised equality for all citizens, and claimed to already be building such a society in Russia – a tempting prospect for a minority with a long history of persecution. As Morry Lebow, secretary of the CPGB's Stepney branch, put it, Jews, particularly those of foreign extraction, found 'in this movement a means of expressing their refusal to accept the inferior social status allotted them'. Alderman believes that the attraction of communism to young, East End Jews 'had about it some of the qualities of group identification, a means, perhaps, of ethnic self-assertion'. It was also 'a visible and practical sign of self-help and of rebellion against an over-docile communal leadership'.[41] Additionally, strong traditions of left-wing political activism, often carried over from eastern Europe, already existed within the Jewish immigrant community.[42]

Nevertheless, there were also undoubtedly many Jews attracted to the CPGB primarily because it offered – unlike the Labour party and many other mainstream political and workers' groups, as well as most existing Jewish bodies – an active and organized means to oppose fascism. Joe Jacobs, an East End Jewish Communist, observed that a lot of the Jews drawn to CPGB in the 1930s 'didn't really know what [communism] was all about'. They joined, Beckman adds, 'purely because the Communist Party were the only ones attempting to take the fight to the fascists'. One such individual, Cyril Spector, outlined his 'simplistic view of politics: the Jews had to be defended at all costs', and the CPGB offered the only effective means of doing so.[43]

This combination of factors drawing young, working-class Jews to the CPGB is perhaps best summarized by Lebzelter, who notes that

> while the apparent militancy of the Left offered a far more satisfying response than the placidity displayed by the Board, its general political message appealed to many East End Jews because it integrated the discontent generated by class-consciousness and the Jew-consciousness arising from anti-Semitism into a coherent ideology. At the same time the idea of fighting anti-Semitism by opposing Fascism, and defeating both permanently by working towards an idealised socialist society, removed the stigma of being preoccupied with paltry self-defence, and allied Jewry to a seemingly progressive movement, advocating peace and social reforms.[44]

The Communist leadership, for its part, was more than aware of these facts, and saw an opportunity to harness Jewish fears by stepping into the vacuum left by the more cautious position of other political parties and the established Jewish leadership. This fitted neatly into a wider aim to forge Britain's disparate anti-fascist forces – working-class organizations, intellectuals, students, liberals and now Jews – into a united front, with the CPGB at its centre. 'The development of the anti-fascist line,' declared Comrade Brisker at a meeting of the party's Central Committee, 'can be the key to the development of the biggest mass movement we have had in the country.' He suggested a particular focus on the East End, where hostility towards fascism was strong among Jews.[45]

Integral to forging this alliance was the Committee for Co-ordinating Anti-Fascist Activity, formed in July 1934, which made particular effort to woo Jews. One of its pamphlets, 'Mosley Attacks the Jews', explained the BUF's use of antisemitism within the framework of the Communists' class-based analysis: as workers became increasingly aware of their exploitation at the hands of the capitalist class, the latter attempted to subdue them through its proxy, fascism, which used racial agitation as a means to divide and rule, settings Jewish and gentile workers against one another. The spuriousness of fascist antisemitism – and the true nature of the 'boss' class – was demonstrated by Hitler's alleged willing acceptance of support from Jewish financiers and industrialists in Germany, and the fact that in Britain rich Jews were not interested in opposing Mosley. The real division was to be found in class, not race or religion; thus, the only effective response was for workers – Jews and gentiles alike – to unite and confront fascism.[46] This argument struck a chord with many Jews, who already felt closer to their fellow British workers than the distant Jewish elites, and provided them a plausible explanation for the latter's apparent reluctance to combat fascism.

The CPGB also did its best to encourage Jewish participation in efforts to directly oppose the fascists. The party's general secretary, Harry Pollitt, warned a Jewish audience that 'mere inaction and stopping quietly at home had never saved Jews from a pogrom'.[47] In the build up to Olympia, Special Branch recorded that the Communists had been particularly active organizing among East End Jews.[48] Prior to a huge protest against the BUF in Hyde Park in September 1934, leaflets were published in Yiddish, warning Jews to heed the lessons of Germany and reminding them of their 'duty' to oppose fascism.[49] Police reports estimated that the east London contingent marching to the event numbered over 1,000, including a large number of Jews, and collections taken during its procession 'were well supported by the Jewish community'.[50]

Recalling an incident that took place a few years later, but which typified the way that the CPGB was able, often cynically, to mobilize Jewish support, the former news editor of the *Daily Worker*, the party's mouthpiece, described what happened when antisemitic chalkings one day appeared on the gateposts of Jewish residences in his neighbourhood. It was clear they were the work of a single person, but nevertheless a big fuss was made, a conference was called, delegates came from all over England, resolutions were passed. The *Daily Worker* fuelled fears by using the antisemitic literature of 'an obscure and … unimportant body on the idiot fringe of the Fascist movement' as further 'ammunition'. As a result, 'new members came rolling into the Party [and] subscriptions from East End clothing and furniture manufacturers skyrocketed'.[51]

Yet it is important not to exaggerate the extent of Jewish support for the Communists in these early stages. At the start of 1933, the CPGB had roughly 5,500 members; by the end of 1934, the figure was only 300 higher. The party's Stepney branch, in the heartland of Jewish communism, was just 115 strong.[52] It appears that, while some Jews saw the CPGB as a useful vehicle through which to express their opposition to fascism, for the time being this usually did not translate into any formal commitment to the party.[53]

The Communists were not the only group to tap profitably into Jewish anger. In March 1934, a leading trade unionist celebrated his organization's 'great success in organising the Jews in the East End of London', noting that 'the fascist menace ... is the main reason why they are flocking to our Union'. His organization produced a pamphlet aimed explicitly at this audience, prominently displaying words of support from three distinguished Jewish figures: Harold Laski, brother of Neville and an influential socialist intellectual; Herbert Samuel, leader of the Liberal Party; and the author Louis Golding. In the publication, Laski attacked fascism on economic, political and class grounds, labelling it 'the form assumed by a capitalist system in distress ... [to] restore profit at the expense of those ... who live by the sale of their labour'. It could 'be defeated only by strong trade unions determined to fight for their rights'; therefore, 'every employed worker who fails to join his union and thus add to its strength is thereby facilitating the growth of Fascism'.[54] Though Laski did not go as far as some on the left in accusing the Jewish elites of supporting fascism, he did (elsewhere) lambast them for their 'complete refusal ... to adopt a fighting attitude towards Mosley', suggesting that they were prepared to 'risk fascism in the hope of buying themselves off rather than strengthening the working-class cause' by joining the anti-fascist ranks.[55]

Trade unions that already had a predominantly or completely Jewish membership were among the keenest to take up the fight against fascism. The East End branch of the National Union of Tailors and Garment Workers, for example, urged 'all Jewish workers to enter the recognised trade unions, and to fight along with their English comrades against capitalism and reaction'. Its counterpart in Manchester made a request to the police for its Jewish members to be allowed to conduct an anti-fascist march in protest against Mosley's Belle Vue meeting.[56] A collection of tailors', bakers' and shop assistants' unions jointly distributed flyers claiming that it was 'the duty of every Jew' not to patronize blackleg cinemas, as doing so would validate fascist attacks on Jewish cinema owners and boost the BUF.[57]

Within Jewish friendly societies, whose membership accounted for a large proportion of Anglo-Jewry, attitudes were divided. The Order Achei Brith, which had around 25,000 members, many drawn from the suburban lower-middle class, used its publication, *The Leader*, to warn young Jews that 'open quarrelling with Fascists ... do[es] a disservice to the fair name of Jewry in this country'. The best means to 'fight against anti-Semitism', it advised, was to 'show the world that the Jew can be as good a citizen as anybody else'. The publication also expressed its approval of the way in which Laski and the Board were running communal affairs.[58]

By contrast, the Workers' Circle, a left-wing Jewish friendly society based in east London with strong roots in the immigrant community, became an active force in the anti-fascist movement. In late 1934 it took the initiative in arranging two conferences of Jewish working-class organizations, at which it was agreed to establish the Jewish Labour Council (JLC), a body whose primary aim was to fight fascism and antisemitism.

The JLC's analysis, outlined in a leaflet entitled 'Sir Oswald Mosley and the Jews', was infused with left-wing rhetoric: antisemitism was a 'safety valve' for the ruling class to 'divert the wrath and discontent of the workers' away from itself; fascism could only be defeated if 'the workers of the world stand together, Jews and non-Jews alike'. But its content also reflected a more peculiarly Jewish perspective. In a clear retort to Mosley's questioning of Jewish loyalties, the leaflet stressed the Jews' contribution to the working-class struggle in Britain, contrasting this to the alien nature of 'imported' fascism. The publication also offered rejoinders to some of the fascists' 'foul lies', in the form of factual information on the Jewish community, fearing that otherwise 'the ordinary English worker ... may wonder whether there is not some truth in them'.[59]

Though the JLC fell dormant over 1935, its brief existence was significant in three chief regards: as the clearest expression yet of the anger felt within working-class sections of Anglo-Jewry towards the passivity of the Board; as a demonstration of their capacity to circumvent the latter's monopoly over communal defence by forming an alternative body to represent them; and in forging the links between various organizations that would, at a conference of the revived JLC in 1936, facilitate the creation of the Jewish People's Council (JPC), which became a leading force within Britain's anti-fascist movement.[60]

It should be noted that it was not only on the left that explicitly political responses to fascism emerged. In May 1934, a few months before the formation of the JLC, Jewish members of the North Hackney Constitutional Club established the National Association. At its inaugural meeting, a motion that the new body should be non-political was overwhelmingly rejected, and instead a declaration was made offering support for the National Government in its efforts to oppose fascism and foster greater understanding between Jew and gentile. The group received backing from two local Conservative MPs, Austin Hudson and John Lockwood, as well as Barnett Janner, the Liberal member for Whitechapel and St Georges and a future president of the Board. Demonstrating that the political right was also not averse to exploiting Jewish fears for its own benefit, Hudson, addressing a meeting of the Association, declared that Jews should oppose not just the extremism of fascism and communism, but socialism too, as a socialist government would cause 'such chaos that it would result in the establishment of Fascism'. Despite its early ambitions, other than organizing a deputation to the home secretary to draw attention to 'scurrilous anti-Jewish pamphlets' being distributed by fascists, the National Association appears to have had few concrete achievements to its name.[61]

There was one significant organization that did explicitly eschew political partisanship, the New World Fellowship (NWF), which described itself as 'the only militant, non-party, non-sectarian organisation preaching anti-Fascism'. Though two Jews were the driving force behind the group – its general secretary, Maurice Isaacs, and director of propaganda, Nathan Birch – it opened its doors to anyone willing to fight fascism. Within the hundreds of 'vigilant anti-Fascist groups' it claimed, with perhaps a touch of hyperbole, to have established across the country, 80 per cent of members were non-Jewish. The NWF was at its most active during 1934, boasting of holding sixty meetings a week, organizing six large anti-fascist demonstrations and distributing one million publications, including Birch's own book, *The Menace of Fascism*, and a weekly newspaper, *Green Band*. The movement argued that fascism was inherently antisemitic, needing Jews as a scapegoat, and pointed out that the BUF had been stirring resentment against Anglo-Jewry since mid-1933. It aimed to repudiate the 'rubbish' spoken by fascists about Jews and to help protect democracy in Britain from the fate that had befallen it in Germany. Its members passed a resolution calling on the home secretary to prevent speeches that incited religious intolerance, while the Board of Deputies was urged to pay greater attention to these worrying developments.[62]

A 'phoney war'

Mosley's vituperative speeches at Belle Vue and the Albert Hall in autumn 1934 decisively ended any lingering pretence over his party's position on the Jewish question, and set British fascism and Anglo-Jewry unequivocally in opposition to one another. But this initially remained something of a phoney war, with the two sides not coming into proper conflict for another year or so. As recounted earlier, this period saw internal disagreement within the BUF over its future direction, one consequence of which was that public expression of antisemitism temporarily diminished in early 1935. Moreover, this inward focus, along with a huge decline in party membership after the violent events of summer 1934, made fascism a far less visible presence. Though incursions into the East End had begun, it was not until late 1935 that large-scale campaigning started there in earnest.

Similarly, Britain's anti-fascist movement lost momentum during this period, with the Committee for Co-ordinating Anti-Fascist Activity winding down its activity after the Hyde Park demonstration and the CPGB focusing its attention on protests against the king's upcoming silver jubilee. Above all, though, it was the BUF's own decline that moderated anti-fascist efforts: the two sides' levels of activity were closely correlated to one another.[63]

These developments appeared to confirm the Board's belief that, with the BUF's true nature having been exposed to a disgusted British public, it could simply be left to fade into obscurity. Thus the Press and Information Committee persisted with its existing policies. It monitored public discourse for signs of antisemitism and kept a careful eye on anti-Jewish organizations, responding to any defamatory charges through private correspondence, letters to newspapers and the dissemination of publications.[64] Meanwhile, the Board's leadership continued to exhort Jews to avoid violence and to maintain a high standard of behaviour. In November 1934, Laski reassured a Jewish audience in north London that domestic antisemitism 'was by no means as serious as many people thought', and reminded them of the 'obligation both to the community and to the country' to 'behave as good citizens'. The 'gangs of silly young men in the East End attending Fascist meetings, making a noise and opposing Fascist arguments ... only increase anti-Semitism'.[65]

While such language may now appear condescending, even provocative, it did not prevent some of those very same young men from seeking an accommodation with the Board. Just a few days after his speech, Laski received a report from Max Bonn, a Jewish banker and patron of the AJY, reporting on a meeting he had held with some 'young hotheads' from the East End who were involved in active forms of anti-fascism. They had warned him that feelings were 'running dangerously high' in the area. Though they understood the 'danger of becoming involved in disturbances', if the Board failed to act, what alternative did they have? The young men suggested that public meetings could be arranged to condemn fascist antisemitism and reassure local residents that the communal leadership understood their concerns.

Bonn expressed his approval of their constructive attitude, and urged Laski to take action as soon as possible. He even proposed that the youths could act as a 'watch committee' in the East End, with the AJY relaying their findings back to the Board.[66] Passing on the report to various other communal leaders, Laski canvassed their opinion on the idea of holding such meetings. He personally viewed the proposal positively, believing that it might allow those who suffered the 'provocative and offensive' behaviour of the fascists with 'some outlet for their emotions'.[67]

Though the Jewish leadership continued officially to oppose directly engaging with the fascists – fearing that 'the resulting controversy would only give [them] considerable publicity'[68] – certain individuals associated with it were prepared to do so in a private capacity. In May 1935, the editor of the *JC* brought the Board's attention to a particularly unpleasant article in *FQ* by the BUF's Fuller, which claimed that the Talmud sanctioned the violation of gentile children and the appropriation of non-Jewish property by fraud or theft. The Board in turn forwarded it to the chief rabbi, with the suggestion that he compose a response.[69] Hertz did indeed take up the case, writing personally to Fuller to repudiate the 'satanic inventions' he was promulgating. With the author obstinately maintaining their veracity, Hertz provided extensive references to Jewish texts to disprove them. A chastened Fuller admitted defeat, and agreed to publish a correction and apology in the subsequent issue of *FQ* – a promise he fulfilled, albeit in as half-hearted and limited a manner as possible.[70]

Another elder statesman, Nathan Laski, issued a much more public challenge, calling on Mosley to name those Jews in the City of London he claimed were financing Indian competition to the Lancashire cotton trade. The BUF did respond, but with a meagre statement on an inside page of *Blackshirt*, irrelevantly offering the names of Jewish directors of the Palestine Electric Corporation. Laski thus repeated his call, asserting that he knew 'a great deal more about Lancashire trade than Sir Oswald' and outlining how Jews boosted British industry, created jobs for native workers and played only a minor role in the City. Moreover, they were as patriotic 'as any Britisher', in contrast to Mosley, whose 'spiritual home is in Germany'.[71] A similar appeal was made by the Anglo-Palestine Club, which invited Mosley to publicly debate his Jewish policy with the club's chairman, Phineas Horowitz (a leading Zionist who later became a member of the Board's defence committee). The Blackshirt leader, however, declined the offer after the club refused to accede to his peculiar and unfeasible demands regarding the conditions of the debate.[72]

Up to this point, Britain's Zionists had paid little attention to the issue of domestic fascism and antisemitism, focusing instead on international affairs in general and Palestine in particular. Where it did touch on the issue of Jewish defence, the *Zionist Review*, the journal of the Zionist Federation of Great Britain and Ireland, had been fairly supportive of the official communal leadership. While it continued to urge reform (and especially greater democratization) of the Board, it also called for 'loyal co-operation against a common danger in time of need'. Although Neville Laski was felt to lack the necessary experience and authority to navigate such a critical period for Jewry in Britain and abroad, he was praised for the 'courage, tenacity and unparalleled industry' with which he had set about his work.[73]

The *Young Zionist* journal, meanwhile, saw in fascism an opportunity. Under the headline 'The Hitler Menace: Will its Effects Prove Beneficial to Jewry?' two contributors urged Anglo-Jewry to learn from the grave consequences of disunity in German Jewish ranks. The indiscriminate nature of Nazi persecution – with the wealthiest, most acculturated Jew being treated as badly as the poorest immigrant – emphasized that assimilation is 'as futile as it is cowardly', and 'force[s] us to realise that we [Jews] are a nation[,] ... segregated in every way from the other nations'. The German Jews' suffering should be treated as a lesson – with the fascists as the 'most cruel of all teachers' – that the only way forward was 'a united Jewry with its own country' in Palestine, which would act as a 'bulwark' against antisemitic attacks.[74]

A subsequent article took this idea even further, effectively conflating the motivation and aims of Zionism and fascism. Its author claimed that both antisemites and Zionists were inspired by 'the eternal foreignness' of diasporic Jewry and its 'continuous economic-national strife with its neighbours', which had brought about a 'fundamental desire' for 'the Jewish nation to substitute for this parasitic basis a better and healthier one'.[75] As we have seen, the BUF would offer virtually the same justification for its official policy of transferring Jews to a new homeland (albeit not in Palestine), where they would be able to 'escape the curse of no nationality' and their 'racialism can take a healthy patriotic instead of an unhealthy parasitic form'.[76]

Following the wave of disruption at BUF events in the summer of 1934, the *Young Zionist* asked 'Should Jews Join Anti-Fascist Societies?', with two authors answering in the negative. To seek 'protective alliances' with gentiles, argued one, would be a sign of Jewish weakness. Moreover, Jewish involvement in anti-fascist activity risked bringing reprisals against the whole community. Jews would always be perceived as different and attract hostility, claimed the other, thereby rendering any attempt to fight antisemitism futile. The best defence against their traducers, both concluded, was to strengthen Jewish identity and national sentiment.[77] As we will later see, however, the *Young Zionist*'s position on this issue would later change radically, as the nature of fascist activity and Jewish communal dynamics shifted over the following years.

The beginning of the East End campaign

As fascist activity became increasingly provocative over 1935, the efforts of the communal leadership appeared ever more inadequate, infuriatingly so for those on the front line, who felt that the Board was out of touch with – or, worse, unconcerned by – the situation on the ground. Previously, direct contact with fascists had tended to arise chiefly when Jews consciously sought it; now, with the BUF encroaching into areas with large Jewish populations in London, Manchester and Leeds, its presence was becoming a far more tangible, indeed inescapable, threat for a substantial portion of Anglo-Jewry.[78] Already by September, Hudson, who represented north Hackney, had complained to the home secretary, John Simon, about fascist attacks on Jews in his constituency. A few months later he noted that 'scarcely a day goes by when I do not receive appeals from my Jewish constituents to stop' fascist provocations. In Hoxton, Jewish shopkeepers and residents similarly appealed to their MP for action to be taken against the fascist intimidation that had become a regular feature of life in the area.[79]

Over 1936 the subject received growing parliamentary attention. Herbert Morrison, the member for Hackney South, described to the House some of the 'innumerable instances' of violence against the Jews he represented. Over the spring and summer various other east London MPs detailed the 'real terror among the Jewish population' and called on Simon to take firmer measures against fascist 'hooliganism'. With the situation still not improving, Dan Frankel, a Jewish MP, warned his colleagues in November of the 'real, living, everyday fear' among his co-religionists.[80] The home secretary also received personal representations from concerned Jews. Lewis Orman, a small business owner from Hackney, wrote to 'draw [Simon's] attention to the scandalous behaviour of certain gangs of hooligans who go around wearing black shirts'. After the fascists' weekly Sunday meeting, local Jews were regularly 'set upon and badly beaten', yet the authorities seemed unable or unwilling to help.[81]

Memoirs further attest to this growing sense of alarm. Morris Beckman, who lived in Hackney, vividly recalls the fascist provocations that 'became part of the fabric of daily life': 'wall daubings, posters, the vandalising of al fresco synagogue furniture, molestations, verbal and physical'. With Blackshirts 'rampaging through the East End streets after dark', many Jews feared to venture out at night. Cordoned off from BUF meetings by the police, 'it was infuriating to stand helplessly outside … and listen to their speakers slagging off … the Yids with the most outrageous of calumnies … [and] to see the crowd actually drinking in the words'.[82] Cyril Spector remembers 'suffer[ing] much personal anti-semitic abuse' at the hands of the 'Fascist thugs and bully boys', while Joyce Goodman describes how, after hearing the fascists 'belting out their message of hate, you learned to hate back'.[83]

These fears were compounded by a widespread feeling of abandonment: not only was the Jewish leadership failing to defend the community, but also the authorities, and in particular the police, were offering scant protection; in some cases, they even appeared to be siding with the fascists. Beckman and Jacobs record the sense of dissatisfaction felt among Jews in the East End at perceived official leniency towards the Blackshirts; Gewirtz and Bergen note similar attitudes in Manchester and Leeds, especially among Jewish youths, who consequently felt obliged to take matters into their own hands.[84]

From the mid-1930s, the National Council for Civil Liberties (NCCL) – which counted the prominent Jewish socialists Victor Gollancz, Harold Laski and Hyman Levy among its vice-presidents – was particularly active in collating and publicizing alleged instances of injustice. Its newsletter accused the police of 'show[ing] marked partiality in the execution of their duty'. At fascist meetings, those heckling 'in a perfectly proper manner' were punished, whereas the 'insulting and provocative' speakers were allowed to continue unimpeded. By contrast, action was rarely taken against Blackshirts who disrupted anti-fascist meetings. Furthermore, judges meted out harsher punishments to anti-fascists than to fascists for similar crimes.[85]

One should, though, be wary of the provenance of such accusations. The NCCL, for example, was a committed adherent to the anti-fascist cause and had close links to the CPGB. Behind closed doors, it actually expressed doubts about some of the testimony it received, noting that one Jewish witness of alleged police brutality 'seems to exaggerate', while another decided to withdraw her charges against the police before they reached court.[86] Many of the Jewish YCL members interviewed by Gewirtz recalled police favouritism towards the fascists, whereas, in fact, the local authorities in Manchester, as we shall see, were at the forefront of efforts to clamp down on fascist provocation.[87]

Yet even those of a more moderate political persuasion expressed concern at the police's attitude. During a five-hour parliamentary discussion of fascist violence, Percy Harris, the Jewish Liberal MP for Bethnal Green, warned of the 'general feeling created right through the East End that somehow or other the police were acting in collusion with the Fascists'. His claim was supported by many fellow parliamentarians.[88] The *JC* had, as early as October 1935, called for courts to 'act with greater sternness and determination' in dealing with cases of fascist violence; the following summer it published accusations of police partiality towards the Blackshirts.[89] Three years later, even the secretary of the Board's defence committee privately alleged that a certain division of the Metropolitan Police was 'notoriously Fascist'. A list of instances demonstrating this bias was forwarded to the deputy commissioner of the Met, with a strongly worded warning that it provided 'justification for those people who persist in saying that the police are on the side of the Fascists and [are] in many cases anti-Semitic'.[90]

Such a perception was to some extent inevitable: the police's principle objective was to preserve public order, and this regularly entailed defending fascist events, which were usually legal, from anti-fascist disruption, which often was not.[91] The Blackshirts regularly invoked Britain's tradition of free speech in their defence. They argued that they had as much right to denounce Jews as any other political party had to criticize those it opposed.[92] Moreover, the BUF could justifiably claim to be speaking for many east London residents, who were attending its meetings and joining the party in large numbers. Such protestations received some sympathy, with MPs from both sides of the House stressing the importance of protecting freedom of expression. The home secretary reminded his colleagues that 'when we talk about civil liberty for all, that means liberty... for the expression and demonstration of opinions that we do not like'.[93]

A further factor feeding the impression of police and judicial inconsistency stemmed from a vagary of the law, which made a distinction between language that was provocative, and should be prevented, and that which was merely offensive, and protected as free speech. This meant that the fascists' anti-Jewish invective was deemed unlawful only if it was likely to occasion a breach of the peace; therefore, the legality of exactly the same words depended largely on the context in which they were uttered. In theory, the law could be interpreted quite broadly: the police, Simon reassured concerned East End MPs, were authorized to arrest fascist speakers for using abusive language in areas with significant Jewish populations.[94] In practice, however, these powers were exercised only if there appeared to be the imminent prospect of disorder – meaning only if Jews were in attendance at a meeting and threatened to respond violently to Blackshirt insults. The resultant discrepancies in the treatment of antisemitic speeches are well demonstrated by three cases from 1936.

In February, 'Jock' Houston had responded to dissent from his audience with the words 'No Yiddish stuff here – with your damned Jewish ignorance'. Although such language was relatively mild by the BUF's standards, it led immediately to disturbances in the crowd. The police, fearing more serious trouble, arrested the speaker, who eventually pleaded guilty to charges of using insulting words whereby a breach of the peace may have been occasioned. The following June, at a meeting in Stoke Newington, loudspeakers were used to provocatively broadcast calls to 'fight the dirty Yid'. Though there were hecklers in the audience, they were seemingly discouraged from physical disruption by the presence of armed fascist stewards. With no prospect of disorder, the police declined to intervene. Just a few days later, Mick Clarke was arrested for, and later found guilty of, using insulting words and behaviour in a speech at Bethnal Green, in which he had called Jews 'greasy scum' and 'lice'. But his sentence was subsequently quashed on appeal, on the grounds that there had been no Jews present at the meeting to take offence.[95]

Perhaps in part because of the legal confusion exemplified by the latter instance, police on the ground were generally reluctant to take action in all but the most clear-cut cases. Despite the Blackshirts' persistently offensive language, and despite the regular presence of Jews in their audiences, Skidelsky calculates that at over 2,000 BUF meetings in east London over 1936–8, speakers were cautioned on just sixteen occasions, leading to only three convictions. A further reason for this, he posits, was that the authorities were prepared to grant speakers some leeway if Jewish opponents in the audience were themselves being vocally abusive towards the fascists, as they often were.[96] An East End magistrate, in justifying his decision to find Alexander Raven Thomson not guilty of using provocative language, explained that although he would come down hard on fascists who made attacks on any 'law-abiding community', if 'a coterie of Jews' challenged a speaker in an offensive manner, the latter had every right 'to deal with the challenge and comment on the Jews in the same way'.[97]

All this left Jews with something of a dilemma: if they stayed away from meetings, as both the Jewish and non-Jewish establishment advised, fascist speakers would be at liberty to say whatever they wished about Jews. If they attended, they could either remain calm under fierce insult, in which case the police would take no action against the speaker; or they could respond, verbally or physically, which often led the authorities to treat the fascists' antisemitic attacks more leniently. Of the three options, the latter – as the only course of action that might result in the meeting being stopped – was clearly the lesser evil, meaning that Jews had every incentive to pursue the most disruptive forms of opposition.

Some scholars have suggested that the limited efforts made by the authorities to prevent BUF incitement were not merely due to the inadequacies of the law, but may also have been caused by official partiality towards the fascists or against communists, anti-fascists and Jews.[98] Yet within the relevant records there is little to suggest any consistent bias. Certainly the state was as concerned with the activity of far left as it was with that of the far right, but there is ample evidence that leading figures within the police and Home Office sympathized with Jews and were keen to restrict fascist antisemitism, not least because it was a primary cause of disorder.

In the wake of Houston's conviction, a senior police officer expressed his hope that there would not 'be any difficultly in … arranging to arrest any other Fascists who use abusive language'.[99] Later in the year, when discussing additional observation of political meetings, one of his colleagues dismissed the idea of doing so at non-fascist events, noting that 'what we are chiefly interested in is "Jew-baiting"'.[100] In 1934, Lord Trenchard, the commissioner of the Metropolitan Police, had actually proposed proscribing the BUF altogether; his successor, Philip Game, was 'even more anti-fascist', Thurlow notes, and regarded fascist antisemitism as a particularly incendiary issue, one that necessitated new legal measures.[101]

Admittedly, the tough line at the top did not always translate into action lower down the ranks. But this was often due to junior officers' difficulties in interpreting the law, rather than any ulterior motive. Moreover, as the deputy assistant commissioner of the Criminal Investigation Department later recalled, the BUF was expert at provoking its opponents into violence but remaining just on the right side of the law itself, something that was 'extremely frustrating for the police'.[102] William Fishman, a historian who as a teenager had been present at Cable Street, points to a 'wealth of evidence' demonstrating that East End policemen were 'disposed to be friendly towards the law-abiding Jews'. He criticizes those who unquestioningly accept contemporary accusations of pro-fascist bias.[103] Kushner and Valman concur, concluding that in the relationship between the police and Jewish immigrants, 'familiarity more often than not brought the opposite of contempt'.[104]

In Manchester, too, the chief of police, John Maxwell, was an ardent opponent of fascism, and pioneered many methods of suppressing the BUF that would later be imitated in London. As early as March 1933, at a time when convention dictated that the police should not enter indoor meetings (as would be the case at Olympia a year later), Maxwell's officers broke up Mosley's Free Trade Hall meeting after disorder had arisen.[105] In mid-1934, the city's Watch Committee, which was chaired and dominated by Maxwell, refused a BUF request to hold a procession, despite permitting other political parties to conduct similar events.[106] Later in the year at Belle Vue, a huge number of officers – under orders from Maxwell to 'carry out their duties in an impartial manner' – were deployed to keep the two sides from coming into conflict (though anti-fascists were not prevented from getting close enough to drown out Mosley's speech with their heckling).[107]

In 1936, the Watch Committee banned the BUF from wearing uniforms in the city and requested greater powers from the Home Office to prohibit marches – both measures that had a significant inhibitory effect on the fascists and were implemented in London the following year.[108] Despite acknowledging Maxwell's efforts to subdue local fascism, Gewirtz criticizes him for being more 'interest[ed] in "keeping the peace" … [than] defend[ing] the right of Jews not to be harassed'. Such an assessment is not only somewhat unreasonable (his primary responsibility *was* to keep the peace), but also not completely accurate: having previously expressed concern at the BUF's 'deliberate provocation of Jews', on at least two occasions in 1936 Maxwell issued general orders for greater effort to be made in investigating and preventing such incidents.[109]

Thurlow also finds that within the Home Office 'the view of British fascism ... was almost uniformly a negative one'. The department was, though, 'nervous, hesitant and often divided' on the question of civil liberties, with a split between 'hawks', who called for greater restrictions on fascist activity, and 'doves', who were wary of infringing freedom of expression. Initially, it had been agreed that changing the law to deal with fascism would stir too much controversy; instead, more surreptitious methods were favoured, such as putting pressure on the media not to report on extremist political activity. However, as the nature of BUF campaigning changed over 1935–6, it came to be accepted that antisemitism had added a new dimension to the disorder surrounding the fascists, necessitating a different approach.[110] In February, an official at the Home Office remarked that the increasing intimidation of Jews was 'very disquieting', and suggested a conference between Game and Simon to discuss more serious measures 'to deal with Fascist behaviour towards the Jews'.[111] While a new policy was being discussed, additional police numbers were diverted to Jewish districts of London in March and again in June.[112]

It was Jewish lobbying that then helped bring about more substantial changes. In early July a deputation of the three most senior figures from the Board, Laski and his two vice-presidents, Robert Waley Cohen and Lionel Cohen, met Simon to express their concern at the abuse Jews were suffering in east London. While Laski understood that free speech had to be protected, and promised to encourage Jews to stay away from fascist events, he stressed that 'human nature has its bounds, and ... the apparent immunity and licence enjoyed by the Fascists' was causing great anxiety among Jews. Laski had no truck with allegations of police partiality, but reminded the home secretary that he had himself declared that antisemitic speeches in Jewish districts were intrinsically provocative, and that the authorities should therefore be making greater efforts to prevent them. Simon admitted that the situation had not been handled in an ideal fashion, but assured Laski a firmer approach was now being taken and was already showing positive results. Waley Cohen, however, disputed this claim. According to his sources, the situation was, if anything, deteriorating. He urged the introduction of stricter punishments for those preaching racial hatred, which he hoped would go some way to allaying the 'feeling of insecurity and alarm among the Jews in the areas affected'.[113]

The meeting clearly had an effect. Simon swiftly circulated a memo outlining that, 'in light of representations' he had received, he wanted to take 'intensive action ... to suppress' fascist antisemitism. 'As many police as can be spared' should be posted in Jewish districts, and they should 'intervene promptly if they hear grossly provocative and abusive language towards the Jews'. Additionally, overzealous stewarding by Blackshirts should be prevented, while any allegations of assault should be investigated thoroughly. To keep track of events, he requested that monthly reports be compiled on the situation in the East End. These demands were quickly translated into formal orders for the Metropolitan Police, who were instructed to ensure that 'the right of free speech ... is not made a cloak for insult and abuse'. When in doubt, officers should always 'err on the side of action rather than inaction', even if it was felt that there was little chance of securing a conviction. The primary aim was 'to make all concerned understand that violence towards, and abuse of, Jews will not be tolerated'.[114]

Yet, whatever the complexities of the law, and however earnest the authorities may have been in their desire to prevent fascist provocation, this should not disguise the extent to which many Jews *felt* that they had been left unprotected, and the powerful psychological effect this had on them. A further area in which perception and reality at times diverged was the nature and extent of the BUF's physical threat to Jews in the East End, which was not as ubiquitous as is sometimes suggested – though, again, this is not to detract from its emotional impact on the community.

First, it is important to remember that while the term 'East End campaign' is useful shorthand, in reality it denotes a complex and evolving patchwork of activity across east, north-east and north London, as well as parts of south-west Essex, taking on a distinct character in each area. Linehan records, for example, that while between September 1935 and July 1936 'Jew-baiting' reached its peak in Hackney and Stoke Newington (roughly 16 per cent of whose populations were Jewish), it was 'confined almost exclusively' to these areas. By contrast, in Stepney and Whitechapel, where Britain's greatest concentration of Jews was to be found, there was 'an almost complete absence of anti-Semitic provocation' at this stage. By the summer of 1936, the authorities had largely succeeded in containing the worst of the provocation in north-east London, but this simply displaced the problem elsewhere, into Bethnal Green and Stepney in particular.[115]

Even where incidents did take place, some doubts have been raised as to their prevalence. Skidelsky has focused on this issue, downplaying the frequency of attacks on Jews, denying the BUF's responsibility for them and criticizing historians for credulously regurgitating the 'press cliché' of 'Fascist terror' in the East End. He provides figures, culled from police files, recording 260 cases of assault, damage, insult and defacement directed against London's Jewish community over 1936–8 – an average of around one incident every four days. These led to just thirty-eight arrests, only half of which were of known fascists.[116]

Yet, as elsewhere, Skidelsky's arguments and supporting evidence are not completely convincing, and there is reason to believe that his numbers understate the extent of the problem. With regard to the arrest figures, it was notoriously difficult to identify culprits, given that attacks usually happened spontaneously and were over quickly, while vandalism often took place under the cover of darkness. Game noted that, though 'numerous complaints were received from Jews of insults and assaults upon them by Fascists[,] ... the great majority were unsubstantiated by any evidence on which action could be taken'.[117] As a consequence – and also because of mistrust of the authorities among some Jews – many offences were never even reported in the first place, and would therefore not register in the police's figures. But most significantly of all, Skidelsky's figures exclude episodes that arose at and around fascist events, which is where a large proportion of anti-Jewish harassment took place.

There may be more justification to Skidelsky's allegation that Jews committed 'just as many assaults on fascists in the period', and were often more violent than their opponents. Certainly there is evidence, which will be discussed in the next chapter, that many Jews took an aggressive approach to opposing fascism, though Skidelsky fails to properly acknowledge the intense provocation that prompted them to do so. He also draws attention to the fact that those guilty of harassing Jews were often very young, claiming it was actually local hoodlums who were responsible for much of the trouble, simply using fascism as a convenient cover.[118] There is some merit to this claim: Game noted that while both Jews and fascists tended to blame their opponents for assaults, 'such incidents are as often as not due to a hooligan element which has no real political affinities'.[119] Moreover, there was a long-standing tradition of hostility – and even physical violence – towards Jews in the East End, established well before the Blackshirts had arrived. In April 1934, at a stage when the BUF had yet to focus any real attention on east London, a Jewish resident in Clapton complained that his co-religionists were 'living under a reign of terror', with gangs of local youths 'bent on victimising the Jewish people around here'.[120]

Nevertheless, whatever the existing traditions of antisemitism, and although many attacks may have been perpetrated by individuals with little genuine interest in fascism, there should be no doubt that the BUF knowingly stoked tensions and fostered an atmosphere in which such incidents would proliferate. Nor, as Mosley himself later admitted, did it have any qualms in accepting the support of thugs and pathological antisemites.[121]

Police reports from February 1936 provide two illustrative examples of the pattern of events that had developed by this stage: the intentional stirring of racial tension by the BUF, which directly inspired incidents of Jew-baiting; the feeling of fear among Jews, resulting in an eagerness to blame the Blackshirts for every incident and to disrupt fascist meetings; and the difficulties the authorities experienced in assuaging such concerns, preventing the two sides coming into conflict and investigating incidents that did arise.

Following a fascist meeting in Stamford Hill, three Jewish teenagers were attacked by what they claimed had been a group of Blackshirts. The police took the incident seriously, escorting the youths to the local BUF branch in an unsuccessful attempt to identify the culprits. The superintendent lamented that, despite great effort by his colleagues to prevent post-meeting violence, the incident represented

> another instance of unprovoked assaults on Jewish looking youths by young men who presumably are, or wish to be considered, Fascists[.] … The assaults are for the most part trivial, but they are certainly disconcerting. There is no doubt we shall hear more of this incident from the Jewish opponents of Fascism, and get the usual complaints of police impotence and partiality. Actually police are giving this a great deal of attention, but whilst Jews and others attend the meetings and indulge in 'Baiting' the speakers, such occurrences as this are almost inevitable.

A fellow officer was less sympathetic, noting clear inconsistencies between the boys' accounts of events and their exaggeration of the severity of the attack when reporting it to their local MP, Hudson. Despite 'an entire absence of evidence that the alleged assaults were committed by fascists', he observed, one of the victims 'and his family are highly excitable and nervous individuals, who appear to be obsessed with the idea that they will be seriously injured by fascists'.[122]

Following a similar case in nearby Clapton, the police were again unconvinced that fascists were directly responsible. In fact, given that the Jewish victims had been wearing black shirts, it was distinctly possible, as even the father of one of the boys admitted, that anti-fascists had unwittingly assaulted them. Nevertheless, one of the youths addressed an angry letter to Hudson, placing the blame unequivocally on 'members of a political party assuming the dress of Blackshirts' (despite never having mentioned to the police seeing a uniform on his assailants) and demanding that action be taken against the fascists.

Given that the letter was sent sixteen days after the event, and in language it is hard to believe was written by a boy recently turned seventeen (who described his clash with the fascists as a 'fistic dispute' and reminded Hudson of his pre-election promises to combat fascism), it is likely that an anti-fascist organization or individual had encouraged him to take his case further. Writing some time later, Game noted 'a tendency on both sides... to magnify any incidents that do take place with a view to reviving public interest'. Nevertheless, whoever might have been responsible for this particular attack, an official at the Home Office was convinced where the ultimate blame lay:

[Although] some of the complaints may be exaggerated or untrue, there can be no doubt that in a large number of cases Jews are being molested by Fascists and that the Fascists are trying to stir up hatred against this section of the population.[123]

The Defence Debate, 1936

Communal divisions

The atmosphere of fear and anger engendered by the East End campaign breathed new urgency into the debate within Anglo-Jewish on the best means of communal defence, transforming an uneasy divergence of opinion into an increasingly antagonistic dispute. The Board, in particular, came in for heavy criticism. Many of those who experienced Blackshirt provocation first hand, who were often already estranged from the communal elites, felt further alienated by the passive line advocated by individuals who were safely distanced from the fascist threat. J.W. Bentley, who would later become the founding chairman of the Jewish People's Council, condemned the 'so-called leaders of Jewry' for their 'inertia [and] over-cautious tactics [which] have contributed directly to the Fascist menace against Jews'.[1] Another anti-fascist activist later recalled how it felt like 'we were fighting both the fascists and the Board'.[2]

Criticism was not restricted to the Board; any Jew in a position of authority who was believed to be shirking the struggle against fascism was targeted. In the November 1935 general election, Barnett Janner was labelled by opponents a 'pro-Fascist', the *JC* reported.[3] Voters in Mile End were similarly urged not to vote for the local Labour candidate, Dan Frankel, on the grounds of his unwillingness to directly confront fascism. Nevertheless, over the following year Frankel continued to exhort his fellow Jews to avoid 'excited and hysterical' behaviour, fearing that visible Jewish anti-fascism could provoke violent retaliation against the community and encourage sympathy for the fascists. As an MP, he explained in parliament, he had made a conscious effort to 'scrupulously...ke[ep] out of discussions with regard to Fascism and with regard to the Jewish people[.]...I was not elected a Member of this House as a Jew...[and] I have not thought it my job to come here as a partisan representative of one creed or one race'. Such a position, he admitted, made him 'unpopular with members of my own race'.[4]

With many Jews feeling abandoned by their official leadership and unprotected by the authorities, other organizations sought to fill the void. The CPGB was one significant beneficiary. An internal party memorandum noted how the growing threat of fascism, alongside the 'negative policy advocated by leaders of the [Jewish] community', had pushed working-class Jews 'beyond elementary forms of anti-fascist activity...[to] demand an organised resistance to anti-semitism'. Moreover, such sentiment was not restricted to 'the Jewish class conscious masses', but also encompassed doctors, lawyers and intellectuals. There was now the real prospect of drawing together these 'scattered and wasted' forces into a 'broad Jewish movement' that would 'becom[e] a powerful weapon in the general fight against Fascism and the Capitalist system'.

There were also concerns, however, that this great potential could be diverted in undesirable directions. Fascist hostility had brought 'Jewish racial consciousness ... to a much higher level', it was noted, and this was strengthening support for Zionism, particularly among less assimilated Jews. The Communists should, therefore, stress that migration to Palestine failed to tackle the real problem, capitalism, and that 'only under a system of society where there is no exploitation of man by man can Jewish culture flower to its full stature and ... full and complete equality be realised'. Jewish party members, in particular, were called upon to evangelize among their brethren by emphasizing that fascism was the common enemy of both Jews and gentile workers, and calling for defensive work to be carried out in 'the closest cooperation and alliance with the ... working class movement'.[5] Numerous publications were produced to carry this message to Jewish workers, while the Committee for Co-ordinating Anti-Fascist Activity was resurrected, making direct appeals to East End Jews for support.[6]

The Zionists, for their part, were equally keen to use this opportunity to boost their support – or at least to neutralize Communist charges against them. In March 1936, the *Young Zionist*, in an article entitled 'Fascism, Communism, Zionism', urged the movement to respond to left-wing claims that Zionism was a reactionary, bourgeois and capitalist force by 'address[ing] itself to the problems of the Jewish worker in daily life', including the threat of fascism. Three months later, the journal suggested that Zionism and socialism were completely compatible with one another; indeed, 'probably the majority of the members of Young Zionist societies are Socialists of one type or another', it pointed out.[7]

As we saw in the previous chapter, only two years earlier contributors to the *Young Zionist* had claimed that seeking alliances with gentiles would be a sign of weakness, arguing instead for a bolstering of Jewish solidarity as the best means of defence. Now, the complete opposite was suggested. In an article that presented many elements of the standard Marxist, class-based analysis of fascism, one of the editors, Phil Harris, warned that if Jews isolated themselves it would 'irritate ... the mass of Englishmen' and allow Mosley 'to reap advantage'.[8] Instead, another contributor advised, the Zionists should regard 'big Jews' as potential enemies and instead seek alliances in 'the ranks of democratic non-Jewish youth', with whom they should arrange protest meetings, counter-demonstrations and the lobbying of local authorities to properly enforce the law. This 'policy of action' was contrasted positively to the Board's stance, which was condemned as 'surrender to Fascist provocation' that would lead to 'isolation from progressive and non-sectarian forces in Britain'.[9] While in 1934 the *Young Zionist* had fatalistically declared antisemitism an inevitable feature of life in the diaspora, and therefore not worth fighting, now another of its editors, L.G. Salingar, argued that 'anti-Semitism is a menace only as and because it is used by the fascists ... [and] and it can be repulsed ... only by the joint effort of democratic, anti-Fascist forces'.[10]

Such words were increasingly translated into action, with many younger elements in the Zionist movement pursing confrontational forms of anti-fascism over 1936, including support for the newly formed JPC. However, in a microcosm of the wider pattern witnessed across Anglo-Jewry, the activist approach of Zionist youths brought them into conflict with the movement's leadership. Although the Zionist Federation had also been keen to refute the Communists' anti-Zionist propaganda – with Jewish Communists described as 'enemies' in the *Zionist Review* – it had not, unlike the *Young Zionist*, felt compelled to compete with them on the issue of domestic fascism, which it continued largely to ignore (the subject was not even mentioned in the *Zionist Review* until June 1938).[11]

These contrasting approaches engendered tension within Zionist ranks. In May 1937, the *Young Zionist*'s chief editor, A.S. Eban, announced that he was stepping down from his position, and used his final editorial to suggest that the journal had been working 'without the full support of all sections of the [Zionist] Federation'. At the same time, two of the publication's most strident voices on Jewish defence, Harris and Salingar, also left their editorial posts.[12] Subsequently, the issue of domestic fascism disappeared almost entirely from the journal's pages. This may in part have reflected changing external circumstances: from mid-1937, Blackshirt and anti-fascist activity both subsided in the East End, while, as we shall see, the Jewish communal leadership began to pursue a defence policy that better satisfied the demands of Jewish anti-fascists. But it is also likely that internal pressure was applied on the publication to moderate its tone and content. That this was the case is suggested by the fact that the Zionist Federation privately reprimanded the president of the Federation of Zionist Youth, Abe Harman, for his decision to affiliate his organization with the anti-fascist JPC, which, one executive council member declared, was 'led by communists and anti-zionists'. This pattern was repeated at various provincial Zionist societies, where young activists were restrained by their elders.[13]

As the latter quote suggests, the Zionist leadership's primary concern was not the growth of British fascism itself, but the fact that it was pushing Jews into the arms of the CPGB. Whereas in 1934 Jews had been willing to work alongside the Communists without committing to membership, more formal connections were now being established. Between February 1935 and October 1936, CPGB membership grew by over 4,500, a 70 per cent rise.[14] It is impossible to know precisely the proportion of this figure constituted by Jews, but certainly it was significant. Jacobs celebrated that Jews 'reacted [to the BUF's East End campaign] by joining our side in ever greater numbers'. At the other end of the social spectrum, Rose Henriques, the well-heeled founder of a prominent Jewish girls club in the East End, wrote with concern to the parents of her young charges that 'a great many … have joined Communist clubs, not because they are Communist, but because they feel that the Communists were the only people who were trying to fight the Fascists'.[15]

There was, however, division within Communist ranks over the form that opposition to fascism should take, and Jewish members were central to this debate. Phil Piratin, a leading East End Communist, described the 'constant discussion' within the party between those who favoured an approach he disparagingly labelled 'Bash the fascists whenever you see them', and others, such as himself, who thought more deeply about the reasons why so many working-class East Enders were attracted to the BUF. Piratin argued that the Blackshirts should be confronted politically and ideologically, not physically; the Communists needed to 'cut the ground from under the fascists' feet' by exposing their true nature and by showing people the real causes of their economic suffering.

Piratin admitted, though, that his ideas were 'not accepted by the majority' at his (predominantly Jewish) branch in Stepney, where meetings became a 'verbal battlefield'. Among the dissenters was Joe Jacobs, who advocated a more aggressive approach. Defending such tactics, he later explained that, because 'almost all Mosley's activity was on the street[,] ... we could [not] allow his efforts to go unchallenged'. Physical opposition to the fascists was a necessity, not a choice, brought about by the Blackshirts' own behaviour and the reluctance of the police to intervene.[16]

In the long run, it would be Piratin's tactics that won out, not least because they mirrored the official line of the party leadership, which now aimed to tone down more aggressive forms of rhetoric and behaviour as part of efforts to attract wider (and therefore more moderate) support for a Communist-led 'Popular Front'. Pollitt – who, his biographer Kevin Morgan notes, was 'no enthusiast for ... physical confrontation with the Blackshirts' – warned his comrades that it would be 'fatal' if their opposition to Mosley was perceived as 'a brawl and not a real political struggle'.[17]

But, in yet another example of how the caution urged by senior figures of all types was ignored by younger Jewish elements on the front line, it was initially the militant approach favoured by Jacobs that won the greatest support, as 'party leaders struggl[ed] to assert their authority over rank-and-file members'.[18] This was particularly the case among new Jewish recruits to the party, whose primary motivation for joining was combating fascism, not the 'solid, slogging work' (as Piratin described it) of winning over the masses to Communist doctrine. Smith notes how, in the East End, the local Communists' tactics of 'direct confrontation' had the greatest effect in attracting Jewish youths.[19] Emanuel Litvinoff, a member of the YCL from Whitechapel, recalled how 'night after night ... I hurried away to join my boisterous guerrillas in another skirmish ... with Mosley's fascists'.[20]

As a result, during 1936 anti-fascist activity took an increasingly violent character.[21] In August, around 60 per cent of fascist meetings in London saw organized opposition of some kind, the police recorded; those responsible demonstrated 'little or no discipline', and contained a strong 'hooligan element [that] includes many Jews'.[22] Yet the police's own figures do not suggest a huge surge in Jewish violence: over 1936–7, 21 per cent of non-fascists arrested at a sample of BUF meetings (mostly in London) were Jews, not much higher than the figure for 1934–5. What is striking is that of the thirty-eight Jews whose arrests were recorded during this period, twenty-two were identified by the police as communists. Cullen, on whose research these figures are based, also shows that of fifty-one assaults on fascists recorded over 1934–8, 29 per cent were committed by Jews.[23]

A similar situation was to be found further north. In Leeds, the YCL, whose membership peaked in 1936–7, was dominated by Jews, and it was they who led the 'active resistance' to Mosley.[24] In Manchester, Gewirtz finds that the calls for restraint issued by the official Communist leadership in London gained no hearing whatsoever. Instead, local Communists, led by the predominantly Jewish YCL, attempted to drive the fascists off the streets by breaking up meetings, intimidating newspaper-sellers and responding to antisemitic abuse with physical violence. Though the YCL's own membership was not large, it could count on widespread sympathy for its anti-fascist activity: there 'was a whole community involvement', remembered one Jewish Communist.[25]

The willingness of many young Jews to respond aggressively to fascist provocation was also expressed outside the context of organized anti-fascism: sometimes in the form of individual, spontaneous scuffles,[26] but also by gangs of youths that deliberately sought out Blackshirts. Beckman remembers 'the notorious Gold brothers' of Hackney, who 'went out after dark with like-minded others and hunted for fascists'. Interestingly – and suggesting that violence was indeed often perpetrated by young trouble-makers rather than the politically motivated – the Golds were on first-name terms with many of their Blackshirt opponents, and clashes between the two sides followed tacitly agreed rules of engagement.[27] An investigation by the *Evening Standard* into this 'gang warfare' concluded that 'East End Blackshirts are in some real danger of physical violence. There are some streets in Whitechapel ... where no Blackshirt could walk at night ... without being badly assaulted'.[28]

In Leeds, meanwhile, where the Jewish community was less well organized and boasted weaker institutions than in Manchester or London, it 'relied [for protection] upon a gang of youths, who seem to have operated almost as vigilantes', records Bergan. As well as their defensive duties, such as guarding synagogues on high holy days, the youths sought out conflict, too, with one interviewee remembering 'a group of tough lads who liked fighting the fascists'. Some even travelled to London to assist East End Jews in their struggle against the Blackshirts.[29]

The period also saw the Communists begin to share responsibility for the coordination of opposition to the BUF with a much broader alliance of groups, one that included far greater Jewish participation than had been the case in 1934.[30] Of the various bodies that comprised London's anti-fascist scene in autumn 1936, the police observed that, while the CPGB remained the most active, the remainder were all predominantly or completely Jewish in character.

Among these, the largest was the Ex-Servicemen's Movement Against Fascism (EMAF), which had been formed in July and aimed to 'attack Fascism in its strongholds and sweep it off the streets'. Ostensibly non-partisan and inclusive, in reality EMAF had close ties to the CPGB and was composed largely of Jews. It claimed to have attracted almost 2,000 members in its first eight weeks, a boast that was substantiated by the impressive turnout for a procession it arranged in August. A column of 3,000 military veterans, the great majority of them Jewish, proudly displaying their medals and waving British flags, marched through the streets of the East End to Victoria Park. A crowd of 7,000, drawn from trade unions, the YCL and Zionist organizations, turned up to show support. Less friendly interest was also attracted: numerous fascists, deliberately out of uniform, bombarded the procession with missiles, chants of 'Hail Mosley' and antisemitic slurs. 'Free fights were frequent', the *JC*'s correspondent recorded, and 'many Jews were assaulted.' The newspaper lauded the 'commendable dignity and discipline' demonstrated by the marchers in not rising to this provocation. The event concluded with the passing of a resolution to fight, 'as true patriots', for the 'constitutional rights of all free citizens, which the foreign menace of Fascism seeks to destroy'.[31]

A few weeks before the establishment of EMAF, another group, the Legion of Blue and White Shirts (LBWS), had also emerged. Its followers, bedecked in the movement's eponymous uniform, took a physical approach, clashing regularly with the BUF, which labelled them the 'storm troops of Jewry'. An LBWS pamphlet, 'The Black Plague: An Exposure of Fascism', noted how the Great Plague of 1664–5 had been eradicated by the Fire of London a year later, and called on individuals of all colours and creeds to unite in ensuring that the disease of fascism now met the same fate. The movement was, like EMAF, eager to emphasize its British credentials. A Union Flag was prominently displayed on its shirts, while propaganda spoke of 'our country' and 'our ancestors', celebrating England's proud history as a 'cradle of freedom' that had always offered 'asylum for refugees'. The fascists, by contrast, were 'foreign-minded political charlatans'.[32] Given their similar approaches, later in the year EMAF and the LBWS discussed a formal merger, a move that was indicative of the broad alliance that developed between various anti-fascist organizations, uniting those who favoured disruptive activism and were opposed to the passive stance offered by more traditional institutions.[33]

At around the same time, the North Manchester Co-ordinating Committee Against Fascism was established, bringing together the city's various left-leaning anti-fascists – Communists, Labourites, the Workers' Circle and trade unions – with Jews again to the fore. One of its first achievements was to gather 3,500 signatures in Cheetham, where the city's working-class Jewish community was concentrated, on a petition to the Lord Mayor demanding that fascist meetings not be permitted in Jewish districts. Over the summer, BUF events in Manchester were confronted by crowds of protesters thousands strong.[34]

Aware of the anger feeding these developments, many figures associated with mainstream political parties did their best to advertise their anti-fascist credentials. In his campaign for the November 1935 general election, Janner, perhaps in response to the abovementioned charges of 'pro-Fascism', had 'offered himself ... as a champion of his race against the Fascists'. According to an NCCL report, he subsequently received three-quarters of the votes of local Jews, who 'abandoned their usual political ties and voted as Jews for a Jew'. (This was not enough, however, to overcome the declining popularity of the Liberal Party and save him from defeat.)[35] A non-Jewish candidate in Mile End took out an advert in the *JC* describing himself as 'the only ... candidate who is definitely against Fascism', while another, contesting East Willesden, reassured voters 'I am not ... Fascist', as his opponents had 'scurrilously' claimed.[36]

Even Frankel came to accept that if he was to 'properly represent the people of my constituency', around half of whom were Jewish, he needed to work harder to oppose fascism. In parliament, he now warned his colleagues that there is 'no longer any use trusting to what we all thought was the common sense of the English people and their spirit of fair play'; traditions of free speech had been 'translated into licence ... [for] expression of hatred ... against the whole of the members of one race'. The time had come, he declared, for fascism 'to be dealt with thoroughly'. In July 1936, Frankel and other prominent political figures in the East End led an anti-fascist march, organized by the East London Trades Councils, to Victoria Park in Hackney, where an audience of thousands, a large proportion of them Jews, was addressed.[37]

The above groups and individuals readily intermixed anti-fascism with their wider political agendas, often using the former to serve the latter. But another body, the British Union of Democrats (BUD), established in early 1935 but largely inactive until the summer of 1936, explicitly eschewed any partisanship. Though open to all, it attracted a largely Jewish membership. One of its leading figures, H.A. Swart, a Jewish ex-serviceman, called on his co-religionists to defend themselves against fascism's 'unclean, unwarranted, un-British attack', warning that they could not complacently rely on the compassion of gentiles. In pursuit of this aim, his organization pioneered an approach that came to be adopted by others, including the Board of Deputies. The BUD held public meetings in areas of intense BUF activity, such as Stoke Newington and Finsbury Park, often in close proximity to ongoing fascist events. These attracted hostile audiences, with one BUD speaker claiming to have been physically attacked by Blackshirts. Yet unlike many other groups of its ilk, the BUD advocated a non-violent response. It urged Jews not to physically confront the fascists, arguing that to do so would be to play into Mosley's hands.[38]

While it is clear that many Jews were involved in activist anti-fascism, it is also important to bear in mind how the availability of sources influences perceptions of their number. Political organizations and defence bodies have left behind a highly visible trail of written material in the form of internal records and publications, as well as press reports and other observations by outsiders. Moreover, Jews involved in more direct forms of anti-fascism have been likelier to publish memoirs and be interviewed by researchers, given the interest in this area of history and because, usually having been in their teens or twenties at the time, they were able to tell their story for long afterwards. By contrast, those uncomfortable with, or simply ambivalent towards, such types of activity have left less of a trace, despite making up a significant portion of the community. This is not to suggest, it should be added, that such individuals were not opposed to fascism – after 1934, it was impossible for a Jew not to be. Merely that they favoured a more discreet approach.

In particular, older working-class Jews appeared concerned that the aggressive anti-fascism favoured by younger elements would serve only to inflame the situation. Often first-generation immigrants who had found in Britain a haven from persecution and pogroms elsewhere, they shared little of the assertive anger expressed by their British-born children at fascism's challenge to the Jews' place in society. Spector, for example, remembered that his mother, who did not mix outside Jewish circles, preferred to 'shield herself' from fascism, while his father and brother remained 'passive'. He was banned from bringing communist literature into the house and discouraged from meeting his more political friends. He ascribes his family's attitude to the fact that they 'felt they were still visitors' in Britain, while his parents were also 'haunted with … the memory of the pogroms in Eastern Europe'. Beckman also recalls a rift between young and old, with the latter's perspective shaped by traumatic memories of persecution in their lands of origin.[39]

In Manchester there was a similar disparity, Gewirtz observes, between the caution advocated by 'a less secure, older generation of recent immigrations', and the 'self-confidence of a younger generation of Jews who had been brought up in Manchester and who felt more secure of their place there and more able to defend it vigorously'.[40]

By contrast, Willy Goldman, another East End resident, believed that rather than fearing a repeat of east-European pogroms in Britain, older Jews simply saw Blackshirt antisemitism as 'comparative[ly] harmless' in relation to their own experiences, and were therefore less exercised by it.[41]

One should also be wary of overstating the number of Jews who supported organizations that pursued confrontational forms of anti-fascism. The CPGB's membership, for example, reached an interwar peak of 18,000 in late 1938.[42] It is impossible to gauge precisely what proportion of these were Jews, but even a generous estimate of 20–30 per cent (Alderman believes that in the mid-1940s the figure was around 10 per cent) would mean that only 1–1.5 per cent of Britain's Jewish population were CPGB members. This would be consistent with a survey of Jews in the immediate post-war period – when overall CPGB membership was higher than in the 1930s – which found that 2.3 per cent of Jews identified themselves as communist supporters (though not necessarily party members). By contrast, 33.1 per cent favoured the Liberal Party, 32.9 per cent Labour and 22.5 per cent the Conservatives.[43] Even in working-class Jewish districts numbers were not high. The CPGB's Stepney branch had just 230 members in 1936, while in Cheetham and Leeds the local YCLs were a similar size.[44] Beckman found it 'surprising how few Jews in the 1930s actually joined the Communists'.[45]

Similarly, membership of another mainstay of Jewish working-class activism, the Workers' Circle, never exceeded 3,000, and during the mid-1930s grew at a net rate of only 200 or so a year.[46] By contrast, the far larger Association of Jewish Friendly Societies (AJFS), which represented around 50,000 Jews (some 15 per cent of Anglo-Jewry), was explicitly opposed to confrontational anti-fascism and generally supportive of the approach favoured by the communal leadership. Its chairman, John Dight, advised that 'it would be wiser for young co-religionists to ignore the Fascists', as Jewish attacks were of 'inestimable propaganda value' to the BUF. In early 1936, the largest organization within the AJFS, the Order Achei Brith, declared itself satisfied with the 'valuable work' the Board was doing to defend the community. It was confident that Jews could rely on the English 'love of fair play [a]s the surest deterrent against the rise of anti-Semitism[.] … Jew-baiting is not the kind of game that appeals to the sporting instincts of the decent Englishmen, particularly the English working classes'.[47]

As the fascist threat worsened over 1936, the AJFS did come to accept that a more active approach was needed. However, rather than activity of a disruptive or political nature, it favoured educational anti-defamation and Jewish self-improvement. The 'one thing', its newspaper, *The Leader*, advised, that 'will contribute more than anything else … is the maintenance by Jews of the high moral standards of Judaism in their public and private avocations'. Meanwhile, it proposed that a campaign 'to combat the spate of lies and calumny circulated about Jews' be initiated.[48]

A further insight is offered by Beckman's claim that there were 'too few Jews' to effectively prevent fascist activity. London Jewry numbered around 200,000 or more (perhaps half of whom lived in the East End), dwarfing the size of the BUF, whose membership in the mid-1930s was never higher than around 15,000 *nationally* (and was much lower over most of 1935–8). This again suggests that a large proportion of the community was not engaged in confrontational activity.[49] After the abovementioned Albert Hall meeting in March 1936, there were complaints among some anti-fascists that the 10,000 protesters outside the venue had included disappointingly few Jews. In June, Mosley was able to address an audience of 15,000 in Hackney with no organized disruption whatsoever. Later in the year, a Scottish anti-fascist wrote to the *JC* to protest at how few local Jews were involving themselves in the cause, accusing them of 'cowardice'. [50] It is also instructive to note that, despite some vociferous criticism of Frankel's allegedly timid response to fascism in late 1935, his election campaign was a success, securing one of the most Jewish constituencies in the country with 57 per cent of the vote, a 13 per cent swing in his favour against the incumbent.[51]

Nor was Frankel the only Jew in his party to advocate a cautious approach towards fascism. Leslie Lever, a Manchester councillor and later an MP and Lord Mayor of the city, in 1936 opposed a proposal to bar the leasing of public halls to fascists, on the grounds that while Jews had every reason to abhor fascism, they, of all people, should understand the importance of protecting basic rights such as free speech.[52] Morris Davis, Labour leader of Stepney Borough Council and a second-generation immigrant who had grown up in Whitechapel, voted in 1937 to allow the BUF to use Limehouse town hall for its meetings, and generally distanced himself from more radical anti-fascist elements on the left.[53]

Moreover, although historians have been quick to depict working-class, activist anti-fascists and the communal elites as irreconcilable antagonists, with the former estranged from and seeking alternatives to the latter, in fact, many of those who expressed dissatisfaction with the Board's policies explicitly renounced any desire to undermine its position, or even to fundamentally reform its structure. They simply hoped to encourage it to take a more robust position on the issue of fascism, and for Anglo-Jewry to present a united front. An East End branch of the Shop Assistants' Union unanimously passed a resolution condemning the 'passive attitude of the leaders of British Jewry'. It added, however, that if the Board toughened up its policy, the union 'promise[d] our assistance in every possible way'.[54] Even the archetypal popular Jewish defence body, the JPC, conveyed from the very start that it did 'not wish to usurp to the functions of the Board', but to work alongside it.[55] As we will see, such sentiment was genuine: once the Board adopted a more vigorous defence policy, many working-class anti-fascists, including the JPC, came to support its efforts.

The most significant development at this stage, though, was that institutions traditionally supportive of the Board, while continuing to profess their loyalty, began to apply substantial pressure on it to act. In July, a member of the council of the United Synagogue put forward a motion that the Board should be pressed to take firmer action against fascism. It was, however, quashed by Waley Cohen, the synagogue's vice-president and dominant figure, who, to the chagrin of many colleagues, attempted to stifle all discussion of non-religious matters within the institution.[56] The same month, the Jewish Ex-Servicemen's Legion (AJEX, as it became known soon after; not to be confused with EMAF) warned Jews of the importance of remaining united, but reminded the Board that it needed to take the lead on defence issues.[57]

More worrying for the Board, the friendly societies, with their large membership, began to express discontent. The Order Achei B'rith warned that 'the hesitant and over-cautious attitude of the leaders is tending to make Jewry look elsewhere for the championship of Jewish rights'. The AJFS, meanwhile, feared that with no 'authoritative body yet enter[ing] the field to combat the menace' of fascism, Jewish 'extremists' were being allowed to monopolize the communal response. As such, it took matters into its own hands, putting together in mid-1936 plans for a campaign of outdoor meetings in areas of fascist activity to disseminate anti-defamation propaganda. This, as we shall see, would come to form the basis of the Board's own defence work, initiated soon after in close cooperation with the AJFS.[58]

But perhaps the most important voice in the defence debate of 1936 was that of the *JC*, which successfully balanced cautious support for anti-fascist groups with calls for responsible behaviour, and demands for greater action from the Board with respect for its authority – all the while continuing to act as an open forum for all elements of Anglo-Jewry to express their views on the issue. Initially, with the BUF in decline over 1935, the newspaper had felt little need to pay it great attention;[59] where it did, the party was treated with ridicule as much as contempt. In many ways the *JC* appeared glad that Mosley's antisemitism was finally out in the open, allowing its mendacity, and fascism's true nature, to be exposed. In September, the newspaper felt confident enough, in its review of the previous Jewish year, to celebrate the failure of British fascism and conclude that the 'race hatred' it was attempting to cultivate 'is a weed which fortunately it is difficult to root in British soil'.[60]

Even during the early stages of the East End campaign, the *JC* provided little coverage, no doubt in the belief that to do so might aggravate the situation and provide the Blackshirts additional 'evidence' of Jewish hostility towards them. The newspaper did, though, express sympathy with the victims of Jew-baiting and concern at the authorities' apparent reluctance to adequately protect them. Following the trial of a fascist for attacking a Jew with an iron bar, it criticized his sentence as too lenient, calling for 'greater sternness and determination' in such cases and firmer measures against provocative language. Otherwise, there was the prospect of 'a veritable reign of terror starting against Jews', and of a violent Jewish response.[61]

However, as the situation worsened, the newspaper showed growing signs of frustration with the Board's continued reluctance to take the lead in communal defence. Under the editorship of Jack Rich, the *JC* had been supportive of Laski, though not afraid to reprimand him on occasion, as it had done in 1933, when the Board had been slow to respond to calls for a Jewish boycott of German goods.[62] Now, with Laski similarly hesitant, it again acted as a mouthpiece for communal demands that defence policy be reformed.

In January 1936, the *JC* warned of widespread 'dissatisfaction and anxiety' towards the 'badly bungled' policies of the Anglo-Jewish leadership, which had 'le[ft] the Community exposed, without adequate protection'. Though the newspaper saw some merit in suggestions, being aired in various quarters, for an independent body to coordinate Jewish defence, it warned that its establishment would damage the pre-eminence of the Board – further reason for the latter to pre-empt such a move by strengthening its policies.[63]

With action still not forthcoming, a further, more urgent exhortation was published in May, condemning the Board's meagre anti-defamation efforts as 'penny-whistle piping' in the face of a 'raucous anti-Jewish blast'. Senior deputies were accused of paying greater attention to internal wrangles over who should be responsible for defence policy than on actually implementing it. Meanwhile, as they dragged their feet, younger members of the community were 'throwing themselves into the arms of extremist anti-Fascist groups ready to help in defending them', the newspaper warned.[64]

By June, the *JC*'s patience had run out. In a piece entitled 'The Question of Self-Defence', its regular columnist 'Watchman' (the penname of Simon Gilbert, an East End journalist with a self-described 'proletarian' style) proposed a detailed framework for defence policy (one that would, by and large, come to be adopted by the Board over subsequent months). There remained, he reassured, 'no ground for panic': Jews could be confident that the fair-minded British people were unlikely ever to turn to a 'second-hand Hitler' like Mosley. But even without political power, fascism had great potential to 'poison the relations between Jew and non-Jew', and it was the duty of Anglo-Jewry to challenge the inflammatory propaganda broadcast by fascists. Gilbert called on the community's 'do nothing' leaders to arrange for anti-defamation meetings to be held in the wake of fascist events; to distribute publications undermining antisemitic lies and outlining Jewish accomplishments; and to collaborate in this struggle with sympathetic gentiles.

While historians have often deemed such an approach as apologetic, reflecting Jewish insecurity, Gilbert thought quite the opposite. He argued that Jews should not 'resign ourselves fatalistically' to forever be seen as 'strangers', but instead confidently assert their position in, and advertise their positive contribution to, British society. 'Respect,' he maintained, 'is reserved for those who stand up for themselves.' The article did finish, however, on a paternalistic and apologetic note. Gilbert reminded the community of its 'duty' to be 'chaste and pure'; it should 'stamp out the plague of ostentation', 'frown on materialism' and avoid 'excessive clannishness'. Every Jewish wrongdoer was 'Hitler's most potent ally'; Anglo-Jewry therefore needed to ensure there were 'as few "horrible examples" as possible for enemy use'.[65]

The article marked the beginning of a period of intense focus on this issue by the newspaper, which two weeks later launched a weekly 'Jewish Defence' section covering fascist and anti-fascist news, incidents of Jew-baiting and discussion of the communal response. Over the course of 1936, David Rosenberg calculates, one-third of editorials (and four-fifths of those that covered domestic issues) were devoted to fascism or antisemitism.[66] The letters pages were also dominated by the issue. Among correspondents, there was almost-unanimous support for determined and united Jewish action, alongside collaboration with like-minded gentiles; nearly all were critical of the Jewish leadership's 'dignified apathy' and 'impotent attitude'.[67]

Yet with the Board continuing to temporize, in mid-July the *JC* felt obliged again to remind it of the 'desperate need for a Jewish reply', warning that the community was 'waiting with ebbing patience' for strong leadership.[68] It also made the pointed decision to advertise and report on the JLC conference in late July that led to the formation of the JPC, and subsequently continued to provide coverage of this new organization's activity.[69]

The establishment of the Co-ordinating Committee

As the *JC*'s growing frustration suggests, the communal leadership had spent much of late 1935 and early 1936 inconclusively wrangling over the issue of defence. Some senior figures had, in fact, accepted as early as the winter of 1934–5 that a new approach was needed. But the variety of competing interests on the Board, the inherently cumbersome workings of a large, umbrella institution (one that had little formal power or revenue-raising ability), the unprecedented nature of fascism's political antisemitism and the fact that the BUF was itself in a state of flux over 1934–6 meant that change came slowly.

Waley Cohen had been one of the first to throw his weight behind the creation of a body dedicated to the production of counter-propaganda. In December 1934, he discussed the idea with Isidore Salmon, a Jewish Conservative MP and vice-president of the Board. Such an organization should, Waley Cohen believed, remain independent of the Board, as any outward association between the two would negate the effectiveness of anti-defamation work. It would be funded, he anticipated, by discreet donations from wealthy Jewish individuals, whose potential generosity Otto Schiff, a prominent Jewish stockbroker with close connections to the Rothschilds, was already gauging.[70]

In early 1935, however, Waley Cohen was involved in a serious car accident, necessitating a lengthy period of convalescence and delaying the pursuit of his plan. In the meantime, a similar proposal was put forward by Bertram Jacobs, a deputy to the Board. It failed, though, to raise significant financial support, leading the chairman of the Press Committee, Philip Guedalla, to conclude that criticism of the Board's anti-fascist efforts was 'merely a pretext for evading money contributions' to defence activity.[71]

Guedalla, a popular writer and former Liberal parliamentary candidate, had himself, in his time heading the committee, demonstrated a willingness, within certain bounds, to oppose fascism. In 1933 he had, to the frustration of Laski, with whom he enjoyed an uneasy relationship, supported the campaign to boycott German goods. On the domestic front, although Guedalla endorsed the Board's official line that visible Jewish hostility would simply play into the fascists' hands, he was keen for it to pursue a more active anti-defamation policy and, in doing so, to collaborate with other Jewish anti-fascist bodies. In this regard, however, he found himself hamstrung by the aforementioned dearth of funds and, more problematically, by a lack of support from the upper echelons of the Board.

These frustrations eventually compelled Guedalla to resign his chairmanship in November 1935. Over the previous three years, he complained, the committee's work had become 'vastly heavier', yet there had not been a commensurate increase in the resources provided to it. Worse, there appeared to be active resistance to its work: of fifteen publications it had proposed, for example, only one had been approved.

Against Guedalla's express wishes, Laski had invited Philip Magnus, a Jewish former member of Mosley's January Club, to advise on defence issues, later appointing him to the Press Committee. The *Jewish Times* claimed that Guedalla was regarded as 'one of the opposition' by the Board's leadership. Certainly from his side there was little love for the Board as an institution, whose protracted decision-making process he found infuriating. Laski himself even apologetically acknowledged to Guedalla 'the inadequacy of the apparatus and weapons which have been given to you', but assured him that he had done all he could to provide greater resources.[72]

Guedalla's angry departure epitomized the discord within and around the Board at this stage. Waley Cohen, now fully recuperated, congratulated Guedalla on his decision to leave the 'absurd [Press] Committee' and reiterated his belief that the Board – whose 'quasi-political' machinations he too found exasperating – was ill equipped to combat antisemitism. Such was Waley Cohen's strength of feeling that he went as far as to urge Lionel de Rothschild not to put his name or entrust any money to the Board's defence work: he could 'not imagine a more disastrous course'. Instead, he resurrected his plans to establish 'a proper communal body trained up to do this work'.[73]

Jacobs, too, continued his agitation, publicly branding the efforts of the Jewish leadership 'cock-eyed' and 'make-shift'. At a meeting of the Board in early 1936, he attempted to introduce a motion to create an independent defence body. However, discussion of the matter was adjourned after Waley Cohen agreed to grant the president more time to put together a new policy.[74] Alexander Easterman, now no longer a deputy, joined the chorus of condemnation. In a letter to the *JC*, he described spending three fruitless years urging the Press Committee to abandon its '*laissez faire* attitude'. He, and many other Jews with journalistic experience, would have 'serve[d] gladly ... given the least glimmer of encouragement'; but their offers of assistance were constantly rebuffed, leaving them 'humiliate[d] and alienate[d]'.[75]

Despite this strident criticism, a change in the Board's approach was ultimately precipitated by pressure from another source. At an AJFS conference in June, a debate on 'strengthening the Community's machinery of defence' was held. There, a decision was made for the friendly societies, in the absence of adequate action from the Board, to formulate a defence policy of their own. Janner, the AJFS's president, prepared a scheme encompassing anti-defamation meetings and intelligence-gathering. But rather than implementing it immediately, he first presented the idea to the honorary officers of the Board, at a meeting between eleven leading figures from the two organizations, held at Waley Cohen's home in early July. There, a plan 'for the counteraction of Fascist and other anti-Semitic activities' along the lines suggested by Janner was agreed. Though the majority of this work would be carried out by the Board, the AJFS would be responsible for outdoor meetings and would be given representation within the Board's defence machinery.[76]

Later the same month, things came to a head publicly at a tetchy gathering of the Board, described by the *JC* and, more colourfully, in a letter from Laski to his father. Following a lively debate on the question of defence, which demonstrated the wide spectrum of opinions represented on the Board, a resolution to transfer defence activity to an independent body of the type suggested by Waley Cohen was moved by Moss Turner-Samuels – accompanied, Laski noted, by 'a most offensive personal speech'. It was seconded by Jacobs, who accused the Board's honorary officers of 'betray[ing] the community ... because of their egregious vanity, their lack of moral courage and their desire, above all things, to preserve their own privilege'. In response, Phineas Horowitz and Morris Davis 'condemned to all eternity' the rebels.

Finally, Laski spoke. He successfully persuaded the dissenters to withdraw their motion and accept the alternative scheme put forward by the AJFS, which had been approved earlier that day by the Board's Law and Parliamentary Committee. This established a new body within the Board, the Co-ordinating Committee (CoC), whose responsibility would be 'to deal with the general subject of Fascism, propaganda and cognate matters'. It was also agreed that Waley Cohen would be free to pursue his own plan independently, and that he would not raise the issue at the Board again.[77]

The president's motivation for taking action at this stage was threefold. First, of course, to maintain harmony within the Board. Ever the mediator, Laski conceded enough to ward off unrest, but not so much as to upset more conservative elements. The Board's secretary, Adolph Brotman, confided privately that the CoC had been designed to bring together the two sides. It would include representatives of both the 'activist' faction – the likes of Janner, Jacobs and M. Gordon Liverman – who favoured 'an open and even aggressive policy of countering Fascist activity', alongside those, such as Horowitz and Magnus, who were happier to pursue 'quiet defensive work'.[78] Laski, who would chair the committee, expressed his satisfaction that giving the rebels a stake in its success – 'convert[ing] the poacher into the gamekeeper' – had proved 'a very successful method of dealing with this problem'.

A second factor was the growing discontent across the wider community. It was vital, Laski confided to his father, to allay 'the obviously deep apprehension of a large section of the Jewish population in the East End'.[79] Such concerns, as we have seen, were pushing Jews to seek alternative sources of representation. So far, these had largely taken the form of existing political parties and workers' organizations – which, the CPGB apart, did not concern the communal leadership too greatly – or newly created defence bodies, which were often relatively small and limited in their scope of activity, offering little challenge to the Board's position. Now, however, a far more significant development was in the offing. A large conference had been called by the JLC for 26 July, at which 131 delegates representing eighty-seven Jewish working-class organizations would be present. Their declared aim was, in the absence of satisfactory leadership from the Board, to establish a popular alternative to it, one that would present a vigorous and unified Jewish response to fascism and antisemitism.[80] This mooted organization was potentially a genuine threat, and it appears to be no coincidence that Laski pre-empted its emergence by ushering through the formation of the CoC just a week before the JLC's gathering.

There was also a third, less cynical reason for Laski's change of heart. As evinced by his urgent tone during the aforementioned meeting with the home secretary earlier in July, he clearly appreciated that fascist campaigning had moved in a more dangerous direction, and sympathized with those Jews who were suffering as a consequence. Realizing the limitations of his own experience, the president had attended a BUF meeting in February 1936. In a private account of the event, he confessed to finding it difficult to 'adequately convey' the 'vulgar, abusive, provocative tirades' he had heard, and admitted that he had 'needed all my self-restraint, not only to refrain from interruptions, but to refrain from physical violence, so horrified, insulted and incited was I'.[81]

Laski also requested a report from the AJY to 'describ[e] the feelings of Jewish citizens on the attacks made upon them by the Blackshirts'. The resultant memo, which Laski forwarded to the home secretary, recounted the sense of alarm among Jews and the perception that the authorities were providing insufficient protection. The author concluded by warning that 'it will take very little to push them over the edge'. With no improvement over the following year, Laski reiterated privately that 'the situation in East London is causing me some anxiety'. He was particularly concerned at the fascists' provocative processions, and began to plan another deputation to Simon to press him for firmer implementation of recently passed public-order laws.[82]

Meanwhile, in a letter to the *JC*, Waley Cohen acknowledged the 'growing and justifiable anxiety among many sections of the Jewish community' at the 'campaign of calumny and falsehood … directed against the[m]' by fascist 'hooligans'. In the circumstances, 'it is not surprising that they are impatient to see the leaders of the community … establish without more delay adequate means of defending … against these calumnies'. 'The leaders of Anglo-Jewry,' he reassured them, 'are fully alive to the poisonous seriousness of the attack and are determined to concert measures which will leave no stone unturned in the wise and effective organisation of defence.' Discussing the Board's change of direction, Brotman explained to a colleague that as the BUF had previously not represented a direct physical threat to Jews, it had been felt that overt anti-fascism would simply provide Mosley with publicity. But the party's penetration into Jewish areas over 1935–6, accompanied by severe verbal and physical intimidation, had necessitated a new approach.[83]

This did not, however, mean that the Board would now take a radically different tack. Instead, the CoC's main role was, initially at least, to coordinate and bolster existing defence activity, which took four main forms: anti-defamation, intelligence-gathering, lobbying the authorities to restrict antisemitic activity and encouraging Jews not to engage in confrontational anti-fascism (the Board's more general policy of encouraging Jewish 'improvement' did not initially fall under the CoC's remit, but was regarded as an important element of the fight against antisemitism).

With regard to the first of these policies, propaganda work was greatly expanded, though still with the twin objectives of debunking antisemitic claims and informing the British public of the positive contribution Jews made to society. This message was propagated through publications, meetings, and letters to newspapers and public figures, often through third parties rather than directly from the Board. No one could accuse the Board of a lack of activity in this direction: in the late 1930s, it organized over 3,000 public meetings, distributed more than two million copies of various publications and sent out up to thirty letters a week.[84]

But many have deemed such efforts to be apologetic, as demeaning Jews in an attempt to prove their worth as citizens. Alderman goes as far as to argue that they may have 'strengthened the anti-Semitic cause', while Kusher describes such propaganda as nothing better than 'sugar-coated antisemitism'.[85] For its part, the Board was aware of such potential criticism, offering the response that, although 'one cannot hope to convert an anti-Semite', the majority of those who felt ill towards Jews did so 'not through prejudice but through ignorance'. It was therefore the Board's duty to ensure that all gentiles were furnished with the truth. Moreover, if 'lies are [left] unanswered' people assume them to be true and 'public opinion is formed from them'.[86]

An investigation into popular antisemitism, commissioned by the Board and conducted by the nascent social-research organization Mass-Observation, found that hostility towards Jews among M-O's nationwide network of 2,000 correspondents was 'almost unanimous' but not deeply rooted. Often, underlying prejudice against an abstract image of 'the Jew' (who was stereotyped as arrogant, greedy, clannish, scheming and so on) was tempered by greater contact with actual Jews. In one report, which M-O's researchers highlighted as typical, a man confessed, 'I do not like the Jewish race as a whole, though I have a few Jewish friends whom I like very much'. There was often even self-awareness at how irrational and unfair such prejudices were, and a desire to rectify them. One correspondent's statement is particularly revealing:

> My own opinion is that the Jew is as good as an Englishman[,] ... that he is neither better nor worse ... But, and it is a big but, I am aware that this opinion has been formed only by reading such books as Louis Golding's 'Jewish Problem', and by making a conscious effort to be fair and tolerant. Instinctively, I've got a prejudice against them ... I instinctively dislike Jews but am trying to teach myself not to.[87]

In this context, the efforts made by the Board (and indeed virtually all Jewish groups concerned with defence) to challenge the fascists' negative portrayal of Jews and to promote a more positive image no doubt had some effect, although precisely how much is impossible to quantify. Rubinstein is one who sees merit in this work, describing the Board's anti-defamation efforts as 'intelligent and valuable, [making] a rationally argued case against whatever anti-semitism was in the air'. He suggests that its public meetings, in particular, 'may well have done some lasting good'.[88] It is also worth noting that Golding's book – credited by the M-O respondent above as having had a particular impact and elsewhere praised by the *Zionist Review* for doing much 'to counteract the anti-Semitic influences that we know only too well are present' – had been funded by the Board.[89]

The CoC's most widely circulated publication, 'The Jews of Britain', of which over 300,000 copies were distributed, aimed to factually confute a wide range of typical fascist accusations. It answered questions such as 'How many British Jews are there?', 'Did they play their part in the war?' and 'Can they control the government?', while also providing quotes from prominent gentiles lauding the Jews' contribution to society. It finished with a reminder that 'the Jewish community in Britain is composed of law-abiding and peaceful citizens, proud of their citizenship and just as mindful of their obligations and duties as any other class'.[90]

Around fifty other titles were published between 1936 and 1940, dealing with the most common charges made by fascists against Jews, while the CoC also sponsored popular books on Jewish history and antisemitism by the likes of Cecil Roth and James Parkes, in addition to Golding. Distribution of publications often took place outside fascist meetings, and copies were sent to politicians, churches, teachers' associations and a variety of other public figures and organizations. The BBC's director of news agreed to broadcast 'subtle propaganda' on the Board's behalf, in the form of reports on Jewish events, religious holidays and the like. A series of thirty sets of speakers' notes on various topics was also produced, to provide those addressing CoC meetings 'ammunition' against fascist calumny.[91]

As the commissioning of the M-O study mentioned above suggests, the foundation for anti-defamation work was an extensive intelligence-gathering operation, which constituted the second plank of defence policy. It was deemed essential that all of the CoC's activity be based upon a comprehensive understanding of exactly what fascists and other antisemites were saying, writing and doing; where this was happening; and how and by whom their words were being received. To this end, the Board began to set up 'vigilance committees', a nationwide network of groups and individuals, both Jewish and non-Jewish, who sent reports on antisemitic activity in their region, which were collated and periodically presented to the CoC.[92] Additionally, numerous other individual correspondents, particularly in London, regularly reported to the Board on fascist activity, with some making substantial efforts to investigate antisemitic organizations and their supporters.[93] The Board also managed, as we will see in the next chapter, to establish a system of informants and moles within fascist organizations, who provided a stream of valuable intelligence.

Further information was provided via extensive high-level contact with the Home Office and police, to whom, Brotman noted, the Board enjoyed 'the readiest access whenever occasion demands it'. Laski, in particular, corresponded regularly with successive home secretaries and commissioners of the Metropolitan Police, as well as various politicians of all stripes. The flow of information travelled in both directions, with the president taking advantage of his privileged position to supply decision-makers with the latest reports of antisemitic incidents – which the Home Office found 'of the utmost value' – and to offer them the perspective of the Jewish community. Moreover, given that Anglo-Jewry was limited in what it could achieve independently to restrict antisemites – Laski angrily reminding one critic that 'the Board is not a police force' – constant pressure was applied on the authorities to take firmer action, and this formed the third prong of the CoC's policy.[94]

Though Laski's tone remained deferential in such exchanges, he had no compunction in frankly demanding stricter measures to be taken against the fascists when necessary, and even in criticizing the conduct of the police. The seriousness with which this aspect of work was treated – and the disparity between the Board's public calls for Jews to respect the authorities and its private attitude – was revealed in CoC correspondence from September 1936. The author remarked that, despite some recent improvement, the police had demonstrated 'a strong pro-Fascist feeling in their ranks'; in particular, it was absurd that 'a speech which is purely a stream of invective against Jews' could be treated as 'political', and thus be protected by law. Worse still, with the BUF importing 'the scum of the surrounding towns to fill their meetings … many streets in the East End [had been allowed to become] quite unsafe after dark for law-abiding citizens'. The Board wanted to avoid 'antagonis[ing] the Home Office', but it was now imperative that they be 'challenged to show that the

Police are adequately performing their duties'. To this end, the recipient of the letter, a left-wing Zionist, was asked to make these observations public.[95]

Soon after, Laski contacted the permanent undersecretary to the Home Office, Russell Scott, to inform him that the reports of official observers at antisemitic meetings in Finsbury Square were 'in considerable contradiction' to the Board's own information, suggesting that perhaps the police 'do not take the serious view which should be taken'. He reminded Scott that the only arrest made so far at this location, of Houston, had come after Laski's own intervention. The following March, he wrote again, this time criticizing the police's tendency to target Jewish hecklers, rather than the speakers, at antisemitic meetings. This was, 'to put it mildly, a little hard on the interrupters', given the 'gross' provocation they faced. In what was perhaps intended as a veiled threat, Laski reminded Scott that he had always defended the authorities, even in front of hostile Jewish East End audiences, but the situation now required 'such drastic measures as are permissible within the law'.[96]

This area of activity also encompassed lobbying for additional legal measures to restrict fascist and antisemitic activity, with one of the CoC's sub-committees dedicated solely to this issue. It immediately began to explore the possibility of modifying libel laws to cover the defamation of entire communities (as things stood, only individuals falsely maligned by fascists could take legal action, whereas slurs against Jews as a whole, however fallacious and offensive, were exempt).[97] Occasionally, the Board explored the possibility of bringing cases against antisemitic individuals or publications, but usually decided against any action.[98] This was in large part because the limitations of the law made securing a conviction difficult, as well as the fact that such cases allowed fascists a public platform from which to advertise their views and perpetuate their image of victimhood.

These problems had been aptly demonstrated during the trial of Arnold Leese in 1936 for ritual-murder accusations he had made against Jews in print. The IFL's leader was convicted on a lesser charge of creating public mischief, but found not guilty of seditious libel, making it appear that his allegations had some legitimacy. Moreover, the trial had thrust an otherwise obscure figure and his vile ideology into the limelight (Leese's defence included the claim that Jews were descended from the devil), while his decision to serve six months' imprisonment rather than pay a fine allowed him to claim 'martyrdom'.[99]

The case made Laski, himself a lawyer, wary of pursuing such avenues. In 1938 he discouraged a Jewish ex-serviceman from taking legal action against a fascist publication, stressing the slim chances of success and warning that 'it would only give publicity on a much wider scale to the infernal impudence and provocation of the [fascist] papers, which really have a very minute circulation'. Laski did, however, endeavour to remedy the situation, pressing the home secretary to revise defamation laws to prevent defendants from exploiting pleas of 'justification', as Leese had done.[100]

Once again, the relationship between Laski and the authorities was of mutual benefit, with officials and politicians keen to use the Board as a conduit through which to moderate the behaviour of elements within the Jewish community. In response to one of Laski's complaints, Scott retorted that even when fascist speakers used 'mild' language, 'offensive heckling on the part of Jews' often caused disorder. Game urged the Board to 'do anything to bring [Jewish anti-fascists] to a more sensible frame of mind', arguing that 'if deprived of publicity and more or less ignored, the BUF's wings would very soon be clipped'.[101] Similarly, at a meeting with the mayors of Stepney, Poplar and Hackney, Laski was informed that many Jews, especially those 'intermeddled with Communist activities', were closely involved in the current cycle of violence in the East End. They asked that he take 'repressive measures of a strong and immediate character'.[102] Herbert Morrison, leader of the London County Council, advised that Jews 'should keep in the background ... and leave it to the Gentiles to fight for them', stressing that it was the authorities' job to deal with the problem.[103]

It was such advice, in part, that informed the fourth strand of the Board's approach: imploring Jews not to involve themselves with militant anti-fascism.[104] This was not due to any lack of sympathy with those who felt compelled to take such action. In correspondence with the Home Office, Laski admitted that, from his own experience of hearing fascist speakers, 'any self-respecting Jew in the crowd would have the greatest difficulty in restraining himself, not only vocally, but even physically'. Sidney Salomon, secretary of the CoC, publicly excused Jewish assaults on fascists on the grounds that 'it is not human nature ... to stand calmly by while Blackshirts shout insults'. Even the Board's solicitor, Charles Emanuel, wrote to the *Times* to complain that while fascists may have been attacked by Jews, 'surely they have asked for it'.[105]

Yet from the more detached perspective afforded to the Board, it was also clear that a confrontational response was in many ways counterproductive. It first of all lent superficial substance to two of the justifications the BUF offered for its use of antisemitism: that it was being victimized by Jews and that the Jews were involved with subversive political activity, particularly communism. Moreover, Jewish anti-fascism, by helping perpetuate the cycle of political violence in London and elsewhere, brought further suffering on the Jewish community and boosted sympathy and support for the fascists, as we shall shortly see with regard to Cable Street. It also helped keep the Blackshirts in the headlines, as newspapers tended to report on their events only when disorder occurred, nearly always as a result of anti-fascist heckling or physical disruption.[106]

The Board's efforts to restrict fascist activity and restrain confrontational anti-fascism were very much in keeping with the approach favoured by the British authorities. There was, Thurlow finds, a 'near consensus' across a 'wide spectrum of opinion' within parliament and the state apparatus that the BUF was a troubling threat to civil liberties and public order, and in particular a menace to Jews. However, in contrast to the 'active' line favoured by many at the grass roots, those in positions of authority favoured a 'passive anti-fascism' that aimed not to tackle the fascists physically, but to 'isolate and marginalise the BUF through denying it the oxygen of publicity and to control its behaviour through changes in the law'.[107]

A further motivation to curb disruptive Jewish anti-fascism was that some of its expressions were illegal. The Board's efforts in this regard fitted a wider policy of 'improving' the conduct of certain elements of the community. It should be noted, however, that this was not initially an area that greatly concerned the CoC. Instead, it remained largely the domain of the Law and Parliamentary Committee, and was also pursued individually by leading communal figures. Only from around 1938 – when it was decided that it had become 'an integral part of the defence problem' – did the CoC begin to focus attention on what it euphemistically labelled the 'internal causes' of antisemitism, appointing a 'public relations' officer and establishing the Trades Advisory Council (TAC), which endeavoured to tackle the factors underlying ill-feeling towards Jews in trade, business and industry.[108] Even then, Waley Cohen, who had been made president of the TAC, warned the Board that Jewish behaviour was, in his opinion, responsible for 'not more than 10 percent of anti-Jewish feeling', and that more effort should be made to tackle 'the other 90 per cent which stemmed from ignorance and prejudice'.[109]

A common misconception is that the CoC's vigilance committees were intended primarily as a tool by which to scrutinize Jewish behaviour.[110] In fact, as noted above, their founding purpose was to observe antisemitic, and particularly fascist, activity (concern was even expressed within the CoC that in areas with no Jewish inhabitants, it was proving hard to establish vigilance committees to keep an eye on local fascists).[111] This always remained the primary aim, though their role was later expanded to include surveillance of potential Jewish misconduct, too.[112]

Nevertheless, the Board's improvement policy was intimately linked to its defence work. Much of the BUF's antisemitism exploited grievances against Jews that resulted from their alleged commercial and social shortcomings: Jewish landlords and employers mistreating their tenants and workers; Jewish businesses killing off gentile competitors with underhand practices; Jews being prominent in the vice trade and other immoral industries; ostentatious and vulgar behaviour. All of this supposedly stemmed from the fact that the Jewish character was incorrigibly alien and undesirable. While fascist accusations were usually selective, exaggerated or simply invented, similar complaints were also heard from friendlier sources.

At his abovementioned meeting with three east London mayors, Laski was warned that Jewish property agents 'resorted to every indecent trick and device, causing an enormous amount of trouble and a great deal of ill-feeling, this being cleverly turned by the Fascists into anti-Semitic feeing'.[113] These allegations were reinforced when, three days later, he met with Morrison and Harry Pollitt, who informed him that the practices of some Jewish landlords, small employers and shopkeepers were stirring discontent.[114] The Board received further protests from various professional groups about Jewish traders and employers, while a London magistrate lamented after the conclusion of one case that this was 'yet another instance ... of a Jewish tradesman cheating the public'.[115]

From a more disinterested perspective, Parkes, a clergyman and noted scholar of antisemitism, warned Laski that his research among East End residents had found 'an extremely critical attitude towards the Jews with whom they had come into contact', stemming from their social and economic behaviour. There was a widespread perception that Jews cared only that their actions were legal, without thought for their morality or the consequences for others. He and Father Grosser, an East End cleric active in the fight against fascism, urged the Jewish leadership to offer firmer moral guidance to the community on the 'un-Jewish' nature of certain activities – though they acknowledged that this would do little for the Board's popularity.[116]

The issue also exercised many elsewhere in the Jewish community. We have already seen 'elite' figures such as Montefiore and Hertz pleading for improved Jewish behaviour; even the popular 'Watchman', despite his humble roots, was not averse to offering paternalistic guidance. His new editor at the *JC* from December 1936, Ivan Greenberg, also expended great energy on the issue, using the newspaper as a pulpit to preach against the supposedly low ethical standards of Jewish businessmen, and condemning even 'vulgar displays' of wealth.[117] One correspondent described in a letter to the *JC* his 'shame' at the tawdry deportment of young Jews, regarding them as 'enemies in our midst, against whom we need defensive measures'. The secretary of Canning Town Synagogue wrote to the Board to warn that the unethical behaviour of a Jewish doctor – undercutting prices and opening on Sundays – was 'being used to advantage by Fascists', leading other local physicians to 'becom[e] quite understandably anti-Semitic'.[118] In Manchester, Gewirtz finds, the older generation of the immigrant community, who retained control of local Jewish institutions, also felt that it was up to 'Jews themselves … to eradicate some of the causes of anti-semitism' by 'conform[ing] to certain standards of behaviour'.[119]

Whatever the validity of such complaints, their sheer weight and the quarters from which they emerged compelled the Board to respond. As the community's representative body, it felt responsible for uncovering and curtailing any genuine cases of illegal or immoral conduct. This, in turn, it was hoped, would weaken at least one of the foundations for anti-Jewish sentiment. Again, this was not a new aspect of policy: the Law and Parliamentary Committee had long been monitoring trade disputes involving Jews, assisting when necessary to find 'amicable arrangements'. But such interventions now became more frequent and urgent. The 1936 Shops Act, which allowed limited Sunday trading by religious Jews, had established a 'Jewish tribunal' to deal with those alleged to have contravened the new regulations, and this was manned by prominent Jews nominated by the Board.[120] Laski himself publicly demanded that Jews needed to 'tidy up our own house', although he was at pains to stress that only a 'few individuals' were guilty of any misconduct and that the community should be judged by the same standards as gentiles, many of whom were also involved in disreputable behaviour.[121]

The glaring omission from the Board's approach – initially at least – was direct and visible opposition to fascism itself. In addition to the concern that this would draw attention to the BUF and feed its carefully cultivated image of victimhood, there were two further motivating factors. The first, another indication of the assimilationist mindset that prevailed at the heights of the community, was that Jews should avoid interfering in British politics *as* Jews. The Board jealously guarded its tradition of apoliticism, and was keen to ensure that Anglo-Jewry should not be perceived as a single interest group. In a memorandum discussing how best to counter the BUF's political ambitions, Percy Cohen, formerly chairman of the Press Committee and now a member of the CoC, recommended that

> whatever lines of policy we adopt must be in accordance with the status which the Jewish community occupies in … the public life and accepted traditions of the country[,] … [particularly] the governing principle of neutrality of Jews as Jews in

political affairs[.] ... Mosley's evident ambition is to create a Jewish problem, and we could assuredly play his game by fighting him as a Jewish Party. Our duty in these circumstances is to fight him on other lines ... [and] to remain politically neutral ... however great the provocation[.] ... Quite clearly, our safety as Jews and citizens depends on the strict observance of these conditions.

Moreover, fascism was a legitimate political ideology and the BUF a legitimate political party; Jews, therefore, had no right to oppose the existence of either. 'It ill befits a Jew,' Laski advised a colleague at the AJFS, 'to try to restrict freedom of opinion, however unpleasant that opinion may be'. All they were entitled to do was respond to antisemitism, but from whichever sources it emanated, not only fascist ones. 'We are free as citizens to defend our good name against those who assail it,' Cohen's report concluded, 'as long as ... [we] act in a constitutional way.'

On a more practical level, it was felt that fascism, despite the trouble it was currently causing in some areas, was not a significant long-term threat. It remained poorly supported, and was in fact regarded with disdain by the majority of gentiles, particularly its violent, explicit prejudice towards Jews. There was no possibility, many leading Jews believed, that Britain, with its long traditions of democracy and tolerance, would ever embrace this brutal, authoritarian and discriminatory ideology. While the authorities should be pressed to curtail the aspects of Blackshirt activity that most threatened the community – marches through Jewish districts, antisemitic speeches and other forms of 'Jew-baiting' – fascism could otherwise be left to fade into obscurity of its own accord.[122]

In 1936, Magnus prepared a report on British fascism that typified the perspective that prevailed at this stage. He argued that the BUF's recent shift towards more militant activity, accompanied by anti-Jewish propaganda aimed at 'simple and uninformed audiences', was a sign of desperation. Mosley was attempting to 'save the ship of his variegated political career from complete and final shipwreck' by moving away from the Italian fascist model, which was not antisemitic, to the German one. As such, the best course of action was not to attack fascism per se – 'with which, as Jews, we have no quarrel' – but only the aspect of it that concerned Jews, namely antisemitism. And rather than responding like for like to fascist agitation, 'the simple truth appears to be the best reply', in the form of counter-propaganda against Blackshirt lies. Jews had always been treated well in Britain, with its 'principles of freedom, tolerance and fair play', and should now endeavour to remind gentiles that they remained loyal and valuable contributors to society.[123]

While the Board was correct to deduce that fascism posed no realistic political threat, and that it thrived off the publicity that violent confrontation brought, the idea that one could so easily disentangle antisemitism from the rest of fascist ideology and activity was misguided and unsustainable. In mitigation, however, it should be remembered that, as was outlined in the first half of this book, the BUF's commitment to and relationship with antisemitism remained outwardly ambiguous at this stage. Its use had fluctuated greatly over 1935, as the movement struggled to settle on its future direction. Over the following year it did develop into the central plank of East End campaigning; but at the national level, only after Cable

Street did it become the dominant aspect of propaganda, and not until 1937–8 was it more comprehensively integrated into the party's wider programme. Meanwhile, as Magnus' report intimated, fascism's archetypal Italian manifestation remained at this stage publicly indifferent towards the Jewish question, suggesting that fascism itself was not necessarily the problem. However, as the East End campaign intensified over 1936–7, and as it became absolutely clear that antisemitism was intrinsic to and inseparable from the BUF's activity and ideology, the Board would come to make corresponding adjustments to its approach.

The establishment of the Jewish People's Council and the Battle of Cable Street

Despite the Board's new emphasis on defence, for the time being its leadership in this area continued to be rejected by certain sections of Anglo-Jewry. Often, though, this was not due to dissatisfaction at the actual form of policy. With the (admittedly significant) exception of a failure to explicitly condemn fascism itself, the scheme put together by Janner and Laski broadly corresponded to the demands of large parts of the community. It closely matched, for example, the proposals put forward by Watchman earlier in the year, which had proved popular among the *JC*'s readership. Tellingly, complaints directed against the Board after the CoC's formation tended not to demand a significantly different approach.

Two young, east London Jews, for example, wrote to the *JC* in August to complain of the Board's 'failing leadership' on defence issues. Yet the alternative proposal they put forward deviated little from the Board's strategy: a body should be formed under the auspices of the *JC* to organize publications and outdoor meetings, with the aim of debunking fascist propaganda; it would be 'absolutely non-political' and its members would be trained to maintain 'self control and ... keep the peace in all circumstances'. Another correspondent, from Liverpool, also called for a focus on anti-defamation, this time to be coordinated by the Zionists.[124] The following month, a new organization, the Jewish Council of Action Against Anti-Semitism, was formed in east London. Though closely linked to the JPC, its functions – researching and collating information to refute antisemitic claims and to advertise the Jewish contribution to British life, which was to be promulgated through meetings and publications – replicated those of the CoC. Indeed, it even distributed thousands of copies of the Board's pamphlets.[125]

The provenance of the above two letters – East End youths and a provincial Zionist – is particularly instructive. Much of the discontent expressed towards the Board's defence policy was rooted not in its substance, but its formulation and implementation – more specifically, that these were monopolized by a narrow and unrepresentative clique. Rapid changes in Anglo-Jewry's socio-economic, political, religious and geographical composition – largely a consequence of the mass immigration that had helped quadruple the size of the community over the preceding fifty years – had not been matched by corresponding reform of Jewish institutions, which were still dominated by the 'old' community.[126]

The Board, for example, drew the majority of its deputies from synagogues (only from 1919 had secular institutions begun slowly to be admitted), embodying, Rosenberg suggests, the assimilationist conception of a 'Jewish community in which its defining and single distinguishing characteristic was religion'. Stringent criteria were laid out for non-religious organizations wishing to elect deputies to the Board. For a friendly society to be eligible, for example, it was required to have at least 2,500 members; other stipulations included that 'the objects of the body should be Jewish' (i.e. not only its membership) and that it 'should not be political'. Even then, decisions were made secretively and could appear arbitrary. In 1936, the suggestion that Jewish trade unions should be granted representation was dismissed; two years later, an application from the Ex-Servicemen's Legion, which cooperated closely with the Board in defence work, was rejected.[127]

This all meant that secular Jewish groups – Zionist organizations, professional and trade bodies, workers' associations, veterans' societies, youth groups – which disproportionately represented working- and lower-middle-class Jews from the immigrant community, were largely absent from the Board. Grievances at this state of affairs had long been simmering, but it was the various crises of the 1930s, combined with the growing self-assertiveness of second- and third-generation immigrants, that brought them to the boil. With urgent action required to mitigate the threat presented to Jews by fascism and antisemitism at home and abroad, the absence of a leadership that adequately reflected the views of Anglo-Jewry was felt even more sharply, and the defence debate became a key battleground in the struggle for institutional reform.

Another correspondent to the *JC*, also from Liverpool, claimed that 'the growth of antisemitism in this country requires an overhauling of our communal machinery'; the current composition of the Board 'no longer represents the Anglo-Jewish community, and consequently is out of touch with rank and file'. This he blamed on the domination of the synagogues, to the exclusion of 'the large mass of Jewry which does not belong to the[m]'. He called instead for 'Jewish Communal Councils' to be established in every district, each reflecting the composition of the local community. These would be responsible for combating antisemitism in their area, under the overall coordination of the Board.[128]

There remained, however, a vocal section of the community that wanted defence activity to be pursued independently of the Board entirely.[129] At the JLC's conference in late July, A.R. Rollin, a leading trade unionist who was chairing proceedings, expressed his satisfaction that, 'as a result of the immense pressure of popular Jewish public opinion', the Board had abandoned its 'policy of inaction'. Nevertheless, he reminded delegates that the institution, which was constituted on 'an obsolete and often farcical basis of representation, does not represent the widest elements of the Jewish people in this country'; nor could they yet trust that there has been 'a sincere change of heart and mind … in [its] leadership'. There remained, therefore, the need for 'a strong and virile popular Jewish body to act as a driving force in our fight against the dangers confronting us'. His sentiment was seconded by Issie Rennap, the joint secretary of the JLC, who condemned the Board's 'ostrich-like policy', calling instead for the formation of a 'Jewish people's front'. A resolution was subsequently passed to form such a body, which was to include representatives of political organizations, youth groups, synagogues, ex-servicemen's associations, trade unions, Zionist bodies and friendly societies.[130]

It was this collective that became known as the Jewish People's Council Against Fascism and Anti-Semitism, setting out, as its name suggested, to combat not only prejudice against Jews, but also the political movement seen as primarily responsible for its newest and most dangerous forms. Jews faced a constant struggle against discrimination, a JPC publication observed, 'but *organised* anti-Semitism is used only by Fascism ... [and] only the defeat of Fascism will remove organised anti-Semitism'. To attempt to oppose merely the fascists' antisemitism would be to 'tackl[e] the symptoms without touching the disease'.[131] It was this feature of the JPC's programme that most obviously set it apart from the CoC at this stage, and both sides justified their position by claiming that the other's risked exacerbating anti-Jewish sentiment.

The Board feared that for Jews, who enjoyed a relatively secure existence in Britain, to make specific demands of gentiles for action to be taken against fascism would appear ungrateful, thereby arousing resentment. The JPC, by contrast, argued that it would be ungrateful for Jews to leave others to deal with the fascist threat, without offering any contribution themselves. Its view was that antisemitism was merely a 'smokescreen behind which Fascism plots the destruction of all those rights and liberties, social, economic, religious, cultural, etc., that today are enjoyed by people in democratic countries'. This meant that antisemitism 'has ceased to be a Jewish problem': 'the issue is not Jews versus their defamers, but Fascism against the whole people'. If Jews focused narrowly on combating only fascist antisemitism, they would 'isolate [them]selves from the people of this country – and thereby strengthen anti-Semitism'. While the Board believed that visible Jewish involvement in the anti-fascist movement would be to 'play [Mosley's] game', the JPC warned that to *not* participate would be to 'fall into the trap laid for the Jewish People by Mosley'. It was imperative that Jews forge alliances with like-minded gentiles, and play their part in this universal struggle. The Board's approach, the JPC argued, amounted to 'an acceptance of inferior status for Jews'; instead, the JPC aimed to cooperate with gentiles as 'equal speaking to equal'.

Moreover, in response to the Board's claim that for Jews as a community to oppose fascism could be construed as political interference, the JPC countered that it was the fascists themselves who had politicized the issue, by making antisemitism a central aspect of their programme. This left Jews no choice but to retaliate politically, by fighting fascism itself. As one member of the JPC's executive committee put it: 'We are not a political body, but that does not mean that when a certain party calls itself a political party and makes its main plank the fight against the Jews, that the Jews should not retaliate by attacking that party and the policy it stands for'. Furthermore, a pamphlet noted, if the BUF chose to treat Jews as an indiscriminate whole, then the JPC 'makes no apology for addressing Jewish voters AS A JEW'.[132]

These contrasting analyses would have been strongly influenced by the environments in which they were formed. Those in elevated positions at the Board, while well aware of fascist activity, remained distanced from it, making a patient, measured response more acceptable. Such a perspective was reinforced by the influential non-Jews with whom Laski and other senior figures had regular contact, who strongly advocated the restriction of fascism by non-confrontational means through the proper channels. As the community's representative body, the Board was in any case obliged to pursue a lawful and reputable line. Additionally, the privileged socio-economic position of the Jewish elites no doubt also made an optimistic prognosis of the Jews' position in Britain easier to reach. Those involved with the JPC, on the other hand, experienced fascist provocation first hand. They also had close ties with organizations that were actively engaged in the anti-fascist fight and who were calling on the working class to unite in this struggle. It is little surprise, therefore, that they felt compelled to play their part, and favoured a more urgent, direct approach.

In the two months following its formation, the JPC set about putting in place a structure and staff to coordinate its work. Only from mid-September, when it took up premises on Commercial Road in the East End, did 'real activities' begin. Almost immediately, it was called upon to undertake the most important operation of its entire existence, when, later that month, the BUF announced its intention to march through the East End on 4 October. Outraged, in particular that many areas of high Jewish population were on the proposed route, the JPC began to organize opposition to Mosley's plans.[133]

Initially, it attempted to persuade the authorities to prevent the event taking place altogether, gathering almost 100,000 signatures in the space of two days in support of a petition to the home secretary that drew attention to the BUF's 'avowed object … to incite malice and hatred' and called on him 'to prohibit such marches and thus retain peaceable and amicable relations between all sections of East London's population'.[134] The document was presented to the Home Office by a deputation comprising four senior JPC officials, as well as A.M. Wall, secretary of the London Trades Council, Ronald Kidd, founder and secretary of the NCCL, James Hall, MP for Whitechapel and St George's, and Grosser. Their demands were, however, rejected, on the grounds that prohibiting the procession would constitute a restriction of freedom of speech and allow Mosley to portray himself as a victim.

Disagreement subsequently emerged within the JPC's executive over the best course of action, with representatives of the Workers' Circle pushing hardest for an aggressive approach. As they formed the strongest faction on the council, their argument prevailed, and it was agreed that people should be encouraged to physically obstruct the fascists' path. A leaflet campaign and a series of street-corner meetings were quickly organized to mobilize support, with the JPC – alongside other Jewish allies such as EMAF and the Jewish Council of Action – becoming the driving force behind the counter-demonstration. Its role was especially significant given that institutions such as the Board, the Labour Party and the *JC* advised people to stay away from the event.[135]

More surprisingly, even the CPGB initially refused to endorse the protest, preferring instead to encourage attendance at a previously arranged rally at Trafalgar Square in support of Spanish Republicans. The party's leadership was, according to Joe Jacobs, keen to avoid association with the disorder that would inevitably arise in east London, advising that 'if Mosley decides to march[,] let him'. A Communist leaflet urged members not to respond to fascist provocation: 'Dignity, Order, and

Discipline must characterise the actions of the great masses of London people in their protest against Fascism'. Only under great pressure from East End members, particularly Jews, did the CPGB's leadership relent, agreeing at the last minute to support efforts to block Mosley's march. Even then, however, followers were warned to 'keep order', so as not to give the government any 'excuse ... to say we, like the BUF, are hooligans'.[136]

The actual events of 4 October have been described abundantly elsewhere, and there is little need to recount them here in great detail. Although estimates vary, a crowd of at least 100,000 protestors congregated in the East End to prevent the passage of Mosley's column of Blackshirts, which was only a couple of thousand strong. Around 6,000 police officers were deployed to keep the two sides apart, and to clear a path for the marchers. Having failed in the latter endeavour – in the face of determined, and often violent, resistance from the demonstrators – they advised Mosley to call off the procession, which he agreed to do. Around eighty anti-fascists had been arrested, at least seventy-three police officers injured – but the fascists did not pass.[137]

It is worth reflecting, however, on the wider significance of what Kushner and Valman describe as 'the most remembered day in twentieth century British Jewish history'.[138] The extent of Jewish participation in the demonstration cannot be gauged precisely. Police records show that of 133 arrests made in London at fascist or anti-fascist events in October (eighty-eight of them at Cable Street), only ten were of Jews. Among reports of individual arrests and ensuing court cases, a handful of Jewish names are apparent. Most prominent among them is the aforementioned Marks Barnett Becow, described by the police as 'one of the most violent communists in London', who received a three-month prison sentence for assaulting a police officer.[139]

But there is no doubt that the crowd contained a significant Jewish presence. This was the moment, Beckman recalls, when 'several thousand' ordinary Jews made clear – not just to their fascist tormenters, but also to the Jewish and gentile authorities that had been failing to protect them – that they 'were sick and ashamed of keeping their heads down'.[140] Moreover, they felt great pride that in doing so they were standing, literally, side by side with their fellow East End residents. Piratin claimed that 'never was there such unity of all sections of the working class as was seen on the barricades at Cable Street'; everyone 'from bearded Orthodox Jews' to 'rough-and-ready Irish Catholic dockers' played their part.[141] This sense of participation in a broad-based act of defiance, Benjamin Lammers argues, epitomized young Jews' 'rejection of the passive, almost hidden, Jewishness favoured by the Anglo-Jewish elites ... [and] demonstrated their vision of an inclusive Englishness'. For young Jewish communists, Kushner and Valman add, 'memories of the "Battle" were a crucial part of political and personal identities'.[142]

For some, Cable Street held another layer of meaning, fitting into a wider pattern of events at home and in Europe. Just as the fascists increasingly regarded themselves as participants in a historic, international struggle, so too many politically orientated Jews aimed to play an integral role in the progressive movement as it fought the forces of reaction across Europe. A JLC publication warned that victory for fascism in one country would mean 'a tremendous increase in Jew baiting all over the world'.[143]

Combating the threat of the BUF was, therefore, not only a domestic concern, but a way for Britain's Jews to support their co-religionists abroad. At Cable Street itself, the widespread adoption of the Spanish Republican slogan of 'no pasarán' ('they shall not pass') as a rallying call was a telling indication that the event was seen to transcend its East End setting. (Indeed, there was a significant number of Jews among the British volunteers who travelled to Spain to fight in the International Brigades.)[144] Jack Pearce, the secretary of the JPC, later wrote that the Cable Street demonstration had been 'the climacteric of a political development that had been maturing for some time', stoked by events abroad, in Germany and Spain, and by domestic unemployment and heightening tensions in the East End. What linked all these issues was fascism, which represented 'the greatest menace' both to Jews and to the wider working classes, binding the two together as the 'strongest allies' in the struggle against it.[145]

One should also remember that this was not just an East End affair. Young, working-class Jews across Britain enlisted in the battle against fascism. As well as travelling from around the country to support their comrades at Cable Street,[146] Jews also carried the fight to fascists in their own localities. Indeed, the events of 4 October were an almost exact replication, albeit on a larger scale, of a less celebrated incident in Leeds one week earlier. There, huge crowds had overwhelmed a Blackshirt rally in a confrontation that Cesarani notes 'was just as nasty' as Cable Street, and 'in fact far more bloody'. The JPC, in advertising the demonstration in east London, drew explicitly on the actions of its northern counterparts for inspiration, demanding that: 'What has been done in Leeds, must be done in East London!' On the same day as the Battle, violent opposition to the BUF was also manifested in Edinburgh and Liverpool.[147]

Over 1936, Leeds, like London, had seen a worrying growth in fascist provocation, 'giving rise', the *Times* noted, 'to intense indignation' among local Jews. Shops and businesses had been attacked, stickers bearing swastikas were plastered over walls, and uniformed marches occurred regularly – though physical assaults, at least, were rare. As a show of strength, the BUF called a huge rally for 27 September. First, a procession would be held, taking in many of the city's Jewish districts on its path, before finishing with a large meeting at Holbeck Moor, addressed by Mosley himself.

Protests were made to the authorities to stop the event taking place, including a petition signed by shopkeepers, both Jewish and non-Jewish, and a deputation led by various local luminaries. Although they failed to attain an outright ban, it was agreed that the march's route would be altered, so as to avoid areas of concentrated Jewish inhabitation. The Board, of course, urged Jews to avoid the event, broadcasting this appeal to synagogue congregations during the preceding High Holy Days period. By contrast, local Jewish Communists took a prominent role in organizing a counter-demonstration.

Although on the day the majority of Leeds Jewry did stay away, significant numbers, especially younger Jews, turned out to oppose the Blackshirts. As at Cable Street, a small BUF contingent, around 1,000 strong, was dwarfed by the gathered crowd, which numbered 20,000–30,000. And like in London, the protest quickly took a violent turn. One local Jew, interviewed by Bergen, admitted that he and his friends had attended because 'we liked a good fight against the fascists'. Whereas at Cable Street the police largely succeeded in keeping the two sides apart, Holbeck Moor saw a number of direct clashes, with the fascists coming off far the worse. As well as scuffles in the crowd, stones were hurled at the platform by protestors. Mosley, making a speech attacking 'Jewish corruption', was struck repeatedly by the hail of projectiles. At the meeting's conclusion, an ambush was made on the departing Blackshirts, leaving forty injured – at least nine seriously enough to be hospitalized – and leading to numerous arrests.[148]

The wave of violent, organized opposition that confronted the BUF in autumn 1936 – and above all Cable Street itself – has come to be regarded, certainly in popular perception, as a momentous victory for Britain's anti-fascists, and in particular the Jewish community. Beckman, for example, recounts how 'the effect on the fascists was devastating'; Cable Street 'proved to be the high water mark of the British Union of Fascists' hubris and arrogance[,] the very moment... the tide began to recede'. The South African-born Jewish Trotskyist thinker, Ted Grant, who had attended the protest, later recalled how 'it induced widespread despondency and demoralisation in the [fascist] ranks', and, as a consequence, 'the East End fascist movement declined'. Both writers argue that the event demonstrated how working-class unity and 'vigorous counter-action hinder the growth of the menace of fascism'. Kusher and Valman, too, claim that it was significant in 'showing [Jews] that... public protest could bring success'.[149] Yet while Cable Street did have certain negative consequences for the BUF, contemporary records reveal a very different picture from the mythology that has subsequently grown around the event.

In the immediate aftermath, the Blackshirts claimed that Cable Street had given fascism 'an immense impetus'. While normally one could dismiss such boasts as disingenuous bluster, in this case they contained some substance. As had been the case after Olympia, Cable Street provided the BUF with enormous publicity (even more welcome now than in 1934, as the press was suppressing reports of fascist activity). It also engendered sympathy for the fascists in some quarters, given that it had been their opponents who were almost completely responsible for disorder on the day. This, ran the BUF's side of the story, had been an entirely legal procession, approved and protected by the police, and planned in an area that contained many of the party's supporters; yet it had been forcibly prevented by an alliance of Soviet-inspired political radicals and foreign Jews, who, unlike the fascists, had failed to respect the rule of law, violently attacked the police, and caused chaos and enormous damage.[150]

The positive impact of Cable Street on the fascist cause was observed by Special Branch, whose monthly report for October noted 'abundant evidence that the Fascism [sic] movement has been steadily gaining ground in many parts of East London'. Police sources suggested an influx of at least 2,000 new BUF members in the capital, a considerable boost given that party membership in the city had been estimated at 2,750 earlier in the year. In the days after Cable Street, the BUF 'conducted the most successful series of meetings since the beginning of the movement', attracting crowds of thousands to events in Stepney, Shoreditch, Bethnal Green, Stoke Newington and Limehouse. Moreover, the meetings passed with little opposition and no disorder. Mosley himself made an 'enthusiastically received' address to an audience of 12,000 at Victoria Park Square, before marching with his followers to Limehouse, facing no disruption en route. By contrast, the Communists' efforts to consolidate on their victory had 'met with a very poor response', with attendances declining – and opposition increasing – at their meetings. 'A definite pro-fascist feeling has manifested itself,' the report concluded; 'the alleged fascist defeat is in reality a fascist advance.'[151]

This boost in popularity was relatively enduring. At March's LCC elections, BUF candidates won the support of over 7,000 voters in Bethnal Green, Limehouse and Shoreditch – a figure rendered even more impressive by the fact that only ratepayers were permitted to vote, thus disenfranchising much of the BUF's disproportionately young support, as well as many of the women who made up a quarter of membership. The party received around 18 per cent of all votes in these districts, and a significantly higher proportion of those cast by non-Jews. (In Bethnal Green, for example, Jews made up almost 20 per cent of the population, meaning that the BUF may have taken as much as 30 per cent of non-Jewish votes in the constituency.) The *Young Zionist* estimated, from the election results, that there were 20,000 fascist followers in the East End.[152] Seven months later, in borough-council elections, BUF candidates received a similar share of the vote in the same districts, despite their campaign not receiving any financial support from central headquarters.[153]

As this all suggests, rather than making life any easier for the East End's Jewish residents, Cable Street served only to aggravate the situation further. Indeed, its aftermath saw the most intensive phase of antisemitic campaigning in the BUF's history, justified on the grounds of Jewish involvement in the protest. A source within BUF headquarters reported that, in retaliation for the embarrassment the party had suffered, it would now embark on a 'renewed anti-Semitic campaign'.[154]

This was manifested, first of all, in increasing harassment of and violence towards Jews. Soon after Cable Street, a Blackshirt speaker declared, 'by God there is going to be a pogrom … [and] the people who have caused this pogrom in East London are the Yids'. True to his word, the next weekend saw the most serious single set of anti-Jewish attacks during the interwar period. In the worst incident, later labelled the 'Mile End Pogrom', a gang of 100–200 youths, some armed with iron bars and hatchets, looted and wrecked Jewish shops, overturned and set alight a car, and threw an elderly Jewish man and young child through a window. A similar episode took place on the same day in Bethnal Green.[155] This backlash was not limited to London: incidences of Jew-baiting increased in Leeds, while the *JC* described how the fascists had escalated their 'campaign of deliberate intimidation' in parts of Manchester.[156]

This growing physical threat was accompanied by a marked hardening of the BUF's rhetoric. As we saw in Chapter 2, immediately after Cable Street there was a large and sudden rise in the quantity of antisemitic material in the party's publications, continuing through to March's elections, which the BUF fought on an almost exclusively anti-Jewish platform. These developments were matched by increasingly vicious verbal attacks on Jews at the BUF's public meetings in the East End. In mid-1937, Game observed with concern that the 'abuse of Jews by Fascist speakers has shown a tendency to increase', and the issue continued to feature prominently in his monthly reports well into 1938. The JPC, too, noted that the LCC campaign had witnessed 'an intensification of fascist Jew-baiting and hooliganism', which, after a brief post-election lull, then developed into full-scale 'terrorism' over the summer.[157]

Compounding the problem was that the BUF increasingly held its meetings in localities inhabited almost exclusively by Jews, no doubt in the hope of inspiring more of the disorder that boosted the movement's fortunes. Laski warned Game that the regular fascist events conducted in Philpot Street and Church Street, which housed large synagogues, were of 'special nuisance value'. Even those Jews who attempted to stay away were now 'compelled to attend the meetings because the loud speakers used are such that every word spoken percolates into the houses'.[158]

Yet these developments should not be seen purely as a reflexive act of vengeance or a cynical attempt to further stoke ethnic tension (though both motivations would have played a part). They were also a response to – and an attempt to harness and amplify – what the BUF believed was genuine anger among some East End residents at the perceived Jewish role in the aggressive tactics of the Cable Street protestors. A set of guidelines for speakers published by the BUF in the build-up to the LCC elections advised them to take advantage of the fact that the

> strong sense of local patriotism in East London ... was gravely offended by the rioting of Jews and Communists last October[.] ... The impudent use of violence in the streets ... den[ied] East Londoners the right to walk through their own part of London ... [and] sent a wave of anti-Jewish resentment through East London.[159]

That this was not merely optimistic self-delusion is suggested by Special Branch's observers, who recorded that among the wave of new Blackshirt recruits after Cable Street were a 'large number of gentiles with grievances against the Jews'.[160] This impression was further substantiated by the party's relative success at the polls in 1937 on the back of its viciously antisemitic campaigning. Unsurprisingly, the BUF itself interpreted the result 'a mandate to Mosley to proceed with his anti-Jewish policy from the people best able to express an opinion on the subject, those who live next door to the Jews'.[161]

A final consequence of Cable Street, and one that has sometimes been regarded as a contributory factor to the BUF's demise, or at least to the diminution of its presence in the East End, was that the disorder of October focused public attention on the issue of political extremism, helping usher through parliament the Public Order Act (POA), which came into force in January 1937.[162] Yet serious doubts can be raised as to the effectiveness of the POA in restricting fascist provocation.

Among its various provisions, the act granted the Home Office greater powers to prohibit marches in the East End, and these were regularly invoked. But rather than diminishing the problem, the result was often simply to shift it elsewhere. In October 1937, for example, Mosley organized a procession in Bermondsey, just south of the river from the East End. Though little remembered, it was remarkably similar to, and perhaps even more violent than, Cable Street – further undermining the idea that the latter event set the BUF on a downward path. A vast crowd of anti-fascists, many of whom, like the Blackshirts, had travelled from the East End for the day, physically attacked the marchers and the police. 'London has not witnessed such bitter street conflicts in years', declared the *Daily Worker* – a claim borne out by other newspaper reports – indicating that the hostilities eclipsed those at Cable Street twelve months earlier. Over 100 arrests were made, predominantly of anti-fascists, with many Jewish-sounding names among them. Special Branch estimated that of 2,000 anti-fascists in a crowd outside Borough station, 75 per cent were Jews.[163]

A further hindrance was that the authorities' new proscriptive powers under the POA did not apply to outdoor meetings, which not only continued in the East End, but proliferated. In August–December 1936, 508 fascist meetings were recorded in the area; in the corresponding period a year later, the number grew to 647.[164] The POA also conferred greater powers on the police to prevent provocative racial language at such meetings. But these were often evaded through coded allusion (Clarke successfully appealed against a conviction with the defence that his use of the terms 'aliens' and 'Shylocks' was 'not intended to refer to Jews'), or were inconsistently applied by officers on the ground, leading Game to reprimand his subordinates in mid-1937 for their continued failure to fully implement his directives on Jew-baiting.[165]

Yet whatever the longer-term consequences of the Battle, there is no doubt that the immediate success of efforts to physically impede BUF events in London, Leeds and elsewhere in October – and the breadth and unity of opposition to fascism that they demonstrated – filled Jewish anti-fascists with renewed vigour. In the wake of Cable Street, the JPC 'took the offensive', organizing a campaign of meetings that aimed to stress to gentiles the dangers that fascism posed to them. One of its publications warned that the present racial agitation was merely a 'foretaste' of what was in store: 'Today Fascists attack the Jews; tomorrow Trade Unionists, Co-operators, Protestants and Catholics, Democrats and all freedom-loving people!' On 5 October it hosted an event at Shoreditch Town Hall, sharing a stage with Wall, Kidd and Grosser; a meeting in Hackney a month later drew an audience of 1,000. EMAF and the YCL, meanwhile, organized a march that attracted 1,500 participants.[166]

The JPC also had ambitions greater than simply organizing anti-fascist protests in east London. It opened branches in the north, north-west and west of the city, and began to publish a monthly bulletin, *Vigilance*. When the BUF was allowed the use of Hampstead Town Hall for a meeting, a gathering was held at the same venue a week later in protest and a delegation sent to the mayor on behalf of local Jewish residents. The JPC lobbied for legal measures to be taken against the wearing of political uniforms and the use of racial incitement, hosting a press conference on the subject in early November 1936 and putting forward draft bills on these questions. When the government presented its own Public Order Bill that month, it was criticized by the JPC for being too vague and difficult to enforce.[167]

These developments gravely concerned the communal leadership. Above all, they worried that the involvement of Jews in October's clashes presented an image of the community – as part of a violent mob that had attacked the police, forcibly prevented lawful events from taking place and was associated with communist agitation – that was not only undesirable in itself, but was one that the fascists were delighted to perpetuate.[168] The *JC* advised that Jews 'have nothing to gain, but everything to lose, by imitating the tactics of their enemies. They merely degrade themselves[,] … compromise the sovereign right of free speech and forfeit the sympathy of their friends'. The newspaper did, though, condone legal disruptive activity, in particular heckling, which had long been a tradition in British political life. Noting how meetings addressed by Joyce and

Raven Thomson had been forced to close due to clamorous opposition, the newspaper concluded that 'heckling and interruptions [are] effective weapons in deflating any anti-Jewish gasbag'. If one 'counter[s] the foul lies and slanders of the Fascists *immediately*', non-Jewish listeners would not take speakers seriously and meetings would quickly descend into farce.[169]

A further concern for Laski was that the broadening scope of the JPC's activity appeared to confirm that this new body presented a genuine challenge to the Board's position, fears that were exacerbated by the enthusiastic support the new organization was able to muster. By contrast, the Board's appeal for donations to its defence fund had met with a 'disappointing' response, it admitted, while early CoC meetings in the East End had been sparsely attended.[170] The president understood, however, that the problem sprung as much from grievances regarding the legitimacy of the Board as it did from the substance of policy. A letter from a CoC official expressed frustration that, despite the Board's new, more active approach, it remained 'in such ill favour in the East End'; he assumed that this unpopularity stemmed from a lack of knowledge of its work.[171] As such, Laski accepted 'that it was the duty of the Board to make itself better known to the Community', and to reassure its poorer elements that their voices were being heard.[172]

In mid-September, a meeting was organized by the Board in Shoreditch, attracting an audience of 1,500 or so local residents, who were provided details of the CoC's 'active campaign' and warned of the dangers of division in the Jewish ranks. Speakers with a presumed appeal in the East End were deliberately chosen: Janner, a Lithuanian-born ex-serviceman, former local MP and Zionist; and Morris Myer, owner and editor of the Yiddish-language, East End-based *Jewish Times*. Finally, Laski himself addressed the crowd, reassuring them that all shades of opinion were represented on the Board. He also took the opportunity to condemn the 'Jewish mushroom organisations' that claimed to be interested in fighting antisemitism, but were in fact 'rackets'. His speech, according to the *JC* at least, 'was punctuated by frequent outbursts of applause', the only serious dissent arising when he attempted to defend the record of the police. Salomon, the CoC's secretary, deemed the event 'a great success'.[173]

Two months later, Laski went even further in his efforts to compete with the JPC, arranging a conference to be held in the East End on exactly the same day as one that had already been organized by the Board's rival. Despite being announced at very short notice, Laski's event managed to attract an impressive 400 delegates from seventy different organizations, including youth clubs, trade unions and friendly societies. The president used the occasion, again, to 'outline in detail the activities and policy of the Board vis-à-vis the anti-Semitic campaign'. He had also intended the conference to lead to the establishment of a 'strong local Defence Committee in the East End' under the Board's auspices. Though the extent to which this was discussed on the day is unknown, Laski's plan would come to fruition a few months later.[174]

Interestingly, while the Board's conference was held in east London, drawing delegates from the area, the JPC also ventured into slightly unfamiliar territory, organizing its event in the West End. Despite Laski's attempts to discourage attendance, representatives from ninety-one organizations were present, and many voiced strident criticism of the Anglo-Jewish elite. One delegate claimed that while 'we represent the

Jewish masses ... the Board d[oes] practically nothing for the Jewish people'. He moved an emergency resolution – which was carried with only five dissenters among the 163 attendees – that condemned the Board's hostility towards the JPC, urging it instead to 'concentrate its energies on fighting our common enemy – Fascism'. In a further, thinly veiled attack, another resolution was passed deploring the 'policy [of] concentrating only against the defamation of the Jews ... [which] plays into the hands of the Fascists by making the issue one of the Fascists versus the Jews'. Instead, the JPC and its working-class allies reiterated the call for 'the Jewish people [to] stand in the front line of [sic] the attack waged by Fascism on democratic rights and liberties[,] ... co-operating with all the democratic forces in the country'.[175]

Communal Convergence, 1937–40

If we were to draw a line at the point we have reached so far, then the preceding account, other than offering greater scope, detail and nuance, does not differ radically from the established historical narrative. By late 1936, we find a community at odds over the question of fascism, with Zionists and Communists competing against one another; a variety of Jewish defence bodies pursuing a range of approaches to anti-fascist activity; the Board internally split and its leadership facing external criticism from all sides, including normally loyal quarters such as the *JC* and AJFS. The problem with the existing historiography, however, is that to a great extent it does indeed stop here, barely taking account of developments after 1936. This has, therefore, left the enduring impression of a community irrevocably divided, led by senior figures who were unable or unwilling to meet the demands placed upon them, in particular to confront the challenge of fascism directly. Yet this picture is misleading: in actual fact, significant developments took place over the following years that transformed Jewish defence and intra-communal relations. This chapter, by exploring this subsequent period comprehensively for the first time, will challenge the established version of events.

It will, first of all, demonstrate how Jewish attitudes towards fascism evolved significantly over the late 1930s, and the ways in which this consequently influenced the form and efficacy of anti-fascist activity. In particular, this will encompass a reassessment of the approach pursued by the Board of Deputies. In the literature on the subject, the Board has been almost unanimously condemned, with researchers variously describing its efforts as 'naive', 'apologetic', 'complacent', 'arrogant', 'apathetic', 'lack-lustre', 'timid' and 'condescending', motivated by an 'extreme reluctan[ce] to combat anti-Semitism'. Indeed, some even argue that its work was not only ineffective, but, by taking fascist slanders at face value and apologetically admitting to alleged Jewish shortcomings, actually counterproductive.[1]

Yet what should have already begun to become clear is that such a negative analysis is, at the very least, exaggerated. As we saw in the previous chapter, the initial defence policy implemented by the Board and its allies was not lacking in breadth, endeavour and, in some areas, ambition. The CoC's anti-defamation and monitoring policies broadly conformed to the demands of the community, while its lobbying of the Home Office and police – Britain's most potent anti-fascist forces – was effective.[2] And the 'improvement' efforts so criticized by historians were not initially part of the Board's defence policy (and even once they were, remained of secondary importance behind intelligence-gathering, lobbying and propaganda). Moreover, while easy to criticize with hindsight, attempts to mitigate certain types of Jewish behaviour were pursued at the urging of many senior figures in politics, law enforcement, trade and industry, as well as a significant number of Jews.

Additionally, aspects of the Board's approach that some have regarded as signs of weakness can just as easily be interpreted as prudence. Encouraging Jews not to attend fascist events or seek out conflict, for example, may have been unpalatable to many, but it was an effective way to break the cycle of violence that, as was shown in the wake of the Battle of Cable Street, boosted the BUF and caused Jews to suffer further. Indeed, as we will see below, many Jews who had been actively involved in organizing that particular event quickly realized the negative consequences of their actions, and radically changed course. Moreover, the secrecy with which the CoC conducted its affairs may have lent an appearance of passivity to outside observers, but was very much a necessity given the sensitive nature of some of its activity.

Yet even if one wishes to dispute negative assessments of the Board's early defence policy, it is undeniable that the central criticism levelled against it – that it failed to include measures directed against fascism itself – remains largely valid if one looks only at events up to the end of 1936. As we have seen, in that year senior figures within the Anglo-Jewish leadership were determined to separate antisemitism, which was to be combated, from its fascist promulgators, whose free speech and political freedom should be respected. However, the failure of historians to take account of later developments has led them largely to miss the significant transformation in the Board's approach that subsequently took place. As will be shown below, it was quickly accepted by Laski and others within the Board's defence apparatus that a neat separation of fascism and antisemitism was unfeasible, and that tackling the latter would inevitably involve taking measures against the former. As such, a directly anti-fascist policy was developed that, far from being limited, naive and inflexible, was comprehensive, sophisticated and constantly evolving.

Where these efforts to combat fascism itself have been acknowledged in the historiography, they receive little attention, overshadowed by a far greater focus on more 'apologetic' policies,[3] dismissed as part of an attempt by the Jewish elite to police the community,[4] or presented as secretive activity of which little is known.[5] Moreover, where it is admitted that the CoC did eventually convert to the anti-fascist cause, it is usually claimed that this happened only very late in the day.

Kushner, for example, argues that the Board 'refused to protest directly against the anti-Semitic threat to Jews, [leaving] the working class Jewish community … to deal with the problem itself'. 'Not until 1939 did [it] realise the unreality of its approach and actually begin to defend democracy', and only once the war had begun did it finally start to cooperate with the JPC. Similarly, Copsey maintains that Laski always 'refused to accept that fascism and anti-Semitism were integrally connected', and that under his leadership the Board 'remained resolutely opposed to direct action against fascism[,] … keep[ing] the response of the Jewish community focused on anti-defamation'. He, too, claims that the Board modified its approach only after the outbreak of war, citing as evidence Laski's attempts to infiltrate a mole into the BUF.[6] Yet in fact, as we will see, Laski's first mole was in place by late 1936, and it was from this time that his, and the Board's, attitude to fascism began to change. Moreover, private discussions with the JPC – which will be detailed over the following pages – begun within weeks of its establishment in 1936; and by 1938 the two organizations were collaborating with one another on defence activity (with this cooperation actually ending, not beginning, with the outbreak of war, when the JPC dissolved itself).

Improving relations with the JPC were representative of another significant set of changes that contradict traditional accounts. A second consequence of the historical focus on 1936 has been to skew perceptions of the impact on the Jewish community of the defence debate, which was at its most antagonistic that year, making it appear far more divisive than it really was. In actual fact, the vociferous criticism the Board received in the build-up to the establishment of the CoC, and the threats by Jews to seek or establish alternative forms of representation, soon subsided. Though certain elements continued to favour a more confrontational approach to fascism, they became an increasingly small minority; where other groups, such as the Zionists, expressed hostility towards the communal leadership, defence was actually one issue on which they tended to respect the Board's authority. Meanwhile, over the latter years of the decade Laski was able to rally practically all sections of the community behind his leadership on defence.

These two developments – the hardening of the Board's anti-fascist position and improvements in communal relations – were closely tied to one another; indeed, they were mutually reinforcing. As it became increasingly clear that the Board was prepared to confront domestic fascism directly, a growing number of Jews were willing to fall behind its leadership. Their voices, which were now given a greater hearing within the Board's defence apparatus, in turn helped to influence the direction of anti-fascist policy. At the same time, many Jews who had previously engaged in direct confrontation with the fascists now began to realize the dangers of such activity, and consequently moderated their approach – making accommodation with the Board easier. These various processes symbolized a convergence among the disparate elements of Anglo-Jewry, as they moved towards a shared understanding of the fascist threat, general agreement on a core of policies that should be pursued in their defence and a consensus that these were best conducted under the auspices of the Board. Throughout this chapter we will explore these developments in detail, beginning with perhaps the most striking rapprochement, that between the erstwhile adversaries, the Board and the JPC.

Early relations between the Board of Deputies and the JPC

Despite the public sparring between Anglo-Jewry's two main defence organizations in late 1936, behind closed doors tentative negotiations had actually already been taking place between them. Though these proved abortive, they were conducted in a congenial spirit and demonstrated a willingness on both sides to come to an accord. It had been the JPC that made the first move, approaching the AJFS – which, as we have seen, was working closely with the Board on defence – in August 1936 'with a view to co-operation'. Leading figures from the two organizations met and, convinced of the JPC's desire for collaboration, the AJFS arranged a second gathering, this time attended by leading figures from the Board, including Laski.

According to the JPC's version of events, it 'offered to place itself under the control of the Co-ordinating Committee ... [but] was refused on the ground that the Board could not accept any organisation fighting Fascism'. Proposals to exchange speakers or to jointly distribute CoC publications were also rejected. Nevertheless, the two sides left on good terms, with Laski declaring that 'we part as friends' and Salomon adding, 'if we can assist you with information at any time, we shall be pleased to do so'.[7] A further meeting, this time with EMAF also invited, was held in October; then in February 1937, Redcliffe Salaman, a prominent scientist and Zionist, brought together the Board and JPC for another discussion. But with the activist anti-fascists 'refus[ing] to remove political colour from their campaign', neither summit produced a positive outcome, the AJFS recorded.[8]

Evidently, the chief sticking point was the JPC's overtly political opposition to fascism. But Laski also had a number of other concerns, which he outlined privately to the CoC: the JPC's close relationship with the Communists; its pursuit of an approach that he believed imparted the image of Anglo-Jewry as being a state within a state; and the fact that its lobbying on the POA arrogated 'functions which only the Board was entitled to exercise', risking damaging Laski's relationship with the Home Office.[9]

Yet Laski's fears were overblown, and the two sides were in actual fact not as far apart on these issues as they seemed. From the start, the JPC had expressed a willingness to work alongside the communal representative body, making explicit that it did 'not wish to usurp the function of the Board', but merely to encourage it to take up an anti-fascist position.[10] Moreover, there was significant overlap between the two organizations' aims. On its founding, the JPC had outlined its three central objectives as:

> 1. To unite the Jewish People in their own Defence against Fascist attack; 2. To co-operate with all anti-Fascist organizations; 3. To point out to the British people the dangers of anti-Semitism, since through Jew baiting the Fascists intend to destroy the liberties of the whole of the people.[11]

On the first issue, plainly the Board shared the aim of presenting a unified Jewish response (albeit under its own auspices, but this was something that the JPC was willing to accept). On the second, too, the two sides took a very similar approach, though initially misinterpreted each other's position. As we have seen, the Board believed that the overtly 'Jewish' nature of the JPC's campaigning, as well as its association with left-wing groups, made Jews appear a single, political entity. The JPC, in turn, interpreted the Board's approach as call for Jews to take a back seat and leave gentiles to do the work, thereby isolating themselves. Both sides, in actual fact, wanted exactly the same thing: for Jews to fight antisemitism not only as Jews, but as part of a wide coalition of democratic forces.

Although the JPC had links to the CPGB – through overlapping membership and activity[12] – there is no indication that the former took orders from the latter. Indeed, as the build-up to Cable Street had demonstrated, the two pursued independent lines.[13] The JPC, moreover, regularly made clear that its position was only political in so far as it opposed any antisemitic political party (a stance the Board also came to adopt). It did not promote or officially favour any particular ideology of its own, other than democracy in general, stating: 'No body claiming to represent Jewry can become identified with any political party or grouping, for Jews belong to all political parties … [The JPC] is essentially non-political'. Again, an identical position to the Board.[14]

Of course, given the background from which many JPC members were drawn, its analysis of fascism had a left-wing flavour. But this did not deter it from seeking collaboration with a wide range of groups and individuals. In April 1937, for example, it co-organized a conference on fascism and antisemitism with the NCCL that attracted representatives from churches, synagogues and the Labour and Liberal Parties. The welcome address was given jointly by Moses Gaster, *hakham* of London's Spanish and Portuguese congregation, and Walter Matthews, the Dean of St Paul's. The next year, the Conservative and Liberal parliamentary candidates for Whitechapel shared a JPC stage.[15]

In a similar vein, many figures associated with the Board had overt political loyalties (there were even some MPs on the CoC), but their defence work was also formally divorced from any particular ideology. And like the JPC, the Board set out to establish contact with as wide a range of individuals, groups and institutions as possible. This often took it to unexpected places, not least when Laski invited the general secretary of the CPGB for a private meeting in October 1936. This encounter has been partially described elsewhere, but accounts focus only on the advice Laski received relating to Jewish commercial misconduct in the East End.[16] In fact, the primary purpose of the meeting was to obtain Communist support in hampering fascist activity in the East End.

In the wake of Cable Street, Laski had convened with Herbert Morrison, the Labour leader of the LCC, and Louis Gluckstein, a Jewish Conservative MP, to hold 'a full and frank discussion on the situation in the East End'. Morrison declared that, because the BUF was thriving off the conflict it had provoked, he was keen to persuade his supporters to stay away from fascist events. But, he believed, this would be of little use unless the Communists did the same. Accordingly, he and Laski arranged, through Harold Laski, to meet with Pollitt the very next day.

At the outset, Neville Laski proposed that he, Morrison and Pollitt could 'use our joint and separate influences to keep those over whom we might be deemed to have some control off the streets and [away] from [the] meetings and processions of Mosley'. To Laski's surprise, Pollitt 'sympathised' with the idea. But, regrettably, he felt it would be impossible to convince his followers of the merits of such a policy. He expressed his willingness, though, to limit Communist activity in particularly volatile areas (and the police did note a significant reduction in Communist meetings in east London the next month). Pollitt also suggested organizing a public gathering to be jointly addressed by Communist, Jewish, Labour and church representatives, an idea Laski felt had 'some genius' to it.[17]

With regard to the JPC's third and final objective – persuading the British public that antisemitism was merely the thin end of the fascist wedge – the Board again pursued a similar line. Its guidelines for CoC speakers advised them to warn gentiles that 'the stirring of racial hatred ... [threatens] the sacred liberties for which Britain has [always] stood', and that therefore 'all right-thinking men and women [should] stand shoulder to shoulder in defence of democracy and humanity'.[18] Laski himself publicly described opposition to fascism as the 'struggle of humanity ... against forces which are not only anti-Semitic, but which seek to destroy every element of liberal, democratic and progressive thought and action'.[19]

It is also important to note that, despite its prominent role in the build-up to Cable Street, the majority of the JPC's work was remarkably similar to the Board's (indeed, the demonstration at Cable Street had not even been its preferred option: initially it had lobbied to have the fascist march banned and, even after this was unsuccessful, its executive was divided over the merits of physical opposition). It, too, undertook an 'educational' anti-defamation campaign, designed to correct antisemitic falsehoods. Its publications – with titles such as 'Fascists say the Jews want War! What are the Facts?' and 'Fascism is Responsible for Refugees' – were often little different to the CoC's. Over a quarter of a million such leaflets had been issued in its first year, the JPC claimed, and hundreds of meetings were held around London.[20] Its leading figures, particularly Rennap, regularly wrote to newspapers in response to letters from BUF supporters, providing evidence to refute their 'slanders and misrepresentations'.[21]

Even on the biggest obstacle to collaboration – the question of how to deal with fascism – a gradual evolution of both sides' positions brought them closer to one another. As had been demonstrated during the internal disagreements in the build-up to Cable Street, many within the JPC's leadership had never been completely comfortable with confrontational tactics. And the intensification of the BUF's anti-Jewish activity in the wake of the event would have made it increasingly apparent to others on the council that such an approach could do more harm than good. In June 1937, an observer noted the JPC was 'becoming more moderate in its views'.[22] When the BUF organized its Bermondsey march in October, the JPC appears to have taken a neutral stance on Jewish involvement in the counter-demonstration, neither advocating nor discouraging it.[23] The Council's publications do most to reveal its dramatic change in direction. One warned supporters not to disrupt an upcoming Blackshirt meeting, declaring that this would be 'just the denial of Free Speech that the fascists want. DO NOT FALL INTO THEIR TRAP!' Another noted that the BUF's 'purpose is ... to cause disorder and incite breaches of the peace'. It advised anti-fascists to complain to MPs, mayors and the Home Office, rather than confront the fascists directly.[24]

This shift coincided with a wider decline in organized disruption of BUF events. The other main anti-fascist force, the CPGB, had by this stage firmly embarked on its 'Popular Front' campaign, aiming to bring together as broad a range of anti-fascist forces as possible. This necessitated an abandonment of the aggressive approach to fascism that tarnished its image in respectable circles. From June 1937, Copsey notes, the party made particular efforts to persuade its members to stay away from fascist events, or at least to avoid violent disruption of them. A Communist leaflet advised East End Jews that 'discipline' was the 'correct attitude' to take in response to 'Mosley's provocation'; if fascist meetings were simply 'left alone' the BUF would 'decline still further'. At the same time, a growing number of East End Communists were in any case beginning to abandon physical confrontation in favour of the policy, advocated by

Piratin and other local leaders, of tackling the underlying socio-economic issues that made fascism attractive to many local residents.[25]

In August 1937, the Metropolitan police were called upon to intervene to prevent potential breaches of the peace at just five of the 530 fascist and anti-fascist meetings held in London. The same month, EMAF abruptly disbanded, due to internal discord and a shortage of funds – both factors suggesting diminishing support for the type of activism it had previously pursued. In November, Game noted that 'the Communist Party and the Jewish Anti-Fascist movement have conducted no special anti-Fascist activities', describing the month as 'the most uneventful since the commencement of these reports [in August 1936]'. By spring 1938, he had concluded that the anti-fascists now 'realise that active opposition is more likely to assist the Fascist cause than to hurt it'.[26]

Finally, the period 1938–9 saw the JPC pay growing attention to international, rather than domestic, events, in particular the ever-worsening persecution of Jews in Central Europe and Italy, the refugee problem this was creating and the growing prospect of war. It now made regular charges that the BUF was simply an extension of German Nazism, proclaiming that ' "British" Fascism uses anti-Semitism in its attempt to introduce Nazism in this country'.[27] This was another perspective that united the various elements of Anglo-Jewry, nearly all of whom came to perceive British fascism through the lens of international developments, in particular as a vehicle through which the Nazis aimed to stir racial animosity in Britain.[28]

The Board's anti-fascist campaign

The JPC's evolution over this period was paralleled by even more striking developments taking placing within the Board's defence apparatus – in particular an increasing willingness to oppose fascism. Just as the JPC accommodated a variety of views within it, with a gradual erosion of the initial majority who favoured disruptive anti-fascism, so too the balance of power swung on the CoC, as those in the centre ground between the conservatives and the 'activists', most notably Laski himself, began to move towards the latter camp.

A willingness to target the fascists directly had become apparent in the Board's activities as early as 1936. Initially, this had largely been for practical reasons: it was quickly becoming apparent that combating fascist antisemitism would inevitably require some measures against those responsible for it. As already noted, a private complaint by Laski to the Home Office had led to the arrest of Houston in 1936, while the president's constant harrying of Simon and Game contributed to stricter police measures against the fascists. The same year, the Board also explored the possibility of bringing legal action against the antisemitic journal *Truth*, published by Graham Seton Hutchison, a former BUF member who subsequently became involved with a variety of radical-right groups. But, following the fiasco of Leese's trial, which the Board had also supported, these plans never came to fruition. The Board did later assist a company, Horatio Myer Ltd, in bringing a libel case against *Blackshirt*, with Cyril Picciotto, chairman of the Board's London Area Council (LAC), representing the prosecution in court. The newspaper was found guilty, forced to issue a front-page apology and retraction of its claim (that the company was founded and run by aliens and abused its staff) and to pay costs.[29]

Propaganda also began to target the fascists more directly. In September 1936, the Board published – and arranged house-to-house distribution of – 50,000 copies of an article by George Lansbury, MP for Bow and Bromley, entitled 'Anti-Semitism in the East End'. It attacked the BUF's 'terrible doctrine of hatred', drew attention to its intimidation of east London's Jews and accused the authorities of bias towards the fascists. Another publication, 'Fascists and Jews', was handed out among crowds at fascist meetings in the East End, while a motion put forward by Laski to ask David Low, the famous political cartoonist, to provide 'anti-Blackshirt' posters was approved by the CoC. By 1937, as part of a campaign against the BUF in March's LCC elections, a leaflet was released drawing attention to some of the hypocrisy behind Mosley's rhetoric: that in the 1920s he had criticized fascists as 'black-shirted buffoons', in 1933 had claimed 'fascism is in no sense anti-Semitic' and that his 'Super-British Party get[s] its money from non-British sources'.[30]

The explicitly anti-fascist nature of the latter publication caused some consternation on the CoC, with certain members expressing concern that its 'political tendencies ... were not in accordance with the traditions of the Committee's publications'. Clearly the development of a more direct defence policy was stoking tension, and its subsequent continuation was indicative of the conservative faction's increasing marginalization. Philip Magnus, the former January Club member, stopped attending CoC meetings in October 1936, while Phineas Horowitz announced his resignation from the committee in July 1937. He was eventually persuaded to remain, but took a less prominent role thereafter.[31]

These developments reflected the fact that a more substantial shift was taking place in the Board's underlying analysis of fascism. In March 1937, Laski confided to a colleague that the CoC was now prepared 'to deal with the Fascist programme', as long as it was not done in the Board's own name. A year later, he expressed satisfaction that Game was 'most strongly anti-fascist[,] ... in entire sympathy with the view [we] had laid before him'.[32] This change stemmed from a growing belief within the CoC that 'the fight against anti-Semitism [was] identified and co-extensive with the fight for democracy'. Because the fascists attacked Jews as part of their campaign to undermine Britain's tolerant, democratic traditions, this meant that the issue now 'transcend[ed] the wrongs or oppression of any particular race of creed ... [and was] one of general humanitarian principle'. Jews, therefore, were entitled to fight back against fascists without being seen to be acting in pursuit of purely sectional interests.[33]

Indications of this new approach were evident in the build-up to the local elections of 1937. Cohen's memorandum on dealing with the fascists' political ambitions, mentioned earlier, had made a careful distinction: though Jews should remain politically neutral as a whole, 'we are free as citizens to defend our good name against those who assail it ... [and] to advise Jewish voters or to supply information on the Jewish questions to those who need it and seek it'. This included the right to 'criticise, canvass against, question or speak against any Fascist candidate'. On these grounds, the Board resolved not to support any party in particular, but to 'give such assistance as was necessary' to anyone standing against a fascist, and to produce and distribute 'leaflets exposing Fascist tactics'.

As we have seen, precisely such leaflets were disseminated in the build-up to the LCC elections. Later in the year, during campaigning for October's borough-council elections, 600 LAC volunteers canvassed Jewish voters; on polling day, 160 cars were used to ferry them to cast their vote (a significant factor in boosting anti-fascist turnout, given the poor weather). In a further sign of convergence, this activity matched closely the JPC's approach to the same election. It accused fascist candidates of standing 'on the contemptible basis of anti-Semitic lies' and urged Jews to 'vote anti-Fascist', rather than for any specific party.[34]

Over the following years, the CoC kept meticulous track of all prospective fascist parliamentary candidates, and provided assistance to those standing against fascists in three by-elections in 1940.[35] Meanwhile, publications became progressively more explicit in their condemnation of the BUF.[36] A favourite tactic was to publicize criticism of the party by former members. Charles Wegg-Prosser, a BUF candidate at the LCC elections who had subsequently abandoned Mosley, was approached by Salomon with a request to use his resignation letter in a CoC leaflet. The ex-Blackshirt agreed, and even offered to write an introduction. In the publication, entitled 'The BUF and Anti-Semitism: An Exposure', Wegg-Prosser described the BUF as 'the negation of everything British': it shamelessly imitated a foreign creed and ignored British traditions of tolerance to 'side-track the demand for social justice by attacking the Jew'. (Wegg-Prosser also worked with the JPC, publishing an article in its journal and speaking at meetings.)[37]

While the Board's name was deliberately left absent from the vast majority of its publications, far more conspicuous work was carried out by its East End defence body, the LAC. Established in stages over 1937, and taking up offices on Whitechapel Road, it aimed to 'fight Fascism systematically' in the East End, coordinating its activity with other local organizations pursuing the same end. Though a subsidiary of the CoC, the LAC was granted a degree of autonomy in its work. Given that the majority of those on the council were representatives of friendly societies, youth and student groups and ex-servicemen's organizations, it often took a far more direct and active line than its superiors were comfortable with. This regularly caused friction between the two bodies (at one stage the entire council tendered its resignation in protest at interference from above), but also helped push the CoC in a more anti-fascist direction.[38]

The LAC's primary function was to organize the Board's outdoor-meeting campaign in the East End, responsibility for which was formally passed to it by the AJFS in June 1937.[39] Here, the aim was to neutralize fascist propaganda as directly as possible by shadowing the Blackshirts. Meetings (around 50–60 of them a month, on platforms inscribed 'The Board of Deputies of British Jews: Anti-Defamation Campaign') were held in the wake of (or occasionally simultaneously to) fascist ones at the same location. As such, speakers often faced 'very hostile' audiences, and even physical violence, necessitating the employment of stewards, who were provided by the Jewish Ex-Servicemen's Legion. Many LAC speakers relished such antagonism, occasionally inviting opponents on to the platform to debate with them. One report noted with satisfaction that a fascist heckler had 'made an ass of himself' after ten minutes on stage with the speaker. In this regard the Board was more effective in presenting to gentiles the Jewish response to fascist propaganda than was the JPC, which generally focused its activity on Jewish areas and attracted sympathetic crowds. Attendance at meetings varied greatly, ranging from thousands to just a handful of listeners. (Low turnout was actually seen as a positive sign, indicating that the 'Jewish question' had become less acute in the area concerned.)[40]

Although it is impossible to assess with any precision the effectiveness of the meetings campaign, the CoC itself believed that through such efforts the LAC had 'literally fought the Fascist open-air campaign to a standstill'. The *JC* agreed, stating that follow-up meetings after fascist events had been the most significant factor in the decline of the BUF's East End activity.[41] Similarly, the *Zionist Review* praised the 'valuable work of enlightenment' being undertaken by the CoC, and later ran an advertisement appealing for volunteer speakers for the LAC's campaign.[42] Certainly it is true that BUF activity declined markedly in the East End from late 1937, although there are a number of reasons for this.

The LAC's work was not only aimed at fascists, or at gentiles susceptible to their propaganda. It was also hoped, Picciotto admitted, that it would 'show the East End Jews that their interests were not neglected'. In this regard, success was mixed. The council did attract a number of local volunteers to assist with campaigning or to monitor fascist activity, though it often complained that too few were coming forward to help.[43] Moreover, at times the LAC faced as much hostility from Jews in its audiences as from fascists. In the summer of 1938, a representative of the CoC reported his observations on the crowd at an LAC meeting. He was amazed by some of the rumours he overheard, including claims that wealthy British Jews were funding the fascists 'in order to disturb East-End Jewry'. It was clear that local Jews still 'felt very abandoned' by the 'aristocratic' Board, 'left to their own devices' in the fight against fascism. The author believed, however, that such attitudes persisted because there remained a lack of awareness of the LAC's work. He noted that the reassurances offered by speakers at the meeting had made a positive impact, and suggested that greater energy be expended on spreading this message among the Jewish community, an idea that was immediately sanctioned by the LAC.[44]

The boldest – and least well known – aspect of the Board's defence activity was its efforts to investigate and infiltrate various fascist organizations. The reason this work has remained so obscure is that, for obvious reasons, it was conducted in absolute secrecy, with even many members of the CoC unaware of its precise nature. The purpose was, Laski explained, to 'enquire very carefully, if necessary by means of skilled responsible private enquiry agents, into Nazi and/or Fascist influences, their funds, their method, their distribution, their sponsors, their sources of revenue, and their method of operation'.[45] This information would then inform and guide the defence campaign, while anything particularly incriminating would be passed on to the appropriate authorities, or even publicly broadcast.

The Board was especially keen to advertise that the ultranationalistic BUF – so quick to attack alien influences – appeared itself to be receiving funding from foreign sources. Though this was widely believed to be the case, Laski was eager to find definitive evidence. 'The search for the source of these funds,' Salomon later wrote, 'was the most difficult problem that [we] faced.' Additionally, it was hoped that shining some light on the BUF's rather murky finances might embarrass or damage the party in other ways. In particular, it often evaded payment of damages in libel cases by putting one of its various publishing arms into bankruptcy. In March 1937, for example, having learned that BUF Publications Ltd had gone into liquidation after being ordered to pay £1,500 to the Amalgamated Engineering Union, the Board contacted the union to confirm whether the money had ever arrived. Later in the year, Salomon instructed solicitors to ascertain what dividend had been paid upon the winding-up of the company. The Board also approached Lord Camrose, owner and editor of the *Daily Telegraph*, with a request for information on the fascists' finances following his successful libel action against the BUF, which had resulted in £20,000 damages.[46]

In late 1937, Laski, through an intermediary, engaged private investigators to examine the financial records of BUF subsidiary companies held at party headquarters. On their first visit, they were not only illegitimately denied access to the files, but endured a succession of uniformed fascists parading in and out of the room, pointedly displaying weapons in their belts. That this was intended as an act of intimidation was confirmed when three Blackshirts subsequently tailed one of the detectives through the streets after he had left. A few days later, the majority of the requested documents were finally produced, but in a form that was 'obviously faked' and contained nothing of interest. Taking matters further would have risked discovery of who was seeking the information, so the issue was dropped. This setback notwithstanding, the Board was able to build up a detailed cache of information on the BUF's various subsidiaries: their directors, registered offices, mortgages, debentures, capital and so on.[47]

But the most striking aspect of the Board's investigative work was its success in placing moles within various fascist groups. This began in 1936, when, 'by devious means', contact was made with a disgruntled senior figure within BUF headquarters – an Irish nationalist referred to as 'Captain A' or 'Captain X' – who began passing weekly reports to the Board. These contained details of developments within the movement, the names of members and news of upcoming events. This information helped guide the Board's defence activity – for example, in deciding where to arrange counter-meetings or leaflet distribution – and was also regularly forwarded to the authorities.

In September 1936, for instance, details of a BUF plan to deliberately court arrest by making provocative antisemitic speeches were sent to the Home Office, along with circulation figures for the party's newspapers. It was the Board's source that revealed the Blackshirts were aiming to launch a 'renewed anti-Semitic campaign' in the wake of Cable Street, information that was passed to the chief constable of Manchester police, along with the names and addresses of 'a few Manchester [BUF] officials worth watching'. The following March, an internal BUF memo was received, detailing the financial cutbacks to be implemented that month and plans to form a new fascist front with the IFL and other groups. Most significant of all, during the war the Board presented a list of BUF members to Scotland Yard, which proved vital in identifying for internment some Blackshirts whose activity had previously been unknown to the police.[48]

Inspired by this success, the Board endeavoured to infiltrate other organizations on the radical right. This proved much harder, however, given the secretive, underground nature of many of these groups. Through his contacts with the police, Laski secured the services of a former Special Branch inspector, Cecil Pavey, who, under an assumed identity, gained membership of the MCP and NL in the late 1930s. His reports – which included meticulous accounts of meetings and profiles of individual members – revealed the degree to which these bodies sympathized with and had connections to the Nazi regime, as well as the extreme nature of their antisemitism. Such was the extent of Pavey's integration that he was invited to an NL summer school in Germany, where links between the organization and senior Nazi figures became further apparent. In addition to providing reports on the potentially treasonous position of the NL, he was able to supply the names of Nazi agents in Britain (at least one of whom was, on the basis of the Board's intelligence, arrested and imprisoned for the duration of the war). It was also thanks to the Board, Salomon claimed, that the government first became aware of Conservative MP Archibald Ramsey's role in this shadowy activity.[49]

Before being called back to police duty after the outbreak of war, Pavey gained access to a number of other groups: the IFL, National Socialist Party, British People's Party and Liberty Restoration League.[50] There have also been claims that further reports on the NL were provided by E.G. Mandeville Roe, a former leading member of both the BF and BUF.[51] This appears to be confirmed by material in the Board's defence archives from summer 1939, which records a number of payments being made to an 'expenses account' for Mandeville Roe (although the tone of the correspondence suggests some dissatisfaction with the arrangement on the Board's part).[52] Another agent, Victor Edwards, provided intelligence on The Link. Additionally, he acted as a 'post office' for the Board in its pseudonymous communication with the BUF and contacts within Nazi Germany.[53] Finally, an individual working for the Board was inducted into the White Knights of Britain, a secretive, occult, obsessively anti-Jewish and pro-Nazi group modelled on the American Ku Klux Klan. In 1940, he compiled a lengthy and detailed report on its membership, ideology and inner workings, concluding that it was 'a menace to the State' and a 'Fifth Column Unit', and recommending that MI5's attention be drawn to it.[54]

This information provided Laski great leverage in his efforts to encourage firmer action from the authorities, whose own investigations into British fascism, Thurlow records, were limited by budgetary constraints, making the Board's intelligence extremely valuable to them. (Even today, Thurlow adds, the Board's reports on the NL remain 'the most important information we have on its activities'.)[55] Meeting with a Home Office official, Laski stressed that the evidence he was conveying clearly indicated that the MCP and NL were not just a threat to the Jewish community, but to the government, to public order and to 'broader national and international questions'. In the subsequent internal Home Office discussion, it was admitted that the reports did 'contain some astonishing material', particularly the revelation that members of the NL were 'knowingly acting as German propaganda agents'; as such, 'it would be necessary to keep them under very close observation'. (Ramsay and others involved with him were later interned during the war.) In addition, the CoC was able to use the material it gathered to publicly embarrass those concerned. When rumours of Ramsay's beliefs began to emerge, the Board felt it their 'duty privately to bring certain aspects of this activity to the attention of his constituents', provoking an angry local reaction towards the MP. Regular reports of NL activity were also sent to the Conservative Chief Whip.[56]

The collation of such detailed intelligence also allowed the Board to formulate a sophisticated understanding of the variegated and evolving nature of the radical right in Britain. Most activist anti-fascists, informed by a left-wing analysis, tended not to differentiate greatly between individual groups on the 'reactionary' far right, and their attention focused mainly on the most visible fascist organization, the BUF. By contrast, the CoC's less partisan and better informed perspective helped it appreciate that, although the BUF 'was the largest and…most vocal' body, 'there were other organisations which also required the most careful watching'. Moreover, the threat presented by each was not static, with Laski's successor as chairman of the CoC, Liverman, noting that 'the miasma of anti-Semitism is very difficult to cope with by a fixed and settled plan, wandering as it does from phase to phase'.[57] The Board was thus keen to construct a comprehensive and flexible defence policy, with individually tailored and constantly evolving responses to different antisemitic threats.

In the case of the BUF, this had originally involved observing its activity for any indications of an antisemitic position. Once it did become a direct menace to Jews, the Board's approach was threefold: working with the authorities to clamp down on the fascists where they most endangered and antagonized the community; attempting to rein in the anti-fascist disruption that drew attention to the Blackshirts; and countering the BUF's political ambitions. By early 1938, it appeared that the party was in decline, with Laski celebrating that it was 'dying with a rapidity which is not surprising but certainly gratifying'. In these circumstances, he felt that giving the BUF too much attention would simply 'fan the dying embers and give them publicity, which is the only thing that can keep them alive'. As such, some of the more direct action against the party was now to be scaled back, with a focus instead on ensuring the enforcement of the POA and continued scrutiny of Blackshirt activity.[58] Equally, however, it was understood from intelligence sources that Mosley had no intention of abandoning his anti-Jewish platform; indeed, there was evidence that he was 'stumping' around the country in preparation for 'an intensified anti-Semitic campaign, but of a more subtle character than before'. This meant there was no place for complacency, and continued vigilance remained vital.[59]

The CoC's intelligence, it transpired, was completely accurate. Over 1938–9, the Board observed the transformation of the BUF's antisemitism from the crude and extreme propaganda aimed at exploiting pre-existing friction between Jews and gentiles in specific areas such as the East End, to a more restrained and calculated anti-Jewish message directed at a broader audience, associating Jews with issues of more general concern, such as the growing prospect of war and the influx of Central European refugees. In mid-1938, the CoC noted that BUF activity had begun to migrate from east to west London, where it employed a brand of antisemitic 'innuendo' that was successfully attracting educated, middle-class audiences. This, it was feared, 'made the situation more dangerous than ever', and necessitated a change in approach, in particular the organization of indoor meetings in the more affluent districts affected.[60]

The Blackshirts' reemphasis on campaigning at the national level had also revealed how pervasive anti-Jewish sentiment was outside the capital. Salomon warned the

CoC that while provincial antisemitism was often 'not conspicuous', appearing to be 'of a superficial nature, and worthy of little attention, it would be entirely erroneous to take this view'. Fascists were making 'full use' of concern over refugees, for example, to feed their propaganda, while also 'taking advantage of the political tension and the international situation to lay all the blame for the present state of affairs on the Jews'.[61] Laski feared that 'there is always anti-Semitism lurking in the background and round the corner'.[62] In 1939, in an effort to better understand such attitudes, the CoC commissioned Mass-Observation to investigate the matter. The resultant report, which was mentioned earlier, demonstrated how widespread negative feeling towards Jews was across Britain, and provided details of the types of attitudes that had been expressed.[63]

Previously, outside the East End the CoC had favoured a lighter touch when it came to defence work: there was no desire to 'create a Jewish problem in localities where it does not exist'.[64] But developments now necessitated a 'completely different' response.[65] Anti-defamation work was readjusted to focus on pertinent subjects. Publications highlighted the economic benefits that refugees brought to Britain and emphasized the humanitarian case for their reception. A booklet was published to help new arrivals adapt to British life.[66] In addition to refuting Mosley's other main charge – that Britain was fighting a 'Jewish war' against Germany – the Board also turned the tables on the fascists, painting them as unpatriotic Nazi agents and encouraging Jews to contribute to the war effort.[67]

To reflect the national spread of fascist activity, Laski proposed a decentralization of defence work, giving local representatives more scope to implement appropriate policies in their own areas.[68] The idea was approved by the CoC, but the subsequent restructuring was interrupted by the outbreak of war, which itself necessitated yet another modification of defence policy. Following an initial lull in fascist activity in September 1939, the LAC decided to suspend its meetings campaign for the time being. But once Blackshirt activity began to re-emerge, exploiting what Laski saw as a 'strong undercurrent of anti-Semitism' in wartime Britain, it was decided to continue the Board's defence work with 'undiminished vigour'.[69]

As mentioned above, the Board also played a role in the mass internments of fascists in 1940. In April, Salomon passed his local MP a list of potential fifth-columnists; two months later, he recapitulated to Game the names of every fascist the Board had brought to his attention over the years. The CoC also protested at the inconsistent way potential traitors had been identified and imprisoned. A query was made as to why Robert Gordon-Canning and Barry Domvile, founder of The Link and a former navy officer, had not been interned. The latter case was described as 'the most amazing piece of favouritism'. Even the home secretary was scolded by a senior CoC figure, who complained that the lacklustre pursuit of Nazi sympathizers made 'one doubt very much the sincerity of the Government in the manner in which it intends to deal with this unmistakeable menace'.[70]

Recognition that the BUF was not the only threat to the Jewish community also meant that by the late 1930s close attention was being paid to an assortment of groups on the radical-right fringe. Their undisguised sympathy for, and clandestine connections with, the German regime were of great concern, especially given the growing prospect of war. In February 1939, Laski informed a colleague that the BUF 'has taken for the time being a back seat', and that groups such as the MCP and NL were 'infinitely more dangerous' at this stage.[71] As such, each group merited a distinct approach.

The IFL, for example, was understood to have 'fewer members but … an even more venomous policy' than the BUF. Consequently, and as Leese's court case had demonstrated, direct attempts to silence the organization accorded it a significance that its size did not merit and drew attention to its hateful message. Observation and anti-defamation were more appropriate tools.[72] The MCP offered a similar but 'somewhat milder version' of IFL propaganda, infused with a 'violent anti-Zionism and anti-Bolshevism'. When it functioned mainly as an underground 'propaganda agency', constant monitoring, anti-defamation and investigation into its sources of funding sufficed; but as soon as it attempted to hold public meetings, these were successfully countered by the Board, which contacted the proprietors of the venues in question and persuaded them to cancel the events.[73]

The NL, meanwhile, was understood to be a 'leaderless and formless … association[,] rather than an organisation', with no aim to establish any formal political functions. Instead, it simply wished to bring together some of the most prominent 'race conscious Britons' to discuss their shared interest in 'frustrating the Jewish stranglehold on our Nordic Realm'. There was little direct action the Board could take against such an amorphous and secretive group, so instead, as we have seen, meticulous intelligence was accumulated and passed on to the authorities, who were pressed to move against the individuals involved. Additionally, a number of other organizations were monitored for signs of antisemitism, with intervention made where appropriate: the Anglo-German Fellowship, the Nationalist Association, the National Socialist Party, the British People's Party, the Link, the Liberty Restoration League, the National Citizens Union, the *Catholic Times*, the NSL, the Social Credit Movement and the Anglo-German Brotherhood.[74]

Many of these, of course, were not on the radical-right fringe, reflecting the Board's awareness that the struggle against antisemitism was a wider one. As a CoC report in late 1938 put it:

> Fascism is not a growth that will take root easily in this soil. But … anti-semitism can and does exist apart from Fascism. It would be far too optimistic to assume that anti-semitism as a whole is on the down-grade. Many competent persons indeed assert the contrary. For us the watchword must be constant and unremitting vigilance for that is the price of freedom.[75]

It is worth mentioning at this juncture the case of Manchester, where events matched in microcosm national developments. In 1936, the Council of Manchester and Salford Jews (CMSJ), the local equivalent of the Board of Deputies, had established a defence committee of its own. At first, like the CoC, this had simply maintained the existing strategy of anti-defamation, reflecting the fact that, as yet, 'the communal leadership had no coherent policy of opposition', Gewirtz observes. But from late 1936, its activity began to change, with 'the Council t[aking] seriously the task of monitoring the BUF and combating its actions', 'play[ing] a much more positive role in the fight against fascism'. This, of course, mirrors precisely the path taken by the CoC. Moreover, some of the impetus for this change in direction, it seems, came from local Jewish friendly societies, just as it had in London.

Gewirtz also notes (with some scepticism) rumours that 'certain communal leaders were engaged in joint anti-fascist action with members of the CPGB'. This claim is based on the testimony of an ex-Communist, who alleged that the CMSJ clandestinely channelled money from wealthy Jews, via intermediaries, to support the Communists' anti-fascist activity. This may not be as far-fetched as it seems, given that, as Barrett records, the CMSJ cultivated links with the Communist-associated NCCL. Indeed, Nathan Laski even applied for membership. The elder Laski was a vocal opponent of fascism, managing, for example, in collaboration with the Manchester Labour Party, to secure the prohibition of uniforms during political processions in 1936 and helping raise funds to cover the legal costs of an anti-fascist successfully sued by Mosley for slander.[76]

Laski's defence alliance

The transformation of the Board's defence campaign over 1936–40 did much to improve intra-communal relations. Its increasingly active and open opposition to fascism had the effect of both warming attitudes towards the communal leadership and making the Board more willing to cooperate with other Jewish anti-fascists. In mid-1937, it used its privileged position to help the JPC forward to Game allegations that Jewish protestors had been victims of police brutality at a fascist meeting in Stepney. Subsequently, the JPC made further approaches to the Board, requesting assistance for an anti-fascist facing allegedly unfair treatment in court and intervention in trade disputes involving Jews.[77]

There was, no doubt, a degree of self-interest in these early interactions. The JPC had quickly realized that its lobbying efforts were hindered by a lack of access to decision-makers, and hoped to make use of the Board's stature and extensive contacts. Following their April 1937 conference, for example, the JPC and NCCL had proposed to make a deputation to the home secretary to call on him to clamp down on racial incitement and antisemitic propaganda. Despite the reputable character of those comprising the delegation – including Walter Matthews and various MPs – the request was rejected, with Home Office officials privately expressing concern that entertaining organizations which opposed a 'lawful ... political philosophy' such as fascism 'might give rise to serious embarrassment'.[78] One of Game's subordinates, meanwhile, asked Laski 'to make .... perfectly clear to' the JPC that 'the Commissioner cannot allow himself to be led into any sort of discussion with the[m]'.[79] The following year, when Game wished to communicate with the JPC he again used Laski as a go-between.[80] Even some Labour MPs were reluctant to publicly associate themselves with Jewish anti-fascists.[81]

For his part, Laski was happy to encourage any indication that the JPC was beginning, for whatever reason, to respect the Board's prerogative to communicate with the authorities on behalf of Britain's Jews. Moreover, he hoped that this might also help Jewish activist anti-fascists appreciate the complications of dealing with fascism, and thus moderate their approach. In response to the JPC's abovementioned complaint, Game had ordered an investigation into the incident in question. Upon learning that no evidence supporting the allegations had been discovered, Laski asked Game for permission to inform the JPC of the results of the enquiry, which had shown that all but one of the casualties at the incident in question had been police officers and that the event had followed the typical pattern: the fascists were deliberately provocative but 'kept within the letter of the law'; the anti-fascists 'let their feelings get the better of them and came into mild conflict with the police'; and then the NCCL and newspapers 'exploited the affair for their own purposes … add[ing] fuel to the flames'.[82]

Equally, though, there was sympathy in the upper reaches of the Board for the plight of those who directly confronted the fascists. In late 1936, Laski hired a lawyer to assist a young East End Jew in bringing proceedings against a group of Blackshirts he alleged had attacked him. Laski believed that a conviction would be of 'high moral value', and indeed, having succeeded in securing one, 'a decided decrease in this class of offence in the Hoxton area' was subsequently recorded. Though the Board was prepared to cover the legal costs, the youth was asked if he could raise a contribution from his family and friends. With nothing forthcoming, however, Salomon chided him for his 'lack of public spirit'. Consequently, it was decided that this was 'too expensive as a policy' other than in special circumstances, and legal assistance was granted to anti-fascists only in a handful of cases over the following years.[83] By 1939, Laski had come as far as to publicly endorse disruptive anti-fascism, writing that such tactics 'on occasion … have their utility'.[84]

Additionally, there was a growing suspicion that the police were not doing all they could to restrict fascist activity and defend the Jewish community. As early as September 1936, as we have already seen, Salomon complained of 'a strong pro-Fascist feeling' in the police force, and that Jewish anti-fascists were receiving harsher judicial treatment than fascists. Laski himself echoed such sentiment privately, suggesting in May 1937 that there was a 'definite … partial[ity]' among the East End police that he found 'deplorable'.[85] The following year, a report by the secretary of the LAC condemned the 'rather truculent attitude of the police', who simply 'harri[ed] the audiences' at fascist events rather than properly enforcing the POA by clamping down on provocative language from fascist speakers. Resentment among local Jews, it noted, was directed more against the police than the Blackshirts. Laski forwarded the document to Game.[86]

By 1939, as mentioned above, Salomon was prepared to describe one division of the Metropolitan Police as 'notoriously Fascist', while Picciotto warned senior police officials that their handling of fascist activity was 'giv[ing] justification for those people who persist in saying that the police are on the side of the Fascists and in many cases anti-Semitic'.[87] By this stage, even Laski was prepared openly to voice such concerns, complaining to the Home Office that 'the vilest accusations were allowed to be made against Jews [at fascist meetings], apparently without any hindrance on the part of the police'. He reminded them that the Board had done all it could to persuade Jews to stay away from meetings, and now called on the police to do their duty, too.[88]

With the Board and JPC now sharing a similar outlook, pursing similar defence activity and showing a willingness to collaborate, the door was open for a resumption of formal discussions between the two sides. In October 1937, the LAC produced a report on the current complexion of Jewish defence. It observed that there were 'but two movements worthy of the name … combating anti-Semitism', the LAC and the JPC; between them, they were 'more or less completely representative of British Jewry'. It seemed a shame, therefore, that they were not working alongside one another, 'especially as we need each other so badly'. While a formal merger was probably not feasible, if the LAC truly aimed to win the support of the entire community, it should consider some form of cooperation. Additionally, this might have the added benefit of producing 'a more moderate policy' from the JPC; at the very least, there would be 'less public mud-slinging'.[89]

No progress was made in this direction over the following months – perhaps due to a restructuring of the LAC that began in late 1937, or, more likely, because the Board felt that it should be the JPC who made the first move. It was not until March 1938 that dialogue between the two was given a kick-start, following a public debate at Whitechapel Art Gallery between representatives of the two sides. The event, which drew a large audience, had been called to 'thrash out' the question of 'how best to combat the menace of the Fascist parties'. It proved to be a pivotal moment in relations between the two sides, doing much to dispel any remaining illusions that the JPC was affiliated to the CPGB, that the Board was not interested in combating antisemitism in the East End and that the two sides had incompatible approaches to fascism.

Opening proceedings, Frank Renton, a senior figure at the AJFS who was responsible for training the LAC's speakers, reminded the audience that he had been fighting antisemitism in east London for two and a half decades, and would continue to do so until 'the last drop of breath in my body'. He hoped that this could be done as part of a united community, but warned that the JPC's political approach, and in particular its close ties to the Communists, made collaboration impossible. Julius Jacobs, speaking for the JPC, responded by pointing out that his organization collaborated with a wide range of political groups: the Conservative MP Austin Hudson, with whom he had recently shared a platform, could hardly be described as a 'flag waving red'! He noted approvingly the LAC's recent willingness to attack fascism, but urged it to do so 'openly and publicly', not apologetically, and in league with all democratic forces.

The three subsequent LAC speakers repeated the same pre-prepared attacks on the JPC's alleged Communist connections, before going on to inadvertently demonstrate once more that the two organizations actually held very similar understandings of fascism. The first quoted a statement by Laski that antisemitism was 'the spear point of the attack on democracy by fascist interests', while the other two described it as a 'smokescreen', 'nothing else but a blind' to the fascists' true intentions. This prompted Bentley, speaking second for the JPC, to observe there really was 'no fundamental difference in our policies'. If 'we are all agreed that anti-Semitism is being used as a smoke screen, then what', he asked, 'is the subject under dispute?' Finally, Rennap complained that while he had come to discuss policy, all he was hearing were attempts to associate the JPC with subversive, revolutionary politics. He reiterated that the JPC understood that the Jews' 'very lives depend on democratic freedom'.

The LAC's last representative, John Dight, appeared at last to grasp that his side had failed to fully appreciate their opponents' position. The JPC, it now dawned on him, wanted Jews to present themselves as a political entity only in as much as they were committed to democracy, like anyone else opposed to fascism. Given that both it and the Board held as their fundamental objective the protection of the rights of the Jewish people, the two sides, he declared, should 'not fight each other' any longer (a plea that met with loud applause from the audience).

Returning to the platform, Jacobs lauded Dight's conciliatory approach, and announced that the offer made in 1936 was still on the table: the JPC would 'go out of existence' and throw 'the whole weight of its organisation … behind the Board' if it promised to 'lead the fight of the Jewish people against Fascism'. But if not, the JPC would continue to 'give them the leadership that the Board is not doing'. In his closing statement, Renton withdrew his earlier accusations, now accepting that the JPC was not an offshoot of the CPGB and proclaiming that should it and the Board come to an accord, 'it will be the greatest day's work that has ever been done'.[90]

The very next day, a letter was sent to the Board by the JPC, proposing a summit to discuss 'the unification of all efforts by the Jewish Community' in defence work. A meeting of the LAC was immediately called, at which a resolution was passed requesting authorization from the CoC to begin informal discussions with the JPC, in order 'to ascertain whether a common basis of action exists'. A week later the CoC gave its approval, but expressed its scepticism as to whether it could 'co-operate whole-heartedly with a body which was primarily a political organisation'.[91]

A series of discussions was subsequently held, the first in late April 1938. The LAC conveyed its pleasure at the 'amicable spirit' in which these negotiations took place, and was now satisfied that the JPC was 'in no way affiliated to any political body'. The JPC was persuaded (with 'much difficulty', Picciotto admitted) to accept that a single organization, 'exhibiting no political bias', should coordinate Jewish defence, with the aim of combating antisemitism and defending democracy in accordance with 'British traditions and ideals'. (This was a carefully constructed compromise, allowing for opposition to antisemitic, anti-democratic fascism, but not explicitly declaring hostility to any particular political ideology or party.) The JPC's leading figures were prepared to dissolve their organization and for defence to be placed under the complete control of the Board, but they were not willing to accept representation only on the LAC, a subsidiary body with a limited scope of activity, in return. They demanded either to be given a role within the CoC, or for the LAC and JPC to be merged into a new council. A committee was established to iron out the details.[92]

In the interim, both sides retired to their respective constituencies to discuss developments. Picciotto implored the CoC to seriously consider a merger with the JPC, as there was 'a great possibility of sincere and unified effort'. Moreover, this would do much to secure support for the CoC among previously hostile elements of the community.[93] The JPC, meanwhile, called a conference of its members, at which senior figures urged 'wholehearted support' for the negotiations. Events in Austria, which Germany had recently annexed, offered a chilling reminder that 'the time is long past when Jewry could afford to be divided'. Supporters were asked to write to the Board to encourage it to work with the JPC.[94]

Yet progress remained gradual, with the Board remaining reluctant to grant the JPC representation on the CoC, and the JPC understandably wary of giving up its autonomy in return for what seemed rather limited influence over communal defence. With attention focused on international events during the Munich crisis in the autumn, the issue was put on the backburner for the time being. The CoC still hoped, though, that a 'satisfactory *modus vivendi*' could soon be reached. Even in the absence of any formal agreement, practical collaboration between LAC and JPC had already begun. By October they had exchanged speakers on twenty occasions, an 'arrangement [that] has been most satisfactory', the LAC's secretary declared. These exchanges continued the following year, while the JPC also distributed thousands of the Board's anti-defamation publications.[95]

The process appeared to be reaching a conclusion in February 1939, when the CoC itself began to negotiate directly with the JPC. The two sides exchanged policy documents in the hope of ironing out any remaining differences. The next month, Picciotto announced that an agreement had in principle been reached for the JPC to dissolve, in return for representation on both the CoC and the LAC. However, at a specially called meeting of the CoC, opinion remained divided. Selig Brodetsky, a recent addition to the committee who would, later in the year, succeed Laski as president of the Board, supported the pact; Laski and Cohen were happy to form an alliance, but on slightly different terms; the chairman of the publications sub-committee, Harry Samuels, opposed the idea altogether, although he appears to have been in a minority of one. Subsequent discussion between these and the other four committee members present failed to produce a consensus. The JPC, for its part, also seemed somewhat hesitant, having requested that the new arrangement be subject to a six-month 'probationary period' before it was finalized.[96]

So, once more, the matter was adjourned; and, again, international events proved a distraction, as attention focused on the growing possibility of war, the refugee situation and the effects of both on domestic fascism and antisemitism. Finally, in late August, the JPC agreed to withdraw all of its policy demands that were unacceptable to the CoC, paving the way for a merger. But just two days later Germany invaded Poland and, after Britain joined the war, the JPC voluntarily disbanded. One of its leading figures, Jacobs, began assisting the Board with defence work, advising on its meetings campaign in London and on relations with trade unions.[97]

Another possible factor behind the CoC's lack of haste in concluding negotiations over 1938–9 was that a large portion of Anglo-Jewry had by this time come to support its leadership of communal defence, thus reducing the urgency in bringing the JPC formally on board. As we have already seen, the AJFS, with its huge membership, was quick to pledge its allegiance, helping establish the CoC in 1936 and relinquishing its own defence work to the LAC the following year. By early 1938, 'satisfied that the campaign for Jewish defence was being conducted on the lines originally planned', it surrendered its entire defence fund, plus any future donations, to the Board. A year later, a conference of the Order Achei Brith agreed that all members would be compelled to pay an annual levy to help finance the CoC's activity. Laski noted with satisfaction that the friendly societies' public support had also encouraged 'other elements [to] co-operate more readily and enthusiastically'. Where friendly society criticism was aired, such as by *The Leader* in the second half of 1938, it was of a constructive character, aimed at helping the CoC better advertise its work to Anglo-Jewry and encouraging wider representation on the committee.[98]

The Board also quickly attracted the support of another important constituency, Jewish ex-servicemen's organizations. AJEX immediately threw its lot in with the newly created CoC, publicly calling in August 1936 for Jews to unite behind the committee and privately offering its own assistance. Its two leading figures, Louis Sarna and J. Weber, were given seats on the LAC, which in 1938 transferred its offices to AJEX's headquarters on Prescot Street.[99] More unexpectedly, in the wake of the CoC's formation, EMAF – an activist organization with close links to the CPGB – published a letter in the *JC* declaring that it wished to work alongside the new body.[100] Beckman recalls that ex-servicemen, in particular, understood that the Board needed to act as a 'responsible law-abiding body[,] ... no matter how great the provocation', and that its 'calls for restraint among Jews in the 1930s carried weight'.[101]

Meanwhile, the Board could continue to count on backing from more traditional sources. In late 1936, Salomon visited communal leaders in Liverpool, Leeds and Manchester, who assured him that they remained 'strong supporters of the policy of the Board, and ready to afford every assistance'.[102] At around the same time, Laski contacted the synagogue congregations represented on the Board to outline his position with regard to the JPC. Almost all replied with expressions of approval and reiterated their continued loyalty.[103] From 1936, the *JC* began advertising the CoC's defence fund, and early the next year its new management, put in place after a period of boardroom upheaval, privately reaffirmed 'their readiness to cooperate with the Board'. Their choice as editor, Greenberg, though like his predecessor Rich an ardent Zionist, shared with Laski an antagonism towards the leadership of the Zionist movement in Britain. He thus became a strong supporter of the president, and Cesarani observes that during this period the *JC*'s 'warmth towards the communal hierarchy was almost without precedent' in the newspaper's recent history.[104]

Although, as mentioned earlier, the CoC's public financial appeals did not initially meet with an enthusiastic response, personal fundraising by Laski had much greater success. At a meeting with Jews involved in the West End textile trade in July 1936, the president secured donations amounting to £2,370 towards the defence fund, as well as a pledge to contribute £5,000 overall. In September, Manchester furniture traders gave £4,000, while further meetings in London, Birmingham, Manchester and Leeds in the autumn raised another £3,000.[105] By April 1938, £18,000 had been collected (75 per cent of which came after personal appeals from Laski), three times the total amount that had thus far been spent on defence activity since the summer of 1936.[106]

Nevertheless, the Board still felt that the community was not being as generous as it could be, especially given the growing support for the CoC's work. The LAC observed in late 1937 'a much greater degree of receptivity on the part of the Community' to its activity. The annual report of the Principal Probation Officer for 1938 noted that a decrease in attendance at provocative political meetings was in large part thanks to 'the fine efforts made by the Board of Deputies[.] ... People now realise that the leaders in the [Jewish] community are not pursuing a diplomatic policy of *lazier-faire*', and so felt less compelled to take matters into their own hands.[107] Yet donations for defence work had not increased commensurately, and so from 1938 fundraising efforts were redoubled, supported by an augmentation of the Board's defence apparatus.[108]

First, in November 1938, the CoC changed its name. The 'co-ordinating' in its title had reflected an original intention to simply harmonize the Board's existing anti-defamation and monitoring work. Now, with its remit stretching much further than had been anticipated, the title 'Jewish Defence Committee' was deemed 'more adequately descriptive'. It might also, it was hoped, raise awareness of the nature of the committee's work among those still unfamiliar with it – and bring in further financial contributions as a result. Yet this was not merely a rebranding exercise; genuine effort was also made to broaden representation on the committee by introducing new voices, many from outside the Board. Among those who accepted invitations to sit on the committee were Brodetsky, a Zionist of international standing (who at this stage was not yet a deputy); two MPs, Gluckstein and Harry Nathan, a former Liberal who had defected to Labour; Cyril Ross, a leading figure in the fur trade; and Lord Rothschild.[109]

The second step was the establishment of the TAC (initially a sub-committee of the Board, but later becoming an independent body). First mooted at a meeting of trade representatives organized by Ross in late 1938, its goal was to ensure good relations between Jews and gentiles in the economic sphere, thus removing what was regarded as a major cause of antisemitism. The TAC's remit encompassed both investigating cases of anti-Jewish discrimination and ensuring that Jews themselves 'establish and maintain [certain] standards of conduct and commercial ethics'. It also aimed to mediate when any friction arose.[110] Additionally, a number of trades agreed to establish vigilance committees, to keep the CoC informed of antisemitic activity and any Jewish misconduct.[111]

Once more, finance was a motivating factor. Laski realized that his most successful fundraising over 1936–8 had come after appeals to trade and business bodies. While many Jewish individuals who suffered fascist provocation first hand were prepared to participate in anti-fascist activity, they often did not (and could not afford to) contribute much money to the cause. (As we have seen, EMAF struggled financially; the JPC also had to work hard to raise funds.)[112] But Jews who suffered economically from antisemitism were often far more prepared (and able) to offer financial resources to fight it. The TAC provided them a greater sense that their concerns were being addressed.

These two changes had a dramatic effect.[113] In the five months after a new campaign for funds was launched in October 1938, £53,000 was received (with a further £15,000 promised). Given that by this stage the annual cost of the Board's defence work was £16,800, this represented a significant reserve to draw upon. The majority was provided by trade groups, while synagogues, many of which introduced a voluntary levy for the purpose, were another important contributor. But Liverman, in charge of fundraising efforts, noted that thousands of individuals had also made donations.

Communities outside the capital were particularly generous. After Laski and Picciotto had addressed a meeting of Jewish businessmen in Leeds, £1,650 per annum for the next three years was pledged – this despite, Laski reported, 'the rich people not [being] there' and Leeds' highly Zionist character. Birmingham's synagogue congregation alone provided £9,000, while the city's Young Israel Society and friendly society branches agreed to distribute CoC publications.[114]

London was not neglected, however. Acknowledging that the Board had yet to win over some elements of the community, Laski arranged his largest East End meeting to date in November 1938, drawing an audience of 4,000. Though 'an attempt was made by certain elements to break it up[,] ... the vast majority of those present express[ed] in no uncertain terms their support of the Board of Deputies and the Defence Committee,' claimed Salomon. The *JC*'s correspondent concurred, arguing that the few who expressed dissent were largely unaware of the Board's defence work. Picciotto did much to 'quiet the discontent' by explaining that the LAC had 'stood up time and again in Fascist infected areas ... fight[ing] the enemy on his own territory', rather than 'wast[ing] time coming to speak to Jews'. His call for Jewish unity – including praise for the 'zeal, enthusiasm and sincerity' of the JPC – prompted great applause. Even Laski's address was met with a relatively warm reception.[115]

Brodetsky's appointment to the CoC also opened the door to better relations with another group hitherto uninvolved with (and, it must be said, largely uninterested in) domestic defence work, the Zionists. The *Zionist Review* had in September 1938 applauded the anti-defamation work being undertaken by the CoC, 'whose endeavours have already earned the gratitude of the Jewish people'. Like the Board, it felt that, while the fascists' anti-Jewish slanders might appear ridiculous, most people in Britain were completely uninformed on such matters, and so educational work was imperative. In November, it ran an advert appealing for contributions to the Board's defence fund.[116]

Given the Zionists' previous silence on this issue, and their hostility towards the communal leadership in other matters, such shows of support may have resulted from a hope that defence funds could be used to further Zionist aims. In February 1939 a meeting was held between the CoC and the Zionist Federation, at the latter's request. The Board's representatives, Laski, Picciotto and Horowitz, were reminded that many Zionists had contributed to the defence campaign and, as such, perhaps a greater emphasis on the issue of Palestine would be appropriate. In response, they indicated that the CoC had a 'completely open mind on the question'; but, while supportive of Jewish interests in Palestine, the Board was not prepared for defence funds to be diverted towards Zionist propaganda. It was agreed that a sub-committee should be established to consider the issue (which came into being in April) and that further discussions would take between the two sides to determine an outline for collaboration.[117]

By 1939, then, Laski had managed to coalesce the most important elements of Anglo-Jewry behind his leadership of communal defence. To a greater or lesser degree, he could now count on the support of trade and professional groups, friendly societies, ex-servicemen's organizations, synagogues, the leaders of provincial communities, the Jewish press, Zionists and large parts of working-class and East End Jewry, including the JPC.

That is not to say that all approved completely of the substance of defence work; but they did now accept the Board's primacy in this area. Dissent was directed through proper channels, with the aim of changing CoC policy, rather than by the pursuit of alternative forms of activity outside the Board's ambit. In a *Jewish Times* editorial,

Morris Myer wrote that, although he and Laski had often been in disagreement, 'no one can deny that as far as actual work, especially in the fight against anti-Semitism … [he has] made great achievements'. In particular, he always attempted 'to keep an even balance between the various sections' of the community.[118]

The communal elites and Jewish defence

In the same editorial, Myer, less approvingly, also alleged that Laski's main objective had been 'to make his views appeal to the privileged circle which had the main say' – a reference to the traditional, anglicized elite that still held great sway in communal affairs (though to an ever-diminishing degree). While Laski, a provincial Jew and the son of an east-European immigrant, was not drawn from the 'Cousinhood', he has often been regarded as an honorary member, helping guard their interests on the Board and retard the process of institutional reform.[119] To whatever extent this may have been true in general, with regard to defence work, it was very much not the case. In fact, quite the opposite: the Jewish 'aristocracy' remained the last group to be won over to Laski's alliance. The development of a more active, anti-fascist position over 1936–8 had been met with little enthusiasm among the community's upper echelons, where the assimilationist mindset was most deeply ingrained. However, given the wealth and influence of such figures, Laski was keen to attain their support, something he eventually achieved, though at great personal cost.

In 1936, Waley Cohen had, as agreed at July's heated gathering of the Board, begun to pursue his own plans for an independent anti-defamation body. While the other two organizations established at this time, the JPC and the CoC, together came to broadly represent the lower and middle social strata of Anglo-Jewry, Waley Cohen's was an unashamedly elite affair, funded by large donations from the community's 'men of substance'. By November, £25,000 had been gathered from just a handful of individuals: the Rothschilds and Lord Bearsted, chairman of Shell, each pledged £1,000 per annum for seven years, for example. It was run in complete secrecy with absolutely no accountability, even to its sponsors, and policy was decided on the whim of Waley Cohen, who laid out his vision and left its implementation to a two-man office. He even admitted to being 'ignorant' of the specific details of the work carried out there, and in fact discovered in 1938 that much of its activity had contradicted his wishes.

Despite the reassurances he had publicly offered to Jewish victims of the BUF, in private Waley Cohen considered that 'the little Mosley organisation is not … worth powder and shot'. It was 'the German attack on civilisation', not 'the silly little Fascist movement in our country', that was the main threat to Jewry in Britain and elsewhere. Consequently, he regarded the CoC as merely a palliative measure to 'satisfy the strong feeling that exists among the general community that something ought to be done'. His own body would carry out the more serious work of investigating and countering Nazi influence in Britain, defending British democratic traditions and forging alliances with influential non-Jews.[120]

In addition to his office's day-to-day work of monitoring Nazi-influenced activity and responding to antisemitic letters in the press, various publishing and research ventures were initiated over 1937–8. Although many never came to fruition, despite significant preliminary investment, one relative success was the commissioning of Colin Coote, a leader writer for the *Times*, to create a series of 'Vigilance Pamphlets' on political extremism in Britain and abroad. By May 1938, 100,000 copies had been produced and distributed. Yet Coote's belief that the Independent Labour Party, trade unions and even elements of the Labour Party itself were among the threats to British democracy, along with the fact that distribution was carried out through Conservative Party channels, was instructive: many of Waley Cohen's schemes had only a tenuous association with the fight against fascism, but were closely linked to Conservative causes. In September 1937, for example, a £1,000 contribution from his defence fund was made to Conservative Central Office, with the vague request that it be used

> to spread in England a sense of the essential importance in our national wellbeing of the democratic system upon which our public life rests… [and the] mutual tolerance and… sense of fellowship and goodwill among all sections of the population.

Such favouritism was in part because of Waley Cohen's own partisan sympathies (he believed that 'Jewish interests are identical with those of the… Conservative Party'), but also because he was concerned that while the political left was alive to the dangers of Nazism, those on the right were 'less immune' to its temptations.

Soon, however, Waley Cohen began to realize that perhaps his endowment was not being disbursed as efficiently as it could be. He complained to the administrator of his office that they had been committing a 'really excessive' outlay on 'rather limited work'. Moreover, he had recently discovered that much of their activity simply duplicated what the CoC was already doing at a cost 'enormously less than ours'. In late 1938, he made the decision to wind up his operation.[121]

A further reason for this move was that Waley Cohen had reluctantly come to accept that Laski should coordinate communal defence, although not through the Board's official defence apparatus. While he had technically been a member of the CoC from its formation, Waley Cohen had only attended meetings intermittently (often to express his opposition to aspects of its policy) and in 1937 rejected an offer to become the inaugural chairman of the LAC. Moreover, he remained wary of the Board as an institution, decrying the 'popular' (i.e. more democratic and representative) direction in which it was heading. It was, he believed, 'not at all a competent administrative body[,] … largely run by lawyers… and a number of not very responsible nonentities'. The only reason it managed to function effectively at all was thanks to the 'superhuman efforts [of] Laski'.[122]

These reservations, along with a continued belief that the most valuable defence work needed to be conducted in private under the direction of just a few responsible individuals, made Waley Cohen reluctant, even after the closure of his office, to place what remained of his defence fund at the disposal of the CoC. Instead, it was set aside as a separate pool of money on which Laski was permitted to draw for the more sensitive aspects of his defence work. Decisions on how it was spent were to be made by a committee composed of Bearsted, Ross, Waley Cohen, Laski and Oscar Deutsch, a cinema magnate, which would meet every Friday.[123]

Additionally, it was decided that some of the fund would be provided to Laski for his personal use. Domestic and international developments had compelled the president to devote almost his entire time to communal duties, particularly work related to defence. His successful legal practice had suffered greatly as a result. By late 1938, with debts mounting, he was torn between his sense of duty to the community at this time of danger and his own welfare. In November, Waley Cohen's committee agreed to use its funds to resolve this problem by paying off Laski's debts and providing him an annual honorarium of £5,000 as compensation for his communal work. Though the payment was approved by the CoC, it was otherwise to remain completely confidential, with Laski maintaining the impression that he continued to practice at the Bar.[124]

Knowledge of this agreement emerged publicly in the 1960s, when Waley Cohen's biographer, Robert Henriques, recorded that Laski was provided 'a very substantial annual sum' to allow him to focus full time on defence.[125] In fact, the claim is only partially accurate, and angered Laski to the extent that, following the book's publication, he located the relevant document in his papers and scribbled in the margin that 'the statement in the life of Sir RWC by Henriques is untrue'.[126] For it appears that Laski never actually received any of the money.

One reason for this was the danger that news might leak out. In August 1939, Laski wrote to his parents of 'tittle-tattle ... behind my back with regard to my alleged receipt and retention of monies from the Defence Fund', mentioning in particular certain letters from an unnamed individual. The next month, Waley Cohen complained that 'on the whisper of some silly judge in New York [Laski] decided publicly to repudiate' their arrangement. To whom they were referring remains unclear.[127]

Yet these developments occurred over eight months after the deal had first been agreed. That no money materialized in the intervening period was largely the responsibility of Waley Cohen himself, whose capricious and intransigent character led to constant interference and outbursts of irrational criticism in his dealings with Laski, obstructing the finalization of arrangements for his salary. The correspondence between the two men over this period does much to reveal their differing interpretations of Jewish defence and of the obligations and responsibilities of the communal leadership, as well as the degree to which Laski's work had become consumed by defence activity, a commitment that, with no financial compensation forthcoming, eventually forced his resignation.

Within days of the original agreement being reached, Waley Cohen was already disputing the amount that had been approved as Laski's annual payment, and over the following months he continued to quibble over such details. A letter to Bearsted revealed the true reason for his equivocation: he believed that defence work was now 'much worse than it was when I was trying to do it alone'. The majority of their Friday meetings, he complained, was being wasted listening to reports of what Laski had been doing, and too little time was devoted to discussion of more important tasks (namely Waley Cohen's own pet projects, previously run by his office).[128]

This prompted a firm rebuttal from a 'much distressed' Laski, who pointed out that the other members of the committee, not he, set the agenda for their meetings.

He also drew attention to the high costs and limited benefit of Waley Cohen's favoured schemes. Finally, he outlined the great success the Board had been having in uniting the community behind its defence work, and reiterated the 'democratic obligation ... incumbent on us' to carry out such activity through the CoC. The latter point was one on which Waley Cohen felt particularly strongly. His brusque reply laid out starkly his view of the choice they faced: either 'observing the forms of democratic obligation' or actually 'rendering real and effective service in directions which don't admit of democratic direction'.[129]

The matter remained unresolved, leading to a further, even more caustic round of letters in May. Waley Cohen again lambasted the CoC, claiming that its spending was extravagant, that it was taking 'almost no steps' to tackle antisemitism and describing the whole situation as a 'farce'. Moreover, he insinuated that Laski had not been working as hard as he should. In a thinly veiled threat, he requested that the two should convene for personal discussions in advance of a meeting he would be holding with Bearsted, Rothschild and Liverman to discuss Laski's remuneration, details of which had still yet to be finalized.

In response, Laski mounted a lengthy and forthright defence – copies of which were pointedly sent to the three men with whom Waley Cohen was due to meet – reiterating the successes of the CoC in fighting domestic fascism, which was now 'at a low ebb'. On his personal efforts, he found it 'difficult to put into words the mingled resentment and distress I feel that you should ... belittle the amount of time I have given to the job'. Communal work occupied his entire time, had 'destroyed ... [his] professional practice and ambitions' and had led to 'the abandonment by me of home life'. Turning the tables, he criticized Waley Cohen's 'impatient' and 'somewhat vigorous character', accused him of speaking with 'incomplete knowledge of the facts', and suggested that if he was keen to save money, perhaps he should abandon some of his own wasteful projects rather than mounting attacks on the person who had done more to raise funds than anyone else.

Waley Cohen, palpably seething, declared that it was now 'doubtful whether we are justified in using Jewish Defence funds for the purpose we had in mind in connection with your work'. Five days later, a second, more conciliatory letter was sent, but the issue of Laski's salary was once more deferred, as Waley Cohen claimed that at their meeting he, Bearsted, Liverman and Rothschild had not found time to discuss it.[130] If this excuse sounded rather implausible, that is because it was a lie. The minutes of the meeting reveal that the honorarium was the first item on the agenda. Moreover, the four had agreed that £5,000 a year was a reasonable amount, and decided to backdate payment to 1 January 1939.[131]

Why Waley Cohen misled Laski is unclear; so, too, is whether or not the committee's decision was revealed to the president over the next two months. But in any case, by July Laski had resolved – presumably due to the 'tittle-tattle' mentioned above – not to take the money in any case.[132] The ramifications of his decision were obvious: he had no alternative but to resign the presidency and return to his professional work. Given that the Board was in recess for the summer, however, he decided to delay any announcement until after autumn, thus giving him time to search for a suitable successor.[133]

In September, the outbreak of war interfered with Laski's plans – by necessitating his supervision of a recalibration of defence work, but also by greatly complicating communal politics. The president's attempts to unify the community behind his defence policy had been taking place against a background of upheaval. Over this period, Cesarani notes, a 'series of power struggles broke out at the apex of communal government', with a 'barrage on the legitimacy of the ruling elite'. In particular, Zionists had succeeded in greatly strengthening their position within the Board.[134]

The opening months of the war brought these developments to a head. First, a proposal was made by the traditional elites for communal affairs to be run by a small executive committee, on the grounds that this was necessary to put Anglo-Jewry on a 'war footing'. The idea was, however, rejected by the Board. The institution, Laski complained, was now dominated by Zionists, as wartime constraints made the attendance of 'more solid and sober' deputies from outside London difficult. The president's problems were compounded by continued interference from Waley Cohen, who still hoped to persuade him to accept the honorarium and stay in his post, yet persisted in making petty complaints about his expenses. In any case, his efforts were in vain, with Laski finally, in early November, announcing his decision to resign. This triggered a by-election to replace him, which, after the outgoing president's failed attempts to install Harry Nathan or Anthony de Rothschild as his successor, was won, uncontested, by Brodetsky.[135]

While one must acknowledge the symbolic significance of a foreign-born, East End-raised Zionist ascending to the apex of Anglo-Jewry, this was not quite the 'takeover' or 'revolution' it has sometimes portrayed as.[136] Just as it had taken time for the power of the traditional elites to be eroded, so, too, was it only gradually redistributed. Indeed, Laski himself had in many ways been a transitional figure (in terms of both his personal background and his policies as president), bridging the gap between the reign of the old elites and the establishment of more representative communal institutions. Laski was, in Rubinstein's opinion, a 'highly typical exemplar … [of] mainstream Anglo-Jewish consensus as it was evolving at the time', representing 'a grafting of the new onto the old'.[137]

Moreover, Brodetsky's outlook was not radically removed from Laski's, and his tenure was marked as much by continuity as it was by change. The new president held 'a fundamental desire to maintain the status quo which was seen to guarantee Anglo-Jewry its position as a tolerated minority in Britain', notes Gewirtz. As Brodetsky explained in correspondence with Rothschild, he was not opposed to the idea of assimilation, and believed strongly that Jews 'should be good citizens, should share to the utmost in the life of the country, and should be identified in their aims and in their secular life with fellow-citizens of other creeds'. His election, Gewirtz concludes, should therefore 'not be viewed as the victory of an alternative immigrant ideology over the "official" ideology of the Anglo-Jewish establishment, but rather as the consolidation of the old strategy of anglicisation on a new "Anglo-Zionist" basis'.[138]

The two men also shared a similar approach to communal politics, seeking to balance the various influences on the Board and to avoid conflict where possible. On his appointment to the presidency, Brodetsky both publicly and in private outlined his aim to 'bring unity in the Community'. As the abovementioned communication with

Rothschild suggests, a central feature of this strategy was to reach out to those who had greatest reason to fear his appointment. He immediately proposed an 'entente' to Rothschild, who agreed to join his executive; later, Waley Cohen was invited to return as vice-president. Brodetsky celebrated the success of these efforts, informing a colleague that a 'number of "assimilationist" Anglo Jewish leaders' had 'offered … their support and cooperation'.[139]

But above all, it was the Board's ongoing defence work that demonstrated how little set Brodetsky apart from Laski, whose analysis of this issue he broadly shared and whose policies he largely maintained. In his autobiography, Brodetsky declared that 'British people have always made me marvel at their extraordinary tolerance and decency';[140] this was, he believed, the reason the country remained relatively free of anti-Jewish sentiment. Of the antipathy that did exist, he felt that much was 'innocent anti-Semitism[,] … caused by ignorance'. He also, however, believed that Jews themselves were to some extent to blame. In 1940, an open letter to the Jewish community was drafted in Brodetsky's name (though it is not clear if it was ever released) warning that 'much anti-Semitism is manufactured from within', by 'unscrupulous business dealing[,] … ostentation, in dress and conversation, loud behaviour in public places, display of jewels and furs, walking and talking in groups'. It called on Jews to hold themselves to an 'even higher code' than gentiles, 'as the Jewish Community is made responsible for the faults of the individual'.[141]

On the basis of this analysis, Brodetsky felt that the Board's efforts to combat antisemitism should take two primary forms: educational anti-defamation work that presented 'impartial statistical and factual information' about Jews to the British public; and 'guidance' for 'Jews who do harm by their misdeeds, their uncouthness, or their strange habits'.[142] With regard to antisemitism in the political arena, he wanted the Board to mount an ardent defence of Britain's democratic values, but warned that such activity should remain divorced from any particular political organization or ideology. Above all, he worried of 'the danger that the enthusiastic [Jewish] anti-Fascist might be converted to Communism'.[143] In other words, Brodetsky argued for precisely the combination of anti-defamation, improvement and political neutrality that had long been favoured by many among the Anglo-Jewish leadership.

This continuity in defence policy was further revealed in the composition of the CoC, where Laski's carefully constructed alliance remained largely in place. Indeed, just a month after his departure as president, Laski himself was invited to return to the committee. While he did not stay on it for much longer, half of those who had sat on the CoC in mid-1937 were still there in 1945: Liverman (now chairman), Waley Cohen, Horowitz, Janner and Percy Cohen. Two further members – Alec Nathan and Brodetsky himself – also remained from before the war. Meanwhile Salomon, the driving force behind much of the CoC's work, was retained as secretary, staying in that position until the late 1950s.[144]

Brodetsky's conception of Anglo-Jewry's position within British society, his desire for a variety of voices to be heard at the Board and his attitude to defence work all, therefore, differed little from his predecessor's approach. In fact, they reflected broad agreement within the community on these issues. This had been demonstrated by the widespread support that emerged for Laski's defence policy over 1936–9, as the

CoC became progressively more inclusive and its activity came to meet communal demands. While the various sub-identities held by different sections of the Jewish community had informed early responses to the BUF, the growing consensus on defence appeared to reflect an overriding, shared sense of Anglo-Jewishness. When challenged by Britain's fascists, who portrayed virtually the entire Jewish community as alien and objectionable, this common identity come to the fore, uniting Britain's Jews against this attack on both their Britishness and their Jewishness.

Conclusion

In drawing together the foregoing, it is apposite to begin with the issue that, in theory at least, most directly connects the two subjects of this study: the idea that Jewish actions – in particular early opposition to British fascism – were to some degree responsible for encouraging the BUF to embrace antisemitism. This is a notion that originated with Oswald Mosley himself, who, in attempting to justify his attitude towards Jews, cautioned in his autobiography that 'in assessing blame for this quarrel it is well to be quite clear on the chronology'.[1] Indeed it is – though not in the way Mosley's self-serving and deceptive version of events suggests.

The simple fact is that no such process of 'interaction' occurred. In 1932–4, those Jews who were involved in active opposition to the BUF represented a small minority of the British anti-fascist movement and an even smaller fraction of Anglo-Jewry. Their participation was wilfully exaggerated – and the initially conciliatory attitude of the official Jewish leadership and the *JC* conveniently ignored – by the BUF to justify its 'adoption' of antisemitism in autumn 1934. This is not to deny that subsequently, over 1935–7, a growing number of Jews engaged in confrontational anti-fascist activity; nor that a mutually reinforcing cycle of violence emerged between the two sides during this period; nor even that the fascists may have fallen victim to disruption and physical assault at the hands of Jews more often than they were guilty of the same offences. It is simply to say that the conflict between them was not the real cause of the escalation of antisemitism in autumn 1934, nor even again two years later, in October 1936. At both junctures, Jewish opposition – imagined or real – merely provided a useful pretext for changes in policy that were implemented for other reasons.

Furthermore, Jewish actions should always be judged in light of the BUF's gross (and calculated) provocation. When, from late 1935, a significant number of Jews did for the first time become regularly involved in disruptive activity, this was at a stage when Mosley had already announced his intention to remove the majority of Anglo-Jewry from the country – with those that remained to be treated as second-class citizens – and unleashed a vicious campaign of verbal and physical harassment in districts of high Jewish occupation.

Indeed, closer examination of the fascists' antisemitism – how it was expressed, its development over time and its relationship to the party's programme and ideology – offers further reason to discount the idea that Jewish anti-fascism, or any other external force, pushed a reluctant BUF into conflict with Britain's Jews. Most obviously, explicit expressions of anti-Jewish sentiment appeared in its discourse from the very start, not least in the pronouncements of its most senior figure. From Mosley's pre-BUF attraction to Jewish conspiracy theories, through his direct attacks on 'subversive' Jewish activity at the party's founding, to his open declaration of opposition to Anglo-Jewry in late 1933 (accompanied by wide-ranging and vicious denigration of Jews in his newspaper), Mosley's antisemitism was manifest well before any serious or consistent hostility had been expressed towards him by the Jewish community.

This was because antisemitism represented an authentic and organic component of Mosley's – and by extension the BUF's – fascist philosophy; the two had developed alongside one another in 1932, and continued to do so over the following years. Every malady Mosley diagnosed in Britain's supposedly corrupt, decadent, decaying society led him to the Jews – or, more accurately, to popular, longstanding representations of 'the Jew' that provided him a tangible personification of the nebulous and disparate set of problems fascism aimed to address. More broadly, his exclusionary, ultranationalistic creed, with its aim of creating a racially (in a cultural sense) pure society, dictated intolerance of distinctive and incompatible out-groups. Jews – who, despite a relatively high degree of assimilation, remained the body most widely regarded in Britain as alien – were an obvious target, the 'other' against which the fascists defined themselves and their idealized vision of Britain and its people.

Consequently, the case Mosley made against Jews represented a 'fascistized' version of existing, indigenous strands of antisemitism, which were woven comprehensively into his programme, made to serve its political, economic and cultural goals, and infused with the millenarian rhetoric regarding degeneration, cleansing and renewal that was characteristic of his 'faith'. The removal of Jews became a necessary prerequisite for the BUF's envisaged national rebirth. This appears typical of the process by which fascism forms and expresses hostility towards minority groups deemed incompatible with its homogeneous vision of society, although this is an area of fascist studies that would benefit greatly from further attention.

This still, of course, begs the question of why Mosley did not immediately choose to fully acknowledge that antisemitism was an intrinsic part of his doctrine. This, it seems clear, was a tactical decision, based on a belief that the British public would not respond positively to any prejudice that appeared indiscriminate and irrational. When Fuller gave Mosley precisely this advice in 1934, the latter expressed his full agreement, revealing that his 'strategy' was to justify antisemitism by placing 'the onus of aggression onto the Jews'. This was a process he had begun in October 1932, highlighting their alleged association with the main enemies of fascism and disruption of his first ever fascist meeting; continued in November 1933, claiming that Jews were agitating for war with fascist Germany; and brought to completion in autumn 1934, when he argued that they had been responsible for physical attacks on his party and putting economic pressure on its supporters. Throughout, it was suggested the cause of this unprovoked aggression was that the fascists' political programme, in attempting to rectify the problems afflicting Britain, had inadvertently challenged the sources of the Jews' wealth and power. Thus Mosley aimed to present his opposition to Jews as completely rational and defensive; as their fault, not his. This justification remained consistent – along with the necessary but entirely theoretical acknowledgement that some Jews could be 'good' – over the remainder of the 1930s.

Mosley's efforts in this regard correspond to the concept of 'licence' Aristotle Kallis uses to explain how fascists 'gear [themselves] towards violence against a specific "other"'. This licence can be expressed in a variety of ways, one of which is on the basis of 'self-defence, regardless of how justifiable or real it may be'. As part of this process, it is first necessary to establish the chosen 'other' as a 'enemy … over a period of time', in particular by ascribing to it 'qualities that render [it] lethally dangerous to the community'. In this way, fascists attempt to create a 'psychological space' in which the removal of this group becomes 'both part and precondition of … the wider project of national regeneration'. Significantly, however, Kallis observes that this image of the 'other' is not created from scratch, but rather builds upon 'a pre-existing, potent but latent … enmity' towards that group, thereby 'transform[ing] [the chosen "other"] from a more-or-less tolerable perceived anomaly into an allegedly immutable and dangerous "threat" that would thwart the project of rebirth'.[2] The parallels to the BUF's justification, presentation and use of its antisemitism are clear.

Environmental factors no doubt played some part in Mosley's calculations, too. Britain's economic recovery and the BUF's loss of respectable support in mid-1934 would have made the use of antisemitism more tempting, just as the rise of Hitler and the alliance with Rothermere had earlier encouraged its suppression. Later, various circumstances – such as the Spanish Civil War, the refugee crisis and growing international tensions – led Mosley to stress or downplay certain elements of anti-Jewish rhetoric. Internal party dynamics also influenced presentation and emphasis at different stages. But at all times Mosley remained committed to this aspect of his programme and – unsurprisingly, given that he was the BUF's primary ideologist, the architect of its programme and one of its main sources of funding – it was always, other than for a brief period from late 1936 to early 1937 during the peak of East End campaigning, his views on the Jewish question that formed the basis of his party's position. While others within the movement may have fleshed out the Leader's vision in various directions, they remained within the parameters he had laid down at the outset.

A final influence on the way in which the BUF's antisemitism was expressed was a growing sense over the late 1930s that the movement was participating in an epochal, pan-European confrontation between fascism and the forces of Jewry. This breathed new confidence into anti-Jewish propaganda, and helped to shape it into a more coherent and focused form. It also facilitated growing cooperation with others on Britain's radical right. This seems to be illustrative of a wider pattern of development in which antisemitism became more prominent among Europe's fascist movements over the decade, as the likelihood of war increased and they united behind the Nazis' leadership in a struggle against the forces of liberal democracy, communism and international finance – all, of course, supposedly controlled by Jews. Given the inherently nationalistic nature of fascism, opposition to Jews, an almost ubiquitous minority across the continent, provided a convenient common cause around which these movements could rally. Yet while their use of antisemitism may have been inspired by the Nazis, it was rarely imitative, building instead upon native traditions of anti-Jewish thought. Again, however, further research into this process, particularly in the form of comparative studies, would be of great value.

A clearer understanding of the chronology has also helped shed new light on the second subject of this study. By moving beyond the relatively static image of Jewish approaches to fascism presented in previous accounts – which focus largely on just two types of response during a relatively brief period – we have observed instead a variegated, nuanced and overlapping spectrum of attitudes and activity, which evolved over time and interacted with one another. Within this framework, three general stages of development have been traced.

Initially, there was uncertainty over the best means of response to the emergence of Britain's first serious fascist organization. This confusion derived, in large part, from the fact that it was unclear at this stage precisely what Jews were responding to: the BUF only revealed its anti-Jewish policy gradually and inconsistently, alternating between episodes of explicit hostility and periods in which the 'Jewish question' was largely ignored, all the while vehemently denying that it was antisemitic at all. Meanwhile, looking abroad, to the only two examples of fascism in power, offered limited guidance as to the potential threat posed by their British counterpart, given Italy and Germany's completely contrasting treatment of Jews at this stage. Even once Mosley had made his position clear in autumn 1934, the BUF's anti-Jewish rhetoric remained erratic over the following year, during which time the party also fell into deep decline, with a consequent drop in its level of activity. It is important to remember, therefore, that not until late 1935, when the East End campaign began in earnest, did the Blackshirts start to become a sustained, serious and direct threat to Jews. As such, before this time, although the vast majority of Anglo-Jewry remained wary of fascism, few actively opposed it. Where specifically Jewish anti-fascist organizations did sporadically appear, they tended to be ephemeral, lacked clear direction and were largely uncoordinated with one another.

Subsequently, once Mosley's commitment to antisemitism had been made explicit and the East End campaign was underway, demands for a cohesive and vigorous Jewish response did emerge. This second stage, where historical attention has previously been most closely focused, saw severe, often vitriolic criticism of the communal leadership for its failure to act. Many Jews, especially among working-class, immigrant communities, sought alternative forms of representation altogether, such as newly established Jewish defence organizations or the Communist Party, which offered a more active approach to fascism.

Yet it is important not to overstate the extent and nature of these divisions. As we have seen, even within groups who were at the vanguard of the physical struggle with the Blackshirts, such as the JPC and the CPGB's East End branches, there were influential voices urging a more measured approach. At the same time, some of the most powerful criticism of the traditional leadership came from its close allies, such as the *JC* and the AJFS, who urged the Board of Deputies to take a more active lead in communal defence. This is illustrative of the fact that this was no straightforward, antithetical division between 'elite' and 'working-class' Jewish approaches, as implied in most accounts. Rather, calls for action came from all sections of Anglo-Jewry and, beneath the surface anger of the defence debate, there was actually relatively broad agreement across the community on the principles that should underlie defence work: the prevention of the most directly threatening forms of fascist activity; countering antisemitic propaganda through anti-defamation work; and collaborating with non-Jews to stymie the progress of political antisemitism, which was to be presented as a precursor to wider attacks on the British people. Moreover, there was widespread acceptance, even among East End Jewish anti-fascists, that this campaign should ideally be overseen by the Board. Consequently, once the official leadership did eventually grind into action, establishing in July 1936 a defence committee whose policies largely conformed to communal demands, much of the criticism was neutralized.

There did, initially, remain two sources of tension. The first was the Board's insistence that Jews should not oppose fascism itself, but only the antisemitism for which it was responsible. The inadequacies of such an approach quickly became apparent, however, and over 1937 the CoC developed an increasingly anti-fascist line, both publicly and behind the scenes.

The second dispute was over the efficacy of confrontational forms of anti-fascism. Yet here the split was not simply between working-class Jews and the Board, or between the 'old' and 'new' sections of the community, or between those of different ideological outlook. Rather, it was a wider division between senior figures and junior ones that cut across a variety of different organizations and groups: from Communist leaders' struggles to restrain their rank and file, through the Zionist Federation's efforts to silence the *Young Zionist*'s increasingly strident anti-fascist line, to the tensions within East End families between cautious parents and their more assertive, British-born children. This often created unexpected bedfellows. When Neville Laski, the president of the Board, met with Harry Pollitt, the general secretary of the CPGB, he was pleasantly surprised by how compatible were their views on defence activity. The *Young Zionist*, which in 1934 had called for Jewish unity as the best response to fascism and rejected collaboration with gentiles as a sign of weakness, was by 1936 instead demanding that its followers shun the 'big Jews', who were their enemies, and instead forge alliances with non-Jewish, progressive anti-fascist forces.

In 1936 it was the advocates of confrontation who were in the ascendency, epitomized by the vast turnout at the Cable Street demonstration, which had been arranged against opposition from both the official Jewish and Communist leaderships. But subsequently the balance shifted, as many of those who had pursued physical opposition to the fascists – often reluctantly, as a last resort in the face of a perceived lack of action by the Jewish and British authorities – began to moderate their approach. This change came about in part because the Board started to take a more active lead in defence; but it also reflected a growing awareness of the limited, even detrimental, effects of physical confrontation. Events such as Cable Street contributed to a vicious circle of violence, with Jews the primary victims; they also boosted the BUF, which deliberately sought conflict to gain publicity and lend some substance to its narrative of victimhood. Consequently, by the end of 1937 those who had been at the forefront of this struggle – the JPC, East End Communists, Jewish ex-servicemen – were now pursuing less violent forms of opposition.

These changing attitudes helped usher in the final stage of development, as different sections of the community – friendly societies, the Jewish press, ex-servicemen, trade and professional groups, synagogues, Zionists and eventually the JPC and many of the working-class Jews it represented – came to support, or at least accept, Laski's leadership in defence matters. Though criticism of the Board's defence work was still occasionally aired, it was of a constructive variety, with no suggestion of seeking alternative forms of representation. Moreover, whatever political machinations were taking place within the Board during this period, they remained separate from the issue of defence. Ironically, given the prevailing historical perception of Laski as an agent of the traditional Jewish elites, it was actually these communal luminaries who were the last to endorse his approach and to accept the Board's leadership in defence, and even then only half-heartedly.

Central to this process was the question of identity. At first, the varying responses to fascism of Britain's fragmented and heterogeneous Jewish community broadly conformed to the non-Jewish social and political milieu in which individual Jews operated, reflecting the various paths of assimilation they had taken. Those Jews who did consistently participate in early anti-fascist activity, for example, tended already to be active within organizations that were in political conflict with the Blackshirts; they therefore often opposed the BUF as, say, communists or trade unionists, rather than as Jews. Dan Frankel, meanwhile, made explicit that he intended to respond to fascism as the Labour MP for Mile End, not 'as a partisan representative of…one race'. At the opposite end of the political spectrum, Robert Waley Cohen favoured reinforcing conservative values as a means of combating Nazi propaganda. He and other established, anglicized Jews exhibited the assimilationist attitude typical of the background they shared, believing that the best answer to antisemitism was for Jews to keep quiet and behave as good citizens. By contrast, the group for whom Jewish identity was paramount, Zionists, initially paid little attention at all to domestic fascism.

But, as the threat from the radical right intensified, the disparate elements of the community were offered a stark reminder of their Jewishness, and of the fact that they remained an alien and undesirable whole in the eyes of many fellow citizens. Meanwhile, the worsening situation for their counterparts in Europe appeared to demonstrate the dangers of allowing disunity to prevent coordinated action against political antisemitism. In this context, the differences that had previously divided the community appeared ever more trivial, and growing calls emerged from all quarters for a united Jewish front against fascism.

Yet equally, this did not mean a retreat into Jewish insularity. In fact, quite the opposite: it was broadly agreed that the communal response to fascism should above all advertise the Jews' Britishness, employing this as their primary defence against fascist charges. Throughout the second part of this book we have seen such sentiment expressed by a diversity of groups and individuals: from the self-proclaimed 'true patriots' of the Communist-linked EMAF and the LBWS, with British flags proudly on display, promising to defend 'our country' from the 'foreign menace of fascism'; through the publications and platform speeches of the AJFS, the Board's LAC and the activist, left-wing JLC, which advertised the positive Jewish contribution to British life; to the articles of the *JC*'s 'Watchman', who called on Jews to defiantly declare that they were not 'strangers' in Britain.

Moreover, all sides concurred that defence work should be carried out in close collaboration with as wide a range of non-Jews as possible, who were warned, by Waley Cohen, Laski and the JPC alike, that political antisemitism was an alien import, and merely a foretaste of the fascists' intended erosion of British values and liberties. Even where one finds disagreement within Anglo-Jewry on this aspect of defence, debate was centred not on whether Jews should ally themselves with other opponents of fascism, but on how this should best be done: the JPC worried that the Board's desire to attack just the fascists' antisemitism made it appear that Jews cared only about their own narrow interests, thereby isolating themselves from the British people's wider struggle against fascism; the Board feared that visible opposition to fascism might give the impression of Jews as an interest group interfering in politics to address their own sectional concerns.

Yet the two managed to find common ground between their positions, agreeing upon a political but non-partisan approach to fascism. Even this kind of compromise was seen to be emblematic of the Jews' assimilation of British values. As the *Zionist Review* explained: 'We have in England a tradition that differences in public life can be compatible with personal friendship and with loyal co-operation against a common danger in time of need.'[3] Whatever separate identities and allegiances had developed among different sections of Britain's diverse Jewish community over preceding decades, the threat of fascism brought out – perhaps even helped form – a shared sense of Anglo-Jewishness.

In this regard, the processes that took place on both the British radical right and among the various elements of Anglo-Jewry were not dissimilar. Initially, although there was broad agreement on the central issue – for fascists, that Jews should be opposed; for Jews, that fascist antisemitism should be opposed – a variety of approaches were taken and mistrust existed between different groups. Moreover, the most prominent figure on each side – Laski and Mosley – failed to win much support outside his own organization. However, on both sides a process of convergence took place over the mid-to-late 1930s, as various actors, realizing, in light of international developments, that bigger issues were at stake, put trivial disagreements aside and accepted that they held broadly the same ambitions, even if the analyses that underlay them, and their preferred means of attaining them, varied slightly. At the heart of the matter were two competing ideas of Britishness: Jews rallied around the democratic, liberal traditions that had provided them a relatively favourable environment in Britain; the fascists promulgated an exclusive and exclusionary vision of the nation, regarding adulteration of the 'race' (however defined) as the root of the problems suffered by the indigenous people of modern Britain.

This was a struggle in which the Jews were largely successful. As Nigel Copsey has shown, Britain's wide array of anti-fascist forces was united by precisely the conception of British values that Jews were keen to emphasize. While there may have remained a relatively widespread conviction that Jews were not entirely British, fascism, and its conception of the nation, was seen as far more alien. At all levels, Jews found allies among their gentile counterparts, from the machinery of the state down to local Communist branches; and at each of these levels, Jews were prominent and influential actors.

Intelligence-gathering and lobbying by the Jewish leadership did much to encourage the authorities to restrict fascist activity. Meanwhile, a sophisticated and extensive anti-defamation campaign undermined the anti-Jewish claims that, as we have seen, lay at the very heart of the BUF's ideology and programme. Because Mosley attempted to portray his opposition to Jews as rational, the Board's well-researched and carefully targeted propaganda was particularly damaging.[4] It may not have won over the most fanatical antisemites, but nor was it intended to. Instead, it provided a necessary rejoinder to insidious calumnies that would otherwise have remained unanswered among a non-Jewish population, the majority of which had little experience or knowledge of Jews beyond the standard (usually negative) images of them in popular discourse.

Meanwhile, although Jewish participation in confrontational anti-fascism had certain negative consequences, it did help associate the BUF with violence, irrevocably tarnishing its reputation. Moreover, with such a high proportion of its meetings and marches descending into disorder, the party's primary method of campaigning was severely hindered. Events such as Cable Street, at which Jews had been the primary organizers, also helped to demonstrate the strength and breadth of public antipathy towards fascism.

Together, then, the Jewish community's efforts over 1936–40 had a powerful inhibitory effect on British fascism, severely restricting the political space available to it. This matches closely the pattern Copsey observes with regard to the wider British anti-fascist movement, in which those engaged in physical confrontation with the BUF 'invited [it] to employ violence against them', thereby 'denying [it] respectability', while those who were 'commit[ted] to political moderation … help[ed] marginalise and delegitimize' the fascists.[5] What he, and others, have failed to fully acknowledge, however, is how integral Jews were to this process, providing an instructive example of how a small minority group can unite to leverage its power and, working alongside other interested parties, counteract, isolate and marginalize the radical right. Just as Anglo-Jewry represented the fascists' primary target, it also constituted Britain's foremost anti-fascist force; and the only real 'interaction' between the two sides was the Jews' highly effective response to the Blackshirts' provocation and harassment.

Appendix One

Data Collection Methodology for Newspaper Analysis

The following methodology was used to survey the expression of anti-Jewish sentiment in the BUF's main propaganda newspaper (variously *Blackshirt*, *Fascist Week* and *Action*, as explained in Chapter 2) over 1933–9.[1]

To create the sample for analysis, data were collected in the following way:

– The first and third issue of the relevant newspaper was taken for every month from March 1933 (the first month in which at least two issues were published) until August 1939 (the last month before wartime censorship restricted the fascists' ability to express themselves freely).[2]
– Up to December 1937, every article[3] on the first four pages of these issues was examined; from January 1938, every article on the first eight pages was examined. (The reason for this change was that *Blackshirt* and *Fascist Week*, which were used for the earlier period, had on average roughly half the number of pages of *Action*, which was used in the latter period. The first four/eight pages were chosen for the sample as these always contained policy articles, editorials and other forms of propaganda, whereas later pages were often used for advertising upcoming events, reports on local activity and other such content.)
– Overall, this produced a very large sample: 4,053 articles over 872 pages, representing approximately 21 per cent of all published content in the BUF's main newspaper over this six-and-a-half-year period.[4]

Each article that mentions Jews was recorded, and then assessed in more detail. (This included articles that employ coded but absolutely clear allusions to Jews: the term 'aliens' being the most common example, but also such references as 'ghetto mob' or 'Asiatic thugs' and offensive slurs on Jewish-sounding names.)[5] Their content was categorized in various ways:

– First, whether the article expressed either a negative or neutral attitude towards Jews (unambiguously positive sentiment was never expressed), and if Jews or Jewish issues were the primary focus of the article.
– If a negative attitude was discerned, whether it could be placed within five broad 'types' of antisemitism: conspiratorial, economic, cultural, religious, and racial-biological.[6]

–   Finally, whether certain themes common to the BUF's anti-Jewish discourse were present: portraying Jews as aggressors towards fascism, as agitators for war, as unwanted refugees/immigrants or as criminals; distinguishing between 'good' and 'bad' Jews; negatively caricaturing Jewish physical features and traits; and attempting to deny that the BUF was antisemitic.

Each article could be (and usually was) placed within more than one of these categories.

Appendix Two

Additional Graphs

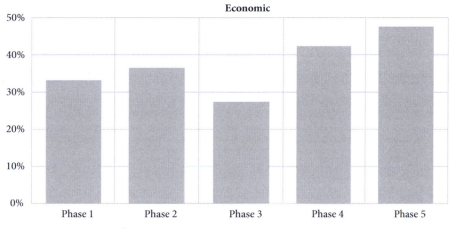

Figure 1 Percentage of articles expressing negative sentiment towards Jews that refer to alleged economic harm caused by them

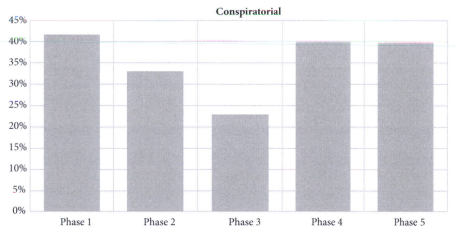

Figure 2 Percentage of 'negative' articles that allude to disproportionate Jewish power or influence

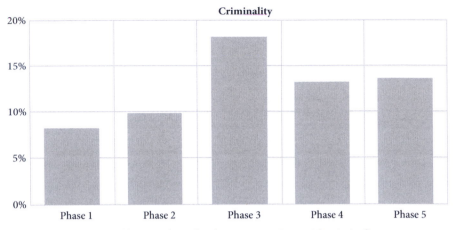

Figure 3 Percentage of 'negative' articles that associate Jews with criminality

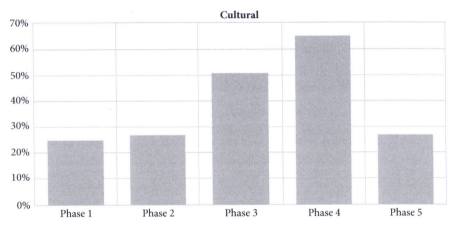

Figure 4 Percentage of 'negative' articles that claim Jews to be distinct from and/or a threat to 'British' culture

Notes

Introduction

1 See section 'Fascism and Antisemitism' in Chapter 1.
2 Richard Thurlow (*Fascism in Britain: From Oswald Mosley's Blackshirts to the National Front* (London: IB Tauris, 2006), pp. xvii, 115, 273) and Stephen Cullen ('The Development of the Ideas and Policy of the British Union of Fascists, 1932–40', *Journal of Contemporary History*, 22 (1987), p. 135) make little reference to such research; Martin Pugh ('*Hurrah for the Blackshirts*': *Fascists and Fascism in Britain Between the Wars* (London: Pimlico, 2005)) and Stephen Dorril (*Blackshirt: Sir Oswald Mosley and British Fascism* (London: Penguin, 2007)) ignore it altogether. Roger Griffin ('British Fascism: The Ugly Duckling', in Mike Cronin (ed.), *The Failure of British Fascism: The Far Right and the Fight for Political Recognition* (London: Macmillan, 1996), p. 141) complains of the insular, 'Anglocentric' treatment of the subject, reminding of 'the need to place British fascism within a wider context'. D.S. Lewis (*Illusions of Grandeur: Mosley, Fascism and British Society, 1931–81* (Manchester: Manchester University Press, 1987), pp. 207–30) was an early exception to this rule, and more recent work by Thomas Linehan (*British fascism 1918-39: Parties, ideology and culture* (Manchester: Manchester University Press, 2000), pp. 1–12, 55–6, 168, 191) and Gary Love ('"What's the Big Idea?": Oswald Mosley, the British Union of Fascists and Generic Fascism', *Journal of Contemporary History*, 42(3) (2007), pp. 447–68) has made greater effort to relate British fascism to the advances made in fascist studies over the past few decades.
3 This will be discussed in more detail throughout Chapter 1.
4 For example, Anthony Julius, *Trials of the Diaspora: A History of Anti-Semitism in England* (Oxford: Oxford University Press, 2010), pp. xx, 304–9.
5 The relevant historiography will be discussed in detail in Chapter 5.
6 A number of other groups were active on Britain's radical right during the 1930s. The majority, however, were negligible in terms of membership, visibility and impact, and often existed only ephemerally. Many also had an extremely limited scope of activity: some were primarily publishing ventures with little other presence; others acted as secretive underground meeting points for various fringe figures; many had little by way of a coherent programme; and, where they did, it often revolved around just one or two narrow issues (keeping Britain out of war with Germany, antisemitism, etc.). Finally, and perhaps most importantly where this study is concerned, while the BUF can readily be defined as 'fascist' by criteria all scholars in the field would accept, doubts surrounds the applicability of this term to some others on interwar Britain's radical-right fringe, who might better be described as extreme conservatives, racial nationalists or various other designations. For discussions of such terms in relation to Britain, see Alan Sykes, *The Radical Right in Britain* (Basingstoke: Palgrave Macmillan, 2005), pp. 1–3. For a small sample of views from the wider debate regarding definitions of fascism, see Zeev Sternhell, 'Fascist Ideology', in Walter

Laqueur (ed.), *Fascism: A Reader's Guide* (Harmondsworth: Penguin, 1976), pp. 325–406; Stanley Payne, *Fascism: Comparison and Definition* (Madison: University of Wisconsin Press, 1980); Roger Griffin (ed.), *Fascism* (Oxford: Oxford University Press, 1995); Robert Paxton *The Anatomy of Fascism* (London: Penguin, 2004); Roger Eatwell, 'Towards a New Model of Generic Fascism', *Journal of Theoretical Politics*, 4(2) (1992), pp. 161–94. The most comprehensive collection of sources can be found in Roger Griffin (ed.) with Matthew Feldman, *Fascism: Critical Concepts in Political Science* (London: Routledge, 2003). None of this is to say that these groups are not significant or relevant, and reference will be made to them, their ideas and activity; but the BUF will be the primary focus.

7   Like the concept of fascism, 'antisemitism' is a disputed, and in some regards unsatisfactory, term. Using a single word to describe negative attitudes and actions towards Jews – which have taken a multiplicity of forms across millennia of history and stem from a variety of motivations and environments – can render such a designation, Gavin Langmuir warns, 'unreliable', 'misleading' and even 'meaningless', *Toward a Definition of Antisemitism* (Berkeley: University of California Press, 1990), p. 16. See also Yehuda Bauer, 'In Search of a Definition of Antisemitism', in Michael Brown (ed.), *Approaches to Antisemitism: Context and Curriculum* (New York: The American Jewish Committee, 1994), pp. 10–23; Shmuel Ettinger, 'Jew-Hatred in Historical Context', in Shmuel Almog (ed.), *Antisemitism Through the Ages* (Oxford: Pergamon Press, 1988), pp. 9–10; Hannah Arendt, *The Origins of Totalitarianism* (London: Andre Deutsch, 1986), p. xi; Richard Levy (ed.), *Antisemitism in the Modern World* (Massachusetts: Heath and Co., 1991), pp. 3–4, 12–13, 16; Herbert A. Strauss (ed.), *Hostages of Modernization. Studies on Modern Antisemitism 1970–1933/39, Vol. 3/1 Germany – Great Britain – France* (Berlin: Walter de Gruyter, 1993), p. v.

   Equally, however, there is utility in having a single term of reference. As David Cesarani argues, although the word 'antisemitism' is 'not very helpful and can be misleading[,] … no longer ha[ving] a clear function', nevertheless, 'as an epithet for anti-Jewish feeling, hostile acts, and so forth … [it] is still useful', 'The Study of Antisemitism in Britain: Trends and Perspectives', in Brown (ed.), *Approaches*, p. 265. For the purposes of this study, 'antisemitism' is used in its widest sense, as any negative sentiment expressed or felt towards Jews as Jews or acts stemming from such sentiment.

8   Stanley Payne, *A History of Fascism, 1914–45* (London: UCL Press, 1995), pp. 303–5.

9   Julius, *Trials*, 309.

10 David Cannadine, 'Cousinhood', *London Review of Books*, 11(14), 27 July 1989, pp. 10–12; William Rubinstein, review of the book *Anglo-Jewry Since 1066: Place, Locality and Memory* by Tony Kushner, *Reviews in History*, www.history.ac.uk/reviews/review/753 [accessed 13 September 2013].

11 Griffin, 'British Fascism', pp. 141–2, 152–5.

12 Sternhell, 'Fascist Ideology', pp. 329, 332.

13 Griffin, 'British Fascism'; Paxton, *Anatomy*, pp. 76–7.

14 Griffin, 'British Fascism', p. 152.

15 Nigel Copsey, 'Communists and the Inter-War Anti-Fascist Struggle in the United States and Britain', *Labour History Review*, 76(3) (2011), pp. 184–5.

16 Jürgen Matthäus and Mark Roseman, *Jewish Responses to Persecution, vol. 1, 1933–1938* (Lanham, MD: AltaMira, 2010), pp. xix–xx. For a discussion of the historiography on Jewish forms of resistance in the restrictive confines of Nazi-occupied Europe, see Robert Rozett, 'Jewish Resistance', in Dan Stone (ed.), *The*

Historiography of the Holocaust (Basingstoke: Palgrave Macmillan, 2004). Interesting work has begun to emerge on the wide array of Jewish interactions with fascism in Italy – ranging from membership of Mussolini's PNF to active opposition to it – and how these changed over time, in particular in response to the party's growing antisemitism. See Joshua D. Zimmerman (ed.), *Jews in Italy under Fascist and Nazi Rule, 1922–1945* (Cambridge: Cambridge University Press, 2005); and Ilaria Pavan, 'An Unexpected Betrayal? The Italian Jewish Community Facing Fascist Persecution', and Elena Mazzini, 'Facing 1938: How the Italian Jewish Community Reacted to the Antisemitic Laws', both in Daniel Tilles and Salvatore Garau (eds), *Fascism and the Jews: Italy and Britain* (London: Vallentine Mitchell, 2010).

17   Richard Thurlow, 'State Management of the British Union of Fascists', in Cronin (ed.), *The Failure*, p. 50. See also Lewis, *Illusions*, pp. 259–60; Dan Stone, *Breeding Superman: Nietzsche, Race, and Eugenics in Edwardian and Interwar Britain* (Liverpool: Liverpool University Press, 2002), pp. 1–2; W.D. Rubinstein, *A History of the Jews in the English-Speaking World: Great Britain* (London: Macmillan, 1996), pp. 313–4.

18   Colin Cross, *The Fascists in Britain* (London: Barrie and Rockliff, 1961); Robert Benewick, *The Fascist Movement in Britain* (London: Allen Lane, 1972); Thurlow, *Fascism*; Lewis, *Illusions*; Linehan, *British fascism*; Sykes, *Radical Right.*

19   Robert Skidelsky, *Oswald Mosley* (London: Papermac, 1990); Oswald Mosley, *My Life* (London: Thomas Nelson, 1968); Dorril, *Blackshirt*; Francis Selwyn, *Hitler's Englishman: The Crime of Lord Haw-Haw* (London: Penguin, 1993); David Baker, *Ideology of Obsession: AK Chesterton and British Fascism* (London: IB Tauris, 1996); Francis Beckett, *The Rebel Who Lost His Cause: The Tragedy of John Beckett, MP* (London: London House, 1999).

20   Thomas Linehan, *East London for Mosley: The British Union of Fascists in East London and South-West Essex* (London: Frank Cass, 1996); John Brewer, *Mosley's Men: The British Union of Fascists in the West Midlands* (London: Gower, 1984).

21   Thurlow, *Fascism*, pp. xi, 62, 114–20. See also Benewick, *Fascist Movement*, pp. 132–64; Neill Nugent 'The ideas of the British Union of Fascists', in Nugent and Roger King (eds), *The British Right: Conservative and right wing politics in Britain* (London: Saxon House, 1977); Cullen, 'Development'; Lewis, *Illusions*, pp. 33–60; Linehan, *British Fascism*, pp. 89–98; Love, 'Big Idea'; Philip Coupland, 'The Blackshirted Utopians', *Journal of Contemporary History*, 33(2) (1998), pp. 255–72 and ' "Left-Wing Fascism" in Theory and Practice: The Case of the British Union of Fascists', *Twentieth Century British History*, 13(1) (2002), pp. 38–61.

22   Paxton, *Anatomy*, p. 75; Payne, *History*, p. 305. See also Griffin (ed.), *Fascism*, pp. 172–3.

23   Pugh, *Hurrah*, pp. 1–6; Webber, *The Ideology of the British Right 1918–1939* (London: St Martin's Press, 1986); Richard Griffiths, *Patriotism Perverted: Captain Ramsey, The Right Club and British Anti-Semitism 1939–40* (London: Constable, 1998).

24   Mike Cronin, ' "Tomorrow We Live" – The Failure of British Fascism?', in Cronin (ed.), *Failure*, pp. 5–6. See also David Baker, 'The Extreme Right in the 1920s: Fascism in a Cold Climate, or "Conservatism with Knobs on"?', and Martin Durham, 'The Conservative Party, the British Extreme Right and the Problem of Political Space, 1967–83', both in Cronin (ed.), *Failure.*

25   Griffin, 'British Fascism'.

26   The following paragraphs contain an overview of this standard, accepted history. Citations will only be included for certain specific pieces of information; the rest can

be gleaned from the abovementioned sources, in particular the general histories cited in note 18 above.

27   On the New Party, see the special issue of *Contemporary British History*, 23(4) (2009), edited by Matthew Worley.

28   The party's programme, which remained remarkably consistent over the years, is outlined in Mosley's founding treatise, *Greater Britain* (London: BUF, 1932).

29   Stephen Cullen, 'Political Violence: The Case of the British Union of Fascists', *Journal of Contemporary History*, 28(2) (1993); Thurlow, *British Fascism*, pp. 67–8.

30   G.C. Webber, 'Patterns of Membership and Support for the BUF', *Journal of Contemporary History*, 19(4) (1984); Thurlow, *Fascism*, pp. 64, 91–9; Arthur Beavan in *Mosley's Blackshirts* (London: Sanctuary Press, 1986), pp. 56, 59.

31   Thurlow, *Fascism*, pp. 34, 37; Pugh, *Hurrah*, p. 61; Andrew Thorpe, 'The Membership of the Communist Party of Great Britain, 1920–1945', *The Historical Journal*, 43(3) (2000), p. 781.

32   Julie Gottlieb, *Feminine Fascism: Women in Britain's Fascist Movement, 1923–1945* (London: I.B. Tauris, 2000); Stephen Cullen, 'Four Women for Mosley: Women in the British Union of Fascists', *Oral History*, 24 (1996), pp. 49–59; Martin Durham, 'Women and the British Union of Fascists, 1932–1940', in Tony Kushner and Kenneth Lunn (eds), *The Politics of Marginality: Race, the Radical Right and Minorities in Twentieth Century Britain* (London: Frank Cass, 1990).

33   Unemployment began to fall in 1932 and continued to do so over the following years in all regions of Britain, W.R. Garside, *British Unemployment, 1919–1939: A Study in Public Policy* (Cambridge: Cambridge University Press, 1990), pp. 5, 10. In 1934, Britain's GDP returned to its pre-depression level, following a year of rapid recovery, 'Some safe haven', *Economist*, 30 July 2011, p. 26.

34   Thurlow, *Fascism*, pp. 71–3.

35   The most detailed survey of BUF's variegated and evolving activity in east and north-east London is provided in Linehan, *East London*. See also Thurlow, *Fascism*, pp. 73–81.

36   Love, 'Big Idea', p. 453.

37   Linehan, *East London*, pp. 153–5.

38   Webber, 'Patterns'; Thurlow, *Fascism*, p. 96.

39   W.F. Mandle, *Anti-Semitism and the British Union of Fascists* (London: Longman, 1968).

40   Gisela Lebzelter, *Political Anti-Semitism1918–1939* (London: Macmillan, 1978), pp. 49–85, and 'Henry Hamilton Beamish and the Britons: Champions of Anti-Semitism', in Kenneth Lunn and Richard Thurlow (eds), *British Fascism: Essays on the Radical Fight in Inter-War Britain* (London: Croom Helm, 1980); Colin Holmes, *Anti-Semitism in British Society 1876–1939* (London: Arnold, 1979), pp. 141–7; Richard Thurlow, *Fascism*, pp. 32, 37–60, and 'Satan and Sambo: The Image of the Immigrant in English Racial Populist Thought since the First World War' in Kenneth Lunn (ed.), *Hosts, Immigrants and Minorities: Historical Reponses to Newcomers in British Society 1870–1914* (New York: St Martin's, 1980); Griffiths, *Patriotism*; John Morell, 'Arnold Leese and the Imperial Fascist League: The Impact of Racial Fascism', in Lunn and Thurlow (eds), *British Fascism*; Graham Macklin, 'The Two Lives of John Hooper Harvey', *Patterns of Prejudice*, 42(2) (2008), pp. 167–90; Dan Stone, 'The English Mistery, the BUF, and the Dilemmas of British Fascism', *The Journal of Modern History*, 75 (2003), pp. 336–58, and 'The Far Right and the Back-to-the-Land Movement', in Julie Gottlieb and Thomas Linehan, *The Culture of Fascism: Visions of the Far Right in Britain* (London: IB Tauris, 2004), pp. 182–98.

41   Colin Holmes, 'Anti-semitism and the BUF', in Lunn and Thurlow (eds), *British Fascism*, p. 114; Kenneth Lunn, 'British Fascism Revisited: A Failure of Imagination?', in Cronin (ed.), *Failure*, p. 177.

42   David Renton, *This Rough Game* (Gloucester: Sutton, 2001), and *Red Shirts and Black: Fascism and Anti-Fascism in Oxford in the 'Thirties* (Oxford: Ruskin College Library, 1996); Nigel Todd, *In Excited Times: People Against the Blackshirts* (Whitley Bay: Bewick Press, 1995); Liz Kibblewhite and Andy Rigby, *Fascism in Aberdeen* (Aberdeen: Aberdeen People's Press, 1978); David Turner, *Fascism and Anti-Fascism in the Medway Towns 1927–40* (Rochester: Kent Anti-Fascist Action Committee, 1993); Neil Barrett, 'The anti-fascist movement in south-east Lancashire, 1933–1940: the divergent experiences of Manchester and Nelson', in Tim Kirk and Anthony McElligott (eds), *Opposing Fascism: Community, Authority and Resistance in Europe* (Cambridge: Cambridge University Press, 1999), pp. 48–62; David Rosenberg, *Battle for the East End: Jewish responses to fascism in the 1930s* (Nottingham: Five Leaves, 2011).

43   Copsey, *Anti-Fascism*, p. 4, and preface to Nigel Copsey and Andrzej Olechnowicz (eds), *Varieties of Anti-Fascism: Britain in the Inter-War Period* (Basingstoke: Palgrave Macmillan, 2010), pp. xiv–xxi.

44   Preface to Copsey and Olechnowicz (eds), *Varieties*, p. xx.

45   A chapter by Thomas Linehan ('Communist Culture and Anti-Fascism in Inter-War Britain', in Copsey and Olechnowicz (eds), *Varieties*, pp. 49–50) deals very briefly with the Jewish contribution to Communist anti-fascism. Of the three émigré intellectuals examined by Dan Stone ('Anti-Fascist Europe Comes to Britain: Theorising Fascism as a Contribution to Defeating It', in Copsey and Olechnowicz (eds), *Varieties*, p. 185), two were Jewish, but neither, of course, British. Moreover, 'their Jewishness was of little significance' to either, Stone notes.

46   A recent article, co-authored with the present author, has begun to address some of these gaps, Nigel Copsey and Daniel Tilles, 'Uniting a Divided Community? Re-appraising Jewish Responses to British Fascism Antisemitism, 1932–9', in Tilles and Garau (eds), *Fascism*.

47   The relevant scholarship is discussed in detail in Chapters 5 and 8.

48   In 2012, as part of a project the present author helped initiate and complete, the defence archive moved to a new home at the Wiener Library in London, making this rich resource far more accessible to researchers.

Chapter 1

1   Thurlow, *Fascism*, p. 86; Bill Williams, 'The Anti-Semitism of Tolerance: Middle-Class Manchester and the Jews 1870–1900', in Alan Kidd and K.W. Roberts (eds), *City, class and culture: Studies of social policy and cultural production in Victorian Manchester* (Manchester: Manchester University Press, 1985), p. 94.

2   Cesarani, 'Antisemitism in Britain', pp. 249–51. See also Todd Endelman, "English Jewish History', *Modern Judaism*, 11(1) (1991), pp. 97–8.

3   Cesarani, 'Antisemitism in Britain', pp. 251–253. For example, James Parkes, *Antisemitism* (London: Valentine Mitchell, 1963), pp. 10–15; Mandle, *Anti-Semitism*; Benewick, *Fascist Movement*; Cross, *Fascists*; Skidelsky, *Mosley*.

4   Lebzelter, *Political Anti-Semitism*, pp. 3–4, 27.

5   Holmes, *Anti-Semitism*, pp. 34, 220–34.

6   Geoffrey G. Field, 'Anti-Semitism with the Boots Off', in Strauss (ed.), *Hostages of Modernization*, pp. 297–8; Holmes, *Anti-Semitism*, pp. 24–30, 75–80. See also Kenneth Lunn, 'Political Anti-semitism Before 1914: Fascism's Heritage?', in Lunn and Thurlow (eds), *British Fascism*.

7   Holmes, *Anti-Semitism*, p. 233; Field, 'Anti-Semitism', in Strauss (ed.), *Hostages*, pp. 299, 308–10, 319.

8   Cesarani, 'Antisemitism in Britain', p. 253; W.J. Fishman, *East End Jewish Radicals 1875–1914* (London: Duckworth, 1975). See also Colin Holmes (ed.), *Immigrants and Minorities in British Society* (London: Allen and Unwin, 1978).

9   Bryan Cheyette, 'Hilaire Belloc and the "Marconi Scandal"1900–1914: A Reassessment of the Interactionist Model of Racial Hatred', in Kushner and Lunn (eds), *Politics of Marginality*, pp. 131–4.

10   Bryan Cheyette, *Constructions of 'the Jew' in English literature and society: Racial representations, 1874–1945* (Cambridge: Cambridge University Press, 1993); Frank Felsenstein, *Anti-Semitic Stereotypes: A Paradigm of Otherness in English Popular Culture, 1660–1830* (Baltimore: Johns Hopkins University Press, 1995), pp. 1, 3, 257; Anthony Julius, *T.S. Eliot, Anti-Semitism and Literary Form* (Cambridge: Cambridge University Press, 1996), and *Trials*, pp. 148–241.

11   Williams, 'Anti-Semitism', pp. 2, 4, 94–5; Holmes, *Anti-Semitism*, 104; Tony Kushner, 'The Impact of British Anti-semitism, 1918–1945', in David Cesarani (ed.), *The Making of Modern Anglo-Jewry* (Oxford: Blackwell, 1990), p. 202.

12   Cesarani, 'Antisemitism in Britain', pp. 257–60.

13   Kushner, 'Impact', pp. 197–200, 206, and 'Beyond the Pale? British Reactions to Nazi Anti-semitism, 1933–39', in Kushner and Lunn (eds), *Marginality*. See also Endelman, 'English Jewish History', pp. 92–3.

14   Julius, *Trials*, pp. xxxvi–xli.

15   For alternative perspectives, see Rubinstein, *Jews in the English-Speaking World*, p. 6; Lloyd Gartner, *History of the Jews in Modern Times* (Oxford: Oxford University Press, 2001), pp. 217–20, 236–7; Werner Mosse, 'Introduction', in Michael Brenner, Rainer Liedtke and David Rechter (eds), *Two Nations: British and German Jews in Comparative Perspective* (London: Leo Baeck Institute, 1999), pp. 8–9.

16   David Feldman, *Englishmen and Jews: Social Relations and Political Culture 1840–1914* (New Haven: Yale University Press, 1994), pp. 13–5, 379–81. See also David Feldman, 'Jews and the State in Britain', in Liedtke and Rechter (eds), *Two Nations*, pp. 141–61.

17   Todd Endelman, 'English Jewish History', pp. 100–1, 'Comparative Perspectives on Modern Anti-Semitism in the West', in David Berger (ed.), *History and Hate: The Dimensions of Anti-Semitism* (Philadelphia: Jewish Publication Society, 1986), and 'The Englishness of Jewish Modernity in England', in Jacob Katz (ed.), *Toward Modernity: The European Jewish Model* (New Brunswick: Transaction Books, 1986), pp. 236–9.

18   Todd Endelman, *The Jews of Britain, 1656–2000* (London: University of California Press, 2002), pp. 257–63.

19   Colin Holmes, 'The German Gypsy Question in Britain 1904–6', in Lunn (ed.), *Hosts*, pp. 149–50.

20   Paxton, *Anatomy*; Payne, *History*; Juan Linz, 'Some Notes Toward a Comparative Study of Fascism in Sociological Historical Perspective', in Laqueur (ed.) *Fascism*; Sternhell, 'Fascist Ideology'; Eatwell, 'Towards'.

21   Griffin (ed.), *Fascism*, p. 7; Payne, *History*, p. 11.

22 Paxton, *Anatomy*, pp. 32, 76–7, 174, 218–20, 253–4.

23 Aristotle Kallis, *Genocide and Fascism: The Eliminationist Drive in Fascist Europe* (New York: Routledge, 2009), p. 85–8, 102–5.

24 Mark Neocleous, *Fascism* (London: Open University Press, 1997), pp. 29–37. See also Eatwell, 'Towards', pp. 178–80.

25 Kevin Passmore, *Fascism: A Very Short Introduction* (Oxford: Oxford University Press, 2002), p. 108.

26 A. James Gregor, *Phoenix: Fascism in Our Time* (New Brunswick: Transaction, 1999), p. 9. Zeev Sternhall is another who argues that racism, let alone antisemitism, 'was not a necessary condition for the existence of fascism' (*The Birth of Fascist Ideology: From Cultural Rebellion to Political Religion* (Princeton, NJ: Princeton University Press, 1994), p. 5). However, in earlier work he does list antisemitism as one of the 'elements which went on to make up fascism' – although exempting the (rather significant) case of Italy ('Fascist Ideology', p. 335).

27 Alan Cassels, *Fascism* (Arlington Heights: AHM, 1975).

28 Griffin, 'British Fascism', pp. 152–5.

29 Sternhell, *Fascist Ideology*, pp. 6–7; Gregor, *Phoenix*, p. 21.

30 Aristotle Kallis, 'Fascism and the Jews: From Internationalisation of Fascism to "Fascist Antisemitism"', in Tilles and Garau (eds), *Fascism and the Jews*. See also, Aristotle Kallis, 'Fascism, "Licence" and Genocide: From the Chimera of Rebirth to the Authorization of Mass Murder', in Antonio Costa Pinto (ed.), *Rethinking the Nature of Fascism* (Basingstoke: Palgrave Macmillan, 2011), pp. 230–1, and *Genocide and Fascism*, pp. 96–9.

31 Dorril, *Blackshirt*, p. 370.

32 Pugh, *Hurrah*, pp. 213–34

33 For example, Skidelsky, *Mosley*, pp. 379–410.

34 As Roger Eatwell ('Towards', p. 173) cautions, one must 'distinguish between *intellectual* and *activist* fascism': while there were some fascist leaders who attempted 'to influence, or themselves were, street-fighters', there were others who 'sought to create and offer a serious level of debate about both current and metapolitical issues'. Much of the academic literature, he complains, has been weighted towards the former, at the expense of the latter.

35 Cross, *Fascists*, p. 123; Benewick, *Fascist Movement*, p. 151.

36 Mandle, *Anti-Semitism*, pp. 1–3, 5, 13–19, 25–45, 64, 67–8.

37 Robert Skidelsky, *Mosley*, p. 18, and 'Reflections on Mosley and British Fascism', in Lunn and Thurlow (eds), *British Fascism*.

38 Holmes, *Anti-Semitism*, pp. 186–9, and 'Anti-semitism', pp. 118–21.

39 Lebzelter, *Political Anti-Semitism*, pp. 95–6, 100.

40 Cheyette, 'Belloc', pp. 132–4.

41 'Editors' Introduction', Kushner and Lunn (eds), *Marginality*. The quote they use is from Cesarani's contribution to the same volume, 'An Embattled Minority: The Jews in Britain During the First World War', p. 76. See also Julius, *Trials*, pp. 304, 306–8, 313. Further criticism of interactionist theories comes from David Renton (*Fascism, Anti-Fascism and the 1940s* (London: Macmillan, 2000), p. 9). He claims that certain scholars (Linehan and Stephen Cullen are named) have allowed their research to be become 'distorted' by a reliance on information from the 'Friends of Mosley' group, resulting, for example, in the perception that the fascists were victims of Jewish aggression. Some scholars have indeed occasionally been too willing to accept the fascists' revisionism at face value, as we shall see; but Renton's accusations go too far.

42   Lewis, *Illusions*, pp. 95-7, 101. The present author, in much much earlier work, has
      also made a similar suggestion, recognising that the BUF's 'increasingly virulent
      anti-Semitism', which had begun to emerge in the movement's early history, 'played
      a large part in stirring Britain's Jews into [anti-fascist] action', but also suggesting
      that, in turn, Jewish 'attacks on the BUF pushed the movement towards stronger
      anti-Semitism'. These views will be thoroughly updated in the present work, Daniel
      Tilles, 'Bullies or Victims? A Study of British Union of Fascists Violence', *Totalitarian
      Movements and Political Religions*, 7(2) (2006), pp. 336, 343.

43   Thurlow, *Fascism*, pp. xiv, 72–5, 78, 86, 126–8. Copsey offers a similarly interactionist
      account, *Anti-Fascism*, pp. 79–80.

44   Pugh, *Hurrah*, pp. 77, 219–20, 230–4.

45   Linehan, *East London*, pp. 24–44, 78–80, 224, 275–6, 302, and *British Fascism*,
      pp. 176–7, 190.

46   The primary exception is Holmes (*Anti-Semitism*, p. 189), who believes that
      antisemitism was a 'useful tactical weapon' for the BUF, helping to 'increase its own
      importance' and providing a means of uniting those from the political left and right
      against a single target.

47   Thurlow, *Fascism*, pp. 61–3, 77, 86. See also, Mosley, *My Life*, p. 341; Copsey, *Anti-
      Fascism*, pp. 40–1; Love, 'Big Idea', p. 467; Field, 'Anti-Semitism', p. 318.

48   Lebzelter, *Political Anti-Semitism*, p. 95; Mandle, *Anti-Semitism*, pp. 1, 64–8, 70.

49   Pugh, *Hurrah*, pp. 172–3, 230–4.

50   See, for various examples, Cross, *Fascists*, pp. 125–6; Holmes, *Anti-
      Semitism*, pp. 120–3, 176–7; Mandle, *Anti-Semitism*, pp. 9–10, 61; Skidelsky, *Mosley*,
      pp. 381–8, and 'Reflections', pp. 84–7; Thurlow, *Fascism*, pp. 73–5, 77; Linehan,
      East London, pp. 12–3, 48, 154–5, 162, and *British Fascism*, pp. 98–9, 103, 109,
      111; Claudia Baldoli, 'Anglo-Italian Fascist Solidarity?: The Shift from Italophilia
      to Naziphilia in the BUF', in Gottlieb and Linehan (eds), *Culture*, p. 156; Paxton,
      Anatomy, p. 75; Geoffrey Alderman, *Modern British Jewry* (Oxford: Oxford
      University Press, 1998), p. 283.

51   Sykes, *Radical Right*, pp. 64–6; Mandle, *Anti-Semitism*, p. 62. See also, Benewick,
      Fascist Movement, pp. 157–8.

52   Skidelsky, *Mosley*, pp. 380, 384–5; Thurlow, *Fascism*, p. 74; Nugent, 'Ideas', pp. 148–9.

53   Linehan, *British Fascism*, pp. 98, 113–4. Elsewhere, Linehan does acknowledge that in
      the late 1930s 'the drift to war also intensified the BUF's hostility towards Jews', *East
      London*, pp. 154–5.

54   Lewis, *Illusions*, pp. 92–110. His focus on the East End campaign leads to a somewhat
      skewed perspective, including the claim that the BUF at times verged on 'the
      holocaust mentality of racial anti-Semitism'. Lebzelter also argues that the BUF's
      turn to antisemitism was 'inaugurated' in November 1933, although she, like others,
      erroneously dates its subsequent re-emergence to after the split with Rothermere,
      Political Anti-Semitism, pp. 91–2. See also, Dorril, *Blackshirt*, pp. 301–4.

55   Mandle, *Anti-Semitism*, pp. 1, 25–45. See also Lebzelter, *Political Anti-Semitism*, p. 96.

56   Holmes, 'Anti-semitism', pp. 114–33, and *Anti-Semitism*, p. 187. Nugent also accepts
      that antisemitism 'was built onto and around' the BUF's existing programme,
      but his brief assessment of its content focuses almost entirely on conspiratorial
      aspects, 'Ideas', pp. 148–52. More recently, Love has also concluded that the BUF's
      antisemitism was 'very much the product of home-grown racism', and differed from
      the more Nazi-like rhetoric used in the East End. His account, however, deals with
      antisemitism only in passing, 'Big Idea', p. 467.

57 Thurlow, 'The Developing British Fascist Interpretation of Race, Culture and Evolution', in Gottlieb and Linehan (eds), *Culture*, pp. 66–79, and *Fascism*, pp. 37, 75, 116–8, 127. Philip Coupland similarly acknowledges that antisemitism was related to the BUF's ideology, but grants it only a 'symbolic role'; it was 'the seasoning rather than the whole dish' (review of *Blackshirt: Sir Oswald Mosley and British Fascism* by Stephen Dorril, *Totalitarian Movements and Political Religions*, 9(4) (2008), p. 610).

58 Cullen, 'Development', pp. 127–8.

59 Baker, *Ideology*, pp. 151–3, 163–5. See also David Baker, *The Making of a British Fascist – The Case of AK Chesterton*, PhD Thesis, University of Sheffield, 1982.

60 Linehan, *British Fascism*, pp. 176, 186–193 (see also pp. 103–112 for outline of BUF's history over 1934–7, which makes some mention of antisemitism's position within this wider context), and *East London*, pp. 275–6.

Chapter 2

1 Leonard Doob's analysis of Ezra Pound's fascist propaganda highlights how such biases can manifest themselves. Using a quantitative survey of a broad sample of Pound's work, he refutes many of the findings of previous scholars and illustrates how a limited and unrepresentative choice of sources has skewed their interpretations. See Leonard Doob (ed.), *'Ezra Pound Speaking': Radio Speeches of World War II* (Westport: Greenwood, 1978), pp. 427–35.

2 Ian Budge, Hans-Dieter Klingemann, Andrea Volkens, Judith Bara and Eric Tanenbaum, *Mapping Policy Preferences: Estimates for Parties, Electors, and Governments 1945–1998* (Oxford: Oxford University Press, 2001); Paul Pennings, 'An Empirical Analysis of the Europeanisation of National Party Manifestos, 1960–2003', *European Union Politics*, 7(2) (2006), pp. 257–70; Matthew Gentzkow and Jesse M. Shapiro, 'What Drives Media Slant? Evidence from US Daily Newspapers', *Econometrica*, 78(1) (2010), pp. 35–71; Michael Evans, Wayne McIntosh, Jimmy Lin and Cynthia Cates, 'Recounting the Courts? Applying Automated Content Analysis to Enhance Empirical Legal Research', *Journal of Empirical Legal Studies*, 4(4) (2007), pp. 1007–39.

3 William Brustein, *Roots of Hate: Antisemitism in Europe Before the Holocaust* (Cambridge: Cambridge University Press, 2003), pp. 8–10, 17–8, 25, 30–1.

4 Brewer, *Mosley's Men*, pp. x, 3–14; Linehan, *East London*, pp. 208–21; Webber, 'Patterns'; Cullen, 'Political Violence'.

5 *Blackshirt*, 1 March 1935, p. 4; March 1938, p. 4.

6 In the mid-1930s, *Blackshirt* and *Action* had circulations of 26,000 and 23,000 respectively, far higher than estimated party membership of 15,000 at that time; Pugh, *Hurrah*, p. 223. In his autobiography, Mosley (*My Life*, pp. 341–2, 348) attempted to distance himself from the content of the BUF's publications, claiming that 'party journals were in other hands ... [and] I often did not see a line of what was being written'. As with much of Mosley's revisionism in regard to his own antisemitism, this claim must be viewed sceptically. Chesterton, who edited both *Blackshirt* and *Action*, confirmed that Mosley approved proofs of every issue each week, *J[ewish] C[hronicle]*, 13 December 1969, p. 8. He would have authorized editorial appointments, and could easily censure or remove them if he wished. Furthermore, he often contributed articles himself, sometimes anonymously (such as November 1933's 'Shall Jews Drag Britain to War'), and the stance of the BUF's

newspapers usually reflected the content of Mosley's own contemporaneous public pronouncements. See also Skidelsky, *Mosley*, p. 385.

7   Nugent ('Ideas', pp. 134–5) sets out the BUF's primary instruments of ideological promulgation, in descending order of importance, as: Mosley's speeches and writings; the output of his 'inner circle'; the party's press; and the pronouncements of others within the party. Given that the BUF's newspapers regularly hosted articles by Mosley and his chief propagandists, reported on speeches made by them, and its content and editorial line was overseen by Mosley and other senior figures (see previous note) they should, in fact, be regarded as the principal means of dissemination.

8   *JC*, 28 October 1932, p. 28; *Times*, 25 October 1932; *Daily Herald*, 25 October 1932.

9   *JC*, 30 September 1932, p. 12; 7 October 1932, p. 8.

10   *Blackshirt*, 1 April 1933, p. 1.

11   *Blackshirt*, 1 February 1933, p. 3; 18 March 1933, p. 4; 17 April 1933, p. 4.

12   *Blackshirt*, 16 May 1933, p. 2. Thurlow (*Fascism*, p. 128) and Benewick (*Fascist Movement*, p. 154) identify Joyce as Lucifer. Certainly the writer's tone and attitude towards Jews matched Joyce's. On Joyce, see Selwyn, *Hitler's Englishman*.

13   *Blackshirt*, 5 August 1933, p. 2.

14   *Blackshirt*, 16 September 1933, pp. 2–3.

15   *Blackshirt*, 30 September 1933, p. 1.

16   *Daily Express*, 24 March 1933, p. 1; Sharon Gewirtz, 'Anglo-Jewish Responses to Nazi Germany 1933–39: The Anti-Nazi Boycott and the Board of Deputies of British Jews', *Journal of Contemporary History*, 26(2) (1991), pp. 256–73.

17   *Blackshirt*, 4 November 1933, p. 1 (emphasis added). See also *F[ascist] W[eek]*, 17 November 1933, p. 4. This new stance was not limited to the movement's newspapers. Speaking in Wolverhampton, Mosley promised to stand up to the 'Jewish interests and organisations who were determined to smash the people in Germany'. A poster campaign on the theme was also initiated, *JC*, 24 November 1933, p. 32.

18   *Blackshirt*, 18 November 1933, pp. 1, 6.

19   *FW*, 23 February 1934, pp. 1–2.

20   *Spectator*, 27 September 1930, p. 1; Nigel Nicolson (ed.), *Harold Nicolson: Diaries and Letters 1930–39* (London: Fontana, 1971), p. 95; Skidelsky, *Mosley*, p. 283.

21   Copsey, *Anti-Fascism*, p. 23; Pugh, *Hurrah*, p. 150.

22   Mandle, *Anti-Semitism*, pp. 6–7; Skidelsky, *Mosley*, p. 385; Holmes, *Anti-Semitism*, pp. 176–7.

23   'Lord Rothermere Attacking Jews Advises Hitler to Eliminate Anti-semitism from Program', *Jewish Telegraphic Agency*, 5 October 1930; *Spectator*, 27 September 1930, p. 1.

24   *Daily Mail*, 10 July 1933; Richard Bourne, *Lords of Fleet Street: The Harmsworth Dynasty* (London: Barrie and Jenkins, 1990), pp. 109–10.

25   *Blackshirt*, 20 July 1934, p. 2.

26   A.K. Chesterton did, however, later claim that Rothermere had actually never understood what the BUF stood for, imagining it to be full of 'right-wing Tories', *Oswald Mosley: Portrait of a Leader* (London: Action Press, n.d), p. 128.

27   Pugh, *Hurrah*, p. 168.

28   *Times*, 20 July 1934, NA HO 144/20142.

29   Mosley, *My Life*, pp. 342–5.

30   Skidelsky, *Mosley*, p. 385; Pugh, *Hurrah*, pp. 168–9.

31   Thurlow, *Fascism*, p. 72

32   *FW*, 20 April 1934, pp. 1, 3. On Beckett, see Beckett, *The Rebel*.

33   *FW*, 4 May 1934, p. 4.

34   *FW*, 11 May 1934, p. 7.
35   *Blackshirt*, 3 August 1934, p. 4.
36   *Blackshirt*, 17 August 1934, p. 4. On Raven Thomson, see Peter Pugh, *A Political Biography of Alexander Raven Thomson*, PhD thesis, University of Sheffield, 2002.
37   *Blackshirt*, 22 June 1934, p. 4; 6 July 1934, p. 2; 3 August 1934, p. 1; 14 September 1934, p. 12.
38   *Daily Worker*, 10 September 1934, p. 1; *JC*, 14 September 1934, p. 10; Mandle, *Anti-Semitism*, p. 9; Skidelsky, *Mosley*, p. 386.
39   *Blackshirt*, 5 October 1934, pp. 1–2. Two weeks later, *Blackshirt* (19 October 1934, p. 12) published a letter by A.H. Lane, author of an infamous antisemitic tract, *The Alien Menace*, warning readers of the powerful 'Hidden Hand' of 'Jew-controlled combines' and international communists. In the next issue (26 October 1934, p. 8), a glowing review of Lane's book appeared, describing it as a 'trusty work of reference' that revealed the 'methods and power' of the 'international racketeers and vice-merchants who command the world's gold and brains', to which 'every citizen should be alive'.
40   *Blackshirt*, 2 November 1934, pp. 1–2.
41   *Blackshirt*, 30 November 1934, pp. 1, 7; 7 December 1934, pp. 4, 7; 14 December 1934, pp. 6–7.
42   The column first appeared in *Blackshirt*, 8 February 1935, p. 2.
43   *Blackshirt*, 2 August 1935, p. 1.
44   *JC*, 7 August 1936, p. 9. From June 1936 the *JC* reported in detail on fascist activity in the area, revealing the extent to which local propaganda comprised, almost exclusively, of antisemitism. The BUF's campaign in east London has been well covered in the historiography. Linehan (*East London*) offers the most comprehensive and detailed account. See also Skidelsky, *Mosley*, pp. 393–410; Thurlow, *Fascism*, pp. 75–81, 85–6; Lewis, *Illusions*, pp. 90–110; Pugh, *Hurrah*, pp. 224–30.
45   *Blackshirt*, 7 November 1936, p. 4.
46   *FW*, 23 March 1934, p. 3; *Blackshirt*, 12 July 1935, p. 2.
47   Blackshirt, 2 August 1935, p. 5; Linehan, *East London*, p. 112.
48   *Blackshirt*, 24 May 1935, p. 5; 17 January 1936, p. 4; 11 July 1936, p. 5.
49   *Blackshirt*, 17 May 1935, p. 5; *JC*, 27 March 1936, p. 25.
50   *Blackshirt*, 2 August 1935, pp. 1, 5; 3 January 1936, p. 3; 6 June 1936, p. 4; 15 August 1936, p. 5; 5 September 1936, p. 1.
51   For an early example, see *Blackshirt*, 14 October 1933, p. 3.
52   *Blackshirt*, 23 May 1936, p. 6.
53   *Blackshirt*, 10 October 1936, p. 1.
54   *Blackshirt*, 18 July 1936, p. 4.
55   'London Country Council Elections' 1937 (London: Hillman, n.d).
56   *Blackshirt*, 13 February 37, p. 5.
57   Over most of 1935 and 1936, the newspaper did not identify its editor. From 20 June 1936 Beckett was named above editorials, the first of which he used to announce the party's adoption of the 'National Socialist' moniker.
58   *Blackshirt*, 8 August 1936, p. 1; 29 August 1936, p. 5; 5 September 1936, p. 1.
59   It is important to emphasize that these are changes in relative levels. In absolute terms, economic and conspiratorial antisemitism remained prevalent, simply to a lesser extent than in earlier and later periods.
60   See *Blackshirt*, 14 November 1936, p. 2; 12 December 1936, p. 5; 6 February 1937, p. 2; 27 March 1937, p. 8.

61   *Blackshirt*, 6 March 1937, p. 2; 3 April 1937, p. 2; 1 May 1937, p. 4.

62   *Blackshirt*, 7 November 1936, p. 1; 13 February 1937, p. 1.

63   *Blackshirt*, 5 December 1936, p. 1; 12 February 1937, p. 3; 6 March 1937, p. 2; 20 March 1937, p. 2; 17 April 1937, p. 2.

64   *Blackshirt*, 5 December 1936, p. 8.

65   *Blackshirt*, 19 December 1936, p. 2.

66   *Blackshirt*, 1 August 1936, pp. 2, 4; 15 August 1936, p. 4; 22 August 1936, p. 1; 29 August 1936, p. 3; 9 January 1937, p. 2; 16 January 1937, p. 5; 23 January 1937, p. 1; 27 March 1937, p. 4; 8 April 1937, p. 3; 1 May 1937, p. 3.

67   At this stage the BUF only managed to attract any substantial interest in the East End, almost collapsing as a national force. In local elections in 1937, none of its candidates in Leeds, Sheffield, Southampton and Edinburgh received more than 106 votes; one attained just twenty-nine (report on municipal elections, L[ondon] M[etropolitan]A[rchives] ACC3121/E3/245/2).

68   The election results will be presented in more detail in Chapter 7.

69   Love, 'Big Idea', p. 453.

70   Linehan, *East London*, pp. 11–12. We will return to this subject in Chapter 4.

71   A.K. Chesterton, 'The Apotheosis of the Jew: From Ghetto to Park Lane' (London: Abbey Supplies, n.d.), and *Portrait of a Leader*. On Chesterton and his antisemitism, see Baker, *Ideology*, and *The Making*. Chesterton left the party after disagreements with Mosley, whom he accused of abandoning true fascist principles.

72   *Blackshirt*, 14 August 1937, p. 4; see also 7 August 1937, p. 5.

73   *Blackshirt*, 21 August 1937, p. 5.

74   Alexander Raven Thomson, 'Our Financial Masters' (London: Abbey Supplies, n.d.).

75   *Blackshirt*, 2 October 1937, p. 2; *Action*, 19 March 1938, p. 7.

76   *Blackshirt*, 24 December 1937, p. 6.

77   *Action*, 2 April 1938, p. 7.

78   *Blackshirt*, 27 November 1937, p. 8; *Action*, 19 March 1938, p. 7.

79   The series ran in *Blackshirt* from April to July 1937.

80   Gordon-Canning also produced individual publications for the BUF, such as 'Mind Britain's Business' (1937) and 'Inward Strength of a National Socialist' (1938). For more on Gordon-Canning, see Graham Macklin, 'A Fascist "Jihad": Captain Robert Gordon-Canning, British Fascist Antisemitism and Islam', in Tilles and Garau (eds), *Fascism*.

81   *Blackshirt*, 14 August 1937, p. 5; 31 July 1937, p. 5; 28 August 1937, p. 1.

82   *Blackshirt*, 31 July 1937, p. 5.

83   *FW*, 20 April 34, p. 4; see *Blackshirt*, 4 January 1935, p. 1; 15 February 1935, p. 7; 1 March 1935, p. 1; 16 May 1936, p. 2; 10 October 1936, p. 2; 6 March 1937, p. 2. On BUF cultural policy and its relationship with antisemitism, see Roger Griffin, '"This Fortress Built Against Infection": The BUF Vision of Britain's Theatrical and Musical Renaissance', in Gottlieb and Linehan (eds), *Culture*.

84   *Blackshirt*, 3 July 1937, p. 5.

85   *Blackshirt*, 4 September 1937, p. 4.

86   *Blackshirt*, 14 August 1937, 4.

87   The diary first appeared in *Blackshirt*, 2 October 1937, p. 8.

88   *Blackshirt*, 26 June 1937, p. 8; 21 August 1937, p. 5.

89   *Blackshirt*, 23 October 1937, p. 3. T.S. Eliot was another to use this device (Bryan Cheyette, 'Jewish Stereotyping and English Literature, 1875–1920: Toward a Political Analysis', in Tony Kushner and Kenneth Lunn (eds), *Traditions*

of intolerance: Historical perspectives on fascism and race discourse in Britain (Manchester: Manchester University Press, 1989), pp. 27–8), and may have been an inspiration for the literary-minded Chesterton.

90 E.G. Clarke, 'The British Union and the Jews' (London: Abbey Supplies, n.d.).
91 'Britain and Jewry' (London: Greater Britain Publications, n.d.).
92 Mosley, *Greater Britain*, pp. 143–6.
93 *Blackshirt*, 4 November 1933, p. 1.
94 *JC*, 6 September 1935, p. 34; letter to Mrs Drummond, 4 February 1936, B[oard][of Deputes]D[efence]A[rchive] C6/9/1/2; *Blackshirt*, 31 July 1937, p. 5.
95 *Action*, 17 September 1938, p. 1.
96 *Action*, 18 June 1938, p. 1; 17 September 1938, p. 1.
97 *Action*, 17 September 1938, p. 2.
98 *Action*, 1 April 1938, p. 8.
99 *Action*, 6 August 1938, pp. 1, 3; 20 August 1938, p. 1.
100 Action, 13 September 1938, p. 3.
101 *Action*, 6 May 1939, p. 4; 30 May 1939, p. 1.
102 *Action*, 5 November 1938, p. 3; 21 January 1939, p. 8; 5 August 1939, p. 1.
103 *Action*, 17 September 1938, p. 3; 7 January 1939, p. 1. Emphasis in original.
104 *Action*, 6 May 1939, p. 2.
105 *Action*, 14 January 1939, p. 5; 21 January 1939, p. 5; 3 June 1938, p. 8.
106 *Action*, 17 December 1938, p. 3.
107 *Action*, 21 January 1939, p. 7; 20 May 1939, p. 3.
108 Robert Gordon Canning, *The Holy Land: Arab or Jew?* (unknown publisher, n.d.).
109 Raven Thomson, 'Financial Masters'.
110 The first front-page anti-war article of 1938, for example, warned against British involvement in conflict with Japan in the Far East and made no mention of Jews (*Action*, 5 February 1938, p. 1). Similarly, opposition was expressed to immigration in general, not only of Jews.
111 *Action*, 2 April 1938, p. 6; 21 May 1938, p. 6.
112 *Action*, 18 July 1938, p. 6; 1 July 1939, p. 6.
113 A similar pattern was apparent in another newly created column, ''Gainst Trust and Monopoly', which was aimed at small traders. In a typical instalment from late 1938, its author, Peter Heyward, used the entire column to outline the baleful influence of large chain stores on small shopkeepers, wholesalers and workers. Throughout the piece, no mention of Jews was made; only at the very end was it explained that these large combines were run for the benefit of 'Jewish fleshpots, whose motto is "Britain last"', *Action*, 5 November 1938, p. 6.
114 *Action*, 3 June 1939, p. 4; 3 December 1938, p. 2; 4 March 1939, p. 4; 21 January 1939, p. 7.

Chapter 3

1 Criticism of Jews that invoked religion or biology appeared in just 2 per cent and 1 per cent, respectively, of all sampled articles that expressed anti-Jewish sentiment. It is important here to note that, although the BUF did speak about different 'races', there were rarely any biological connotations to the term. Rather, it was used to refer to distinct ethnic groups. This is in keeping with what Kenan Malik (*The

Meaning of Race: Race, History and Culture in Western Society (New York: New York University Press, 1996), p. 81) notes was an 'imprecise … notion of race' across the post-Enlightenment Western world, in which 'the idea of "peoples", "nations", "classes" and "races" all merged together'. By the time the BUF came into being, narrower, biologically based understandings of race had emerged, but the older, more nebulous conceptions continued to exist alongside them. This was reflected in the BUF's inconsistent use of the term, always denying that it attacked Jews on 'racial grounds' (that is, because of inherent biological traits), yet regularly making attacks on Jews as a 'race' (that is, a distinct ethnic group).

2   *Letters from Lucifer* (London: BUF Publications, n.d.), pp. 100–1.
3   Emphasis added. William Joyce, 'Fascism and Jewry' (London: BUF Publications, n.d.).
4   *Blackshirt*, 1 April 1933, p. 1; 30 September 1933, p. 1.
5   Mosley, *Tomorrow We Live* (London: Greater Britain Publications, 1938), p. 64; *Blackshirt*, 2 August 1935, p. 5; Chesterton, *Mosley*, pp. 125–7.
6   In quantitative terms these three areas of concern – cultural, conspiratorial and economic – represented by far the most significant elements of the movement's anti-Jewish discourse, appearing, respectively, in 31 per cent, 35 per cent and 39 per cent of all sampled articles that contained anti-Jewish sentiment.
7   On British fascism's cultural prognosis and policies, see Linehan and Gottlieb (ed.), *Culture*.
8   *Action*, 17 September 1938, p. 4.
9   Speaking at Earl's Court, 16 July 1939, www.oswaldmosley.com/britain-first.htm [accessed 27 August 2011].
10   Quoted in Linehan, *East London*, pp. 64, 249.
11   *Blackshirt*, 7 December 1934, p. 9; Pugh, *Hurrah*, p. 30; Thomas Linehan, 'Reactionary Spectatorship: British Fascists and Cinema in Inter-War Britain', in Gottlieb and Linehan (eds), *Culture*, pp. 27–39; Griffin, 'Fortress', pp. 45–63; Julie Gottlieb, ' "Motherly Hate": Gendering Anti-Semitism in the British Union of Fascists', *Gender and History*, 14(2) (2002), pp. 308–9.
12   *Action*, 17 September 1938, p. 4. His analysis was remarkably similar to that presented in *Blackshirt* exactly five years earlier, 30 September 1933, pp. 1, 4.
13   Report of debate at National Liberal Club, 12 November 1938, LMA ACC3121/E3/245/1; 'Resignations from the B.U.F', BDA C6/9/1/3.
14   Report of debate at National Liberal Club.
15   *JC*, 13 March 1936, p. 28.
16   *Blackshirt*, 9 January 1937, p. 7. See also, Gordon-Canning, *Holy Land*, p. 9; Clarke, 'British Union'.
17   Mosley, *Greater Britain*, p. 27.
18   *JC*, 2 February 1934, pp. 12–13; *Blackshirt*, 18 November 1933, p. 1.
19   Joyce, 'Fascism and Jewry', p. 6; Clarke, 'British Union'; Oswald Mosley, *Fascism: 100 Questions Asked and Answered* (London: Action Press, 1936), pp. 35–6, and *Tomorrow*, p. 64; Gordon-Canning, *Holy Land*, p. 5; *JC*, 1 May 1936, p. 31; *Daily Mail*, 19 July 1934.
20   'Britain and Jewry'.
21   Skidelsky, *Mosley*, p. 388.
22   Linehan, *East London*, pp. 240–1; Mandle, *Anti-Semitism*, pp. 28–9, 30–1; Joyce, 'Fascism and Jewry', pp. 3, 5, 7; J.F.C. Fuller, 'March to Sanity' (London: Greater Britain Publications, n.d.); *Action*, 19 March 1938, p. 7; 6 May 1939, p. 4.

23 Raven Thomson, 'Financial Masters'; A.K. Chesterton, 'Why do Food Prices Rise?' (unknown publisher, n.d.); 'Britain First – Mosley's speech at Earl's Court, 16 July 1939' (unknown publisher, n.d.), p. 10.

24 *Blackshirt*, 18 December 1933, p. 1; 3 January 1936, p. 3; 6 June 1936, p. 4; 15 August 1936, p. 5; 5 September 1936, p. 1.

25 *JC*, 30 November 1934, p. 18; 15 February 1935, p. 16; 'Is Lancashire Doomed?' (London: Abbey Supplies, n.d.).

26 'Yorkshire Betrayed – British Union Textile Policy (Wool)' (London: Abbey Supplies, n.d.).

27 'Help Fascism to Save the Miners' (London: British Union, n.d.); *JC*, 1 May 1936, p. 31.

28 *JC*, 17 July 1936, p. 31; Peter Heyward, 'Menace of the Chain Stores' (London: Greater Britain Publications, n.d.); Raven Thomson, 'Financial Masters'; John Beckett and Alexander Raven Thomson, 'Private Trader and Co-operator' (unknown publisher, n.d.), pp. 1–3, 13–4; F.D. Hill, 'Gainst Trust & Monopoly! Shopkeepers Action' (London: Abbey Supplies, n.d.).

29 Heyward, 'Menace of the Chain Stores'; Clarke, 'British Union'; 'Draft Election Address for Municipal Elections', U[niversity of]B[irmingham]S[pecial]C[ollections] OMD/B/7/3; Hill, 'Gainst Trust & Monopoly!'; Linehan, *East London*, pp. 33–6, 76–7, 80; Alderman, *Modern British Jewry*, pp. 290–1; Pugh, *Hurrah*, p. 210.

30 *Blackshirt*, 17 August 1934, p. 4. See also Alexander Raven Thomson, *The Coming Corporate State* (London: Greater Britain Publications, 1938), p. 16; John Rumbold, 'Dangers of our Film Censorship', *British Union Quarterly*, 1(3) (1937), pp. 44–55 (cited by Griffin, 'Fortress', p. 49); and Hill, 'Gainst Trust & Monopoly!'.

31 Chesterton, 'A Spiritual Typhus', *Fascist Quarterly*, 2(1) (1936), pp. 377–95 (cited by Griffin (ed.), *Fascism*, pp. 178–80).

32 This particular intersection of the BUF's cultural concerns and its antisemitism has been well covered in the existing literature. See 'Introduction', Gottlieb and Linehan (eds), *Culture of Fascism*, p. 5; Linehan, 'Reactionary Spectatorship', pp. 27, 30–2, 36–8; Griffin, 'Fortress', pp. 49–56; Pugh, *Hurrah*, p. 30.

33 Linehan, *East London*, pp. 31, 86–7.

34 Jorian Jenks, 'The Land and the People. British Union Agricultural Policy' (London: Greater Britain Publications, n.d.). See also Hill, 'Gainst Trust and Monopoly!'; Joyce, 'Fascism and Jewry'; *JC*, 29 March 1935, p. 20.

35 *Blackshirt*, 2 November 1934, p. 1; *JC*, 25 September 1936, pp. 28, 30.

36 *Blackshirt*, 26 June 1937, pp. 1, 4, 8.

37 *Blackshirt*, 3 July 1937, pp. 1, 4.

38 *Blackshirt*, 18 December 1937, p. 2.

39 *Blackshirt*, 2 August 1935, p. 5; 3 October 1936, p. 1.

40 *Blackshirt*, 14 October 1933, p. 3.

41 *Action*, 3 December 1938, p. 3. See also Joyce, 'Fascism and Jewry', report of Mosley's speech at the Criterion, Co[-ordinating] C[ommittee] minutes, 13 December 1937, BDA C6/1/1/1–2.

42 *Blackshirt*, 5 October 1934, p. 2.

43 *Blackshirt*, 2 November 1934, pp. 1–2. Mosley was still making a near-identical rallying call six years later, report of Mosley 'Peace Meeting' at Friends House, 13 April 1940, BDA C6/9/1/3.

44 Ilaria Pavan, 'An Unexpected Betrayal?', and Salvatore Garau, 'Between "Spirit" and "Science": The Emergence of Italian Fascist Antisemitism through the 1920s and 1930s', both in Tilles and Garau (eds), *Fascism*, pp. 48–9, 51, 55–6, 153–5. The

persecution of homosexuals in Fascist Italy remains a neglected subject. See Eszter Andits, '*Sore on the nation's body': Repression of homosexuals under Italian Fascism* (Master's thesis, Central European University, 2010).

45   Michele Sarfatti, *The Jews in Mussolini's Italy: From Equality to Persecution* (Madison: University of Wisconsin Press, 2007); Paxton, Anatomy, p. 167.
46   Holmes, Anti-Semitism, pp. 175–90.
47   Kenneth Lunn, 'Political Anti-semitism Before 1914: Fascism's Heritage?', in Lunn and Thurlow (eds), *British Fascism*, p. 21
48   David Cesarani, 'Joynson-Hicks and the Radical Right in England after the First World War', in Kushner and Lunn (eds), *Traditions*, pp. 134, 139.
49   Kushner, 'Impact', pp. 197–8, and 'The paradox of prejudice: The impact of organised antisemitism in Britain during an anti-Nazi war', in Kushner and Lunn (eds), *Traditions*, pp. 79–80.
50   Lunn, 'British Fascism', pp. 175–6, 179.
51   Stone, 'English Mistery', pp. 337–8, 'Far Right', p. 183, and *Breeding*, p. 2.
52   Griffiths, *Patriotism*, pp. 11–33.
53   Baldoli, 'Fascist Solidarity?', pp. 156–7.
54   Thurlow, 'Developing', pp. 66–79, and *Fascism*, p. 127.
55   Love, 'Big Idea', pp. 452–3, 458–9, 467.
56   Thurlow, *Fascism*, pp. 11–2.
57   Pugh, *Hurrah*, pp. 77, 230–4.
58   Linehan, *East London*, pp. 78–80.
59   Linehan, *British Fascism*, pp. 13, 177–186, 190–3.
60   In November 1938, 77 per cent of those surveyed by the British Institute of Public Opinion believed that Nazi persecution of Jews represented an obstacle to Anglo-German relations, Harry Schneidermann (ed.), *The American Jewish Year Book 5700*, vol. 41 (Philadelphia: Jewish Publication Society of America, 1939), p. 234.
61   Both quotes come from articles by 'Lucifer', *Blackshirt*, 16 May 1933, p. 4; 5 August 1933, p. 2; see also, 1 March 1933, p. 1. Mosley later tried to explain away *Kristallnacht* as a 'mob got out of hand', rather than officially sanctioned policy, *Action*, 19 November 1938, p. 1.
62   *Blackshirt*, 2 November 1934, p. 2. Mosley had given a similar, though less explicit, message a year earlier, *Sunday Graphic*, 2 July 1933.
63   *Blackshirt*, 3 October 1936, p. 1. See also Mosley, *Fascism*, p. 35.
64   *Action*, 15 October 1938, p. 2.
65   'The Split in the British Union of Fascists', W[iener]L[ibrary]P[ress]C[uttings]2/315c.
66   Fuller to Mosley, 8 February 1936, UBSC OMD/B/7/4.
67   'Speakers' Notes No 21 – LCC Elections' (Policy Propaganda Department of the BUF, February 1937), W[orking]C[lass]M[ovement]L[ibrary]. See also 'The Mosley Meeting at Earl's Court', BDA C6/9/1/3 F3.
68   See note 1 above. On the BUF and the Church, see Thomas Linehan, '"On the Side of Christ": Fascist Clerics in 1930s Britain', *Totalitarian Movements and Political Religions*, 8(2) (2007), pp. 287–301. Linehan admits (p. 297) that only a handful of low-level clergy were attracted to the BUF, and that Christian principles had little direct impact on the party's leadership and ideology. Indeed, 'Mosley's religious philosophy was infused with decidedly non-Christian elements'.
69   Kushner, 'Impact'; Holmes, *Anti-Semitism*, p. 104; Williams, 'Anti-Semitism', pp. 94–5; 'Note on Interview Between L[aski], M[orrison] and P[ollitt]', 14 October 1936, P[arkes]L[ibrary]J[ewish]A[rchives] MS134 AJ33(90).

70   Cheyette, 'Belloc', p. 137.

71   Chesterton, *Mosley*, p. 126; Cheyette, 'Stereotyping', pp. 13–20, 29.

72   David Cesarani, 'The Anti-Jewish Career of Sir William Joynson-Hicks, Cabinet
      Minister', *Journal of Contemporary History*, 24(3) (1989), pp. 461–4, 466, 472, 475.

73   Cesarani, 'Anti-Jewish', p. 471. See also Peter Stansky, 'Anglo-Jew or English/
      British? Some Dilemmas of Anglo-Jewish History', *Jewish Social Studies*, 2(1)
      (1995), pp. 165–6.

74   T.S. Eliot, *After Strange Gods: A Primer of Modern Heresy* (London: Faber and Faber,
      1934), pp. 19–20; David Cesarani, 'The Forgotten Jews of London: Court Jews
      Who Were Also Port Jews', in David Cesarani (ed.), *Port Jews. Jewish Communities
      in Cosmopolitan Maritime Trading Centres, 1550–1950* (London: Frank Cass,
      2002), p. 122; Jonathan Morse, 'T.S. Eliot', in Richard S. Levy (ed.), *Antisemitism:
      A Historical Encyclopedia of Prejudice and Persecution*, vol. 1 (Santa Barbara, CA:
      ABC-CLIO, 2005), p. 200–1; Julius, *Eliot*.

75   Holmes, *Anti-Semitism*, p. 12.

76   Colin Holmes, *Anti-Semitism*, pp. 67–8, and 'Boer War', in Levy (ed.), *Antisemitism:
      A Historical Encyclopedia of Prejudice and Persecution*, vol. 2 (Santa Barbara, CA:
      ABC-CLIO, 2005), p. 76; Claire Hirshfield, 'The Anglo-Boer War and the Issue of
      Jewish Culpability', *Journal of Contemporary History*, 15(4) (1980), pp. 621–9.

77   J.A. Hobson, *The War in South Africa: Its Causes and Effects* (London: Nisbet, 1900),
      pp. 11–3, 189–97, 217, 310.

78   Holmes, *Anti-Semitism*, p. 84.

79   Julius, *Trials*, p. 287; Harry Defries, *Conservative Party Attitudes to Jews, 1900–1950*
      (London: Frank Cass, 2001), pp. 4–5.

80   Keith M. Wilson, 'The Protocols of Zion and the Morning Post, 1919–1920', *Patterns
      of Prejudice*, 19(3) (1985), pp. 5–14; Julius, *Trials*, pp. 287–9; Cesarani, 'Anti-Jewish',
      pp. 466, 477; Robert Wistrich, *Antisemitism: The Longest Hatred* (London: Thomas
      Methuen, 1991), pp. 107–8.

81   William Evans-Gordon, *The Alien Immigrant* (London: Heineman, 1903), pp. 247–8,
      276–94.

82   David Feldman, 'The Importance of Being English: Immigration and the Decay of
      Liberal England', in David Feldman and Gareth Stedman Jones (eds), *Metropolis
      London: Histories and Representations Since 1800* (London: Routledge, 1989), pp. 76–8.

83   'Speakers' Notes No 21'.

84   Cesarani, 'Anti-Jewish', p. 471. See also Field, 'Anti-Semitism', pp. 202–3.

85   Linehan, *East London*, pp. 78–80.

86   Julius, *Trials*, pp. 148–241.

87   Holmes, *Anti-Semitism*, pp. 65–79; Hobson, *War in South Africa*, p. 189. See also
      Alan Lee, 'Aspects of the Working-Class Response to the Jews in Britain, 1880–1914',
      in Lunn (ed.), *Minorities*.

88   Holmes, *Anti-Semitism*, pp. 63, 75–6, 81; Lunn, 'Fascism's Heritage?', pp. 21–2, 25;
      Cheyette, 'Hilaire Belloc', pp. 131–42; Wistrich, *Antisemitism*, pp. 105–6.

89   On the 'spectral-syncretic' nature of fascism, see Eatwell, 'Towards'.

90   *Time*, 31 December 1934; *JC*, 21 December 1934, pp. 7–8; 4 January 1935, p. 25.

91   Kallis, 'Fascism and the Jews'.

92   *JC*, 8 September 1933, p. 8; 31 August 1934, p. 15.

93   'The Fascist Movement in the United Kingdom Excluding Northern Ireland',
      Report Nos II and III, June-September 1934, N[ational]A[rchives]H[ome]O[ffice]
      144/20142/108–22, 215–35.

94   Mosley, *Fascism*; *Sunday Graphic*, 2 July 1933.
95   Cited by Baldoli, 'Fascist Solidarity?', pp. 154–5; James Drennan [W.E.D. Allen], 'The Nazi Movement in Perspective', *Fascist Quarterly*, 1(1) (1935), p. 47.
96   *Manchester Guardian*, 11 May 1935; *JC*, 7 June 1935, p. 40. Two years later, a Blackshirt delegation met with Streicher in Nuremberg, reportedly 'rejoic[ing] that we have seen the world leader in the fight against Semitism', *News Chronicle*, 28 August 1937.
97   Joyce, 'Fascism and Jewry', pp. 5–6.
98   'Britain and Jewry'.
99   *Action*, 17 September 1938, p. 4.
100 *Action*, 15 April 1939, p. 8.
101 *Action*, 19 March 1938, p. 7.
102 Action, 6 January 1938, p. 6.
103 Report of Mosley 'Peace Meeting' at Friends House.
104 *Action*, 17 December 1938, p. 7; see also, 15 July 1939, p. 8.
105 NA ME[tropolitan]PO[lice] 2/10646, 3/1256.
106 'Our Political Uniform', IFL, 1933; 'The Workers' Empire' (London: British Fascists, n.d.); Thurlow, *British Fascism*, p. 51.
107 Letter from BUF headquarters to all districts, 12 March 1937, BDA C6/9/1/3; Special Branch report, September 1937, NA MEPO 2/3041/147.
108 NA HO144/21381/233, 234–8, 259–65, 270–93; HO144/21382/28–31, 299–300; Griffiths, *Patriotism*, p. 47; Linehan, *East London*, pp. 142–4.
109 *JC*, 2 June 1939, p. 21.
110 Linehan, *British Fascism*, pp. 141–2; Pugh, *Hurrah*, pp. 230–3.
111 Stone, 'Far Right', p. 189, and 'English Mistery', pp. 347–8; Schneiderman (ed.), *American Jewish Year Book 5700*, p. 318.
112 See, for example, Lebzelter, 'Beamish', p. 41; Morell, 'Leese', pp. 68–9.
113 *The Patriot*, 8 June 1933. It should be noted that the IFL's leader, Leese, was prepared to countenance more radical measures, including his tragically prescient suggestion in 1935 that 'the most certain and permanent way of disposing of the Jews would be to exterminate them by some humane method such as the lethal chamber', *The Fascist*, February 1935, p. 2. Nevertheless, forced emigration remained the only solution his party officially endorsed.

Chapter 4

1   Mosley, *My Life*, pp. 144, 200, 336–42, 347–8.
2   Thurlow, *Fascism*, pp. 116, 126.
3   Pugh, *Hurrah*, pp. 131, 218–20; Lewis, *Illusions*, pp. 98–101. Lewis does acknowledge that Mosley's own 'deeply-held convictions would have played their part too', particularly 'the concept of collective social harmony … which lay at the very root of fascism as a doctrine'. See also, Griffin (ed.), *Fascism*, p. 172; Nugent, 'The Ideas', pp. 152–5; Baker, *The Making*, p. 246.
4   Skidelsky, *Mosley*, pp. 17–8, 383, 390–3, and 'Reflections', p. 87.
5   Linehan, *British Fascism*, p. 191.
6   Mandle, *Anti-Semitism*, pp. 31–4, 69–70.
7   Dorril, *Blackshirt*, pp. 212, 231–2, 254, 291, 302–6, 326. Dorril's work is characterized by methodological and analytical flaws that suggest caution in

assessing his findings, and the sources he uses to support them. Most troublingly, the book contains no footnotes. A more detailed list of sources is provided on the author's personal webpage, but is difficult to decipher and appears to be incomplete. (To make matters worse, that website is, at the time of writing, offline, denying even this limited resource to those wishing to authenticate Dorril's findings.) Moreover, Dorril's interpretation of his evidence is at times dubious. Sources are recounted uncritically, with little questioning of the motives of those responsible for them or the context in which they appear; conclusions are often based on a seemingly limited amount of supporting material; quotes regularly appear without attribution; and a number of errors are apparent. For examples of these deficiencies – and more general criticism of Dorril's book – see William Rubinstein, review of *Blackshirt: Sir Oswald Mosley and British Fascism* by Stephen Dorril, *The Social Affairs Unit*, 15 May 2006, www.socialaffairsunit.org.uk/blog/archives/000920.php [accessed 12 December 2013], and Coupland, review of *Blackshirt*, p. 609.

8   These instances are both cited by Skidelsky, *Mosley*, pp. 291, 378–80. See also Thurlow, *Fascism*, p. 66.

9   Mosley, *Greater Britain*, p. 115.

10   See notes 8 and 9, Chapter 2.

11   *Blackshirt*, 4 November 1933, pp. 1, 4; *JC*, 24 November 1933, p. 32.

12   *JC*, 26 January 1934, 8; 2 February 1934, p. 8; 23 February 1934, p. 8.

13   *JC*, 2 February 1934, p. 8.

14   There words are paraphrased in a report by Neville Laski, with whom Forgan was meeting. Geoffrey Alderman, 'Dr Robert Forgan's resignation from the British Union of Fascists', *Labour History Review*, 57(1) (1992), pp. 37–40; Cross, *Fascists*, p. 123.

15   Charles Dolan, *The Blackshirt Racket. Mosley Exposed* (unknown publisher, n.d.), p. 11.

16   Selwyn, *Hitler's Englishman*, p. 41; Thurlow, *Fascism*, p. 112; Skidelsky, *Mosley*, pp. 342–4; Pugh, *Hurrah*, p. 133; *FW*, 26 January 1934, p. 5; *JC*, 2 February 1923, pp. 8, 16.

17   *JC*, 20 April 1934, pp. 7, 12–3.

18   'Fascism: The Enemy of the People' (London: National Council of Labour, 1934); Mandle, *Anti-Semitism*, p. 7; *Blackshirt*, 15 June 1934, p. 5.

19   Mosley, *My Life*, pp. 337–40.

20   A.K. Chesterton, *Mosley*, pp. 125–6, and (with Joseph Leftwich) *The Tragedy of Anti-Semitism* (London: Robert Anscombe, 1948), pp. 65–6; Skidelsky, *Mosley*, pp. 387–8; *Action*, 7 November 1936, p. 7.

21   *Blackshirt*, 2 August 1935, p. 5.

22   *Blackshirt*, 4 November 1934, pp. 1, 4; 18 November 1933, pp. 1, 6.

23   *JC*, 27 April 1934, p. 15.

24   Thurlow, *Fascism*, pp. 73–5; Mosley, *My Life*, pp. 346–7.

25   Indeed, some of Skidelsky's evidence is questionable: he speculates that the British Union of Democrats (BUD) 'may have been the "organised band of Communists" whom Mosley complained' attacked him in the early days, *Mosley*, pp. 381, 385–7. Yet the BUD, which we will meet in Chapter 7, was not formed until 1935 and remained largely inactive until 1936. Moreover, it advocated a non-confrontational approach to anti-fascism.

26   For various accounts of these factions' composition and dynamics, see Thurlow, *Fascism*, pp. 111–3, Linehan, *East London*, pp. 5–8, and *British Fascism*, pp. 99–100; Dorril, *Blackshirt*, pp. 321–2, 330–2.

27   G.S. Gueroult, 'Apathy', UBSC OMN/B/7/2; *Streatham News*, 14 July 1933.

28   NA HO 144/20142/108–322.

29   Dorril, *Blackshirt*, pp. 288, 301, 306.

30   James Barnes and Patience Barnes, *Nazis in Pre-War London, 1930–1939: The Fate and the Role of German Party Members and British Sympathisers* (Eastbourne: Sussex Academic Press, 2010), pp. 128–31.

31   'The Fascist Movement in the United Kingdom Excluding Northern Ireland', Report No II, June-July 1934, NA HO 144/20142/108–22.

32   Barnes and Barnes, *Nazis in Pre-War London*, p. 130; NA HO144/20142/138.

33   Forgan to Mosley, 1 August 1934, OMN/B/7/2; Barnes and Barnes, *Nazis in Pre-War London*, p. 130; 'The Fascist Movement in the United Kingdom Excluding Northern Ireland', Report No III, August–September 1934, NA HO 144/20142/215–28.

34   Pfister to Mosley, 19 March 1935, OMN/B/7/2.

35   Dorril, *Blackshirt*, pp. 341–3.

36   Barnes and Barnes, *Nazis in Pre-War London*, p. 131; Dorril, *Blackshirt*, p. 338.

37   Pugh, *Hurrah*, p. 221; Thurlow, *Fascism*, pp. 111–2; Linehan, *East London*, p. 9, and *British Fascism*, pp. 100–5, 109–11; Dorril, *Blackshirt*, p. 366.

38   Harry Schneiderman (ed.), *The American Jewish Year Book 5697*, vol. 38 (Philadelphia: Jewish Publication Society of America, 1936), p. 251; *JC*, 29 March 1935, p. 20.

39   *Manchester Guardian*, 11 May 1935; *JC*, 17 May 1935, p. 18.

40   Report on the BUF, UBSC OMD/B/7/4.

41   Skidelsky, 'Reflections', p. 87.

42   Commissioner's Reports, August–September 1936 (this and all subsequently referenced Commissioner's Reports from NA MEPO 2/3043); Pugh, *Hurrah*, p. 226.

43   *Blackshirt*, 3 October 1936, p. 1; Commissioner's Report, August 1936.

44   There are discrepancies in the historiography over who was primarily responsible for the LCC campaign. Mandle (*Anti-Semitism*, pp. 56–7) argues that this was 'more of a Mosley campaign than a Joyce or Chesterton one', though on the questionable basis that if Joyce had been in charge, propaganda would have been even more anti-Jewish. It is hard to imagine how. Linehan (*British Fascism*, pp. 109–11), by contrast, believes that responsibility was assumed by Francis Hawkins, whose 'quasi-military "Blackshirt"' faction gained control of the party over late 1936 and early 1937. This sidelined 'the Joyce-Beckett power base' and brought about 'a re-orientation away from the more violent forms of anti-semitism'. Yet, as we have seen, it was not until after the LCC campaign that anti-Jewish rhetoric began to decline, while subsequently the likes of Chesterton, Raven Thomson and Gordon-Canning continued to offer a powerful anti-Jewish voice in the movement. Moreover, the BUF election manifesto's call for voters to join the 'National Socialist Revolution', as well as its saturation with antisemitism, bore all the hallmarks of Joyce's influence.

45   Joyce to: Mosley, 14 December 1936, and Raven Thomson, 1 January 1937, UBSC OMD 4/2; Linehan, *East London*, pp. 12–13; 'Resignations from the BUF', BDA C6/9/1/3; 'The Split in the British Union of Fascists'; *Manchester Guardian*, 1 November 1968; Jeffrey Hamm, *Action Replay* (unknown publisher, 1983), p. 79.

46   Fuller to Luttman-Johnson, 30 June 1937, I[mperial]W[ar]M[useum] HL-J1; Commissioner's Report, November 1937; 'Resignations from the BUF'; Linehan, *East London*, pp. 47–8.

47   Thurlow, *Fascism*, pp. 116–17; Mosley, *Tomorrow*, pp. 42–3.

48   Mosley's large Earl's Court rally in July 1939, for example, attracted an audience of 20,000. The *Picture Post* (29 September 1939) noted that 'all through the evening the

anti-Jewish outbursts were the line that got the big applause'. The event prompted the *Daily Mirror's* columnist 'Cassandra' to ask 'Can Mosley succeed? Is Fascism on the way up?', U[niversity of]S[heffield]A[rchive] MS338/1/i.

49 Frustrated that the BUF was now dominated by an 'isolated … little clique', Gordon-Canning relinquished his official positions by the end of 1938, but officially remained a member of the party, Macklin, 'Fascist "Jihad"', p. 102.

50 Skidelsky (*Mosley*, p. 330) claims that, over 1938 and 1939 alone, for example, Mosley put £100,000 of his own money into the party. He also ('Reflections', p. 87) agrees that Mosley was the party's 'supreme policy-maker'.

51 Compare *Blackshirt*, 4 November 1933, pp. 1, 4, with Mosley, *Tomorrow*, pp. 42–3.

52 Nicolson (ed.), *Nicolson*, p. 87.

53 Skidelsky, *Mosley*, p. 379.

54 Israel Sieff, *Memoirs* (London: Wiedenfeld and Nicolson, 1970), pp. 170–1.

55 UBSC OMD/8/14.

56 Skidelsky (*Mosley*, pp. 72–3) admits that Mosley's determination to secure 'Britain for the British' led him to oppose various 'aliens': first Germans in 1918, then Jews in the 1930s and finally blacks in the 1950s.

57 Mosley, *Tomorrow*, p. 43. Chesterton offered precisely the same argument, *Blackshirt*, 29 August 1936, p. 5.

58 This may reflect Mosley's incipient idea of a European 'nationalism', which manifested itself in his post-war calls for 'Europe a Nation'. Mosley, *Tomorrow*, pp. 64–5. Thurlow believes Mosley's separation of 'good' and 'bad' Jews grew from the influence of Spenglerian philosophy, developing after he had read *Decline of the West* in 1931, 'Satan and Sambo', pp. 47–8.

59 Skidelsky, *Mosley*, pp. 391–2.

60 *Blackshirt*, 15 June 1934, p. 5; 'Britain and Jewry'.

61 Stone, 'English Mistery', pp. 357.

62 Baker (*The Making*, pp. 326–8, 343, 350, 355, 420–2, 428) finds that Chesterton went through a similar process of development. Although, in contrast to Mosley, he had expressed anti-Jewish beliefs in his pre-BUF days – and, moreover, these were already tied into his gloomy prognosis of Britain's 'cosmopolitan' society and encompassed conspiracy theories of Jewish power – Chesterton's transition to fascism was not simply a means to 'rationaliz[e] … his anti-Semitic prejudices'. As with Mosley, it was vice versa: only as his fascist thought developed was his antisemitism 'amplif[ied]' to become a central 'ideological theme', helping to 'focus' his longstanding opposition to various manifestations of 'decadence'. Baker, however, incorrectly believes that Chesterton's 'cultural and conspiratorial anti-Semitism separates him from Mosley'; in actual fact, the two men shared a great deal in common in this regard. Also, despite acknowledging the ideological basis of Chesterton's fascist antisemitism, Baker still places some of the blame for its development on the 'intimidation and violence' of Jewish anti-fascists.

Chapter 5

1 David Cesarani, *Reporting Anti-Semitism: The Jewish Chronicle 1879–1979* (Southampton: University of Southampton, 1993), p. 24; Joe Jacobs, *Out of the Ghetto* (unknown publisher, 1978), p. 148.

2 Cesarani, 'The Transformation of Communal Authority in Anglo-Jewry, 1914–1940', in Cesarani (ed.), *Modern Anglo-Jewry*, p. 118.

3   On the breadth of opposition to British fascism, see Copsey and Olechnowicz (eds), *Varieties*.

4   Sharon Gewirtz, 'Anti-Fascist Activity in Manchester's Jewish Community in the 1930s', *Manchester Region History Review*, 4(1) (1990), p. 18; 'Introduction', Kushner and Valman (eds), *Remembering Cable Street: Fascism and Anti-Fascism in British Society* (London: Vallentine Mitchell, 2000), pp. 19–20; Geoffrey Alderman, *London Jewry and London Politics 1889–1986* (London: Routledge, 1989), pp. 98–9.

5   Stuart Cohen, 'Anglo-Jewish Responses to Antisemitism: Suggestions for a Framework of Analysis', in Jehuda Reinharz (ed.), *Living With Antisemitism: Modern Jewish Responses* (Hanover: University Press of New England, 1987), p. 87.

6   We will return in Chapter 8 to scholars' views on the effectiveness of the Board's defence work.

7   Lebzelter, *Political Anti-Semitism*, pp. 138–46, 169.

8   Cesarani, *Reporting*, p. 25, and 'Transformation', pp. 128–30; Endelman, *Jews of Britain*, pp. 203–4, 212; Elaine Smith, 'Jewish Responses to Political Antisemitism and Fascism in the East End of London, 1920–1939', in Kushner and Lunn (eds), *Traditions*, p. 67, and 'But What Did They Do? Contemporary Jewish Responses to Cable Street', in Kushner and Valman (eds), *Remembering*, p. 54; David Rosenberg, *Facing up to Antisemitism: How Jews in Britain Countered the Threats of the 1930s* (London: JCARP, 1985), p. 13, and *Battle*, pp. 14, 171, 252–3; Lebzelter, *Political Anti-Semitism*, p. 152.

9   Lebzelter, *Political Anti-Semitism*, pp. 138–9; Alderman, *Modern British Jewry*, pp. 289–90; Cesarani, 'Transformation', pp. 128–9; Endelman, 'English Jewish History', p. 102; Gewirtz, 'Anglo-Jewish Responses', p. 257; Rubinstein, *Jews in the English-Speaking World*, pp. 340–1.

10 Cited by Kushner and Valman, 'Introduction', p. 17.

11 David Cesarani's foreword to Morris Beckman, *The Hackney Crucible* (London: Vallentine Mitchell, 1996), pp. vii–xi; Kushner and Valman, 'Introduction', pp. 4, 17–8. See also Rosenberg, *Facing Up*, pp. 10, 13; Barrett, 'Anti-Fascist Movement', p. 62; Smith, 'Jewish Responses', pp. 62, 67.

12 Cohen, 'Anglo-Jewish Responses', pp. 99–102.

13 Elisa Lawson, ' "Scientific monstrosity" yet "occasionally convenient": Cecil Roth and the idea of race', *Patterns of Prejudice*, 42(2) (2008), pp. 209–227; John M. Efron, *Defenders of the Race: Jewish Doctors and Race Scientists in Fin-de- Siècle Europe* (New Haven: Yale University Press, 1994), p. 176.

14 Neil Barrett, 'The Threat of the British Union of Fascists in Manchester', in Kushner and Valman (eds), *Remembering*, pp. 56–73. Elsewhere, Barrett is even more critical of the Jewish leadership, 'Anti-Fascist Movement', pp. 52–5.

15 Gewirtz, 'Anti-Fascist Activity', pp. 17–26.

16 A.C. Crouch, *Jews are News* (Leicester: Wolsey, n.d.), pp. 24–5.

17 Amanda Bergen, *Leeds Jewry, 1930–1939: the challenge of anti-Semitism* (Leeds: Thoresby Society, 2000), pp. 37–9.

18 Skidelsky, *Mosley*, pp. 380–3, 385–7, 391–3, 397. For example, in referring to an incident in 1933 in which two anti-fascists were arrested, Skidelsky not only misquotes the relevant police report, but claims one of the two, a 'mental case', was Jewish, when in fact there is no indication that he was, NA MEPO 2/3069. For a further instance, see note 25, Chapter 4. See also Mandle, *Anti-Semitism*, p. 5.

19 For example, Thurlow, *Fascism*, pp. 74, 78–9.

20 Linehan, *East London*, pp. 35–6, 78, 83, 119, 160, 163–4, 233.

21 Copsey, *Anti-Fascism*, pp. 4, 13, 20–1, 26, 34, 42–54, 74–6, and preface to Copsey and Olechnowicz (eds), *Varieties*, pp. xiv–xix.

22 Thurlow 'State Management', and 'Passive and Active Anti-Fascism: The State and National Security, 1923–45', in Copsey and Olechnowicz (eds), *Varieties*. See also Philip Williamson, 'The Conservative Party, Fascism and Anti-Fascism 1918–1939', in Copsey and Olechnowicz (eds), *Varieties*.

23 For example, Smith's work on the East End relies extensively on such sources; Gewirtz bases her Manchester study on interviews with former Young Communist League (YCL) members.

24 Jacobs, *Ghetto*; Phil Piratin, *Our Flag Stays Red: An account of Cable Street and political life in the East End of London* (London: Wishart and Lawrence, 1978). See also Beckman, *Hackney*; Jack Pearce, 'The Fascist Threat', in *The Circle: Golden Jubilee, 1909-1959* (London: Central Committee of the Workers' Circle Friendly Society, 1961), pp. 20–1.

25 Rosenberg, *Facing Up*, and *Battle*; Barrett ('Threat', p. 71) acknowledges their existence, but goes no further.

26 Lebzelter, *Political Anti-Semitism*, p. 144.

27 Cesarani, 'Transformation', pp. 128–9.

28 Gewirtz notes that the Board's archive 'reveals attitudes which would either not have been aired in public or not have been expressed in such a candid way', thus 'provid[ing] an insight into the motivations of the BoD's leadership which public statements or minutes of meetings will often conceal or distort', 'Anglo-Jewish Responses', p. 256.

Chapter 6

1   *JC*, 8 April 1932, p. 12; 22 April 1932, p. 6; 11, 26 August 1932, p. 7.

2   *JC*, 26 August 1932, p. 7.

3   *JC*, 7 October 1932, p. 8; 4 November 1932, pp. 8–9; 13 January 1933, p. 9.

4   Assistant Secretary to Guedalla, 30 September 1932, LMA ACC3121/E3/69/1; Raphael Langham, *250 Years of Convention and Contention: A History of the Board of Deputies of British Jews, 1760-2010* (London: Vallentine Mitchell, 2010), p. 148.

5   NA MEPO 2/3069; *JC*, 12 May 1933, p. 8; *Times*, 15 July 1933; Copsey, *Anti-Fascism*, pp. 20–1.

6   Terry Wyke, *A Hall For All Seasons: A History of the Free Trade Hall* (Manchester: Charles Hallé Foundation, 1996), p. 86; David Brennan, *Mosley and Manchester: Sir Oswald Mosley, the BUF, and Manchester in the 1930s*, Master's thesis (unknown institution, 1988), p. 27.

7   *Daily Dispatch*, 13 March 1933; 14 March 1933.

8   *JC*, 5 May 1933, p. 8.

9   *JC*, 12 May 1933, pp. 8, 35.

10 *JC*, 7 July 1933, p. 8.

11 *JC*, 4 August 1933, p. 6.

12 *JC*, 12 May 1933, p. 33; Langham, *Convention and Contention*, pp. 152–3.

13 *JC*, 26 May 1933, p. 32.

14 *JC*, 15 June 1934, p. 12; *Sunday Observer*, 29 September 1935. The latter words are paraphrased by the newspaper's correspondent.

15   Laski to Cripps, 11 May 1933, L[abour]H[istory]A[rchive and]S[tudy]C[entre]LP/
     JSM/210/103.
16   Pugh, *Hurrah*, p. 226.
17   'Annual Report – Press and Information Committee' (draft) and memorandum, 13
     March 1934, LMA ACC3121/E3/69/1; secretary to Guedalla, 10 May 1934, LMA
     ACC3121/E3/69/1; Sidney Salomon, 'The Deputies – A Short Historical Survey'
     (London: V.W.H. Press, 1937), pp. 14–15; Lebzelter, *Political Anti-Semitism*, p. 138;
     Langham, *Convention and Contention*, p. 148.
18   *JC*, 24 November 1933, pp. 20–1.
19   His words are paraphrased by the *JC*'s correspondent, *JC*, 20 April 1934, p. 37.
20   *JC*, 10 November 1933, p. 8; 24 November 1933, p. 8; see also 8 September 1933, p. 8;
     12 January 1934, p. 8.
21   David Cesarani, *The Jewish Chronicle and Anglo-Jewry, 1841–1991* (Cambridge:
     Cambridge University Press, 1994), p. 145.
22   *JC*, 15 September 1933, p. 22; 29 September 1933, p. 16; 13 October 1933, pp. 23–4.
23   Earlier in the year, a group called the Jewish Lads' Brigade Anti-Fascist Group had
     appeared, but was almost immediately disbanded following an injunction taken out
     against it by the Jewish Lads' Brigade itself, *JC*, 5 May 1933, p. 20.
24   *JC*, 20 October 1933, p. 11; 15 December 1933, p. 33; 16 March 1934, p. 33; 4 May
     1934, p. 43; 9 November 1934, p. 17; 14 December 1934, p. 37.
25   *JC*, 20 October 1933, p. 10; 12 January 1934, p. 31; 26 January 1934, p. 30; 16
     February 1934, p. 38; 27 April 1934, p. 35; 'Obituary', *British Medical Journal*, 1(6110)
     (1978), p. 448.
26   *JC*, 23 March 1934, p. 26; Cross, *Fascists*, p. 123; Skidelsky, *Mosley*, p. 383; Dorril,
     Blackshirt, pp. 309–10.
27   One Jew, Philip Magnus, remained a member of the January Club until the end
     of 1934. He had decided to leave much earlier, after Mosley's antisemitism had
     become clear, but, rather than resigning, decided on 'the more unobtrusive method
     of permitting his membership to lapse', Guedella to Laski, 25 January 1935, LMA
     ACC3121/E3/69/1. Magnus also admitted that he was 'not quite the only one of my
     faith who was a member of the Club', Geoffrey Alderman, *The Jewish Community in
     British Politics* (Oxford: Oxford University Press, 1983), p. 195. Ralph Blumenfeld,
     the former editor of the *Daily Mail* and *Daily Express*, was one such member, Dorril,
     Blackshirt, p. 292; Ted Grant, *The Menace of Fascism: What it is and how to fight it*
     (London: Revolutionary Communist Party, 1948), pp. 5–7.
28   *JC*, 30 March 1934, p. 16.
29   Skidelsky, *Mosley*, p. 383.
30   Alderman, 'Forgan', pp. 37–40.
31   Sources indicate only sporadic, minor incidents during this period: Linehan, *East
     London*, p. 59; *Morning Advertiser*, 30 March 1933; *Golders Green Gazette*, 31
     March 1933; *Blackshirt*, 16 September 1933, p. 3; *JC*, 10 November 1933, p. 29; *Irish
     Independent*, 27 April 1934; *Mail and Newcastle Daily Chronicle*, 2 October 1933.
32   Copsey, *Anti-Fascism*, pp. 24–5; *JC*, 15 June 1934, p. 10; 24 August 1934, p. 11; 7
     September 1934, p. 8; *Red Violence and Blue Lies: An Answer to 'Fascists at Olympia'*
     (London: BUF Publications, 1934).
33   NA HO 144/20142/199–200; Jacobs, *Ghetto*, pp. 138–9; Emanuel Litvinoff, *Journey
     Through a Small Planet* (Oxford: Isis, 1993), p. 169. The Clyne sisters – five Jewish
     women from Manchester – remembered the many 'skirmishes' in the city from 1933

onwards, with violence perpetrated by those on both sides, M[anchester] J[ewish] M[useum], oral history J61.

34 *Times*, 29 October 1934; *Daily Express*, 2 June 1934; *Blackshirt*, 8 June 1934, p. 7; 29 June 1934, p. 7; LHASC FAS 1/1–120; Copsey, *Anti-Fascism*, pp. 28–30.

35 *Blackshirt*, 15 June 1934, p. 11; 22 June 1934, pp. 4, 7; Special Branch report, October 1936, (this and all subsequently referenced Special Branch reports from NA MEPO 2/3043); Cullen, 'Political Violence', pp. 250–2.

36 *Blackshirt*, 20 July 1934, p. 2; *Birmingham Daily Mail*, 9 March 1936; *Action*, 12 March 1936, p. 5.

37 Henry Srebrnik, *London Jews and British Communism, 1935–1945* (London: Vallentine Mitchell, 1995), p. 34.

38 William Zukerman, *The Jew in Revolt: The Modern Jew in the World Crisis* (London: Secker and Warburg, 1937), pp. 72–4; Barrett, 'Threat', p. 55. One of the Clyne sisters admitted that being a communist cut one off from the 'ordinary' Jewish community, MJM, oral history J61.

39 Rose Clyne, MJM, oral history J61; Litvinoff, *Journey*, p. 111; Gerwirtz, 'Anti-Fascist Activity', p. 21; Bergen, *Leeds Jewry*, pp. 16–7.

40 Smith, 'Anti-Fascist Activity', p. 62; Alderman, *London Jewry*, p. 96.

41 Cited by Griffiths, *Patriotism*, p. 17; Alderman, *Modern British* Jewry, pp. 317–8, and *London Jewry*, p. 96; Litvinoff, *Journey*, p. 112.

42 Gerwirtz, 'Anti-Fascist Activity', pp. 21–2, 26; David Cesarani, *The Left and the Jews. The Jews and the Left* (London: Labour Friends of Israel, 2004), pp. 34–40.

43 Jacobs, *Ghetto*, p. 56; Cyril Spector, *Volla Volla Jew Boy* (London: Centreprise, 1988), pp. 49–50. See also Cesarani, 'Transformation', p. 131; Smith, 'Jewish Responses', pp. 60–1; Beckman, *Hackney*, pp. 155–6; Alderman, *Modern British Jewry*, pp. 316–7; Srebrnik, *London Jews*, pp. 53–5.

44 Lebzelter, *Political Anti-Semitism*, p. 152.

45 Minutes of CPGB Central Committee meetings, 10 August 1934, C.I. Reel Nos. 5&6, page 136, LHASC; Copsey, *Anti-Fascism*, p. 21.

46 'Mosley Attacks the Jews' (London: Committee for Co-ordinating Anti-Fascist Activities, n.d.). An identical message was conveyed by a YCL leaflet, '10 Points Against Fascism' (London: YCL, 1934). For more on the committee, see Copsey, *Anti-Fascism*, pp. 30–4.

47 His words are paraphrased by the *JC*'s correspondent, *JC*, 21 December 1934, p. 34.

48 Copsey, *Anti-Fascism*, p. 26. See also *Daily Worker*, 20 July 1934.

49 Jacobs, *Ghetto*, p. 145.

50 Cited in Nigel Copsey and Daniel Tilles, 'Uniting a Divided Community? Re-appraising Jewish Responses to British Fascism Antisemitism, 1932–9', in Tilles and Garau (eds), *Fascism*, p. 183. See also Copsey, *Anti-Fascism*, p. 34; *Daily Worker*, 10 September 1934, p. 1.

51 Douglas Hyde, *I Believed* (London: Heinemann, 1950), p. 141.

52 Thorpe, 'Membership', p. 781; Smith, 'Jewish Responses', pp. 60–1.

53 Beckman, *Hackney*, p. xxiv.

54 Allott to Leslie, 5 March 1934, and 'Fascism or Freedom – Which?' (National Amalgamated Union of Shop Assistants, Warehousemen and Clerks, n.d.), University of W[arwick]M[odern]R[ecords]C[entre] MSS.431/3/2/2.

55 Barrett, 'Threat', pp. 56, 68–9, 70–1n4.

56 Smith, 'Jewish Responses', pp. 62–3; Brennan, *Mosley*, pp. 52–3.

57   'The Cinema Strike. An Appeal to Jewish Workers!', H[ackney]A[rchives]
     D/S/24/4/13.
58   *Leader*, May 1933, p. 199; January 1934, pp. 12–4; January 1935, pp. 9–11; February
     1935, pp. 43–4.
59   'Sir Oswald Mosley and the Jews' (JLC, n.d). See also, 'Jewish Labour Council
     Manifesto' (JLC, 1936).
60   *Kentish Independent*, 12 March 1937; Pearce, 'Fascist Threat', p. 20; Cesarani,
     'Transformation', p. 129; Elaine Smith, 'Jewish Responses', pp. 62–3, and 'Jews and
     Politics in the East End of London, 1918–1939', in Cesarani (ed.), *Modern Anglo-*
     Jewry, p. 159.
61   *JC*, 11 May 1934, pp. 8, 23; 2 November 1934, p. 13.
62   *JC*, 15 June 1934, p. 11; 6 July 1934, p. 21; 26 October 1934, p. 21; 2 November 1934, p. 6.
63   Copsey, *Anti-Fascism*, pp. 38–40.
64   L[aw]P[arliamentary][and]G[eneral]P[urposes]C[ommittee] minutes (this, and
     all subsequent references to LPGPC minutes, from LMA ACC3121/C/13/1/12):
     15 October 1934, 10 December 1934. Acting secretary to Guedalla, 21 November
     1934, 26 November 1934, 25 June 1935; Guedalla to Laski, 25 January 1935, LMA
     ACC3121/E3/69/1.
65   Laski's words are paraphrased by the *JC*'s correspondent, *JC*, 2 November 1934, p.
     18; LPGPC minutes: 14 April 1935; William W. Simpson, *Youth and Antisemitism*
     (London: Epsworth Press, 1938), pp. 84–5.
66   Bonn to Laski, 5 December 1934, U[niversity]C[ollege]L[ondon]S[pecial]
     C[ollections], uncatalogued archive of Institute of Jewish Affairs.
67   Laski to various, 11 December 1934, LMA ACC3121/E3/244. Unfortunately, there is
     no record of any further discussion.
68   Guedalla to Brotman, 19 November 1934, LMA ACC3121/E3/69/1.
69   Acting secretary to Guedalla, 17 May 1935, LMA ACC3121/E3/69/1.
70   Various letters between Hertz and Fuller, May–November 1935, PLJA MS175 53/4.
71   *JC*, 22 March 1935, 21; 12 April 1935, p. 23.
72   Harry Schneiderman (ed.), *The American Jewish Year Book 5696*, vol. 37
     (Philadelphia: Jewish Publication Society of America, 1935), p. 170; unlabelled press
     cutting, LHASC CP/CENT/SUBJ/04/13.
73   *Z[ionist] R[eview]*, June 1934, p. 53; January 1935, p. 166.
74   *Y[oung] Z[ionist]*, September 1933, pp. 13, 18.
75   *YZ*, February 1934, p. 8.
76   See note 47, Chapter 4, and note 91, Chapter 2.
77   *YZ*, August 1934, p. 6; September 1934, pp. 12, 19.
78   Thurlow, *Fascism*, pp. 76–7; Rosenberg, *Facing Up*, p. 7. On the BUF's anti-Jewish
     activity in Leeds and Manchester at this time, see *JC*, 21 February 1936, p. 23; 15
     May 1936, p. 9; 3 July 1936, p. 17; 14 August 1936, p. 10; 21 August 1936, p. 18; *New*
     Statesman and Nation, 31 October 1936; Rusholme Ward Labour Party to Laski, 21
     July 1936, LMA ACC3121/E3/245/2; 'The BUF by the BUF' (Essex: Anchor, n.d.);
     Copsey, *Anti-Fascism*, p. 46; Mandle, *Anti-Semitism*, p. 50; Bergen, *Leeds Jewry*, p. 12.
79   Linehan, *East London*, p. 23; Hudson to Simon, 13 February 1936, NA MEPO 2/3087;
     BDA C6/9/1/2.
80   Linehan, *East London*, p. 23; Schneiderman (ed.), *American Jewish Year Book 5697*,
     pp. 250–1; *Civil Liberty*, April 1937; *Times*, 11 July 1936; Hansard H[ouse] [of]
     C[ommons], vol. 317 cols 162–5 (4 November 1936).
81   Orman to Simon, 16 January 1936, NA MEPO 2/3085.

82   Beckman, *Hackney*, pp. xxii–xxiii, 78, 107–8, 155–6, 169.

83   Spector, *Volla*, p. 49; Goodman quoted in Kushner and Valman, 'Introduction',
     pp. 16–8. See also Jacobs, *Ghetto*, p. 148.

84   Beckman, *Hackney*, p. 191; Jacobs, *Ghetto*, p. 151; Gerwirtz, 'Anti-Fascist Activity',
     p. 23; Bergen, *Leeds Jewry*, pp. 9–10.

85   *Civil Liberty*, April 1937. For allegations of police bias see, for example, *Free Speech
     and Assembly Bulletin*, November 1936; *Hackney Gazette*, 7 October 1936.

86   H[ull]U[niversity]A[rchives] DCL/39/3.

87   Gewirtz, 'Anti-Fascist Activity', pp. 23–4.

88   *Times*, 11 July 1936; *Buenos Aires Herald*, 11 July 1936; *JC*, 17 July 1936, pp. 26–31.
     See also Beckman, *Hackney*, p. 191.

89   *JC*, 4 October 1935, p. 11; 19 June 1936, p. 18; 26 June 1936, pp. 20–1.

90   Unsigned to Picciotto, 20 November 1939, BDA C6/10/32; Picciotto to Ralph, 28
     November 1939, BDA C6/9/1/3.

91   Mandle, *Anti-Semitism*, p. 67.

92   *Action*, 12 March 1936, pp. 8, 10.

93   Hansard HC, vol. 314 cols 1618–25 (10 July 1936); *Manchester Guardian*, 7 March
     1936; *Times*, 11 July 1936.

94   *JC*, 13 March 1936, pp. 28, 31–3.

95   *Times*, 22 February 1936; *JC*, 19 June 1936, p. 18; Skidelsky, *Mosley*, pp. 399–401.

96   Skidelsky, *Mosley*, pp. 399–401.

97   Cutting from unknown newspaper, 28 September 1936, W[iener] L[ibrary],Press
     Cuttings 2/315c.

98   Pugh, *Hurrah*, pp. 165, 225–6; John Stevenson, 'The BUF, the Metropolitan Police
     and Public Order', in Lunn and Thurlow (eds), *British Fascism*.

99   NA MEPO 2/3087.

100 NA MEPO 2/3043.

101 Thurlow, 'State Management', pp. 37–9, *Fascism*, p. 84, and 'Blaming the Blackshirts:
     the authorities and the anti-Jewish disturbances in the 1930', in Panikos Panayi
     (ed.), *Racial Violence in Britain in the Nineteenth and Twentieth Centuries* (London:
     Leicester University Press, 1996), pp. 119–20. See also Pugh, *Hurrah*, pp. 173, 226.
     Thurlow notes, however, that some magistrates were comparatively hard on anti-
     fascists, *Fascism*, p. 84.

102 Ronald Howe, *The Pursuit of Crime* (London: Arthur Baker, 1961), pp. 40–3;
     Thurlow, 'State Management', p. 39.

103 Cited by Kushner and Valman, 'Introduction', p. 7.

104 Kushner and Valman, 'Introduction', p. 7.

105 *Daily Despatch*, 13 March 1933.

106 G[reater]M[anchester]P[olice]M[useum] M[anchester] W[atch] C[ommittee]
     P[apers], vol. 182; Brennan, *Mosley*, pp. 18–9, 35.

107 GMPM MWCP, vol. 187; GMPM G[eneral] O[rders] 25/207.

108 *JC*, 24 July 1936, pp. 34–5; Thurlow, *Fascism*, p. 81.

109 Gewirtz, 'Anti-Fascist Activity', pp. 23–4; Brennan, *Mosley*, pp. 50–2; GMPM GO
     27/48, 27/271.

110 Thurlow, 'State Management', pp. 29, 31–4, 42, 'Blaming', pp. 114–5.

111 NA MEPO 2/3087.

112 Unlabelled press cutting, 6 March 1936, HUA DCL/40/4; *JC*, 19 June 1936, p. 19.

113 Report of meeting, 8 July 1936, LMA ACC3121/E3/245/2.

114 NA MEPO 2/3043/229–34.

115	Linehan, *East London*, pp. 22–4, 26–7.
116	Skidelsky, *Mosley*, p. 397.
117	*Report of the Commissioner of Police of the Metropolis for 1936* (London: House of Commons, 1937), p. 26. In a sample of 24 reported assaults by fascists over 1934–8, Cullen finds that in one-third of cases Jews were the victims, 'Political Violence', p. 253.
118	Skidelsky, *Mosley*, p. 397; Commissioner's Report, September 1936; Gewirtz, 'Anti-Fascist Activity', p. 25; Bergen, *Leeds Jewry*, p. 12. See also Mandle, *Anti-Semitism*, p. 52.
119	Commissioner's Report, March 1937.
120	*News Chronicle*, 20 April 1934.
121	See note 1, Chapter 4.
122	NA MEPO 2/3085, 2/3087.
123	NA MEPO 2/3087; Commissioner's Report, March 1937.

Chapter 7

1	*JC*, 19 June 1936, p. 16.
2	Quoted by Beckman, *Hackney*, pp. xxiv, xxix, 155–7.
3	*JC*, 22 November 1935, p. 8.
4	Smith, 'Jews and Politics', p. 152, and 'Jewish Responses', pp. 59–60; Hansard HC, vol. 317 cols 162–5 (4 November 1936).
5	Minutes of CPGB Central Committee meetings, 5 June 1936 (including untitled document, 21 May 1936), reel 8, p. 9, LHASC; Alderman, *Modern British Jewry*, pp. 305–6. On the political and ideological conflict between Zionists and Communists in the East End, see Elaine Smith, *East End Jews in Politics, 1918–1939: A Study in Class and Ethnicity*, PhD thesis, University of Leicester 1990, pp. 165–223.
6	Copsey, *Anti-Fascism*, p. 43; LHASC CP/CENT/SUBJ/04/09 (see CP/CENT/SUBJ/04/02 for examples of publications).
7	*YZ*, March 1936, pp. 8–9; June–July 1936, pp. 8–9.
8	*YZ*, August 1936, pp. 5–6.
9	*YZ*, December 1936, p. 11.
10	*YZ*, January 1937, p. 9.
11	David Cesarani, *Zionism in England, 1917–1939*, PhD thesis, University of Oxford 1986, pp. 342–5; *ZR*, August–September 1935, pp. 91–2; October 1935, pp. 113–15; November 1935, pp. 125–7; 23 June 1938, p. 13.
12	*YZ*, May 1937, p. 21.
13	Cesarani, *Zionism in England*, pp. 342–5.
14	Thorpe, 'Membership', p. 781.
15	Jacobs, *Ghetto*, p. 148; Henriques to parents of members of Oxford and St George's Girls' Club, 28 October 1936, PLJA MS60 17/16; Alderman, *Modern British Jewry*, pp. 316–17; Copsey, *Anti-Fascism*, pp. 43–4.
16	Piratin, *Our Flag*, pp. 17–9; Jacobs, *Ghetto*, pp. 151, 159; Srebrnik, *London Jews*, p. 55; Copsey, *Anti-Fascism*, pp. 72–3; Rosenberg, *Battle*, pp. 158–9; Commissioner's Report, June 1938.
17	Minutes of CPGB Central Committee meetings, 6 January 1934, reel nos 5 and 6, pp. 15–16, LHASC; Kevin Morgan, *Harry Pollitt* (Manchester: Manchester University Press, 1993), p. 94; Copsey, *Anti-Fascism*, pp. 49–50. Copsey ('Communists', p. 184) warns against 'making too much of physical confrontation as the single most important feature defining the British Communist anti-fascist experience'.

18   Copsey, 'Communists', p. 199.
19   Smith, 'Jewish Responses', p. 60.
20   Litvinoff, *Journey*, p. 169.
21   Copsey, *Anti-Fascism*, p. 48; Gewirtz, 'Anti-Fascist Activity', p. 24.
22   Commissioner's Reports, August and September 1936.
23   Cullen, 'Political Violence', pp. 250–4.
24   Bergen, *Leeds Jewry*, pp. 15–6.
25   Gewirtz, 'Anti-Fascist Activity', pp. 17, 24; Copsey, *Anti-Fascism*, p. 46; Barrett, 'Anti-Fascist Movement', p. 50.
26   *JC*, 31 July 1936, p. 24; 21 August 1936, p. 17.
27   Beckman, *Hackney*, pp. 155–6, 159.
28   *Evening Standard*, 2 November 1936.
29   Bergen, *Leeds Jewry*, pp. 7, 11–12; Copsey, *Anti-Fascism*, p. 61.
30   Copsey, *Anti-Fascism*, pp. 42, 52–4; Jacobs, *Ghetto*, p. 159; Thurlow, 'Blaming', pp. 113–4; Linehan, *British Fascism*, pp. 106–7.
31   Commissioner's Reports, August–October 1936; Special Branch report for October 1936; Copsey, *Anti-Fascism*, p. 54; *Blackshirt*, 5 September 1936, p. 1; report on march, 31 August 1936, BDA C6/9/1/3; *JC*, 31 July 1936, p. 25; 14 August 1936, p. 13; 4 September 1936, p. 15.
32   *JC*, 28 August 1936, p. 15; 'The Black Plague: An Exposure of Fascism' (London: The Legion of Blue and White Shirts, 1936); HO MEPO 2/3043/234–7.
33   Copsey, *Anti-Fascism*, pp. 54, 78–9; Thurlow, 'Blaming', pp. 113–14; Gewirtz, 'Anti-Fascist Activity', p. 24.
34   Gewirtz, 'Anti-Fascist Activity', p. 26; *JC*, 19 June 1936, p. 36; 3 July 1936, p. 17; Copsey, *Anti-Fascism*, p. 46.
35   'Fascism and the Jews' (NCCL, n.d.); Bernard Wasserstein, 'Barnett Janner', *Oxford Dictionary of National Biography*, www.oxforddnb.com/view/article/31285 [accessed 21 August 2011].
36   *JC*, 8 November 1935, pp. 8, 20.
37   Hansard HC, vol. 317 cols 162–5 (4 November 1936); *JC*, 10 July 1936, p. 16; 17 July 1936, p. 32.
38   *JC*, 22 March 1935, pp. 32; 19 June 1936, p. 18; 26 June 1936, p. 20; 17 July 1936, p. 33; 24 July 1936, pp. 36–7; 10 July 1936, p. 16; Copsey, *Anti-Fascism*, p. 52.
39   Spector, *Volla*, pp. 49–50; Beckman, *Hackney*, p. xxiv. Kushner and Valman view such explanations sceptically, suggesting that the influence of persecution in eastern Europe may have been 'distorted in later autobiographical writings of the younger generation anxious to explain tension with their parents' generation', 'Introduction', pp. 17–18.
40   Gewirtz, 'Anti-Fascist Activity', p. 24. Bergen finds a similar situation in Leeds, *Leeds Jewry*, p. 12.
41   Cited by Kushner and Valman, 'Introduction', pp. 17–18.
42   Thorpe, 'Membership', p. 781.
43   Alderman, *Modern British Jewry*, pp. 317, 338.
44   Smith, 'Jewish Responses', pp. 60–1; Gewirtz, 'Anti-Fascist Activity', p. 24; Bergen, *Leeds Jewry*, p. 16.
45   Beckman, *Hackney*, p. xxiv.
46   See 'Record of Membership', *The Circle*.
47   *JC*, 11 January 1935, p. 18; 1 February 1935, p. 16; *Leader*, January 1936, pp. 6–9; April 1936, p. 89.
48   *Leader*, February 1936, p. 7; June 1936.

49   Beckman, *Hackney*, pp. 155–7; Webber, 'Patterns'; Rosenberg, *Facing up*, p. 7; N.
      Barou, *The Jews in Work and Trade: A World Survey* (London: TAC, 1945), p. 4;
      Crouch, *Jews are News*, pp. 24–5.

50   Copsey, *Anti-Fascism*, pp. 45, 199; *Times*, 8 June 1936; *JC*, 11 September 1936, p. 17.

51   F.W.S. Craig, *British Parliamentary Election Results 1918–1949* (London: Macmillan,
      1977), p. 52. After the war, Frankel would lose the seat to Phil Piratin, the CPGB's
      candidate.

52   *JC*, 19 June 1936, p. 36.

53   It is possible Davis' reluctance to take firmer action against the fascists resulted from
      a desire to avoid alienating his support in the local Irish community. He was also,
      Alderman claims, 'an utterly corrupt petty dictator', *Controversy and Crisis: Studies
      in the History of the Jews in Modern Britain* (Brighton, MA: Academic Studies Press,
      2008), pp. x, 263–4, 268; Smith, 'Jewish Responses', pp. 57–9, 67.

54   *JC*, 26 June 1936, p. 22; 21 August 1936, p. 18.

55   'Jewish People's Council Against Fascism and Anti-Semitism and the Board of
      Deputies', (London: JPC, n.d.) (hereinafter: 'JPC and the Board').

56   *JC*, 10 July 1936, p. 17; 17 July 1936, p. 36.

57   *JC*, 10 July 1936, p. 18.

58   *Leader*, August 1936, p. 168; *JC*, 21 August 1936, p. 18; untitled report, 29 October
      1936, BDA C6/9/1/3; Co[-ordinating]C[ommittee] minutes: 26 July 1936 (this, and
      all subsequent references to CoC minutes, from BDA C6/1/1/1–2).

59   The newspaper later admitted that it had adopted a policy of 'quietism' towards the
      BUF, avoiding reporting fascist activity as far as possible, *JC*, 17 July 1936, p. 13.

60   *JC*, 27 September 1935, p. 34.

61   *JC*, 4 October 1935, p. 11.

62   Cesarani, *Jewish Chronicle*, pp. 142–3, 145–6.

63   *JC*, 17 January 1936, p. 9.

64   *JC*, 15 May 1936, p. 9.

65   *JC*, 5 June 1936, pp. 13–14; 7 July 1936, p. 13; Cesarani, *Jewish Chronicle*, pp. 143–4.

66   Rosenberg, *Facing Up*, p. 13.

67   *JC*, 12 June 1936, p. 29; 19 June 1936, pp. 16–17; 26 June 1936, pp. 20–4.

68   *JC*, 10 July 1936, p. 16; 17 July 1936, pp. 32–3. For more on the *JC*, its response to
      fascism and its relationship with the Board, see Cesarani, *Jewish Chronicle*.

69   *JC*, 26 June 1936, p. 22; 17 July 1936, p. 36; 31 July 1936, p. 22.

70   Waley Cohen to Salmon, 19 December 1934, PLJA MS363 A3006 1/3/61. On Schiff,
      see A.J. Sherman and Pamela Shatzkes, 'Otto Schiff (1875–1952), Unsung Rescuer',
      Lae Baeck Institute Yearbook, 54(1) (2009), pp. 243–71.

71   Guedalla to Laski, 30 April 1935, 19 September 1935, LMA ACC3121/E3/69/1.

72   Guedalla to [Lollier?], 14 September 1933; Guedalla to Brotman, 7 November 1934;
      Brotman to Guedalla, 15 November 1934; Guedalla to Laski, 25 January 1935, 11
      September 1935 and 18 November 1935; Laski to Guedalla, 22 November 1935;
      translated extract from *Jewish Times*, 20 November 1935, LMA ACC3121/E3/69/1.
      On Magnus and the January Club, see note 27, Chapter 6. On Guedalla, see Elton,
      'Guedalla, Philip', rev. Mark Pottle, *Oxford Dictionary of National Biography*, www.
      oxforddnb.com/view/article/33595 [accessed 29 August 2011].

73   Waley Cohen to: Guedalla, 20 November 1935; d'Avigdor Goldsmid, 11 December
      1935; Rothschild, 17 December 1935, PLJA MS363 A3006 1/3/123, 151.

74   *JC*, 15 May 1936, p. 9; Waley Cohen to Laski, 3 December 1935, PLJA MS363 A3006
      1/3/150.

75   *JC*, 10 July 1936, pp. 17–18.

76   *JC*, 14 August 1936, p. 12; 18 September 1936, p. 18; untitled report, 29 October 1936, BDA C6/9/1/3; minutes of meeting between executive officers of Board and of AJFS, 9 July 1936, LMA ACC3121/E3/245/2; LPGPC minutes: 14 July 1936; CoC minutes: 23 September 1936.

77   Neville to Nathan Laski, 22 July 1936, LMA ACC3121/E3/245/2; *JC*, 24 July 1936, pp. 28–9.

78   Brotman to Secretary of the South African Board of Deputies, 24 August 1936, LMA ACC3121/E3/245/2.

79   Neville to Nathan Laski, 22 July 1936, LMA ACC3121/E3/245/2.

80   *JC*, 26 June 1936, p. 22; 31 July 1936, p. 22; 'JPC and the Board'; 'Report of Activities: July–November 1936', PLJA MS60 17/16.

81   'Meeting at Finsbury Square', 17 February 1936, BDA C6/9/1/2.

82   Neville to Nathan Laski, 22 July 1936, LMA ACC3121/E3/245/2; *JC*, 24 July 1936, p. 29; unsigned (Laski) to Webber, 11 May 1937, LMA ACC3121/E3/245/1.

83   *JC*, 26 June 1936, pp. 22–3; Brotman to Secretary of the South African Board of Deputies, 24 August 1936, LMA ACC3121/E3/245/2.

84   'The Problem and Meaning of Jewish Defence' (Jewish Defence Committee, n.d.), p. 5, LMA ACC3121/G1/3/34; Sidney Salomon, 'The Jewish Defence Committee: Some Lesser Known Aspects of its Work', p. 5, PLJA MS134 AJ33/158; untitled document, BDA C6/2/1/1.

85   Lebzelter, *Political Anti-Semitism*, pp. 144–5; Tony Kushner, *The Persistence of Prejudice: Antisemitism in British Society During the Second World War* (Manchester: Manchester University Press, 1989), p. 167; Alderman, *Modern British Jewry*, pp. 285–6.

86   Sidney Salomon, *Anti-Semitism and Fascism in Post-War Britain. The Work of the Jewish Defence Committee* (London: Woburn Press, 1950), pp. 12–13; Emanuel to *Sunday Times*, 21 July 1936, LMA ACC 3121/E3/245/2.

87   For the M-O's fascinating – and in places bizarre – report, as well as the CoC's discussion of it, see BDA C6/10/26.

88   Rubinstein, *Jews in the English-Speaking World*, p. 341.

89   *ZR*, 15 December 1938, pp. 3, 14; Salomon, 'Lesser Known Aspects', p. 23. According to Lawson ('Cecil Roth and the idea of race', p. 211, no. 6), it is likely that the book was actually written by Cecil Roth, possibly with some contribution from James Parkes, but published under Golding's better-known name to increase its readership.

90   'The Jews in Britain' (London: McCorquodale, 1936); 'The Jews of Britain' (London: Woburn Press, 1938).

91   Salomon, 'Lesser Known Aspects', p. 23; Frank Renton, *Jewish Defence Campaign – Speakers' Handbook* (London: Woburn Press, 1937), pp. 9–11; letters between Salomon and Parkes, 12 December 1936, 18 December 1936, 22 December 1936, PLJA MS60 17/16; 'Memorandum of interview with Mr John Coatman', 4 November 1936, BDA C6/10/7/1/1; CoC minutes: 'Report on Distribution', 13 April 1937, 'The Defence Committee – How it Works', 3 January 1939, 'Memorandum on Publications', 15 February 1940. Many of these publications, as well as a collection of speakers' notes, can be found in the Zaidman Collection at the University of Sheffield Archives. For more on Roth's engagement in communal defence, see Lawson, 'Cecil Roth and the idea of race'.

92   'Vigilance Committees in Great Britain. A General Survey', PLJA MS60 17/16;
      minutes of meeting between executive officers of the Board and of the AJFS, 9 July
      1936, LMA ACC3121/E3/245/2; CoC minutes: 12 November 1936, and 'Vigilance
      Committee Reports', 10 December 1936, 1 July 1937, 13 February 1939.
93   See, for example, BDA C6/9/1/3.
94   Secretary to Liverman, 17 June 1936, LMA ACC3121/E3/245/1; Laski to Waldman,
      21 April 1937, LMA ACC3121/E3/245/2; 'Interview with Mr JF Henderson', 23 May
      1939, LMA ACC3121/E3/247.
95   Unsigned to M. Rosetté, 30 September 1936, BDA C6/9/1/3.
96   Laski to Scott, 19 October 1936, BDA C6/9/1/3, and 8 March 1937, LMA
      ACC3121/E3/245/1. On Laski's complaint to the home secretary that helped bring
      about Houston's arrest, see Brotman to Magnus, 13 March 1936, BDA C6/9/1/2.
97   CoC minutes: 26 July 1936.
98   For example, Secretary to Liverman, 17 June 1936, LMA ACC3121/E3/245/1; Laski
      to Secretary of South African Board of Deputies, 13 September 1936, WL S[pector]
      P[apers]610/1/8–9; Webber to Laski, 10 July 1939, LMA ACC3121/E3/247.
99   HO 144/24967/45, 52; Thurlow, *Fascism*, pp. 50–1.
100   Letters between Laski and Selincourt, 26 November 1938, 28 November 1938, LMA
      ACC3121/E3/247; 'Interview with Mr JF Henderson'. See also Barrett, 'Threat', p. 64.
101   Scott to Laski, 14 December 1936, LMA ACC3121/E3/245/1; Game to Laski, 15
      June 1938, BDA C6/10/32.
102   Memorandum on meeting at Stepney Town Hall, 11 October 1936, LMA
      ACC/3121/E3/245/2.
103   'Note on Interview Between L, M and P'.
104   Harry Schneiderman (ed.), *The American Jewish Year Book 5698*, vol. 39
      (Philadelphia: Jewish Publication Society of America, 1937), p. 295.
105   Laski to Scott, 8 March 1937, LMA ACC3121/E3/245/1; *Evening Standard*, 4
      November 1936; Emanuel to *Sunday Times*, 21 July 1936, LMA ACC 3121/
      E3/245/2.
106   Letter from Brotman to secretary of the South African Board of Deputies, 24
      August 1936, LMA ACC/3121/E3/245/2; Salomon, *Anti-Semitism and Fascism*,
      p. 3. A leading Mosleyite lamented the 'campaign of total silence' against the BUF
      in the press, complaining that its meetings were only mentioned after 'violence
      initiated ... by the extreme Left', *Mosley's Blackshirts*, p. 63. Another expressed with
      satisfaction, 'now that we have active opposition in Exeter ... we shall make great
      progress here', Pugh, *Hurrah*, p. 159.
107   Ruchard Thurlow, 'Passive and Active Anti-Fascism: The State and National
      Security, 1923–45', in Copsey and Olechnowitz (eds), *Varieties*, p. 163.
108   'Jewish Defence. Work in the past; policy of the future', PLJA MS150 AJ110/4; 'The
      Defence Committee – How it Works'.
109   Waley Cohen's words are paraphrased by his biographer, Robert Henriques, *Sir
      Robert Waley Cohen* (London: Secker and Warburg, 1966), pp. 382–3.
110   Endelman, *Jews of Britain*, p. 211; Lebzelter, *Political Anti-Semitism*, p. 148; Barrett,
      'Threat', p. 61; Langham, *Convention and Contention*, p. 151.
111   CoC minutes: 1 July 1937.
112   'The Defence Committee – How it Works'.
113   Memorandum on meeting at Stepney Town Hall.
114   'Note on Interview Between L, M and P'.

115 See minutes of LPGPC (including 16 November 1937 for magistrate's comment); Alderman, *London Jewry*, pp. 91–4.

116 Parkes to Laski, 30 December 1936; Parkes to Henriques, 13 December 1936, PLJA MS60 17/16.

117 Cesarani, *Jewish Chronicle*, pp. 156–9.

118 *JC*, 31 July 1936, p. 27; Linehan, *East London*, p. 120.

119 Gewirtz, 'Anti-Fascism Activity', p. 24.

120 It should be noted that Laski aimed not only to help the authorities implement these measures, but also sought to speak in the interests of the Jewish community, for example by alleviating some of the restrictions on Jewish traders, who he was concerned were suffering economically as a result. See LPGPC minutes: 10 January 1939.

121 Neville Laski, *Jewish Rights and Jewish Wrongs* (London: Sorcino Press, 1939), pp. 123–5, 139–41.

122 CoC minutes: 'Fascist Parliamentary Candidates' (written 23 November 1936), 1 July 1937; Lebzelter, *Political Anti-Semitism*, p. 142; Laski to Dight, 21 August 1936, LMA ACC3121/E3/245/2.

123 ' "British Fascism" and the Jews', ACC 3121/E3/245/2.

124 *JC*, 7 August 1936, p. 11.

125 *JC*, 21 August 1936, p. 18; 28 August 1936, p. 16; 11 September 1936, p. 16.

126 Gewirtz, 'Anglo-Jewish Responses', p. 257.

127 Rosenberg, *Facing Up*, p. 11; Langham, *Convention and Contention*, p. 139; LPGPC minutes: 30 December 1937, 15 February 1938.

128 *JC*, 7 August 1936, p. 11.

129 Parkes to Laski, 30 December 1936, PLJA MS60 17/16; Lebzelter, *Political Anti-Semitism*, p. 142.

130 *JC*, 31 July 1936, p. 22; Copsey, *Anti-Fascism*, pp. 52–3.

131 Emphasis added. 'JPC and the Board'; Pearce, 'Fascist Threat', p. 21.

132 'JPC and the Board'; report on JPC conference, 15 November 1936, PLJA MS60 17/16; Pearce, 'Fascist Threat', p. 21; 'The Jewish People and the Borough Council Elections' (JPC, 1937); 'What Fascism means to you!' (JPC, n.d.); CoC minutes: 'Memorandum to the Board of Deputies on the Policy of the Jewish People's Council Against Fascism and Anti-Semitism', 13 February 1939.

133 'Report of Activities'.

134 PLJA MS116/6 AJ10; 'Report of Activities'.

135 Pearce, 'Fascist Threat', pp. 20–1; 'Report of Activities'; Copsey, *Anti-Fascism*, pp. 54–5.

136 'Beware of Provocation!' (London District Committee of the Communist Party, n.d.); District Bulletin No 24 of London District Committee of CPGB, 1 October 1936, LHASC CP/CENT/SUBJ/04/02; *Daily Worker* supplement, 3 October 1936; Copsey, *Anti-Fascism*, pp. 55–8, and 'Communists', p. 199; Smith, 'Jewish Responses', pp. 61–2; Lewis, *Illusions*, pp. 123–5.

137 On Cable Street, in addition to sources referenced in the note above, see Skidelsky, *Mosley*, pp. 405–6; Thurlow, *Fascism*, pp. 79–82.

138 Kushner and Valman, 'Introduction', p. 5.

139 Commissioner's Report, October 1936; *Evening Standard*, 8 October 1936.

140 Beckman, *Hackney*, p. xxix.

141 Piratin, *Our Flag*, pp. 23–4. See also Audrey Gillan, 'Day the East End said "No pasaran" to Blackshirts', *Guardian*, 30 September 2006, www.guardian.co.uk/uk/2006/sep/30/thefarright.past [accessed 16 September 2011].

142   Cited by Kushner and Valman, 'Introduction', p. 15; see also, pp. 17–18.

143   'Spain and the Jewish People' (Jewish Labour Council, n.d.).

144   Reliable numbers are hard to come by, but there appear to have been at least a
       couple of hundred British-Jewish volunteers fighting in Spain. Richard Baxell,
       British Volunteers: The British Battalion in the International Brigades, 1936–1939
       (London: Routledge, 2004); Martin Sugarman, 'Against Fascism – Jews who served
       in the International Brigade in the Spanish Civil War', *Jewish Virtual Library*, www.
       jewishvirtuallibrary.org/jsource/History/spanjews.pdf [accessed 4 March 2013];
       Bergen, *Leeds Jewry*, pp. 17–8.

145   Pearce, 'Fascist Threat', pp. 20–1; Kushner and Valman, 'Introduction', p. 19.

146   Copsey, *Anti-Fascism*, p. 61; Kushner and Valman, 'Introduction', p. 19; Clyne
       sisters, MJM, oral history J61.

147   'Stop Racial Incitement in East London', (JPC, 1936); Schneiderman (ed.) *American
       Jewish Year Book 5698*, p. 294; David Cesarani in Peter Catterall (ed.), 'The Battle of
       Cable Street', *Contemporary Record* 8(1) (1994), p. 124.

148   Bergen, *Leeds Jewry*, pp. 12–6; *JC*, 2 October 1936, p. 5; *Times*, 28 September 1936;
       Blackshirt, 3 October 1936, pp. 2, 8; Copsey, *Anti-Fascism*, pp. 46–7.

149   Beckman, *Hackney*, p. xxix; Grant, *Menace*, p. 42; Kushner and Valman,
       'Introduction', p. 18.

150   *Blackshirt*, 10 October 1936, p. 1; Skidelsky, *Mosley*, pp. 405–6; Linehan, *East
       London*, p. 256.

151   Special Branch Report, October 1936; Skidelsky, *Mosley*, pp. 406–7; Linehan, *British
       Fascism*, p. 107; Thurlow, *British Fascism*, pp. 63–4.

152   *Blackshirt*, 6 March 1937, p. 1; *YZ*, March 1937, p. 4; *Daily Telegraph*, 20 February
       1937; Copsey, *Anti-Fascism*, p. 63; Skidelsky, *Mosley*, pp. 393, 409; 'County
       Report Part I', *Vision of Britain*, www.visionofbritain.org.uk/census/census_page.
       jsp?yr=1931&show=DB [accessed 27 August 2011].

153   Mandle, *Anti-Semitism*, p. 59; Salomon, *Anti-Semitism and Fascism*, p. 2; report
       on municipal elections, LMA ACC3121/E3/245/2; *Blackshirt*, 6 November 1937,
       p. 4.

154   Laski to chief constable of Manchester police, 7 October 1936, BDA C6/9/1/3.

155   NA MEPO 3/551; *News Chronicle*, 12 October 1936; *Civil Liberty*, April 1937. See
       also Cesarani, 'Transformation', p. 130.

156   *News Chronicle*, 9 October 1936; *JC*, 11 December 1936, p. 35.

157   Commissioner's Reports, June and September 1937 and June 1938; 'Further
       Disturbances in East London', July 1937, PLJA MS60 17/16; *Times*, 20 April 1937.

158   Laski to Game, 22 July 1938, LMA ACC3121/E3/247; CoC minutes: 21 June 1938;
       LPGPC minutes: 5 July 1938. See also Copsey, *Anti-Fascism*, pp. 62–3; Pugh,
       Hurrah, pp. 227–8.

159   'Speakers' Notes No 21'.

160   Special Branch report, October 1936; Copsey, *Anti-Fascism*, pp. 79–8.

161   Clarke, 'British Union and the Jews', p. 10.

162   Mandle (*Anti-Semitism*, p. 67), Thurlow ('State Management', pp. 46–7) and
       Linehan (*British Fascism*, p. 109) believe that the POA had some success in
       moderating the BUF's East End campaigning; Copsey (*Anti-Fascism*, pp. 66–7) and
       Pugh (*Hurrah*, pp. 173–6) are less convinced.

163   *Daily Worker*, 4 October 1937; *Manchester Guardian*, 5 October 1937; *New York
       Times*, 5 October 1937; *South London Press*, 15 October 1937; USA MS338/1/a;
       HUA DCL/39/2; Copsey, *Anti-Fascism*, p. 171.

164   Commissioner's Reports for relevant months.

165 *JC*, 30 September 1938, p. 20; memo from Commissioner's office to London DACS, 29 June 1937, NA MEPO 2/3043/185–6; Thurlow, 'State Management', pp. 39–40.

166 Pearce, 'Fascist Threat', p. 21; 'Fascist Hooliganism' (London: JPC, n.d.); 'Report of Activities'; *JC*, 16 October 1936, p. 31; Special Branch report, October 1936.

167 *North London Recorder*, 26 March 1937; memorandum of Willesden branch of JPC, PLJA MS60 17/16; *JC*, 16 April 1937, p. 18; *Times*, 3 November 1936; *Daily Worker*, 16 November 1936.

168 Waley Cohen to Cohen, 28 October 1936, PLJA MS363 A3006 1/3/125.

169 *JC*, 7 August 1936, p. 9; 21 August 1936, p. 16; 2 October 1936, p. 5.

170 *JC*, 11 September 1936, p. 18; 25 September 1936, p. 29; Special Branch Report, October 1936.

171 Unsigned to Henriques, 30 October 1936, BDA C6/9/1/3.

172 CoC minutes: 10 December 1936.

173 *JC*, 18 September 1936, p. 18; Commissioner's Report, September 1936; CoC minutes: 'Report to the Coordinating Committee', 23 September 1936. Laski's accusation was not mere politicking. The police noted, for example, that the former leaders of the BUD and the LBWS were both 'only concerned with any possible monetary gain' they could attain from wealthy Jews 'who can be persuaded to subsidise an organisation to combat anti-Semitism'. A group that had splintered from EMAF, meanwhile, was 'more concerned with collecting money than propaganda', Commissioner's Reports, June and July 1937.

174 CoC minutes: 29 October 1936, 12 November 1936, Secretary's Report, 25 November 1936.

175 Report on JPC conference of 15 November 1936, pp. 5–6, 8–10, PLJA MS60 17/16.

Chapter 8

1 Lebzelter, *Political Anti-Semitism*, pp. 139, 144–5; Barrett, 'Threat', p. 67; Endelman, *Jews of Britain*, p. 212; Rosenberg, *Facing Up*, pp. 41–2, 50, and *Battle*, p. 141; Cesarani, 'Transformation', pp. 130–1; Alderman, *Modern British Jewry*, pp. 285–6. Cesarani does accept that, in its response to fascism specifically, the Board's record was 'mixed'.

2 Lebzelter (*Political Anti-Semitism*, pp. 144–5) and Copsey (*Anti-Fascism*, p. 95) concede this point.

3 Lebzelter, *Political Anti*-Semitism, pp. 144–51. Rosenberg believes that the Board was 'solely concerned with countering anti-Jewish defamation and would not embroil itself with the issue of fascism', *Facing Up*, pp. 56, 70, and *Battle*, pp. 177, 181, 183. See also Smith, 'What Did They Do?', p. 53; Barrett, 'Anti-fascist activity', p. 54.

4 Alderman (*Modern British Jewry*, pp. 285–6, 290, 293) claims that Laski had only 'accepted the need for a Defence Committee … in the context of a more systematic effort by the Board to police Anglo-Jewry' and that its 'main thrust' was to deal with 'the internal causes of antisemitism'. As we have already seen, this was not the case. See also Endelman, *Jews of Britain*, p. 211; Lebzelter, *Political Anti-Semitism*, p. 148; Barrett, 'Threat', p. 61; Langham, *Convention and Contention*, p. 150.

5 Smith ('Jewish Responses', p. 67) acknowledges that 'much of the Board's defence work was unpublicised and conducted in private', and mentions that meetings with the Home Office and police took place, but fails to elaborate further. Barrett ('Threat', p. 61) notes that Laski 'seems to have assisted the intelligence services, regarding the activities of certain right-wing groups, on a number of occasions' without offering details. See also Lebzelter, *Anti-Semitism*, p. 144.

6   Kushner, *Persistence*, pp. 166–7; Copsey, *Anti-Fascism*, pp. 50–1, 74–6. Smith ('Jewish Responses', p. 66) dates this change of heart a little earlier, to 1938, as does Lebzelter (*Political Anti-Semitism*, pp. 152–3), who cites the introduction of anti-Jewish legislation in Italy that year as a motivating factor. See also Rosenberg, *Facing Up*, p. 59; Langham, *Contention and Contention*, p. 153.

7   'JPC and the Board'; 'Report of Activities'.

8   For details of the first meeting, see BDA C6/2/1/2. The second is described in Salaman's papers at Cambridge University Library, box 14, CUL. Add. MS 8171/51, cited in Todd Endelman's conference paper 'Who Spoke for Anglo-Jewry in the Nineteenth and Twentieth Centuries?', *The Board of Deputies of British Jews at 250*, August 2010.

9   CoC minutes: 12 November 1936; Lebzelter, *Political Anti-Semitism*, p. 142.

10   'JPC and the Board'.

11   Report by Newsam, 11 June 1937, NA MEPO 2/3112.

12   Issie Rennap and Julius Jacobs were both active communists, for example.

13   Lewis (*Illusions*, pp. 123–5) warns that contemporary police reports have given a false impression that the CPGB controlled a variety of 'front' organizations, such as the JPC. But opinion on this issue remains divided. See Copsey, *Anti-Fascism*, p. 53; Lebzelter, *Political Anti-Semitism*, p. 141; Thurlow, *Fascism*, p. 79; Smith, 'Jewish Responses', p. 64; Srebrnik, *London Jews*, pp. 55–6.

14   'JPC and the Board'; Srebrnik, *London Jews*, pp. 55–6.

15   'Conference on Fascism and Anti-Semitism', PLJA MS60 17/16; *Daily Herald*, 23 April 1937; advertisement for JPC meeting in Whitechapel, 14 November 1938, LHASC CP/ORG/MISC/07/06. On Gaster's attitude to antisemitism, see Cohen, 'Anglo-Jewish Responses', p. 90.

16   Alderman (*Modern British Jewry*, p. 286) and Barrett ('Threat', pp. 61–2) both imply that the meeting was called to discuss resentment towards Jews in the East End. While this theme came to dominate proceedings, it was not Laski's original purpose.

17   'Note of Interview with Mr Herbert Morrison', PLJA MS134 AJ33/89; 'Note on Interview Between L, M and P'; NA MEPO 2/3043/238-44. Laski also held discussions with Ben Tillett, the prominent trade unionist, about dealing with antisemitism in the unions, Laski to Rothschild, 5 December 1938, PLJA MS363 A3006/1/3/54.

18   Renton, 'Jewish Defence Campaign', p. 23.

19   Laski, *Jewish Rights*, p. 134.

20   Both pamphlets, which are undated, can be found in LHASC CP/ORG/MISC/07/06; 'What the Jewish People's Council Against Fascism and Anti-Semitism Has Done!' (JPC, 1937).

21   *East London Observer*, 27 January 1937; *Hackney Gazette*, 24 February 1937; *East London Recorder*, 23 April 1937.

22   Untitled document, 24 June 1937, WL SP610/1/12.

23   'Debate between Mr Jacobs and Mr Renton, Whitechapel Art Gallery, 21st March 1938', LHASC CP/ORG/2/20.

24   'Do the Democratic British People Want Fascism?' and 'Fascist Provocation' (both JPC, n.d.), LHASC CP/ORG/MISC/07/06.

25   Copsey, *Anti-Fascism*, pp. 49–50, 68, 72, and 'Communists', p. 199; Grant, *Menace*, pp. 42–3; Noreen Branson, *History of the Communist Party of Great Britain 1927–1941* (London: Lawrence and Wishart, 1985), pp. 110–28, 145–57; Commissioner's Report, June 1938. On Piratin's favoured approach, see note 16, Chapter 7. For

a contrasting view on the Communists' Popular Front campaign, see Linehan, 'Communist Culture', p. 39.

26 Commissioner's Reports for August and November 1937 and April 1938.

27 Undated JPC leaflets: 'Hitler Said..."British" Fascism Echoed', 'Fascists say the Jews want War! What are the Facts?', 'Fascism is Responsible for Refugees', LHASC CP/ORG/MISC/07/06.

28 *ZR*, 11 August 1939, p. 5; *Leader*, June 1938, p. 143; 'Interview with Mr JF Henderson'; Waley Cohen to Rothschild, 14 May 1936, PLJA MS363 A3006 1/3/124.

29 Laski to Scott, 19 October 1936, BDA C6/9/1/3; secretary to Gordon Liverman, 17 June 1936, LMA ACC3121/E3/245/1; Laski to secretary of the South African Board, 13 September 1936, WL SP610/1/8-9; Salomon, 'Lesser Known Aspects', p. 6; Pugh, *Hurrah*, p. 226; Thurlow, *Fascism*, p. 50; BDA C6/10/32; *East London Blackshirt*, May 1939; CoC minutes: Secretary's Report, 13 February 1939.

30 CoC minutes: 23 September 1936, 29 October 1936, 21 January 1937; George Lansbury, 'Anti-Semitism in the East End' (London: Woburn Press, 1936); 'Do you these facts about Mosley and his Fascists?' (London: Woburn Press, 1937).

31 CoC publications Sub-Committee minutes, BDA C6/1/4/2; CoC minutes: 13 April 1937; 1 July 1937.

32 Laski to Webber, 19 March 1937, BDA C6/9/1/3; CoC minutes: 21 June 1938.

33 'Memorandum re Mr Montague Bell', 23 June 1939, PLJA MS363 A3006 1/3/55; CoC minutes: 'Memorandum to the Jewish People's Council on the Policy of the Board of Deputies', 13 February 1939.

34 'Fascist Parliamentary Candidates'; Salomon, 'Lesser Known Aspects', pp. 7–8; 'The Jewish People and the Borough Council Elections' (JPC, 1937); CoC minutes: 'Work of the London Area Council', 15 November 1937.

35 Salomon, 'Lesser Known Aspects', pp. 7–8; Laski to Waley Cohen, 16 July 1937, PLJA MS363 A3006/1/3/54; Laski to Waley Cohen, 19 May 1939, PLJA MS134 AJ33/150; CoC minutes: 1 July 1937.

36 'The BUF by the BUF', 'Be on your guard! How fascists work', both Tiptree: Anchor Press, n.d.

37 Letters between Salomon and Wegg-Prosser, 13 June 1938, 14 June 1938, 15 June 1938, BDA C6/9/1/3; 'The B.U.F. and Anti-Semitism: An Exposure' (London: CH Lane, n.d.); C. Wegg-Prosser, 'Fascism Exposed! Political Use of Anti-Semitism' (JPC, 1938); 'I was a Fascist!' (JPC), LHASC CP/ORG/MISC/07/06.

38 *JC*, 20 August 1937, p. 15; letters between Laski and Picciotto, 12 November 1937, 14 November 1937, 9 June 1939, 15 June 1939; Salomon to Picciotto, 17 May 1938, BDA C6/10/32; CoC minutes: 'Summary of the Situation', 4 June 1937; 15 November 1937; 19 June 1939.

39 Bermel to Brotman, 9 June 1937, PLJA MS363 A3006/1/3/54.

40 CoC minutes: 'London Area Council Monthly Reports', 29 March 1938 and 24 May 1938; LAC minutes (BDA C6/1/2/1): 1 February 1938; Smith, 'Jewish responses', p. 65. See BDA C6/3/1B/4 for reports of LAC-organized meetings.

41 CoC minutes: 'The Jewish Defence Committee – Retrospect and Prospect', 3 January 1939; *JC*, 4 February 1938, p. 22.

42 *ZR*, 30 September 1938, p. 6; 4 May 1939, p. 7.

43 CoC minutes: 'Proposed Scheme Prepared by Mr Picciotto for the Reorganisation of the East End Office', 13 December 1937; 21 June 1938. See 'Emanuel's' monthly column in *Leader* from February 1939.

44 'Memorandum from Mr Gellman', LMA ACC3121/E3/247; LPGPC minutes: 'Co-ordinating Committee Report', 11 January 1938. For other examples of Jewish hostility towards the Board, see BDA C6/3/1B/4.

45 'Notes on the work of the Defence Committee', BDA C6/2/1/6; Laski to de Rothschild, 5 December 1938, PLJA MS363 A3006/1/3/54.

46 Kraft to Salomon, 23 February 1937; Salomon to Secretary of AEU, 11 March 1937; Smith to Salomon, 15 March 1937, BDA C6/9/1/3; unknown to Salomon, 6 November 1937, BDA C6/9/1/6; unknown to Iwi, 11 February 1938; 'Memorandum of certain activities in reaction', LMA ACC3121/E3/245/1; Salomon, 'Lesser Known Aspects', pp. 1–2.

47 BDA C6/9/1/6; Salomon, 'Lesser Known Aspects', pp. 1–2.

48 Salomon, 'Lesser Known Aspects', pp. 13–14; Sidney Salomon, 'Now it can be told', BDA C6/9/2/1; unknown to Scott, 20 September 1939, 22 September 1939, LMA ACC3121/E3/245/2; Laski to chief constable, 7 October 1936; Brotman to chief constable, 20 October 1936; secretary to Keebles and Scott, 22 January 1937; letter from BUF HQ, 12 March 1937, BDA C6/9/1/3; 'Interview with Mr JF Henderson'; Linehan, *East London*, p. 180.

49 Salomon, 'Lesser Known Aspects', pp. 12, 14–17, and 'Now it can be told'; NA HO 144/21381/248-93, 270–93; NA HO 144/22454/47-82.

50 Salomon, 'Now it can be told'.

51 Griffiths, *Patriotism*, pp. 29–30, 38, 45; Thurlow, *Fascism*, p. 53.

52 Treasurer to Samuel Montagu & Co, 26 June 1939, BDA, C6/7/4/1; Laski to Brotman, 25 July 1939, BDA C6/2/1/3.

53 See various letters to and from Edwards, BDA C6/9/1/3.

54 Letter from [illegible] to Salomon, 2 [November?] 1940 and attached report, BDA C6/9/1/3.

55 Thurlow, 'Passive and Active', pp. 164–5, 169–70, and *Fascism*, pp. 48–50, 52–3. Linehan also notes that the Board gathered some of 'the most detailed and informative data' on BUF membership of any contemporary anti-fascist organization, *British Fascism*, p. 152.

56 NA HO 144/21381/239-45; Salomon, 'Lesser Known Aspects', pp. 14–15, and 'Now it can be told'; 'Interview with Mr JF Henderson'.

57 Salomon, 'Lesser Known Aspects', pp. 9–10; CoC minutes: Liverman to Nathan, 7 March 1940.

58 Unsigned (Laski) to Iwi, 11 February 1938, LMA ACC3121/E3/245/1.

59 CoC minutes: Secretary's Report, 13 December 1937.

60 CoC minutes: Secretary's Report, 'LAC Monthly Report, 24 May 1938; Addendum to Secretary's Report, 8 November 1939; LAC minutes (BDA C6/1/2/1): 1 March 1938.

61 CoC minutes: Secretary's Reports, 13 February 1939, 13 March 1939 and 24 April 1939; 3 October 1939.

62 Laski, *Jewish Rights*, p. 133.

63 When Laski initially contacted M-O about conducting such research, he was not motivated purely by a desire to better understand antisemitism. He had learned that the organization was already planning to conduct research into this issue and publish a book on it, something Laski was concerned could create an unrepresentative picture of attitudes towards Jews, given the exceptional circumstances of 1939. Thus, as part of its agreement with the Board, M-O agreed not to publish any findings for at least five years. Nevertheless, Laski also believed that the research would be 'useful to our work, whatever the result'. 'Mass Observation on Anti-Semitism', 17 January

1939, BDA C6/10/26. For further analysis of the M-O's report and its dealings with the Board, see Tony Kushner, *We Europeans? Mass-Observation, 'Race' and British Identity in the Twentieth Century* (Aldershot: Ashgate, 2004), pp. 82–97.

64 CoC minutes: 13 April 1937.

65 CoC minutes: 17 July 1939.

66 'How Refugees Help Lancashire – New Industries and Secret Processes', (London: Watts & Co., 1939); 'Refugees – The Plain Facts', (London: Woburn Press, n.d.); 'While you are in England: Helpful information and guidance for every refugee' (Tiptree: Anchor Press, n.d.).

67 'True Blue Patriots of the BUF' (London: Lane, n.d.); 'Britain's Fifth Column' (Tiptree: Anchor Press, n.d.); CoC minutes: Secretary's Report, 7 March 1940.

68 CoC minutes: Secretary's Report, 24 April 1939.

69 CoC minutes: 3 October 1939.

70 Salomon to Broadbridge, 22 April 1940; unknown to Game, 4 June 1940; Salomon to Morris, 1 July 1940, 4 July 1940; unknown to Davidson, 2 July 1940, 8 July 1940, 12 July 1940; unknown to Anderson, n.d., BDA C6/9/1/3.

71 CoC minutes: 'Memorandum by the Chairman', 13 February 1939.

72 Salomon, 'Lesser Known Aspects', pp. 2, 9–10.

73 Salomon, 'Lesser Known Aspects', p. 10; secretary to Berridge, 10 July 1939, BDA C6/9/1/3; NA HO144/21381/270-93; CoC minutes: Secretary's Report, 13 February 1939.

74 Salomon, 'Lesser Know Aspects', pp. 2–3, 6–7, 10–12, 20, and 'Now it can be told'; CoC minutes: Secretary's Report, 13 March 1939; NA HO144/21381/270-93.

75 LPGPC minutes: 15 November 1938.

76 Gewirtz, 'Anti-Fascist Activity', pp. 24–6; Barrett, 'Threat', p. 65; *JC*, 25 September 1936, pp. 30–1; Nathan Laski to Waley Cohen, 28 September 1936, BDA C6/9/1/3.

77 Game to Laski, 30 July 1937, LMA 3121/E3/245/2; LPGPC minutes: 16 November 1937, 14 December 1937 and 15 February 1938.

78 HUA DCL/8/5; NA MEPO 2/3112.

79 Unknown to Laski, 16 August 1937, LMA ACC3121/E3/245/2.

80 Game to Laski, 15 June 1938, BDA C6/10/32.

81 Laski to Rothschild, 5 December 1938, PLJA MS363 A3006/1/3/54.

82 Letters between Game and Laski, 30 July 1937, 15 August 1937, LMA ACC 3121/E3/245/2.

83 BDA C6/9/1/4; Laski to Livermore, 15 October 1937; 'Memorandum on Certain Activities', LMA ACC3121/E3/245/1; CoC minutes: Secretaries Reports, 19 June 1939, 17 July 1939.

84 Laski, *Jewish Rights*, p. 133.

85 Unsigned to Rosetté, 30 September 1936, BDA C6/9/1/3; Laski to Waley Cohen, 7 May 1937, BDA C6/3/1b/6/2.

86 'Conditions in the East End of London'; unsigned (Laski) to Game, 22 September 1938, LMA ACC3121/E3/247.

87 Unknown to Picciotto, BDA C6/10/32; various correspondence between Salomon, Picciotto and the police, Nov-Dec 1939, BDA C6/9/1/3.

88 'Interview with Mr JF Henderson'; NA HO 144/21381/233.

89 'Memorandum Submitted by Mr G Levine', 26 October 1937, BDA C6/10/32.

90 'Debate between Mr Jacobs and Mr Renton, Whitechapel Art Gallery, 21st March 1938', LHASC CP/ORG/2/20; *JC*, 25 March 1938, p. 46.

91 CoC minutes: 29 March 1938.

92 CoC minutes: 24 May 1938, 26 July 1938; Picciotto to Laski, 16 June 1938.

93   CoC minutes: 26 July 1938.

94   Pearce to Fine, 30 March 1938; Jacobs to secretary of ULTTU, 11 May 1938;
     invitation from Jacobs, 13 May 1938, HA D/S/24/4/13.

95   'Memorandum on Amount of Distribution', BDA C6/7/3/1; CoC minutes: 1
     November 1938, 3 January 1939, 'London Area Council – Secretary's Report',
     13 February 1939.

96   CoC minutes: 13 February 1939, 30 March 1939.

97   'Memorandum by Mr Jacobs of the JPC', BDA C6/9/1/3; Solomons to Salomon,
     30 August 1939, BDA C6/3/1b/6/4; CoC minutes: 3 October 1939, 'Combating
     Anti-Semitism in the Trades Unions', 8 November 1939, 23 January 1940.

98   Bermel to Brotman, 9 June 1937, PLJA MS363 A3006/1/3/54; Laski to Waldman,
     6 July 1937, PLJA MS134 AJ33/132; *Leader*, January 1937, pp. 6–7; March 1937,
     p. 49; August 1937, pp. 155–6; January 1938, p. 6; July 1938, p. 168; November 1938,
     p. 241; January 1939, pp. 8–9; May 1939, p. 106; CoC minutes: 29 March 1938.

99   *JC*, 14 August 1936, p. 13; 'Anti-Defamation Campaign – Basis for Organisation',
     5 November 1936, BDA C6/9/1/3; CoC minutes: 4 June 1937; Secretary's Report,
     3 February 1938.

100 *JC*, 14 August 1936, p. 13.

101 Beckman, *Hackney*, p. xxvi.

102 CoC minutes: Secretary's Report, 4 January 1937. Extended report of trip in LMA
     ACC3121/E3/245/1.

103 Minutes of Meetings Sub-Committee of CoC: 30 November 1936, BDA C6/1/4/1b.

104 *JC*, 7 August 1936, p. 11; 24 June 1938, p. 10; Cesarani, *Jewish Chronicle*, pp. 154–60;
     CoC minutes: 4 January 1937.

105 Commissioner's Report, September 1936; CoC minutes, 31 July 1936, 23 September
     1936, 29 October 1936.

106 Minutes of Finance Sub-Committee of CoC: 11 April 1938, BDA C6/1/4/1b.

107 CoC minutes: 'Work of the London Area Council', 15 November 1937; 'Extract
     from Report of the Principal Probation Officer', 13 March 1939.

108 LPGPC minutes: 'Co-ordinating Committee Report', 11 January 1938.

109 CoC minutes: 1 November 1938, 29 November 1938; LPGPC minutes:
     15 November 1938.

110 'Jewish Defence – Outline of the Policy and Proposed Programme of the Trades
     Advisory Council', PLJA MS363 A3006 1/3/157. CoC minutes: 'Memorandum on
     Discussion at Luncheon Given by Mr Cyril Ross', 1 November 1938.

111 Seigal to Salomon, 16 June 1939, BDA C6/9/1/3; CoC minutes: 1 November 1938.

112 'What the Jewish People's Council Against Fascism and Anti-Semitism Has Done!'
     (JPC, 1937), 'Not for Nothing' (JPC, n.d.), LHASC CP/ORG/MISC/07/06.

113 It is also possible that the increasing generosity was influenced by concurrent
     events in Europe, where German aggression, both towards its neighbours and its
     own Jewish citizens, was watched with concern by Anglo-Jewry. As we have seen,
     many Jews regarded the BUF and other domestic fascist organizations as conduits
     for Nazi efforts to stir racial tension in Britain.

114 'Comments on Receipts and Expenditure of the Jewish Defence Committee', PLJA
     MS134 AJ33/144; copy of Laski's diary for 18 January 1939, PLJA MS363 A3006
     1/3/56; CoC minutes: Finance Sub-Committee Reports, 26 July 1938, 1 November
     1938, 6 December 1939; 'Memorandum on Distribution', 13 March 1939.

115 *JC*, 2 December 1938, p. 39 (quotes paraphrased by correspondent); CoC minutes:
     Secretary's Report, 'The Jewish Defence Committee – Retrospect and Prospect',
     3 January 1939.

116 *ZR*, 30 September 1938, p. 6; 24 November 1938, p. 13.

117 CoC minutes: 13 February 1939, 13 March 1939, 24 April 1939.

118 Translated extract from *Jewish Times*, 22 November 1939, LMA ACC3121/E3/69/1. See also Harry Schneiderman (ed.), *The American Jewish Year Book 5701*, vol. 42 (Philadelphia: Jewish Publication Society of America, 1940), p. 325.

119 Translated extract from *Jewish Times*, 22 November 1939, LMA ACC3121/E3/69/1; Cesarani, 'Transformation'; Lebzelter, *Political Anti-Semitism*, p. 139; Langham, *Convention and Contention*, pp. 130–2; Barrett, 'Threat', p. 57.

120 Waley Cohen to: Robson, 28 September 1936; Bearsted, 4 November 1936, MS363 A3006 1/3/125; Lazarus, 27 July 1936, MS363 A3006 1/3/124; Bell, 10 October 1937, 6 November 1937, MS363 A3006 1/3/176/3.

121 The above account is compiled from Waley Cohen's personal papers (files PLJA MS363 A3006/1/3/54–6, 59, 124–5, 176/1–3, 177 /1–2, 178/1–2) which detail the establishment and work of his defence office. Quotes taken from Waley Cohen's letters to (file numbers in brackets): Gluckstein, 22 March 1937 (176/1); Rothschild, 28 June 1937 (59); Bell, 24 September 1937 (176/3); Hacking, 27 September 1937 (176/3). Henriques' biography of Waley Cohen also details his defence activity, though in an unwarrantedly positive light, with the author claiming that, of all British Jews involved in defence work, 'Bob was certainly the most effective', *Waley Cohen*, pp. 361–4, 382–3.

122 Waley Cohen to: Cohen, 12 January 1937, 15 January 1937, 11 May 1937; Laski, 16 May 1938; letters between Waley Cohen and Salomon, 6 June 1939, 7 June 1939, PLJA MS363 A3006 1/3/153, 155, 157; see CoC minutes for Waley Cohen's attendance record and contribution to the committee.

123 Unknown to Laski, 3 January 1939, PLJA MS363 A3006 1/3/56; letters between Laski and Waley Cohen, 22 February 1939, PLJA MS134 AJ33/137.

124 Laski to: Deutsch, 24 November 1938, 1 December 1938; Oates, 24 November 1938, PLJA MS363 A3006 1/3/177/2; emergency JDC resolution, 3 January 1939, PLJA MS363 A3006 1/3/178/1; CoC minutes: 3 January 1939.

125 Henriques, *Waley Cohen*, p. 364.

126 'Minutes of Special Meeting of Defence Committee', 13 July 1939, PLJA MS134 AJ33/148.

127 Laski to parents, 4 August 1939, PLJA MS363 A3006 1/3/56; Waley Cohen to Liverman, 15 September 1939, PLJA MS363 A3006 1/3/178/2.

128 Laski to Deutsch, 1 December 1938; Waley Cohen to Laski, 7 February 1939, 9 February 1939 and 28 February 1939; Laski to Waley Cohen, 6 February 1939; Waley Cohen to Bearsted, 28 February 1939, PLJA MS363 A3006/1/3/54, 56, 177(2), 178(1); Waley Cohen to Laski, 22 February 1939, PLJA MS134 AJ33/137a.

129 Laski to Waley Cohen, 1 March 1939; Waley Cohen to Laski, 2 March 1939, PLJA MS363 A3006 1/3/178/1.

130 Letters between Waley Cohen and Laski, 15 May 1939, 16 May 1939, 17 May 1939, 22 May 1939, PLJA MS363 A3006 1/3/56, 178(2).

131 Minutes of meeting at Helens Court, 19 May 1939, PLJA MS363 A3006 1/3/178/2.

132 Greenberg to Laski, 7 July 1939, PLJA MS150 AJ110/4; 'Minutes of Special Meeting of Defence Committee'.

133 Laski to parents, 4 August 1939, PLJA MS363 A3006 1/3/56.

134 Cesarani, 'Transformation', pp. 127–8, 132–7.

135 Alderman, *Modern British Jewry*, pp. 312–4; Cesarani, 'Transformation', pp. 127–8, 132–7; Langham, *Convention and Contention*, pp. 132–5; letters between Waley Cohen and Laski, 7 February 1938, 16 May 1938, 19 May 1938, 19 April 1939,

7 September 1939, 15 September 1939, 18 September 1939, 14 November 1939;
Waley Cohen to Liverman, 15 September 1939, PLJA MS363 A3006 1/3/56, 155–6,
178(2); Laski to Rothschild, 7 November 1939, PLJA MS150 AJ110/4.

136   Israel Finestein claims that Brodetsky's election is 'universally acknowledged'
        as the start of 'a new era in Jewish affairs', with the 'newcomers and their
        children … integrated into English and Anglo-Jewish life and inherit[ing] the
        institutions and the stability of earlier Anglo-Jewry', *Scenes and Personalities in
        Anglo-Jewry, 1800–2000* (London: Vallentine Mitchell, 2002), p. 229.
137   Rubinstein, *Jews in the English-speaking World*, p. 233.
138   Gewirtz, 'Anglo-Jewish Responses', pp. 268–71, 273; Brodetsky to Rothschild,
        16 January 1941, PLJA MS119 AJ3. See also introduction to Cesarani (ed.), *Modern
        Anglo-Jewry*, p. 6.
139   Brodetsky to: Chanasasha, 27 December 1939; Bakstansky, 23 June 1943; Moss, 23
        June 1943, PLJA MS119 AJ3; Schneiderman (ed.), *American Jewish Year Book 5701*,
        pp. 319–20.
140   Cited by Bergen, *Leeds Jewry*, p. 38.
141   CoC minutes: 13 February 1939, 4 June 1940.
142   CoC minutes: 13 February 1939; 'Problems and Policy of Defence', 11 April 1940.
143   CoC minutes: 30 March 1939.
144   'The Problem and Meaning of Jewish Defence'; LPGPC minutes: 1 June 1937.

Conclusion

1   Mosley, *My Life*, p. 340. He claimed that the 'Jewish attack on us at
        Olympia … occurred well in advance of the first occasion that I ever raised the
        subject [of opposition to Jews], at my Albert Hall meeting on October 23, 1934'.
        This, as we have seen, is completely untrue.
2   Kallis, *Genocide and Fascism*, pp. 110–12.
3   *ZR*, June 1934, p. 53.
4   On various occasions, the BUF felt compelled to offer replies to the Board's anti-
        defamation publications. For example, *Blackshirt*, 8 August 1936, p. 1.
5   Copsey, *Anti-Fascism*, pp. 40–1, 48.

Appendix One

1   A similar data-collection methodology has been used by Doob (*Pound Speaking*,
        pp. 413–425) in analysing Ezra Pound's propaganda broadcasts; by HeeMin Kim
        and Richard Fording ('Party Manifesto Data and Measures of Ideology in Western
        Democracies', pp. 1–3, mailer.fsu.edu/~hkim/Ideology_Measures_Paper-Final.
        pdf [accessed 22 August 2010]) and Andrea Volkens (*Manifesto Data Set. MDS
        2005 Data Handbook* (Berlin: WZB, 2005), Appendix II) with regard to political
        manifestos; and Brustein (*Roots of Hate*, pp. 355–9) in relation to manifestations of
        antisemitism. (The problems with Brustein's work outlined in Chapter 2 relate to
        his interpretation of data, not to their collection.)
2   The newspapers were usually published weekly, but in the first four months of the
        sampled period only two issues were published per month, so these were used for

the sample. Where an issue was missing altogether, the next week's issue was used. Similarly, if a certain page was missing or illegible, the next page was used.

3   Editorials and regular columns were often divided into smaller, separate parts, each covering a different topic. Each of these was counted as one 'article'.

4   By comparison, Brustein's sample for his newspaper analysis comprised about 4.5 per cent of all content.

5   The term 'alien' (as well as similar ones, such as 'Oriental') did not always refer to Jews, however, and instances of their use were only counted when such a meaning is clear. For example, in one issue of *Blackshirt* (15 June 1934, pp. 2, 4) one finds a reference to 'cheap Oriental competition' relating to sweated labour in the Far East, while the term 'Oriental agitators' is used to describe Jewish opponents at a meeting. In this case, only the latter instance would be counted.

6   For a similar system of classification, see Louis Harap, *Creative Awakening: The Jewish Presence in Twentieth-Century American Literature, 1900s–1940s* (Westport: Greenwood, 1987), p. 24.

Bibliography

Archival sources

Primary material was consulted at the following institutions (with particularly important collections named individually). The abbreviations used in endnotes to refer to these sources have also been indicated:

- Hackney Archive (**HA**)
- House of Commons Parliamentary Papers
  - Reports of the Commissioner of Police of the Metropolis for 1932–8
- Hull University Archives (subsequently moved to Hull History Centre) (**HUA**)
  - Archives of Liberty (National Council for Civil Liberties)
- Imperial War Museum (**IWM**)
- Labour History and Archive Study Centre (at People's History Museum, Manchester) (**LHASC**)
  - Archives of the Communist Party of Great Britain
  - Fascist and anti-fascist pamphlets and leaflets
- London Metropolitan Archives (**LMA**)
  - Board of Deputies of British Jews
    - Minutes of the Board's Law, Parliamentary and General Purposes Committee (file: LMA ACC3121/C/13/1/12) (**LPGPC minutes**)
- Manchester Jewish Museum (**MJM**)
  - Fascist and anti-fascist pamphlets and leaflets
  - Oral-history recordings of Jewish life in Manchester
- Manchester Police Museum (**MPM**)
- National Archives (**NA**)
  - Metropolitan Police (**MEPO**)
    - Monthly Commissioner's and Special Branch reports (file: NA MEPO 2/3043)
  - Home Office (**HO**)
- Parkes Library Jewish Archives (**PLJA**)
  - The papers of Selig Brodetsky
  - The papers of Neville Laski
  - The papers of James Parkes
  - The papers of Robert Waley Cohen
- University College London Special Collections (**UCLSC**)
  - Archives of the Institute for Jewish Affairs
  - Archives of the Trades Advisory Council
- University of Birmingham Special Collections (**UBSC**)
  - Oswald Mosley Papers
- University of Sheffield Archives (**USA**)
  - British Union Collection
  - Cooper Collection

- Peroni Scrapbooks
- Zaidman Papers
- University of Warwick Modern Records Centre (**UWMRC**)
- Wiener Library (**WL**)
  - Defence Archive of the Board of Deputies of British Jews (held by the Community Security Trust until late 2011) (**BDA**)
    - Minutes of the Board's Co-ordinating Committee/Jewish Defence Committee (file: BDA C6/1/1/1-2) (**CoC minutes**)
  - Collection of fascist and anti-fascist pamphlets and leaflets
  - David Spector: Miscellaneous Papers
- Working Class Movement Library (**WCML**)

Contemporary newspapers and journals

The BUF's three weekly newspapers were drawn upon heavily:
- *Action*
- *Blackshirt*
- *Fascist Week* (**FW**):

The following Jewish publications were also used extensively:
- *Jewish Chronicle* (**JC**)
- *The Leader*
- *Young Zionist* (**YZ**)
- *Zionist Review* (**ZR**)

Additionally, many collections of contemporary press cuttings held by various archives have been used (where reference is made in the text to such items, page numbers are unfortunately often not available). In particular those at:
- Hull University Archives (files DCL/70/1, DCL/1/3, DCL/40/4)
- Labour History and Archive Study Centre (file FAS 1/1–120)
- University of Birmingham Special Collections (files OMN/B/3/3, OMD/9/1/4 and 5)
- Wiener Library (files PC2/315a, b and c)

Selected contemporary publications, memoirs and diaries

The following list includes full-length books but not leaflets and pamphlets, which can be accessed in the archival collections mentioned above:

Beckman, Morris, *The 43 Group*, London: Centerprise, 1992.

———, *The Hackney Crucible*, London: Vallentine Mitchell, 1996.

Charnley, John, *Blackshirts and Roses*, London: Brockingday, 1990.

Chesterton, A.K., *Oswald Mosley: Portrait of a Leader*, London: Action Press, n.d.

———, (with Joseph Leftwich), *The Tragedy of Anti-Semitism*, London: Robert Anscombe, 1948.

The Circle: Golden Jubilee, 1909–1959, London: Central Committee of the Workers' Circle Friendly Society, 1961.

Drennan, James (pen name of Allen, W.E.D), *BUF: Oswald Mosley and British Fascism*, London: Murray, 1934.

Golding, Louis, *The Jewish Problem*, Harmondsworth: Penguin, 1938.

Gordon-Canning, Robert, *The Holy Land: Arab or Jew?*, unknown publisher, n.d.

Grant, Ted, *The Menace of Fascism: What it is and how to fight it*, London: Revolutionary Communist Party, 1948.

Grundy, Trevor, *Memoir of a Fascist Childhood: A Boy in Mosley's Britain*, London: Heinemann, 1998.

Hamm, Jeffrey, *Action Replay*, unknown publisher, 1983.

Hobson, J.A., *The War in South Africa: Its Causes and Effects*, London: James Nisbet, 1900.

Hyde, Douglas, *I Believed*, London: Heinemann, 1950.

Jacobs, Joe, *Out of the Ghetto*, unknown publisher, 1978.

Kops, Bernard, *The World is a Wedding*, London: Mayflower, 1970.

Laski, Neville, *Jewish Rights and Jewish Wrongs*, London: Soncino Press, 1939.

Levine, Maurice, *Cheetham to Cordova: A Manchester Man of the Thirties*, Manchester: Neil Richardson, 1984.

Litvinoff, Emanuel, *Journey Through a Small Planet*, Oxford: Isis, 1993.

Mosley, Oswald, *The Greater Britain*, London: BUF, 1932.

——, *Fascism: 100 Questions Asked and Answered*, London: Action Press, 1936.

——, *Tomorrow We Live*, London: Greater Britain Publications, 1938.

——, *My Life*, London: Thomas Nelson, 1968.

Mosley's Blackshirts, London: Sanctuary Press, 1986.

Nicolson, Nigel (ed.), *Harold Nicolson: Diaries and Letters 1930–39*, London: Fontana, 1971.

Pearce, Jack, 'The Fascist Threat', in *The Circle: Golden Jubilee, 1909–1959*, London: Central Committee of the Workers' Circle Friendly Society, 1961.

Piratin, Phil, *Our Flag Stays Red: An account of Cable Street and political life in the East End of London*, London: Wishart and Lawrence, 1978.

Raven Thomson, Alexander, *The Coming Corporate State*, London: Greater Britain Publications, 1938.

Red Violence and Blue Lies: An Answer to 'Fascists at Olympia', London: BUF Publications, 1934.

Salomon, Sidney, *Anti-Semitism and Fascism in Post-War Britain. The Work of the Jewish Defence Committee*, London: Woburn Press, 1950.

Schneiderman, Harry (ed.), *The American Jewish Year Book 5696*, vol. 37, Philadelphia: Jewish Publication Society of America, 1935.

—— (ed.), *The American Jewish Year Book 5697, vol. 38*.

—— (ed.), *The American Jewish Year Book 5698, vol. 39*.

—— (ed.), *The American Jewish Year Book 5699, vol. 40*.

—— (ed.), *The American Jewish Year Book 5700, vol. 41*.

—— (ed.), *The American Jewish Year Book 5701, vol. 42*.

Sieff, Israel, *Memoirs*, London: Wiedenfeld and Nicolson, 1970.

Simpson, William W., *Youth and Antisemitism*, London: Epsworth Press, 1938.

Spector, Cyril, *Volla Volla Jew Boy*, London: Centreprise, 1988.

Zukerman, William, *The Jew in Revolt: The Modern Jew in the World Crisis*, London: Secker and Warburg, 1937.

Selected secondary sources

Alderman, G., *The Jewish Community in British Politics*, Oxford: Oxford University Press, 1983.

——, *London Jewry and London Politics 1889–1986*, London: Routledge, 1989.

———, 'Dr Robert Forgan's resignation from the British Union of Fascists', *Labour History Review*, 57(1), 1992, pp. 37–41.

———, 'English Jews or Jews of the English Persuasion? Reflections on the Emancipation of Anglo-Jewry', in P. Birnbaum and I. Katznelson (eds), *Paths of Emancipation: Jews, States and Citizenship*, Princeton: Princeton University Press, 1995.

———, *Modern British Jewry*, Oxford: Oxford University Press, 1998.

———, *Controversy and Crisis: Studies in the History of the Jews in Modern Britain*, Brighton, MA: Academic Studies Press, 2008.

Almog, S. (ed.), *Antisemitism Through the Ages*, Oxford: Pergamon Press, 1988.

Baker, D., *Ideology of Obsession: AK Chesterton and British Fascism*, London: IB Tauris, 1996.

———, 'The Extreme Right in the 1920s: Fascism in a Cold Climate, or "Conservatism with Knobs on"?', in M. Cronin (ed.), *The Failure of British Fascism: The Far Right and the Fight for Political Recognition*, London: Macmillan, 1996.

Baldoli, C., 'Anglo-Italian Fascist Solidarity?: The Shift from Italophilia to Naziphilia in the BUF', in J. Gottlieb and T. Linehan (eds), *The Culture of Fascism: Visions of the Far Right in Britain*, London: IB Tauris, 2004.

Barrett, N., 'The anti-fascist movement in south-east Lancashire, 1933–1940: The divergent experiences of Manchester and Nelson', in T. Kirk and A. McElligott (eds), *Opposing Fascism: Community, Authority and Resistance in Europe*, Cambridge: Cambridge University Press, 1999.

———, 'The Threat of the British Union of Fascists in Manchester', in T. Kushner and N. Valman (eds), *Remembering Cable Street: Fascism and Anti-Fascism in British Society*, London: Vallentine Mitchell, 2000.

Bauer, Y., 'In Search of a Definition of Antisemitism', in M. Brown (ed.), *Approaches to Antisemitism: Context and Curriculum*, New York: The American Jewish Committee, 1994.

Beckett, F., *The Rebel Who Lost His Cause: The Tragedy of John Beckett, MP*, London: London House, 1999.

Benewick, R., *The Fascist Movement in Britain*, London: Allen Lane, 1972.

Bergen, A., *Leeds Jewry, 1930–1939: The challenge of anti-Semitism*, Leeds: Thoresby Society, 2000.

Berger, D. (ed.), *History and Hate: The Dimensions of Anti-Semitism*, Philadelphia: Jewish Publication Society, 1986.

Birnbaum, P. and Katznelson, I. (eds), *Paths of Emancipation: Jews, States and Citizenship*, Princeton: Princeton University Press, 1995.

———, 'Emancipation and the Liberal Offer', in P. Birnbaum and I. Katznelson, *Paths of Emancipation: Jews, States and Citizenship*, Princeton: Princeton University Press, 1995.

Black, G., *Living Up West: Jewish Life in London's West End*, London: London Museum of Jewish Life, 1994.

Bourne, R., *Lords of Fleet Street: The Harmsworth Dynasty*, London: Barrie and Jenkins, 1990.

Branson, N., *History of the Communist Party of Great Britain 1927–1941*, London: Lawrence and Wishart, 1985.

Brenner, M., Liedtke, R. and Rechter, D. (eds), *Two Nations: British and German Jews in Comparative Perspective*, London: Leo Baeck Institute, 1999.

Brewer, J., *Mosley's Men: The British Union of Fascists in the West Midlands*, London: Gower, 1984.

Brown, M. (ed.), *Approaches to Antisemitism: Context and Curriculum*, New York: The American Jewish Committee, 1994.

Brustein, W., *Roots of Hate: Antisemitism in Europe before the Holocaust*, Cambridge: Cambridge University Press, 2003.

Cassels, A., *Fascism*, Arlington Heights: AHM, 1975.

Catterall, P., 'The Battle of Cable Street', *Contemporary Record*, 8(1), 1994, pp. 105–32.

Cesarani, D., 'Joynson-Hicks and the radical right in England after the First World War', in T. Kushner and K. Lunn (eds), *Traditions of intolerance: Historical perspectives on fascism and race discourse in Britain*, Manchester: Manchester University Press, 1989.

———, 'The Anti-Jewish Career of Sir William Joynson-Hicks, Cabinet Minister', *Journal of Contemporary History*, 24(3), 1989, pp. 461–82.

——— (ed.), *The Making of Modern Anglo-Jewry*, Oxford: Blackwell, 1990.

———, 'The Transformation of Communal Authority in Anglo-Jewry, 1914–1940', in D. Cesarani (ed.), *The Making of Modern Anglo-Jewry*, Oxford: Blackwell, 1990.

———, *Reporting Anti-Semitism: The Jewish Chronicle 1879–1979*, Southampton: University of Southampton, 1993.

———, *The Jewish Chronicle and Anglo-Jewry, 1841–1991*, Cambridge: Cambridge University Press, 1994.

———, 'The Study of Antisemitism in Britain: Trends and Perspectives', in M. Brown (ed.), *Approaches to Antisemitism: Context and Curriculum*, New York: The American Jewish Committee, 1994.

——— (ed.), *Port Jews. Jewish Communities in Cosmopolitan Maritime Trading Centres, 1550–1950*, London: Frank Cass, 2002.

———, 'The Forgotten Jews of London: Court Jews Who Were Also Port Jews', in D. Cesarani (ed.), *Port Jews. Jewish Communities in Cosmopolitan Maritime Trading Centres, 1550–1950*, London: Frank Cass, 2002.

———, *The Left and the Jews. The Jews and the Left*, London: Labour Friends of Israel, 2004.

Cheyette, B., 'Jewish Stereotyping and English Literature, 1875–1920: Toward a Political Analysis', in T. Kushner and K. Lunn (eds), *Traditions of intolerance: Historical perspectives on fascism and race discourse in Britain*, Manchester: Manchester University Press, 1989.

———, 'Hilaire Belloc and the "Marconi Scandal" 1900–1914: A Reassessment of the Interactionist Model of Racial Hatred', in T. Kushner and K. Lunn (eds), *The Politics of Marginality: Race, the Radical Right and Minorities in Twentieth Century Britain*, London: Frank Cass, 1990.

———, *Constructions of 'the Jew' in English literature and society: Racial representations, 1874–1945*, Cambridge: Cambridge University Press, 1993.

Cohen, S., 'Anglo-Jewish Responses to Antisemitism: Suggestions for a Framework of Analysis', in J. Reinharz (ed.), *Living With Antisemitism: Modern Jewish Responses*, Hanover: University Press of New England, 1987.

Copsey, N., *Anti-Fascism in Britain*, London: Macmillan, 2000.

———, 'Communists and the Inter-War Anti-Fascist Struggle in the United States and Britain', *Labour History Review*, 76(3), 2011, pp. 184–206.

——— and Olechnowicz, A. (eds), *Varieties of Anti-Fascism: Britain in the Inter-War Period*, Basingstoke: Palgrave Macmillan, 2010.

——— and Tilles, D., 'Uniting a Divided Community? Re-appraising Jewish Responses to British Fascism Antisemitism, 1932–9', in D. Tilles and S. Garau (eds), *Fascism and the Jews: Italy and Britain*, London: Vallentine Mitchell, 2010.

Coupland, P., 'The Blackshirted Utopians', *Journal of Contemporary History*, 33(2), 1998, pp. 255–72.

——, '"Left-Wing Fascism" in Theory and Practice: The Case of the British Union of Fascists', *Twentieth Century British History*, 13(1), 2002, pp. 38–61.

Cronin, M. (ed.), *The Failure of British Fascism: The Far Right and the Fight for Political Recognition*, London: Macmillan, 1996.

——, '"Tomorrow We Live" – The Failure of British Fascism?', in M. Cronin (ed.), *The Failure of British Fascism: The Far Right and the Fight for Political Recognition*, London: Macmillan, 1996.

Cross, C., *The Fascists in Britain*, London: Barrie and Rockliff, 1961.

Cullen, S., 'The Development of the Ideas and Policy of the British Union of Fascists, 1932–40', *Journal of Contemporary History*, 22, 1987, pp. 115–36.

——, 'Political Violence: The Case of the British Union of Fascists', *Journal of Contemporary History*, 28(2), 1993, pp. 245–67.

——, 'Four Women for Mosley: Women in the British Union of Fascists', *Oral History*, 24, 1996, pp. 49–59.

Defries, H., *Conservative Party Attitudes to Jews, 1900–1950*, London: Frank Cass, 2001.

Dorril, S., *Blackshirt: Sir Oswald Mosley and British Fascism*, London: Penguin, 2007.

Dudley Edwards, R., *Victor Gollancz: A Biography*, London: Victor Gollancz, 1987.

Durham, M., 'Women and the British Union of Fascists, 1932–1940', in T. Kushner and K. Lunn (eds), *The Politics of Marginality: Race, the Radical Right and Minorities in Twentieth Century Britain*, London: Frank Cass, 1990.

——, 'The Conservative Party, the British Extreme Right and the Problem of Political Space, 1967–83', in M. Cronin (ed.), *The Failure of British Fascism: The Far Right and the Fight for Political Recognition*, London: Macmillan, 1996.

Eatwell, R., 'Towards a New Model of Generic Fascism', *Journal of Theoretical Politics*, 4(2), 1992, pp. 161–94.

Endelman, T., 'Comparative Perspectives on Modern Anti-Semitism in the West', in D. Berger (ed.), *History and Hate: The Dimensions of Anti-Semitism*, Philadelphia: Jewish Publication Society, 1986.

—— 'The Englishness of Jewish Modernity in England', in J. Katz (ed.), *Toward Modernity: The European Jewish Model*, New Brunswick: Transaction Books, 1986.

——, 'English Jewish History', *Modern Judaism*, 11(1), 1991, pp. 91–109.

——, *The Jews of Britain, 1656–2000*, London: University of California Press, 2002.

Ettinger, S., 'Jew-Hatred in Historical Context', in S. Almog (ed.), *Antisemitism Through the Ages*, Oxford: Pergamon Press, 1988.

Feldman, D., 'The Importance of Being English: Immigration and the Decay of Liberal England', in D. Feldman and G. Stedman Jones (eds), *Metropolis London: Histories and Representations Since 1800*, London: Routledge, 1989.

——, *Englishmen and Jews: Social Relations and Political Culture 1840–1914*, New Haver: Yale University Press, 1994.

——, 'Jews and the State in Britain', in M. Brenner, R. Liedtke and D. Rechter (eds), *Two Nations: British and German Jews in Comparative Perspective*, London: Leo Baeck Institute, 1999.

—— and Stedman Jones, G. (eds), *Metropolis London: Histories and Representations Since 1800*, London: Routledge, 1989.

Felsenstein, F., *Anti-Semitic Stereotypes: A Paradigm of Otherness in English Popular Culture, 1660–1830*, Baltimore: Johns Hopkins University Press, 1995.

Field, G., 'Anti-Semitism with the Boots Off', in H. Strauss (ed.), *Hostages of Modernization. Studies on Modern Antisemitism 1870–1933/39, Vol. 3/1 Germany – Great Britain – France*, Berlin: Walter de Gruyter, 1993.

Finestein, I., *Scenes and Personalities in Anglo-Jewry, 1800–2000*, London: Vallentine Mitchell, 2002.

Fishman, W., *East End Jewish Radicals 1875–1914*, London: Duckworth, 1975.

Garau, S., 'Between "Spirit" and "Science": The Emergence of Italian Fascist Antisemitism through the 1920s and 1930s', in D. Tilles and S. Garau (eds), *Fascism and the Jews: Italy and Britain*, London: Vallentine Mitchell, 2010.

Garside, W., *British Unemployment, 1919–1939: A Study in Public Policy*, Cambridge: Cambridge University Press, 1990.

Gartner, L., *History of the Jews in Modern Times*, Oxford: Oxford University Press, 2001.

Gewirtz, S., 'Anti-Fascist Activity in Manchester's Jewish Community in the 1930s', *Manchester Region History Review*, 4(1), 1990, pp. 17–27.

——, 'Anglo-Jewish Responses to Nazi Germany 1933–39: The Anti-Nazi Boycott and the Board of Deputies of British Jews', *Journal of Contemporary History*, 26(2), 1991, pp. 255–76.

Gottlieb, J., *Feminine Fascism: Women in Britain's Fascist Movement, 1923–1945*, London: IB Tauris, 2000.

——, ' "Motherly Hate": Gendering Anti-Semitism in the British Union of Fascists', *Gender and History*, 14(2), 2002, pp. 294–320.

—— and Linehan, T. (eds), *The Culture of Fascism: Visions of the Far Right in Britain*, London: IB Tauris, 2004.

Gregor, A., *Phoenix: Fascism in Our Time*, New Brunswick: Transaction, 1999.

Griffin, R. (ed.), *Fascism*, Oxford: Oxford University Press, 1995.

——, 'British Fascism: The Ugly Duckling', in M. Cronin (ed.), *The Failure of British Fascism: The Far Right and the Fight for Political Recognition*, London: Macmillan, 1996.

—— (ed.), with Feldman, M., *Fascism: Critical Concepts in Political Science*, London: Routledge, 2003.

——, ' "This Fortress Built Against Infection": The BUF Vision of Britain's Theatrical and Musical Renaissance', in J. Gottlieb and T. Linehan (eds), *The Culture of Fascism: Visions of the Far Right in Britain*, London: IB Tauris, 2004.

Griffin, R., *Patriotism Perverted: Captain Ramsey, The Right Club and British Anti-Semitism 1939-40*, London: Constable, 1998.

Henriques, R., *Sir Robert Waley Cohen*, London: Secker and Warburg, 1966.

Holmes, C. (ed.), *Immigrants and Minorities in British Society*, London: Allen and Unwin, 1978.

——, *Anti-Semitism in British Society 1876–1939*, London: Arnold, 1979.

——, 'Anti-semitism and the BUF', in K. Lunn and R. Thurlow (eds), *British Fascism: Essays on the Radical Right in Inter-War Britain*, London: Croom Helm, 1980.

——, 'The German Gypsy Question in Britain 1904–6', in K. Lunn (ed.), *Hosts, Immigrants and Minorities: Historical Reponses to Newcomers in British Society 1870–1914*, New York: St Martin's, 1980.

Iordachi, C. (ed.), *Comparative Fascist Studies: New Perspectives*, London: Routledge, 2009.

Julius, A., *TS Eliot, Anti-Semitism and Literary Form*, Cambridge: Cambridge University Press, 1996.

——, *Trials of the Diaspora: A History of Anti-Semitism in England*, Oxford: Oxford University Press, 2010.

Kallis, A., *Genocide and Fascism: The Eliminationist Drive in Fascist Europe*, New York: Routledge, 2009.

———, 'Fascism and the Jews: From Internationalisation of Fascism to "Fascist Antisemitism"', in D. Tilles and S. Garau (eds), *Fascism and the Jews: Italy and Britain*, London: Vallentine Mitchell, 2010.

———, 'Fascism, "Licence" and Genocide: From the Chimera of Rebirth to the Authorization of Mass Murder', in A. Costa Pinto (ed.), *Rethinking the Nature of Fascism*, Basingstoke: Palgrave Macmillan, 2011.

Katz, J. (ed.), *Toward Modernity: The European Jewish Model*, New Brunswick: Transaction Books, 1986.

Kibblewhite, L. and Rigby, A., *Fascism in Aberdeen*, Aberdeen: Aberdeen People's Press, 1978.

Kidd, A. and Roberts, K. (eds), *City, Class and Culture: Studies of Social Policy and Cultural Production in Victorian Manchester*, Manchester: Manchester University Press, 1985.

Kirk, T. and McElligott, A. (eds), *Opposing Fascism: Community, Authority and Resistance in Europe*, Cambridge: Cambridge University Press, 1999.

Kushner, T., *The Persistence of Prejudice: Antisemitism in British Society During the Second World War*, Manchester: Manchester University Press, 1989.

———, 'The paradox of prejudice: The impact of organised antisemitism in Britain during an anti-Nazi war', in T. Kushner and K. Lunn (eds), *Traditions of intolerance: Historical perspectives on fascism and race discourse in Britain*, Manchester: Manchester University Press, 1989.

———, 'Beyond the Pale? British Reactions to Nazi Anti-semitism, 1933–39', in T. Kushner and K. Lunn (eds), *The Politics of Marginality: Race, the Radical Right and Minorities in Twentieth Century Britain*, London: Frank Cass, 1990.

———, 'The Impact of British Anti-semitism, 1918–1945', in D. Cesarani (ed.), *The Making of Modern Anglo-Jewry*, Oxford: Blackwell, 1990.

———, *We Europeans? Mass-Observation, 'Race' and British Identity in the Twentieth Century*, Aldershot: Ashgate, 2004.

——— and Lunn, K. (eds), *Traditions of Intolerance: Historical Perspectives on Fascism and Race Discourse in Britain*, Manchester: Manchester University Press, 1989.

——— (eds), *The Politics of Marginality: Race, the Radical Right and Minorities in Twentieth Century Britain*, London: Frank Cass, 1990.

Kushner, T. and Valman, N. (eds), *Remembering Cable Street: Fascism and Anti-Fascism in British Society*, London: Vallentine Mitchell, 2000.

Langham, R., *250 Years of Convention and Contention: A History of the Board of Deputies of British Jews, 1760–2010*, London: Vallentine Mitchell, 2010.

Langmuir, G., *Toward a Definition of Antisemitism*, Berkeley: University of California Press, 1990.

Laqueur, W. (ed.), *Fascism: A Reader's Guide*, Harmondsworth: Penguin, 1976.

Lawson, E., ' "Scientific monstrosity" yet "occasionally convenient": Cecil Roth and the Idea of Race', *Patterns of Prejudice*, 42(2), 2008, pp. 209–27.

Lebzelter, G., *Political Anti-Semitism in England, 1918–1939*, London: Macmillan, 1978.

———, 'Henry Hamilton Beamish and the Britons: Champions of Anti-Semitism', in K. Lunn and R. Thurlow (eds), *British Fascism: Essays on the Radical Right in Inter-War Britain*, London: Croom Helm, 1980.

Levy, R., *Antisemitism in the Modern World: An Anthology of Texts*, Massachusetts: Heath, 1991.

Lewis, D., *Illusions of Grandeur: Mosley, Fascism and British Society, 1931–81*, Manchester: Manchester University Press, 1987.

Linehan, T., *East London for Mosley: The British Union of Fascists in East London and South-West Essex*, London: Frank Cass, 1996.

——, *British Fascism 1918–39: Parties, Ideology and Culture*, Manchester: Manchester University Press, 2000.

——, 'Reactionary Spectatorship: British Fascists and Cinema in Inter-War Britain', in J. Gottlieb and T. Linehan (eds), *The Culture of Fascism: Visions of the Far Right in Britain*, London: IB Tauris, 2004.

——, ' "On the Side of Christ": Fascist Clerics in 1930s Britain', *Totalitarian Movements and Political Religions*, 8(2), 2007, pp. 287–301.

——, 'Communist Culture and Anti-Fascism in Inter-War Britain', in N. Copsey and A. Olechnowicz (eds), *Varieties of Anti-Fascism: Britain in the Inter-War Period*, Basingstoke: Palgrave Macmillan, 2010.

Linz, J., 'Some Notes Toward a Comparative Study of Fascism in Sociological Historical Perspective', in W. Laqueur (ed.), *Fascism: A Reader's Guide*, Harmondsworth: Penguin, 1976.

Love, G., ' "What's the Big Idea?": Oswald Mosley, the British Union of Fascists and Generic Fascism', *Journal of Contemporary History*, 42(3), 2007, pp. 447–68.

Lunn, K. (ed.), *Hosts, Immigrants and Minorities: Historical Reponses to Newcomers in British Society 1870–1914*, New York: St Martin's, 1980.

——, 'Political Anti-semitism Before 1914: Fascism's Heritage?', in K. Lunn and R. Thurlow (ed.), *British Fascism: Essays on the Radical Right in Inter-War Britain*, London: Croom Helm, 1980.

——, 'British Fascism Revisited: A Failure of Imagination?', in M. Cronin (ed.), *The Failure of British Fascism: The Far Right and the Fight for Political Recognition*, London: Macmillan, 1996.

—— and Thurlow, R. (eds), *British Fascism: Essays on the Radical Right in Inter-War Britain*, London: Croom Helm, 1980.

Macklin, G., 'The Two Lives of John Hooper Harvey', *Patterns of Prejudice*, 42(2), 2008, pp. 167–90.

——, 'A Fascist "Jihad": Captain Robert Gordon-Canning, British Fascist Antisemitism and Islam', in D. Tilles and S. Garau (eds), *Fascism and the Jews: Italy and Britain*, London: Vallentine Mitchell, 2010.

Mandle, W., *Anti-Semitism and the British Union of Fascists*, London: Longman, 1968.

Morell, J., 'Arnold Leese and the Imperial Fascist League: The Impact of Racial Fascism', in K. Lunn and R. Thurlow (eds), *British Fascism: Essays on the Radical Right in Inter-War Britain*, London: Croom Helm, 1980.

Morgan, K., *Harry Pollitt*, Manchester: Manchester University Press, 1993.

Neocleous, M., *Fascism*, London: Open University Press, 1997.

Nugent, N., 'The ideas of the British Union of Fascists', in N. Nugent and R. King (eds), *The British Right: Conservative and right wing politics in Britain*, London: Saxon House, 1977.

—— and King, R. (eds), *The British Right: Conservative and Right Wing Politics in Britain*, London: Saxon House, 1977.

Overy, R., *The Morbid Age: Britain Between the Wars*, London: Allen Lane, 2009.

Panayi, P. (ed.), *Racial Violence in Britain in the Nineteenth and Twentieth Centuries*, London: Leicester University Press, 1996.

Parkes, J., *Antisemitism*, London: Valentine Mitchell, 1963.

Passmore, K., *Fascism: A Very Short Introduction*, Oxford: Oxford University Press, 2002.

Pavan, I., 'An Unexpected Betrayal? The Italian Jewish Community Facing Fascist Persecution', in D. Tilles and S. Garau (eds), *Fascism and the Jews: Italy and Britain*, London: Vallentine Mitchell, 2010.

Paxton, R., *The Anatomy of Fascism*, London: Penguin, 2004.

Payne, S., *Fascism: Comparison and Definition*, Madison: University of Wisconsin Press, 1980.

——, *A History of Fascism, 1914–45*, London: UCL Press, 1995.

Pugh, M., 'The British Union of Fascists and the Olympia Debate', *The Historical Journal*, 41(2), 1998, pp. 529–42.

——, *'Hurrah for the Blackshirts': Fascists and Fascism in Britain Between the Wars*, London: Pimlico, 2005.

——, *We Danced All Night: A Social History of Britain Between the Wars*, London: Vintage, 2009.

Reinharz, J. (ed.), *Living With Antisemitism: Modern Jewish Responses*, Hanover: University Press of New England, 1987.

Renton, D., *Red Shirts and Black: Fascism and Anti-Fascism in Oxford in the 'Thirties*, Oxford: Ruskin College Library, 1996.

——, *Fascism, Anti-Fascism and the 1940s*, London: Macmillan, 2000.

——, *This Rough Game: Fascism and Anti-Fascism*, Gloucester: Sutton, 2001.

Rosenberg, D., *Facing up to Antisemitism: How Jews in Britain Countered the Threats of the 1930s*, London: JCARP, 1985.

——, *Battle for the East End: Jewish responses to fascism in the 1930s*, Nottingham: Five Leaves, 2011.

Rubinstein, W., *A History of the Jews in the English-Speaking World: Great Britain*, London: Macmillan, 1996.

Sarfatti, M. (trans. Tedeschi, J. and Tedeschi, A.), *The Jews in Mussolini's Italy: From Equality to Persecution*, Madison: University of Wisconsin Press, 2007.

Selwyn, F., *Hitler's Englishman: The Crime of Lord Haw-Haw*, London: Penguin, 1993.

Skidelsky, R., 'Reflections on Mosley and British Fascism', in K. Lunn and R. Thurlow (eds), *British Fascism: Essays on the Radical Right in Inter-War Britain*, London: Croom Helm, 1980.

——, *Oswald Mosley*, London: Papermac, 1990.

Smith, E., 'Jewish responses to political antisemitism and fascism in the East End of London, 1920–1939', in T. Kushner and K. Lunn (eds), *Traditions of intolerance: Historical perspectives on fascism and race discourse in Britain*, Manchester: Manchester University Press, 1989.

——, 'Jews and Politics in the East End of London, 1918–1939', in D. Cesarani (ed.), *The Making of Modern Anglo-Jewry*, Oxford: Blackwell, 1990.

——, 'But What Did They Do? Contemporary Jewish Responses to Cable Street', in T. Kushner and N. Valman (eds), *Remembering Cable Street: Fascism and Anti-Fascism in British Society*, London: Vallentine Mitchell, 2000.

Srebrnik, H., *London Jews and British Communism, 1935–1945*, London: Vallentine Mitchell, 1995.

Stansky, P., 'Anglo-Jew or English/British? Some Dilemmas of Anglo-Jewish History', *Jewish Social Studies*, 2(1), 1995, pp. 159–78.

Sternhell, Z., 'Fascist Ideology', in W. Laqueur (ed.), *Fascism: A Reader's Guide*, Harmondsworth: Penguin, 1976.

——, *The Birth of Fascist Ideology: From Cultural Rebellion to Political Religion*, Princeton: Princeton University Press, 1994.

Stevenson, J., 'The BUF, the Metropolitan Police and Public Order', in K. Lunn and R Thurlow (eds.), *British Fascism: Essays on the Radical Right in Inter-War Britain*, London: Croom Helm, 1980.

—— and Cook, C., *The Slump: Britain in the Great Depression*, London: Longman, 2009.

Stone, D., *Breeding Superman: Nietzsche, Race, and Eugenics in Edwardian and Interwar Britain*, Liverpool: Liverpool University Press, 2002.

——, 'The English Mistery, the BUF, and the Dilemmas of British Fascism', *The Journal of Modern History*, 75, 2003, pp. 336–358.

——, 'The Far Right and the Back-to-the-Land Movement', in J. Gottlieb and T. Linehan (eds), *The Culture of Fascism: Visions of the Far Right in Britain*, London: IB Tauris, 2004.

——, 'Anti-Fascist Europe Comes to Britain: Theorising Fascism as a Contribution to Defeating It', in N. Copsey and A. Olechnowicz (eds), *Varieties of Anti-Fascism: Britain in the Inter-War Period*, Basingstoke: Palgrave Macmillan, 2010.

Strauss, H. (ed.), *Hostages of Modernization. Studies on Modern Antisemitism 1870–1933/39, Vol. 3/1 Germany – Great Britain – France*, Berlin: Walter de Gruyter, 1993.

Sykes, A., *The Radical Right in Britain*, Basingstoke: Palgrave Macmillan, 2005.

Thorpe, A., 'The Membership of the Communist Party of Great Britain, 1920–1945', *The Historical Journal*, 43(3), 2000, pp. 777–800.

Thurlow, R., 'Satan and Sambo: The Image of the Immigrant in English Racial Populist Thought since the First World War', in K. Lunn (ed.), *Hosts, Immigrants and Minorities: Historical Reponses to Newcomers in British Society 1870–1914*, New York: St Martin's, 1980.

——, 'Blaming the Blackshirts: The authorities and the anti-Jewish disturbances in the 1930', in P. Panayi (ed.), *Racial Violence in Britain in the Nineteenth and Twentieth Centuries*, London: Leicester University Press, 1996.

——, 'State Management of the British Union of Fascists', in M. Cronin (ed.), *The Failure of British Fascism: The Far Right and the Fight for Political Recognition*, London: Macmillan, 1996.

——, 'The Developing British Fascist Interpretation of Race, Culture and Evolution', in J. Gottlieb and T. Linehan (eds), *The Culture of Fascism: Visions of the Far Right in Britain*, London: IB Tauris, 2004.

——, *Fascism in Britain: From Oswald Mosley's Blackshirts to the National Front*, London: IB Tauris, 2006.

——, 'Passive and Active Anti-Fascism: The State and National Security, 1923–45', in N. Copsey and A. Olechnowicz (eds), *Varieties of Anti-Fascism: Britain in the Inter-War Period*, Basingstoke: Palgrave Macmillan, 2010.

Tilles, D. and Garau, S. (eds), *Fascism and the Jews: Italy and Britain*, London: Vallentine Mitchell, 2010.

Todd, N., *In Excited Times: People Against the Blackshirts*, Whitley Bay: Bewick Press, 1995.

Turner, D., *Fascism and Anti-Fascism in the Medway Towns 1927–40*, Rochester: Kent Anti-Fascist Action Committee, 1993.

Vital, D., *A People Apart: The Jews in Europe, 1789–1939*, Oxford: Oxford University Press, 1999.

Webber, G., 'Patterns of Membership and Support for the BUF', *Journal of Contemporary History*, 19(4), 1984, pp. 576–606.

————, *The Ideology of the British Right 1918–1939*, London: St Martin's Press, 1986.

Williams, B., 'The Anti-Semitism of Tolerance: Middle-Class Manchester and the Jews 1870–1900', in A. Kidd and K. Roberts (eds), *City, Class and Culture: Studies of Social Policy and Cultural Production in Victorian Manchester*, Manchester: Manchester University Press, 1985.

Wistrich, R., *Antisemitism: The Longest Hatred*, London: Thomas Methuen, 1991.

Theses

Andits, E., *'Sore on the nation's body': Repression of homosexuals under Italian Fascism*, Master's thesis, Central European University, 2010.

Baker, D., *The Making of a British Fascist – The Case of AK Chesterton*, PhD Thesis, University of Sheffield, 1982.

Brennan, D., *Mosley and Manchester. Impact and Reaction: Sir Oswald Mosley, the BUF, and Manchester in the 1930s*, Master's thesis, unknown institution, 1988.

Cesarani, D., *Zionism in England, 1917–1939*, PhD thesis, University of Oxford, 1986.

Pugh, P., *A Political Biography of Alexander Raven Thomson*, PhD thesis, University of Sheffield, 2002.

Smith, E., *East End Jews in Politics, 1918–1939: A Study in Class and Ethnicity*, PhD thesis, University of Leicester, 1990.

Srebrnik, H., *The Jewish Communist Movement in Stepney: Ideological Mobilisation and Political Victories in an East London Borough, 1935–1945*, PhD thesis, University of Birmingham, 1983.

Index

Printed in Great Britain
by Amazon